AVANT-GARDE
POLITICIAN
LEADERS FOR A NEW EPOCH

YEHEZKEL DROR

The Hebrew University of Jerusalem

Westphalia Press
An imprint of the Policy Studies Organization
Washington, DC
2014

Avant-Garde Politician:
Leaders for a New Epoch
All Rights Reserved © 2014 by Policy Studies Organization.

Washington, DC: Westphalia Press, 2014.

ISBN 10: 1935907859
ISBN 13: 978-1-935907-85-5

Printed in the United States of America

Westphalia Press
An imprint of Policy Studies Organization
1527 New Hampshire Ave., NW
Washington, D.C. 20036
dgutierrezs@ipsonet.org

Requests for updated material, review copies, and comments on this edition
can be made via the Westphalia Press website:
www.westphaliapress.org

To Rachel, my Remonstrative Soul Mate
Our Three Sons, Asael, Otniel, Itiel
And Our Eight Grandchildren
Naama, Yotam, Lorit, Lidal, Shahar, Liran, Litan, Shani

CONTENTS

Eine grosse Epoche hat das Jahrhundert geboren,
Aber der grosse Moment findet ein kleines Geschlecht
Und noch kleinere Politiker

Our century has given birth to a great epoch,
But the great moment finds a stunted generation
And even more stunted politicians

Friedrich Schiller, "The Present Moment," 1796,
with an added verse of mine marked in bold.

AVANT-GARDE
POLITICIAN

LEADERS FOR A NEW EPOCH

ACKNOWLEDGMENTS

The Hebrew University of Jerusalem is my academic home. It supplies a stimulated academic habitus and essential research resources, for which I am most grateful.

Many fellowships at institutes for advanced study and guest appointments at universities facilitating strenuous writing and provided opportunities for intensive readings and stimulating conversation, which contributed much to my thinking.

It would be inappropriate to mention by name the large number of political leaders and their advisors with whom I had the privilege to work, with wide access to internal documents. Without them this book could not have been written.

In addition to governments around the world who invited me as a consultant, I owe a large debt of gratitude to the United Nations, UNDP, OECD, the European Union Commission, and the European Institute for Public Administration, for providing access to the centers of governments on all Continents and much enlightening discourse. These inputs were of utmost importance for this book.

I benefited a lot from my more than six years as Founding President of the Jewish People Policy Institute, including close acquaintance with the rather special types of Jewish People leadership. I would like to thank especially Avinoam Bar-Yosef, my partner as Director who succeeded me as President, and the Project Manager, Ms. Ita Alcalay, for many insights, stimulating discourse, and unfailing friendly and efficient support. And many thanks to the Institutes staff as a whole for the privilege of working with them.

For important comments on drafts of the book I thank Professor Shalom Saada Saar and Dr. Shalom Salomon Wald, as well as anonymous reviewers. Senior editor Rami Tal has been most helpful with structuring this book.

Special thanks are due to my friend Ricardo Díez-Hochleitner Rodríguez, a distinguished political leader and diplomat, as well as outstanding personality, and Honorary President of the Club of Rome, for encouragement, support and friendship.

Needless to add, but still needing emphasis, only I am responsable for the in part quite controversial contents of this book.

I am most grateful to Westphalia Press, an imprint of the Policy Studies Organization, Paul Rich, the President of the Policy Studies Organization, and especially Daniel

Gutierrez-Sandoval, Executive Director of the Policy Studies Organization, for deciding to publish this book and doing so outstandingly. Not less so do I appreciate the creative help of Matthew Brewer, Director of Outreach and Open Source Materials.

Similarly, thanks are due to Arik Puder, CEO & Founder of Puder Public Relations, New York, and his staff, for high-quality contributions to making this book and its inputs into public and professional discourse widely available.

On my family I maintain, as always, privacy, other than apologizing for neglect caused my over-commitment to what I regard, probably with a good measure of hubris, my "missions."

PROEM
THE WAY OF THE BOOK

TIME HORIZON

Most of my discourse is located within a time horizon of about one hundred Years. This is by two orders of magnitude longer than the time horizon of most mainstream politicians, for whom one year is often a long time. It is also by one order of magnitude longer than most long-term policy planning, which takes into account 10 years at most. However, even relatively longer-range outlook exercises, such as those dealing with Global Trends 2030 (National Intelligence Council 2012), adopt too short a time horizon to permit adequate consideration of alternative long-term futures that require action now. There are exceptions, such as Chinese tendencies to think somewhat in terms of generations, but as far as is known these too fail to consider the metamorphosis into which humanity is moving and its radical implications.

Therefore, a time perspective of 100 years, however guesstimated, is essential, though most action deals with shorter time ranges. Lest this looks prohibitive, it is important to take into account that life expectancy approaches one hundred years in highly developed countries and especially their elites. This makes one hundred years much shorter in terms of social and personal time than the same one hundred years when life expectancy was around 45 years not very long ago. Our thinking is slow in adjusting to such changes in the meanings of "time" however important, such as for personal life planning, policy composing, and the desired length of electoral cycles.

But more is needed for considering the future of humanity and trying to shape its futures. Therefore, in this book I also take into account a long-term evolutionary time horizon, as an essential perspective.

SHAPING FUTURES

Anatomically, modern Homo sapiens emerged about 200 thousand years ago—perhaps more. It made simple and then somewhat complex tools and was able to influence the environment and its future to a very limited extent. About 70 thousand years ago probably a "great leap" resulted in behavioral modernity, accompanied by the emergence of complex societies and cultures and growing impacts on environments and human futures. The industrial revolution and the emergence of modern science and technology, in the eighteenth and nineteenth centuries, radically increased human capacities to shape its future. This is expressed in the novel term "Anthropocene," which refers to the recent period, in most opinions since the industrial revolution, in which the earth is altered significantly by human activities (Ehlers and Krafft, eds. 2010).

The most fateful further leap in human capacities to shape its future, in interaction with the environment, started around the middle of the twentieth century with the development of the atomic bomb. As clearly put by Karl Jaspers, "An altogether novel situation has been created by the atom bomb. Either all mankind will physically perish or there will be a change in the moral-political condition of man" (Jaspers 1963, vii).

The atom bomb was only a beginning. The leap in human capacities to impact on the future becomes more and more gigantic and turns out to be a quantum jump, thanks to scientific and technological breakthroughs, such as in synthetic biology. The results include rapidly escalating human capabilities to destroy humanity, or change its very nature, or move into unprecedented and largely inconceivable pluralistic thriving.

This development constitutes a totally unprecedented turning point in the history of the human species pushing it through an "event horizon," in the sense of "the surface of no return" of a black hole (Deutsch, 2011: 3), which truly deserves to be called a "singularity" (in a broader sense than Kurzweil, 2006). Humanity is cascading into a metamorphosis while being only partly aware of doing so, keeping the mind fixed most of the time on rear mirrors instead of preparing for what is coming.

UNPREPARED HUMANITY

In 1968, Donald Michael published a perceptive book on humanity being unprepared for coping with future challenges (Michael 1968). The most insightful diagnosis for its time was provided by Robert L. Heilbroner, in a book published in 1991, which foresaw the need for a strict global regime in order to contain mass killing weapons supplied by science and technology (Heilbroner 1991). But these and later writers who present fateful challenges to humanity (e.g., Rees 2003; Seielstad 2012; Bostrom and Ćirković, eds. 2012; Newitz 2013; Guterl 2013), even if in part widely read and discussed, are politically treated as Cassandras not to be taken seriously, with the exception of some inadequate measures to protect the environment. Some global bodies do survey "future global shocks" (OECD 2011); some global risk studies are widely diffused, such as at the Davos meetings of the World Economic Forum (World Economic Forum 2014); and some dire outlooks are hotly debated, such as the size of the global population which the earth can carry (Boserup 1981; Brown and Kane 1994; Dorling 2013) and the

Green House effect (Hulme 2009; Dessler and Parson 2010). Even though most of these and other outlooks are partial, the overall diagnosis is clear: "Humanity is cascading into an epoch of metamorphosis, posing fateful challenges of "to be, what to be, not to be?"

SLEEPWALKING POLITICAL LEADERS

The vast majority of humanity is not aware of the existential challenges. And most of the discourse and publications deal only partly with the emerging challenges facing humanity, if at all. For example, the Flagship Report prepared by a consortium of distinguished research institutes (MCRIT et al. 2013), however impressive, hardly mentions the serious dangers posed by synthetic biology and human enhancement, neglects the serious unemployment crises likely to be produced by 3M printing, half-intelligent robots, and other human labor saving devices, and does not even hint at the need for a decisive global regime essential for regulating the production and diffusion of dangerous knowledge and materials. A major project on "Modes of Existence," headed by a distinguished researcher and thinker and financed by the European Research Council (Latour 2013), is very sophisticated but misdirected by ignoring the unprecedented potentials for better or worse of human metamorphosis. And so on.

The most serious misapprehension of the existential challenges is by political leaders, who are supposed to serve as a prime agency coping with them.

The vast majority of political leaders continue to live in what may be viewed, in a perhaps too pessimistic mood, as a kind of "Grand Hotel Abyss" as far as the future of humanity is concerned, described by Georg Lukács as "a beautiful hotel, equipped with every comfort, on the edge of an abyss, of nothingness, of absurdity. And the daily contemplation of the abyss between excellent meals or artistic entertainments can only heighten the enjoyment of the subtle comforts offered" (Lukács 1962, 757, translated from German by Anna Bostock).

To put it more mildly, the vast majority of political leaders are sleepwalkers (to use the term of Clark 2013) as far as the future of humanity is concerned. Some are aware of the main challenges, but the vast majority suffers from mental blind spaces on their significance. The Atoms for Peace policy inaugurated by U.S. President Dwight D. Eisenhower in 1953, which contributed to the proliferation of nuclear weapons, is a striking illustration.

Continuing sleepwalking by political leaders on critical issues assures disasters. To be happy as proposed "so long as [leaders of the Great Powers] realize their responsibility to prevent any actions that might lead to a world war" and to regard their job as "simply to hold firm the iron frame that keeps the international system secure" (Kennedy 2013) is analogous to having a couple of strong drinks in Grand Hotel Abyss, while ignoring the emerging serious dangers to humanity and absolving political leaders from their increasingly fateful responsibilities. As Martin Wolff wrote, comparing the present situation to the eve of World War I, "Complex societies rely on their elites to get things, if not right, at least not grotesquely wrong …the elites need to do better. If they do not, rage may overwhelm us all." (Wolff, 2014).

Descriptions of history as an oil tanker which can change directions only very slowly are true for much but not all of it. To stay for a moment with the metaphor, a tsunami can surely turn a tanker in a minute, and a torpedo can blow it up in a second. Our epoch is one of history taking a sharp turn into a new "space," not only another direction, driven by science and technology together with value transformations. All in all, our epoch is one of metamorphosis, which can lead to thriving, to transformation of the species into Homo sapiens superior or human monsters; or to dismal catastrophes up to the demise of humanity.

To decrease the likelihood of calamity and increase the prospects of thriving, radical changes are essential in values, institutions, and behavior, such as strict regulation of dangerous technologies, containment of fanatic aggressive values, and setting up of decisive but circumscribed global governance. However humanity is not prepared for what is essential. Scholars are not providing enough of the necessary theoretic understandings. Philosophers, religious leaders and other thinkers are not innovating needed values. And political leaders, who should take charge of coping with metamorphosis as far as is humanly possible, are clearly sleepwalking in critical domains.

CONSTITUTION AND LEADERSHIP

Given this diagnosis, this book fuses two leitmotifs: One, the need for a radically novel "Humanity Constitution," together with constantly expanding global law, which postulate basic norms concerning humanity as a whole and establish a decisive global regime headed by a Global Authority, adding up to what can be called metaphorically a Circumscribed Global Leviathan. It will develop in stages; probably following major catastrophes which compel humanity to do what at present is anathema, such as radically limiting "sovereign states."

And two, developing and bringing to the fore a novel type of political leaders which I entitle "avant-garde politician," which has the qualities needed for coping with an era of metamorphosis, including founding the required Humanity Constitution. This book tries to clarify and help with meeting this need, by exploring the qualities of mind required by avant-garde politicians and providing guidelines for becoming one, belonging in this respect to the classical genre of "mirrors" for leaders.

NEW TYPE OF POLITICIANS

The metamorphosis raises the fateful question whether the mental equipment of the human species and its collective learning capacities, as based on the brain and constrained and conditioned by it, are adequate for coping with the dangers and opportunities provided by the soaring human capacities to shape human futures, as supplied by science and technology. The only way to answer this question is by trying our very best. But whatever human potentials may be, as a matter of fact the vast majority of historic and contemporary political leaders lack at least some of the qualities essential for meeting the challenges posed by metamorphosis.

In 1831 on the Isle of Lewis in the Outer Hebrides, Scotland, a number of chess figures were found, known as the Lewis Chessmen. They were apparently crafted in Norway in the twelfth century. The kings, queens, bishops, knights, and warders look rather puzzled and stupefied (Caldwell, Hall, and Wilkinson 2010). My hunch is that the outstanding craftsmen who produced them knew the truth about the inadequacies of most political leaders. But also knowing that speaking truth about power will cost them their heads, the craftsmen put their opinion into the language of art when sculpturing the chess figures.

Today, much is publicly known about the failings of politicians, as glaringly reflected in bad results and uncovered by investigative mass media, committees of inquiry, and multiple forms of leaks. But much still remains hidden. Based on my personal acquaintance with the corridors of power in many countries having different regimes, my finding is that many political leaders perform much worse than is publicly known. If I had the skill to craft a set of chess figures, then most kings, queens, bishops, knights, and warders would look much worse than only "puzzled and stupefied".

However educated, intelligent, and experienced, and often though far from always well intentioned and hardworking they may be, the vast majority of political leaders lack many qualities of the mind essential for coping with increasingly novel critical issues, such as deep globalization, vexing economic crises, unprecedented geopolitical shifts, aggravating greenhouse effects, explosive demographic pressures, disruptive technologies, growing human enhancement possibilities, fanatics armed with new mass-killing devices, bloody clashes of cultures, and more.

Spontaneous, automatic, and self-managing societal processes, such as free markets and self-regulation by scientists, however important, cannot be relied upon to ward off the dangers and prudently utilize the potentials for the betterment of the increasing human capacities to shape the future, despite many unwarranted optimistic outlooks (e.g., Postrel 1999; Innerarity, 2012), but neither can prevailing imaginaries and modalities of politics and types of political leaders. This is all the more dangerous as the importance of politics and political leaders will increase by orders of magnitudes, because they are the only ones legitimately in charge of regulating societal actions impacting on the future and controlling in principle the instruments for doing so.

Every type of regime depends on myths. Most of those of democracies, such as assuming the wisdom of multitudes, are morally honorable and have more good than bad consequences, if not taken too seriously. However, the myth that being elected assures ipso facto fitness to serve as a political leader capable to cope with the challenges of an epoch of metamorphosis is not only wrong but dangerous. It is all the more troubling that most of the discourse on "good governance" (e.g., Ahrens, Caspers, and Weingarth, eds. 2011; Berggruen and Gardels 1913) deals with important subjects, such as corruption, participation, right to know, accountability, and so on, but ignores what is most critical for the future of humanity, including the quality of the minds of political leaders.

There are a small number of outstanding political leaders who sometimes come to the fore, often by a partly accidental convergence of historic situations and personal attributes. But the increasingly fateful role of political leaders in avoiding unprecedented calamities and utilizing radically novel opportunities makes relying on such "accidents" very risky. Therefore, clarifying the core qualities required from political leaders for coping with an epoch of metamorphosis is a priority task, together with the needed redesign of political systems as discussed in another book of mine (Dror 2002).

MIND MIRROR

Classical "Mirrors for Princes" belong to four types: giving advice on gaining and holding on to power, as illustrated by the Indian Arthaśāstra by Chāṇakya and by Machiavelli's The Prince; moral exhortations, as illustrated by Erasmus, The Education of a Christian Prince and Thomas Muntzer, Sermon to the Princes; books on statecraft, as illustrated by various Islamic Mirror books (Boroujerdi, ed. 2013); and teaching fables for future princes, often accompanied by beautiful illustrations which are a pleasure to behold (e.g., Grube 1992). To be added are modern versions of mirrors which mainly recommend personal and statecraft behavior (e.g., Morris 1999; Lord 2003; Codevilla 2009).

This volume joins the family of mirror books, being in part propaedeutic, but is different from most in two respects: adopting the future of the human species is its main perspective; and focusing on core qualities of the "mind" required from avant-garde politicians.

Plato was very concerned with issues of political order and the quality of rulers, as evidenced by his famous book The Republic and his less known but very important book The Laws. In-between is his dialogue The Statesman, which deals with the politikos, in the sense of a future-weaving ruler who has the qualities required for structuring and directing a political community. The Greek term politikos is usually translated as "Statesman." But, as explained by one of the better translators (Plato 1995, xi), this "is a pallid but unavoidable equivalent."

As argued in Plato's dialogue, a politikos differs substantially from those who actually rule, but who merely claim or give the appearance of possessing the required qualities. This evaluation strikingly fits the vast majority of contemporary political leaders, as is becoming glaringly obvious. But little is done to overcome this increasingly dangerous malaise. Serious books on "statesmen" are scarce (an exception is Schwinge 1983). Most of the literature on leadership, politicians, and so on lacks relevant ideas and the very notion of seeking an improved type of political leader is usually ignored and often regarded as taboo.

My "mind mirror" tries to redress this omission by proposing and developing a model of "avant-garde politicians," to serve as a cardinal political agency (Ypi 2012) in advancing what I call raison d'humanité, thanks to appropriate qualities of their mind.

IMPACT POTENTIAL

There are historians and thinkers, such as Leo Tolstoy, who are of the opinion that the impact of political leaders on more than immediate history is minimal. They are right on most political leaders on most ordinary issues. But a few do impact significantly on the trajectories of history, as illustrated in Chapter 8. But, to provide a first look at this question, which is of crucial importance for the raison d'être of this book, let me take up the controversial example of the world-changing First World War. I tend to agree that "Absent the Sarajevo incident, a great power war might still have broken out at some point in 1914 or shortly thereafter. But there are good reasons to think otherwise" (McMeekin 2013, 385), the assassination could easily have been avoided, and that "people carried in them the seeds of other, perhaps less terrible futures" (Clark 2013, xxxi). As well put by Margaret MacMillan (2013, 140) "It so easily could have been different." Taking into account that "the decisions that took Europe into the war – or failed to prevent it – were made by a surprising small number" (MacMillan, 2013, 247 and 249), the absence of adequate virtù of main political leaders clearly played a critical role in bringing about the catastrophe, despite opinions to the contrary (Tuchman 2004). This applies with a large multiplier to the fateful options facing humanity in the era of metamorphosis.

Relevant is a quotation from a 2008 U.S. National Intelligence Council publication:

> **Leadership Will Be Key**…human actions are likely to be the crucial determinant of the outcomes. Historically, as we have pointed out, leaders and their ideas—positive and negative—were among the biggest game-changers during the last century. Individually and collectively over the next 15-20 years, leaders are likely to be crucial to how developments turn out, particularly in terms of ensuring a more positive outcome. As we have emphasized, today's trends appear to be heading toward a potentially more fragmented and conflicted world over the next 15-20 years, but bad outcomes are not inevitable. International leadership and cooperation will be necessary to solve the global challenges and to understand the complexities surrounding them (National Intelligence Council 2008, 98-99).

I could write a history of the last 200 years in which political leaders are marionettes acting as pushed and pulled by the threads of history. Probably I would have to make an exception at least for Adolf Hitler, discussing him as a kind of "mutant," in line with the *Foundation* science fiction book series by Isaac Asimov.

But a "marionette" narrative of history would be fundamentally incorrect, for sure for shorter time spans and partly for very long ones too. Many political leaders make a significant difference to the immediate future, from 5 to 10 years, and also the near future from 10 to 25 years. Some make a difference to the intermediate future, from 25 to about 100 years. A few have significant impacts on the long-term future of 100 to 500 years. And the impact potential of highly qualified political leaders on the future is sure to increase and include the fate of humanity as a species, because of their critical role in determining the uses and misuses of humanity's leaping capacity to shape its evolutionary future.

LINE OF REASONING

I start with an expanded version of Hamlet's question "to be, or not to be," adding "what to be?" applied to the future of humanity. Then the book discusses the need to channelize metamorphosis, followed by a chapter taking the form of a think tank executive report. It suggest the founding of a Humanity Constitution establishing a strong global regime and a decisive Global Authority as an institutional imperative essential for the future of humanity. The Part One concludes with an exploration of the values which should guide avant-garde politicians, including three existential imperatives and a detailed value compass.

Part Two presents the extraordinary mission of an avant-garde politician as a total calling, requiring all of a person and imposing many demands, including a personal code of ethics.

The following two chapters explore necessary qualities of the mind at the core of being an avant-garde politician. Then a number of historical prototypes of avant-garde politicians are presented, demonstrating that the model of an avant-garde politician is not utopian.

Part Three discusses the images of reality in the mind of an avant-garde politician, which must be of high veracity so as to enable fulfillment of the extraordinary mission. This involved understanding very complex ultra-dynamic metamorphosis with special attention to thick uncertainty; realistically taking into account the contradictory nature of human beings as between "good" and "evil"; and thinking and acting in terms of plausible images of alternative futures.

The next part of the book takes up composing humanity-craft. After presenting the main modalities for pondering, ways to reduce error propensities are presented. Then the essence of humanity-craft as efforts to influence the trajectories of history, together with the difficulties posed by the nature of humanity-craft as bounded fuzzy gambles for high stakes, is explored and ways to do better are suggested.

The fifth and last part deals with the personal resources needed by an avant-garde politician. These include "public interest Machiavellianism" essential for achieving adequate power; helpmates who contribute to the qualities of an avant-garde politician and compensate for weaknesses; and a fitting innermost philosophy, including inter alia an "inner citadel" and a good dose of "stoic enthusiasm." The part ends with the "afterglow" appropriate for an ex-avant-garde politician.

An epilogue poses the personal critical choice of yes/no to try becoming an avant-garde politician and suggests ways for doing so.

AUDIENCES

The audience at which this book is directed is global. Despite the deep and intensifying globalization and the emergence of quite some "flat" elites and institutions, the earth is not flat (despite the interesting arguments of Friedman 2007). Geography in all its dimensions, such as physical, environmental, cultural, economic, political, military, and so on, matters a lot and will continue to do so (Kaplan 2012), with all its advantages, such as diversity in cultural learning, and many disadvantages, such as bloody conflicts, which have to be constrained. This implies that the details of this book have to be adjusted to local circumstances. But this will come easy for knowledgeable readers, all the more so as I keep treatment to a general level applicable to most of the world, with exceptions that I note.

Given its global or panhuman scope, the book is intended primarily for all who are or should be in interested in politics and policy studies, writ large, including scholars and students, as well as political leaders eager to improve themselves and persons considering choosing political leadership as their life meaning. The book is also intended for advisors to political leaders; and, with easily made adjustments, for the large variety of non-political leaders and decision makers who desire to impact for the better on the future of humanity.

A new cohort of innovative moral, value and spiritual leaders is also needed, as illustrated by Pope Francis (due disclosure: I am a Jew, not a Catholic), perhaps even more urgently than avant-garde politicians. This subject is to my regret beyond my competence. But there is a significant overlap between their needed qualities and those of avant-garde politicians. Therefore, a large part of the discourse on avant-garde politicians may also be relevant to moral, value and spiritual leaders.

The book is also aimed at all who want to understand the qualities that should be required from political leaders. This includes mass media commentators, enlightened parts of the public, and indeed all voters or agencies otherwise involved in selecting political leaders.

Taking into account such audiences, this book tries to minimize academic jargon. Footnotes are avoided. Full references are provided, but are inserted in easily ignorable brackets so as not to disturb continuous reading. An included annotated list of recommended readings may be useful for many readers.

This book being published both in print and in e-book (kindle) version, with the latter being cheaply available to buyers of the printed version, no index is included. The search program of the e-book being clearly superior to any printed index, the latter is superfluous. However, to ease orientation, the Contents also includes the subchapters.

All in all, I join Confucius in characterizing the readers whom I wish:

> The Master said: I will not open the door for a mind that is not eager to get knowledge, nor provide help to anyone who is not eager to explain himself. When I have presented one corner of a problem and the student cannot understand from it the other three, I teach him no further (Analects 7.8).

COMPOSING THIS BOOK

The responsibility and presumption of writing this book weighed heavily on me. I hesitated for a long time, despite many years of studying political leaders and working with them. However, I sense that the somewhat "taboo" nature of critical discourse on widely accepted values and on the need to radically improve political leaders result in dangerous conservatism and even dogmatism in mainstream thinking, studies, theories, teaching, and practice.

"Political correctness" will not do for the serious concerns of this book. Rather, it speaks frankly on disturbing issues, in the spirit of Norbert Elias:

> At the present stage in the development of humanity some of its representatives have the power to destroy each other, themselves and perhaps humanity altogether. In such a situation it is dangerous not to be completely sincere, not to make an effort to shed disguises, idealistic, materialistic or whatever. They are a luxury one can no longer afford (1992, 163).

I am aware that this book will cause quite some controversy. From the reactions of some readers of the manuscript, however often politely formulated, I sense that they are sorry that they cannot put the book in an index of prohibited books, as happened to the main writings of Machiavelli in 1559 (after he died in 1527). But none of the negative and also hostile reactions to main themes of the book offered plausible arguments demolishing its main contents, expressing instead emotional resistance to its partly iconoclastic approach. Many seem to prefer avoiding bearable costs of changing some widely accepted values and institutions willingly to the very high costs of calamities and subsequent much more painful adjustments.

All the more so, guided by the Jewish canonic adage "In a place where there are no men strive to be a man" (Ethics of the Fathers, Chapter 2, 6), but with many trepidations, I submit this book to the readers.

Readers are invited to share their frank reactions and suggestions with the author, writing to my email address msdror@mscc.huji.ac.il. But please do so after finishing reading the book as a whole, so as to have a coherent view of the diagnoses, prognoses, and prescriptions elaborated and explained in it.

PART ONE

HUMANITY:
TO BE,
WHAT TO BE,
NOT TO BE?

CHAPTER 1
CHANNELING METAMORPHOSIS

HAMLET'S QUESTION EXPANDED

Hamlet's question "To be, or not to be" (Shakespeare's play *Hamlet*, Act 3, scene 1) needs expansion so as to apply to the human species, which for the first time in its history faces squarely and urgently the question "to be, what to be, not to be?" thanks to its leaping capacities to impact on the future as provided by science and technology.

Only very little philosophic discourse deals with "Thinking About Human Extinction" (Kateb 1994, 127-171). On the question to be or not to be, most philosophers and surely the vast majority of humans would reply, "for sure the human species should continue to exist." Exceptions include expectations for a "Day of Judgment" and an end to time. But only a few extremists support deliberate human self-extinction. Accordingly, I accept as axiomatic an existential imperative to assure as far as humanly possible the long-term existence of the human species.

But this leaves open the radically different and more difficult issue "what to be?" Answers depend on different transcendental views and a variety of opinions concerning the nature of a "good life," a "meaningful life," a "worthy community," and so on, accompanying humanity since prehistory. Philosophy, ideologies, religions, utopias, and politics are full with discourses on "what to be?" But here too modern science and technology make a tremendous difference by posing radically novel possibilities.

Most aporetic of all (in the *Oxford English Dictionary* meaning of "to be at a loss," and "impassable," related to the noun "aporia") are the dilemmas posed by the emerging possibilities to "enhance" humans, ranging from lengthening life expectancy to changing bodily and mental attributes, perhaps up to human cloning, a synthesis of living multicellular organisms and other possibilities when the future "does not need us" (Joy 2000; Kurzweil 2006). These lead to increasingly likely alternative futures, which are largely inconceivable in terms of presently available knowledge, analogues, and concepts.

Some pertinent issues are discussed in bioethics, though without adequate consideration of dangers and needed countermeasures (Basl and Sandler eds. 2013; Steinbock, ed. 2009; Kaebnick and Murray, eds. 2013; Kuhse and Singer, eds. 2012; Schmidt, M. et al., eds. 2009). It is troubling that discussions of the future of theology too tend to ignore such issues (e.g., Ford 2011; Kepnes 2013). All the more so, frames of thinking will have to change a lot when far-reaching human enhancement becomes possible, posing acute questions on what to permit, encourage, and prohibit, and how to do so effectively.

Contemporary societies, including political leaders, are completely unequipped to take up such critical questions, in addition to being unwilling to do so because of their divisive nature. But waiting till the unthinkable becomes real will carry a high cost. Therefore, a new type of avant-garde politician is all the more essential for taking up in earnest the fateful question "humanity, what to be?" Adequate responses require creative values, radically novel political cultures, and global decision-making processes, all lacking at present with a few inadequate partial exceptions. This becomes all the clearer when put into evolutionary perspectives and in lights of disruptive technologies and the emerging era of metamorphosis.

EVOLUTIONARY PERSPECTIVE

The history of the human species within the history of the universe is as far as reasonably known well covered in the literature (e.g., Wood 2006; Christian and McNeill 2011; Christian et al. 2013; Scientific American 2013a). Still, an approximate timeline is needed here to provide an initial perspective, with attention to natural catastrophes, which played a crucial role and can do so again (Prothero 2011; Kolbert 2014).

As a starter, let me commence with the most recent near extinction of the human species, which occurred between 195 to 123 thousand years ago. Probably due to an icy climate period "the number of people plummeted perilously - from more than 10,000 breeding individuals to just hundreds…" Genetic studies "indicate that everyone alive today is descendent from a small population that lived in one region of Africa sometime during this global cooling phase" (Marean 2013, 53-54).

Earth formed about 4.600 billion years ago. The first shapes of life appeared about 4 to 3.5 billion years ago, by processes which are in debate and basically unknown. Over billions of years life developed slowly by adaption, natural selection, and genetic drift, together perhaps with presently unknown factors, interrupted in part by three to five main extinction events, the largest of which was the end-Permian extinction which took place around 200 million years ago and caused about 96% of all species to die out. It was probably caused by vast eruptions in Siberia or the continental drift. The most recent extinction took place about 65 million years ago, after vast expansion of life forms and in the age of the dinosaurs. That extinction was most probably caused by a massive meteorite hitting earth. It cleared the ground for modern types of animals and plants, leading to apes and then humans.

Divergence between humans and chimps took place at least 6–7 million years ago. It took about four million years for the difference between the brain cases of earliest ape-like ancestors and our species to develop. The best measure of intelligence-related differences in brain size is the Encephalization Quotient (EQ), which compares the relative brain size defined as the ratio between actual brain mass and predicted brain mass for an animal of a given size. The EQ of humans is 7.4–7.8; of Bottlenose dolphins 4.14; of Chimpanzee 2.2–2.5; and of dogs 1.2.

Homo sapiens sapient is a subspecies of the species Homo sapiens, which belongs to the genus Homo, which in turn is a part of the Homininae. Another subspecies of Homo sapiens was *Homo sapiens idaltu* ("elder wise human'), which became extinct. Some additional subspecies seem to have existed, as shown by modern genetic studies.

Homo sapiens sapiens (to be referred to in short as "Homo sapiens") most probably developed first in Africa between 120 and 150 thousand years ago. It became fully behavioral modern in our sense between 60 and 20 thousand years ago. There was some intermarriage between our subspecies and homo Neanderthals, as shown by modern genetic studies, but homo Neanderthals disappeared.

Neanderthals ruled for more than 200 thousand years, disappearing around 24 thousand years ago, after some interbreeding with our species, which contributed to our genes up to four percent. The reasons are not clear, after the conjecture that they were killed off by Homo sapiens having been rejected. They had more intelligence than was supposed till recently. But it seems that their mental equipment was inadequate for coping with changing climate conditions, with the result, whether inevitable or being influenced by luck, being that Homo sapiens survived and they did not (Finlayson 2009).

In some view, human evolution has accelerated in the past 10,000 years, rather than slowing or stopping, and is now happening about 100 times faster than its long-term average over the 6 million years of its existence. The pace has been so rapid that humans have changed significantly in body and mind over recorded history. (Cochran and Harpending, 2010, 1). But further evolution of our species was mainly cultural, including more advanced tool making, language, agriculture and husbandry, larger settlements, more complex social structures, and later symbolic writing.

Behavioral modernity involved language, symbolic thought, and accelerated cultural creativity. One school of history thinks that this was a relatively rapid development, called the "great leap forward" or the "upper Paleolithic Revolution," related to mainly functional changes in the brain. Another school thinks that a small accumulation over hundreds of thousands of years was involved.

Homo sapiens spread throughout Europe and Asia about 40 thousand years ago and continued to spread to all continents, being the only primate species doing so. It was partly enabled to move from continent to continent by changes in climate related to small ice ages, which lowered sea levels and resulted in land bridges and the gigantic landmass known as Sahul combining Australia with New Guinea and Tasmania, from about 40 thousand to eight thousand years before the present time, together with early narrow sea crossing skills. These resulted in a multiplicity of human settlements with nearly no difference in genes, other than the very few related to variations in bodies, but very significant differences in cultures starting in prehistory.

Cosmologies, tools, attitudes to nature, ways of life, social structures, and so on are very different between, say, Europeans, Australian aborigines, tribes in Papua New Guinea, and small Indian settlements in the Amazon forest. These differences are qualitative in nature and cannot be rated as "more" or "less" developed and "civilized," other than by parochial standards widely accepted in Western (and other) civilization till recently and also nowadays. Still, there clearly are civilizations which had more impact on most of humanity, among which only "Western Civilization" produced the "enlightenment," democratic regimes, and modern science and technology. However, human beings from all cultures and localities constitute one species with the same mental capacities and feelings, interbreed, share many dimensions of culture, and can communicate once language and some conceptual barriers are overcome.

Developments of symbolic language and other cultural learning impacted on some acquired mental capacities, as may modern behavior habits, such as spending much time interacting with computers and related instruments, for example iPhones. These influence some patterns of the brain as shown by fMRI studies (which measure brain activities), but are not inheritable. But there is no discernible difference in the mental capacities of human beings for the last 5 to 10 thousand years at least and probably more. This fits with all we know on evolutionary processes of living beings, as distinct from collective cultural learning, which can be, and for humans is much faster.

Evolutionary processes being slow, human development depended largely on what is often called "memes". A meme acts as a 'unit for carrying cultural ideas, symbols, or practices that can be transmitted from one mind to another through writing, speech, gestures, rituals, or other imitable phenomena, such as "tunes, ideas, catch-phrases, clothes fashion, ways of making pots or building arches" (Dawkins 2006, 192). Some regard memes as cultural analogues to genes in that they self-replicate, mutate, and respond to selective pressures. However the concept is useful even if related processes are very different from biological evolution, leading to the conclusion that the foreseeable future of humanity depends on memes and not genes. A possible exception is human enhancement by genomic engineering, leading to crucial issues concerning the future of the human species.

In our period, thanks to the accelerating and radically innovative cultural learning, something unprecedented is happening, which justifies characterizing the emerging epoch as one of metamorphosis. As mentioned, starting around the middle of the twentieth century, based on developments in the eighteenth and nineteenth centuries, cultural learning of the human species in science and technology provides humanity with the capacity to radically transform its future, including terminating itself. This completely new capacity poses a totally novel fateful human predicament. As mentioned, it is unknown and unknowable whether the mental equipment of the human species and its collective learning capacities, as constrained and conditioned by the brain and bound by the past, are adequate for handling well these predicaments.

In any case, humanity is rushing into a radically new phase in its evolutionary history which requires far-reaching and in part revolutionary innovations in self-perception, perspectives, values, thinking, emotions, social processes, structures, institutions, and so on, and also in grand policies. This existential requirement poses and conditions, inter alia, the unique extraordinary mission of avant-garde politicians. This is well illustrated by the proliferation of disruptive technologies.

DISRUPTIVE TECHNOLOGIES

To introduce the idea of "disruptive technologies," a rather simple but revealing example will serve. Let us assume that a cheap and easily available technology is developed which enables cheap production of large top quality diamonds and other expensive gemstones, such as Jadeites, which are completely identical with naturally found ones. Prices drop, such as from about 3 million dollars per carat of Jadeite to about 200 dollars.

This will have dramatic consequences for owners of expensive gems or investors in them, countries where they are found, and all the trade nets and professionals specializing in them. Secondary consequences are likely to include changes in fashions and perhaps invention of substitute luxury items that serve as status symbols of the rich and very rich. However, all these disruptions are relatively limited, much more so than other possible and in part likely science and technology innovations, such as cheap nonpolluting energy and mass-killing but self-limiting synthesized viruses that can be produced in kitchen laboratories.

Moving on to what is very likely in the near future, let me mention 12 disruptive emerging technologies, as analyzed by the McKinsey Global Institute (Manyka et al. 2013):

1. Mobile Internet;
2. automation of knowledge work;
3. the Internet of things;
4. cloud technology;
5. advanced robotics;
6. autonomous and near-autonomous vehicles;
7. next-generation genomics;
8. energy storage;
9. 3D printing;
10. advanced materials;
11. advanced oil and gas exploration and recovery; and
12. renewable energy.

Also mentioned in the document, but not discussed in detail, are next-generation nuclear fission; fusion power; carbon sequestration; advanced water purification; and quantum computing.

The publication concentrates on economic and business implications viewed through optimistic lenses. But it recognized dangers: "Low-cost desktop gene-sequencing machines will not only put the power of genomics in doctor offices, but also potentially in the hands of terrorists. Even well-intentioned experiments in garages using inexpensive sequencing and DNA synthesis equipment could result in the production and release of dangerous organisms. ….It will be up to business leaders, policymakers, and societies to weigh these risks and navigate a path that maximizes the value of these technologies while avoiding their dangers" (Manyka et al. 2013, 19).

The document concludes with the statement: "Technology continues to advance on many fronts, and many developments bring new challenges for society and government. Governments cannot afford to be passive or reactive. If policy makers wait until bioterrorists show what they can do with a low-cost gene-sequencing machine, it will be too late. Policy makers should also have well-thought-out, structured methods for assessing technologies, to add rigor to their analyses" (Manyka et al. 2013, 151). However what needs to be done to meet these requirements is left open. Not a word on the necessity to improve the quality of politicians, the urgency of which, together with a Humanity Constitution and a novel global regime, become all too clear when the overall nature of the emerging era of metamorphosis is considered.

METAMORPHOSIS

The concept "metamorphosis" refers to a radical transformation making an entity into a very different one. It has also a second meaning, in respect to insects or amphibians, namely the transition from an immature to a mature form, such as a caterpillar becoming a beautiful butterfly. A counterexample is provided by the 1915 Franz Kafka novella *The Metamorphosis* in which a human being becomes a monstrous vermin. The butterfly and vermin can serve as metaphors for the fateful question "to be, what to be, not to be?" Not providing an answer and letting spontaneous developments determine the future can result in the fate of Hamlet and Kafka's vermin.

Yet it is difficult to provide an answer, however provisional, to a question that has no clear meaning. It is nearly certain that the metamorphosis is partly produced by the leaping human capacity to impact on the future, including the very nature of human beings, provided by science and technology. This, together with the likely but unknowable value changes, justifies regarding the foreseeable future as a fateful epoch of metamorphosis—with unknown, partly inconceivable, but at least partly controllable outcomes. Hence comes the extraordinary mission of avant-garde political leaders to guard humanity against undesirable results by channelizing the overflowing streams of metamorphosis (to apply a metaphor used by Niccolò Machiavelli when discussing ways to confine *Fortuna)*.

But the actual forms which the metamorphosis will take, including human reactions to its main features, are largely unknown and also unknowable in advance as well as underdetermined by the past. Not all is undergoing rapid change, significant strands of history remaining probably quite stable for extended periods, such as the basic features of human beings. Some mega-trends can be foreseen some time ahead. But the overall features of the evolving metamorphosis cannot be predicted on the basis of a different past. And encompassing theories on the rise and decline of humanity or other salient Grand Theories are lacking, not plausible, and may be inherently not more than a mixture of guesstimates and speculations. In a nutshell: the future is not here and therefore cannot be "studied"; and the past is a weak basis for outlook into the future in an epoch of radical change.

Three implications follow: (1) the many unknowns do not negate what is foreseeable, including unprecedented opportunities and deadly dangers posed to humanity; (2) therefore, measures to reduce the likelihood of bad futures and increase the likelihood of desired futures are essential; (3) these measures have to be very elastic and need constant adjustment to actually emerging salient realities, including those caused by earlier efforts to channelize metamorphosis.

Clearly, such efforts to steer critical streams of the metamorphosis are very demanding. A novel understanding of turbulent historical processes has to be developed, new social science paradigms are needed, and both value and institutional innovations become essential. All these need a long-term perspective rooted in the history of our species within the evolution of life as a whole—which the vast majority of political leaders lack.

LEADERSHIP FOR METAMORPHOSIS

As noted, contemporary political leaders fail to cope well with present challenges. All the more so they lack the qualities essential for dealing well with the emerging challenges increasingly posed by metamorphosing humanity within its ecological setting. This conclusion is justified both by historic experience and the situational and contingency theories of leadership (Northhouse 2013, 99-136), which explain that different types of leaders succeed or fail under different conditions. The reasoning underlying this proposition was clearly recognized by Machiavelli, especially in Chapter XXV of *The Prince*, where he puts the matter succinctly in two insightful statements: "the man who adapts his methods of procedure to the nature of the times will prosper, and likewise, …the man who establishes his procedures out of tune with the times will come to grief" (Machiavelli 2008, 85); but "No man is so prudent that he knows how to adapt himself to this fact, both because he cannot deviate from that to which he is by nature includes, and also because he cannot be persuaded to depart from a path after having always prospered by following it" (Machiavelli 2008, 85-86).

More is required, namely qualities of the mind leading to a new global politics. As put by Jaron Lanier, "We've never faced genuinely global long-term political issues before, so never needed genuinely global politics" (Lanier 2013, 81). At the center of that new politics a novel type of political leaders is essential the qualities of whom enable them to function well in the new epoch of metamorphosis. Accordingly, the proposed model of an avant-garde politician is based on a functional analysis, together with historic data and relevant theories, as far as available and fitting radically novel situations. It follows that a deeper understanding of the emerging epoch of metamorphosis is the main key to specifying the required qualities of avant-garde politicians.

PROSPECTS

Main religions foresee an end to humanity in its present form, and also an end to "time" itself, such as some kind of apocalypse and Final Judgment. This is not necessarily a prophecy for a far-off future, an end of history having been expected occasionally by religious believers as imminent. But, in line with the overall this-worldly metaphysical stance of this book, such beliefs can be left aside.

Some years ago I read the science fiction story *"The Weapon,"* authored *by* Frederic Brown in 1951. Its gist is that a stranger gives a loaded revolver to the retarded son of a scientist developing an ultimate weapon. This is in my reading a striking metaphor for science providing rather unwittingly immature humanity with instruments to destroy itself.

We can be sure that humanity, as all live on earth, will not exist forever. Cosmic evolution will make the earth, the planets and, later on, our Milky Way and our universe as a whole, and also parallel universes, if they exist, unfit for maintaining organic life. This is an outlook for astronomic time scales, which you can safely ignore, though an avant-garde politician should in a corner of the mind be aware of it. But within the much shorter evolution of life on earth too there is no reason to assume that the human species is the ultimate climber to the peak of "mount improbably" (Dawkins 1997) and will survive for eons. There are very impressive other life forms which arrive at amazing achievements thanks to other paths of evolution, such as the so-called "superorganism" formed by termites, bees, and ants (Hölldobler and Wilson 2008).

The disappearance of humanity may fit into the dynamics of biological evolution, with some species of superorganisms, or some kind of homo superior, or some other entity, sentient in our sense or not, taking over. However, the future of humanity is not determined by biological evolution alone, but largely and increasingly so by cultural developments which can easily influence the life span of our species.

It is far from certain that cultural dynamics will assure a thriving future for humanity. The opposite is also possible and perhaps likely, with cultural achievements providing humanity with instruments for destroying itself, which may be used because of limitations and propensities built into the human mind, which were useful at earlier phases of human evolution but become dangerous when supplied with the capacities provided by science and technology.

To sharpen the analysis, let me refer to Jay Wright Forrester's systems dynamics (Forrester 1969). The relevant parts of his models claim that in a dynamic system main trends may develop in ways which produce antinomies and contradictions that cannot coexist and thus lead to some kind of implosion of the system. This model was applied to humanity by the well-known Club of Rome Report *Limits to Growth* (Meadows et al. 1974; Meadows, Randers, and Meadows 2004), which claimed that rapidly growing populations and consumption on the one hand and lesser increases in resource supplies, on the other, lead unavoidably to an implosion, unless some of the trends change direction. Without using a formal model, the theory of population proposed by Thomas Robert Malthus was similar, claiming that unavoidable gaps between growing populations and limits on the capacity to produce food would produce self-correcting catastrophes, such as large-scale famines. However, these are models, not fate. Alternative thriving futures are also possible, given the adequate channeling of metamorphosis processes.

ALTERNATIVE SCENARIOS

Presentation of a few scenarios illustrating components of possible alternative global futures in the next one hundred years may provide some sense of the potentials of the metamorphosis. They are divided between mainly desirable, disastrous, and problematic ones, with some overlaps and mixed outcomes. Comprehensive alternative futures serving as bases for humanity-craft are presented in Chapter 12.

Mainly desirable scenarios:

- Climate engineering eliminates environmental degradation, greenhouse effects, and other pollutions.

- Cheap and easy to use human enhancement technologies provide immunity against many diseases, result in a live expectancy in good health till the age of about 150, increase IQ by 20 to 30 points, and strengthen altruistic human solidarity.

- Quasi-intelligent robots, together with three-dimensional (3D) printing, atomically precise manufacturing (APM) (Drexler 2013) and other new technologies, take over nearly all human manual work and growing parts of routine intellectual work. Labor markets are disrupted and mass unemployment becomes endemic. But, after a relatively short adjustment period, release from wearisome work facilities cultural thriving.

- Future technologies reduce human dependence on scarce materials, enable space travel, and have many other beneficial consequences (Highfield 2013).

- Escape into amusement machines, virtual hedonistic realities, and new "happiness"-producing drugs becomes widespread. If subjective happiness is a main goal, this provides a way to "tranquilize" societies. If maturing humanity is a main goal, this is a bad scenario.

Disastrous scenarios:

- Devastating pandemics are caused by mutated or created viruses and bacteria produced by human efforts and released by accident or on purpose.

- Nuclear or other mass-killing wars and multiple mega-terror attacks add up to global mayhem.

- Doomsday devices are activated by martyr apocalyptic actors.

- Irreversible damage to the environment is caused by human actions, which hurts the narrow band of natural conditions essential for human life, such as CO_2 balance, average temperatures, sweet water, and cosmic radiation.

- Radical demographic imbalances between genders are produced by easily available pre-selection technologies widely used to prefer males over females.

- Large-scale famines and scarcity of critical materials caused by increasing global population and breakdowns of the global economy devastate societies.

- Experimental production of a self-propagating nano-based material intended to serve medical diagnostics gets out of control and kills most children under the age of about 12 worldwide.

- Continuous and aggravating breakdowns of the global financial system and of the global market economy result in decreasing standards of living and large-scale scarcities of essential food, materials, and energy, which in turn result in uncontrollable violence.

- Live-enhancing technologies become available, but are very expensive and can be used only by a small part of humanity, causing much antagonism, social disruptions, and massive bloodshed.

- A large meteor hits earth, or one of the at least twenty supervolcanoes on earth erupts, causing havoc with most of the human species being killed.

Problematic scenarios:

- Enhancement of critical human features producing a new kind of "super-humans" breaks the basic unity of the species.

- Brain enhancement technologies enhance the intelligence of animals, raising profound ethical issues with bitter differences of opinion.

- Cloning of human beings becomes feasible.

- Breakthroughs in synthetic biology result in artificial production of multicellular living beings.

- New technologies permit easy worldwide intrusive, but nearly impossible to sense and regulate, surveillance.

- Brain scans permit reliable findings on whether a person is lying or telling the truth in judicial proceedings.

SECOND AXIAL AGE?

Assuming that a catastrophe is prevented, which is not at all assured, developments during the next one to two hundred years may lead into a new Axial Age, which will be much more than a "Next Renaissance" (Khanna 2011), Neo-humanism (Sarkar 2012), and similar visions. The Second Axial Age, if and when it emerges, will be driven by socio-technical innovations together with peak value creators (very much neglected in Joas 2000), with radically novel cultural and spiritual contents changing the self-understanding of humanity and human societies in presently inconceivable ways.

The term "Axial Age" was coined in 1949 by Karl Jaspers (2010, 1-21) referring to the period from about 800 to 200 BCE, during which relatively similar radical innovations in thinking appeared in China, India, and the Occident, apparently independent of one another. These transformed human self-understanding and transcendental views and inaugurated a new epoch in human intellectual and spiritual history which in many respects continues till now.

In contrast to the mainly spiritual–philosophical–religious nature of the First Axial Age and it's not really understood drivers, the Second Axial Age is likely to be driven initially by the capacity of humanity to destroy or transform itself. But unforeseeable spiritual, cultural, and social consequences are very likely to follow, with unpredictable value transformations, which can be "good" or "bad" in terms of contemporary values. Beyond such guesstimates and speculations the nature of a Second Axial Age is shrouded in thick uncertainty impenetrable with our present modes of thinking, dependent as they are on analogies with the past—and therefore making it difficult to ponder seriously on futures beyond a hiatus in historic continuity.

It may well be that the increasing academic interest in the First Axial Age (Eisenstadt, ed. 1986; Bellah and Joas, eds. 2012) is a tacit symptom of a feeling that a new Axial Age is in the making. But this too is a speculation.

CAN HUMANITY COPE?

Let me return to the crucial open question whether humanity has the potential to cope adequately with the existential dangers and mind-popping potentials inherent in the metamorphosis. Humanity is moving through a deep hiatus in its history, which in some crucial respects is more fundamental than all earlier transformations (with the crucial exception of the invention of stone tools by proto-humans around 1.5 million years ago), such as the use of fire, transition to agriculture, increasing populations, leaps in self-understanding and transcendental views, enlightenment, industrialization, democratization, and globalization. Therefore, the overall successes of the species in the past, never mind their high costs, do not guarantee abilities to succeed in the future.

It is possible that physical limits determine that "we probably cannot get much smarter" (Fox 2011). This implies that "normal" evolutionary processes, including Lamarckian inheritance applied to cultural learning, according to which an organism can pass on characteristics that it acquired during its lifetime to its offspring, cannot be relied upon to enable coping with problems the difficulties of which may go beyond the capacities of human individuals and collectives.

Relevant is the theory of punctuated equilibrium evolution, as propounded mainly by Stephen Jay Gould (2007), according to which periods of relatively rapid biological evolution take place dispersed among periods of biological stability. But such accelerated biological evolution too takes many generations and therefore cannot be expected to augment human mental capacities in the foreseeable future, perhaps with exceptions related to the plasticity of the human brain.

It might be possible to increase human mental qualities with the help of science and technology, so as to enable coping adequately with the challenges of the epoch of metamorphosis. This can be an impressive evolutionary leap, with Homo sapiens being enabled by cultural evolution to achieve the mental qualities essential for coping with the dangers and opportunities provided by that same science and technology.

Therefore, augmentation of mental qualities may be a main goal for humanity-craft, even if the consequences are inconceivable. And avant-garde politicians would have to be among the first to be subjected to such enhancement. But this is a speculative contingency, which cannot be relied upon and which may have dangerous "side effects."

Till salient qualities of the human mind can be reliably enhanced, which may or may not become possible before metamorphosis-generated catastrophes strike, it is up to Homo sapiens with its present minds to do its very best, including facilitating the gestation of avant-garde political leaders.

PRELIMINARY CONCLUSIONS

Desirable, dismal, and problematic alternative futures become increasingly within human reach. Which one is regarded as more likely depends on optimistic or pessimistic views. Marquis de Condorcet and quite a number of modern thinkers assume that there are no limits to the ability of humanity to produce a utopia on earth, thanks to "the power of ideas" being an "infinite resource" (Naam 2013). The tragic-ironic fact that Condorcet was one of the victims of the French Revolution has not hindered most of modern culture to cling to optimistic notions on the future of humanity, with the exception of recent worries concerning nuclear weapons, the environment, synthetic biology, and other pessimistic outlooks. But these suffer from the curse of Cassandra, having little impact on mainstream cultures and policies—other than much "green" rhetoric without decisive action.

When the future of humanity and large-scale suffering are at stake, I recommend prudence, which takes pessimistic contingencies seriously. At least limited calamities are likely to occur, till lessons of experience produce adequate safeguards. And large-scale catastrophes are far from unlikely and definitely not impossible. Prudence therefore requires guarding against bad possible futures, combined with grand-policies increasing the likelihood of futures desirable by a majority of humans. Also essential are pathways for deciding what to do about problematic possible futures. All these are at the core of the extraordinary mission of avant-garde politicians and provide a basis, together with personal ethics considerations, for mapping the qualities required from their minds.

CHAPTER 2
CIRCUMSCRIBED GLOBAL LEVIATHAN

INSTITUTIONAL IMPERATIVE

As demonstrated by contemporary realities, existing institutions, societies, and cultures, as well as political leadership and global governance bodies as presently constituted, cannot handle in an adequate and timely manner most global issues, such as protracted conflicts, bloodshed, financial crises, glaring disparities, global warming, and so on. All the more so they are unable to deal with emerging existential challenges. Therefore, a foundational process setting up novel humanity institutions, facilitating a fitting global society and culture and developing a new type of political leadership, is essential for the future of the species.

Political leaders here face a double catch: To fulfill their increasingly important and demanding extraordinary mission they need enabling institutions, societies, imaginaries, and cultures. But the emergence of these prerequisites depends significantly on top quality political leaders, who are hardly available.

Urgently needed is a Humanity Constitution which institutionalizes a suitable global regime and decision-making bodies, while avoiding "structural sin," such as expanding interventions beyond what is essential. But an endeavor to found them, even if in bits and stages, is sure to be opposed by prevailing values and power structures. Untangling and, if necessary, cutting through this knot is the main task awaiting, among others, avant-garde politicians. In doing so, an avant-garde politician has to act in some respects as a revolutionary leader from within.

Leaving development of avant-garde politicians to later chapters, this chapter takes up the idea of a "Humanity Constitution," postulates its basic norms, and specifies the required global regime and Global Authority, adding up to a "Circumscribed Global Leviathan." To do justice to their futuristic nature, they are presented in the literary form of an executive report by a fictitious think tank (somewhat on line with Lewin 1967).

The presented proposal is counterfactual and will remain so for quite some time. It is also contrarian, only single thinkers having realized and publicly said what is very likely to become necessary, in one form or another, for assuring the future of humanity. But let me quote an already mentioned exception. Robert Heilbroner, after diagnosing the need for an "alternative to the present order," concludes that "the order…most likely to satisfy… requirements is one that blends a 'religious' orientation with a 'military' discipline' as 'needed to reach a 'new stable socio-economic basis'" (Heilbroner 1991, 176-177). Arnold Toynbee had some even more radical ideas which, though at present ignored, have much to recommend themselves subject to adjustments (Toynbee 1963a; 1963b).

Should it prove possible to meet the needs of human survival and related requirements making superfluous a Global Leviathan however circumscribed, with all its costs, this is much for the better. However, this seems quite unlikely. Various more conventional proposals for a revised global order (e.g., Ikenberry 2011; Kupchan 2012) most probably err in clinging to contemporary paradigms (Suganami 1989) which are unlikely to be sustainable for long. Therefore, it is very likely that "forcing events" (in the sense of Fukuyama, ed. 2008) will cause main powers to do what at present seems far-fetched.

NOT A DYSTOPIA

The presented outline vision is nor a fantastic dystopia. Rather, the sketched foundations are likely to become glaringly essential within the twenty-first century and perhaps somewhat later, however contradicting what at present is often viewed as "obvious" and "immutable" and is deeply rooted in widely accepted imaginaries and "common sense." This assessment becomes even more convincing when the constant changes in forms of governance throughout history (Finer 1999; Bobbitt 2003; Fukuyama 2012) are taken into account. Such clear lessons of history should serve as an antidote to rather childish beliefs that the present institutions and their underlying belief systems and power structures somehow are in line with an "end of history" (Fukuyama 2006, including an important updating new afterword).

Political institutions have to fit historic dynamics as changing with time, in order to fulfill essential functions, all the more so when humanity is cascading into a radically novel era of metamorphosis.

It is absurd to believe than everything is going to change, but politics will and can remain the same. Foreseeing a civilization-changing revolution in nanotechnologies and then postulating that "Potential paths forward will be constrained by politics, and politics is the art of the possible. What is possible, however, will depend on the state of opinion, and opinions, as they take form, are shaped by conversation," (Dexler, 2013, 272) contradicts itself. Such an opinion demonstrates total misunderstanding of what must be done, namely restructuring of most of politics by avant-garde leadership, which makes what is necessary possible, inter alia by shaping opinions and building high-quality consensus, as discussed in Chapter 17.

Required is global super-cooperation, avoiding "free riders" and the "Tragedy of the Commons" (Nowak and Highfield, 2013), but it cannot be relied upon to emerge on its own, nor can less demanding forms of cooperation, such as based on reciprocity and feeling of identity. Therefore some approximation of what is presented below is probably essential for the future of the human species for an interim period of a couple of generations. Then, if surviving more or less intact, humanity will hopefully advance into another era of novel flourishing, whether taking the form of a Second Axial Age or not, making the coercive elements of the proposed Circumscribed Global Leviathan a part of the future past. But this is in the further off future.

THINK TANK OMEGA-ALPHA EXECUTIVE REPORT

You probably do not know about our existence. We are the Omega-Alpha think tank, our name signifying that we are dealing with the transition from the end of the long history of the human species since its beginning till the middle of the twentieth century, during which, luckily, it lacked the ability to destroy itself, to the new era of metamorphosis, when the human species becomes increasingly capable of terminating its existence and also changing its very nature.

We are a group of 15 select thinkers with different backgrounds and qualifications, set up and financed by an anonymous philanthropist. Our charge is to make proposals on the form of global governance needed for preventing termination of the human species, controlling its "enhancement," and advancing pluralistic thriving. We have concluded our main study and sum up its main findings and recommendations in this short Executive Report.

Our overall conclusion is that a vigorous but strictly and in part narrowly circumscribed Global Leviathan, based on a Humanity Constitution and "global law," is essential for the survival of humanity. The term "global law" is reserved for laws strictly based on the Humanity Constitution and directly aimed at implementing the survival and species changing inhibition imperatives, including parts of international law explicitly adopted as global laws by the Global Authority as set down below. For the foreseeable future, most of international law, augmented by laws aiming at realizing increasing parts of the human flourishing imperative, will continue to be based mainly on agreements between states as developing with time. It will be applied separately. But global law has superior standing overriding incompatible international law.

We know that our assessment and proposals contradict presently widely accepted values and require radical changes in the prevailing power structures. However, we are convinced that without a firm global regime the very existence of humanity is increasingly endangered.

No one can bring about adoption of the needed constitution and establishment of the required global regime in one big leap. But political leaders and other future-shapers can and should take steps to compensate temporarily for the absence of a suitable Humanity Constitution and its executive organs, while preparing the ground for their founding and proceeding as far as possible with their establishment.

Progress may be slow till calamities, hopefully limited ones, will teach humanity what needs to be done. Utilizing such opportunities requires advance thinking and preparatory action, which should be commenced urgently.

The Humanity Constitution and related global law and institutions must cope with the fateful and increasingly likely possibility of serious damage being caused, inadvertently or purposefully, to the human species or large parts of it by human action or lack of action. To do so, the proposed Humanity Constitution should be based on fitting and explicit basic norms, in the sense of the Pure Theory of Law (Kelsen 1949). These include three existential imperatives dealing respectively with human species survival, human enhancement controls, and advancement of pluralistic flourishing of humanity. They are axiomatic, though if you wish you can regard them as grounded in one or another transcendental belief.

The Humanity Constitution should set down rules of global law and outline human rights and duties and other main values derived from the basic norms as applied to the changing conditions of an era of metamorphosis. Also to be included are principles of a global regime and its main institutions, as discussed below.

The Humanity Constitution is in no way a utopia. Indeed, we reject any utopian or quasi-utopian construct, not only for the dangers of utopias and their impossibility in a pluralistic global world (on line with Lacan, Stavrakakis 1999), but as sure to become rapidly obsolete in the emerging era of metamorphosis. But it is in some respects harsh when compared with present values and hopes, however inadequately that these are realized in practice. The needed Humanity Constitution is of global scope and involves a lot of global surveillance with quite some invasive monitoring, strict regulation, and painful sanctions. At the same time, the scope of the proposed constitution, global law and global regime is circumscribed, most ordinary governance tasks being left to states, lower level authorities and multiple public and social agencies, on the principle of subsidiarity. This principle, as first developed in the Catholic Church and accepted in the European Union, postulates that authority, functions, and responsibility should be located at the lowest level that can do the job, subject to higher level supervision and override if necessary.

In essence we propose a Humanity Constitution, which establishes a "Circumscribed Global Leviathan." We know that this terminology will not make our proposals easier to digest. But the seriousness of the issues at stake requires in this Executive Report frank terminology. However, we do not suggest that the term "Circumscribed Global Leviathan" should be used to propagate the proposed constitution and regime, which can be fairly and more effectively presented as "humanity survival norms and regime," or some other attractive and truthful concept.

Let us sum up the basic rationale of our proposal, though the details are tentative and subject to deeper studies as well as changing situations: because of the emerging capacity of individuals, small groups, states, and other actors to cause great harm to large parts of humanity and the species as a whole, up to terminating its existence or changing its core nature, strict regulation and partial prohibition of development, diffusion, and use of knowledge and technologies that may endanger humanity is mandatory. This regulation and prohibition, as set down in a partly new category of "global law," has to be on a global scale and of maximal effectiveness, strictly enforced on all actors. To do so while providing adequate safeguards against misuse, a Humanity Constitution and a fitting global regime are essential, with a decision-making Global Authority at their core—

which is authorized to legislate global law and give directives of global applicability and enforce them, subject to limitations and an overview as set down in the constitution.

While operating as far as possible by agreement, guidance, convincing, and a variety of incentives, forceful action will be necessary to impose some rulings of the Global Authority. The Global Authority has to erect a global surveillance system, however intrusive, which assures early detection of potentially humanity-endangering activities, but strictly avoids collection of irrelevant personal information and fully safeguarding all data. Also, however radical this requirement may be, in order to safeguard humanity the Global Authority needs a monopoly over all types of mass-killing weapons and an overwhelming preponderance of other instruments of coercion—as necessary for avoiding nuclear and other mass-killing events (Cirincione 2013; Schlosser 2013) and, mainly, for enforcing decisions effectively on whatever scale necessary, ranging from coercing states to surgical operation against non-state toxic leaders and actors.

This requirement clearly changes the basic paradigm of statehood as postulated by Max Weber (2004, 33) and widely accepted, according to which "the state is the form of human community that (successfully) lays claim to the *monopoly of legitimate physical violence* within a particular territory" (emphasis in original). Leaving aside doubts on the validity of this definition in view of the proliferation of non-state actors possessing potent instruments of violence, the Humanity Constitution should postulate that "the Global Authority has a monopoly on all weapons and other means of mass killing and is entitled to impose further limitation on the weapons possessed by states and other actors." This rule and its enforcement worldwide are an essential feature of the needed new global regime.

The disturbing and in part disruptive nature of our conclusions requires an explanation of the reasoning behind them, all the more so as nearly all of classical and contemporary political philosophy and of the discourse on modernity and postmodernity as a whole is increasingly inadequate, largely irrelevant and often misleading on what is essential for human survival and thriving in an epoch of metamorphosis.

We started with the possibility, and indeed likelihood, of accidental or purposeful misuses of the emerging human capabilities to shape the future supplied by science and technology. These can cause serious harm to the future of humanity, up to its extinction, as a result of aggregated unintended effects, such as greenhouse climate changes; accidents, such as escape of mass killing synthesized viruses; or purposeful action by fanatic aggressive states, groups, or individuals. Neglect of defending humanity against natural catastrophes, such as asteroid impacts, adds to the dangers which require a decisive global regime commanding adequate resources.

Also needed are central resources, to equalize environmental damages distributed unfairly between different physical locations and for large-scale science projects, possible experimental human settlements beyond earth and other human thriving-oriented activities of a scale requiring global action, as already taking place in some domains though inadequately so.

We went on to consider a number of additional cardinal issues related to radical human enhancement, human cloning, creation of multicellular life, total emersion pleasure machines, and intelligent robots. Such possibilities are very problematic in terms of human values and possible results, including inconceivable ones.

Our recommendation is not only to keep options open, but also to limit salient research and experimentation to closed and carefully monitored facilities, and strictly regulate commercialization. Definite choices can wait till issues mature, which will take quite some time. However, we want to emphasize that whatever and however choices on human enhancement and related issues are made, they cannot be reliably implemented without some kind of Global Authority.

Having identified grave dangers to humanity, we accepted as our working assumption the moral necessity and human desire to reduce their likelihood to a minimum, giving priority to risk reduction also at the cost of foregoing potential benefits of developing multi-use knowledge and instruments. Therefore, the Global Authority should operate according to the principle of minimum regret together with cost–benefit–risk considerations. Thus, when a contingency, which is very dangerous, is considered, large-scale countermeasures are justified even when the realization probability of the contingency is low or unknown. But when a less serious contingency is at stake and countermeasures are costly in terms of values and materials, then only a high realization probability justifies taking full-scale counteraction.

We considered whether and to what extent presently operative or expectable societal processes can be relied upon to institutionalize and realize required controls. This involved examining the propensities of states, the dynamics of markets, the preferences of civil societies, the clusters of activists, the self-regulating abilities of science and technology, and so on. We reached the conclusion that all these can be helpful if steered in the needed direction, but are unable to meet the requirements. Thus, even assuming, however unrealistic, that an international agreement signed by all states prohibits experiments on synthesizing multicellular life and that salient professional associations worldwide adopt a code of ethics prohibiting such experiments, this assures nothing. Individual scientists and laboratories, on their own or clandestinely supported by governments, fanatic groups, or commercial interests, are likely to engage in such experiments despite all agreements to the contrary. Even a highly effective Global Authority may be unable to stop some well-hidden efforts, but it provides maximal protection by imposing global law and rulings on states, large international corporations, predatory fanatic organizations, and other salient actors and assuring compliance by mobilizing support and providing incentives together with surveillance, enforcement, and harsh punishments.

We paid special attention to the potentials of emerging elements of global governance such as the United Nations and its affiliated organizations. However important for handling a variety of humanity issues they may be, clearly much more is needed. Typical is the United Nations *Global Compact* launched in July 2000 (UN Global Compact Office 2011). However worthy in other respects, with the exception of some principles on protecting the environment, the main dangers and opportunities facing humanity and the critical importance of preventing businesses from promoting and marketing dangerous information and goods are neither mentioned nor at least hinted at. Little wonder that books for business managers presenting the *Global Compact* (e.g., Lawrence and Beamish, eds. 2013) follow suit. This is not an accident but a manifest symptom of the structural inadequacies of the United Nations Organization in its present form for coping with the serious challenges posed by the metamorphosis into which humanity is cascading at increasing speed. Such inadequacies are widely recognized, but nearly all reform proposals (e.g., Goldin 2013) are insufficient.

Throughout history changes in modes of production and in population sizes and density, accompanied by increasing complexity, always required and in part brought about new forms of regimes, otherwise decline followed. This was the case with the evolution from families and clans, through tribes, to states and empires, and emerging proto-forms of global governance. Accordingly, we studied the history of main attempts to establish large-scale and partly global regimes, such as the unified Chinese Empire after the Warrior State period, *Pax Romana*, Mongol Empire, attempts to achieve a unified Catholic world, British Empire, Communist visions of a peaceful just world, hopes for cooperation between the willing to bring about universal peace as positioned by Emmanuel Kant, and the history of modern global governance starting with the League of Nations and continuing with the United Nations family of organizations, and the European Union. We also studied the experience of special organizations such as the International Committee of the Red Cross and the International Red Cross and Red Crescent Movement, relevant non-governmental organizations, humanitarian law combined with global jurisdiction and international courts, and philanthropic initiatives.

We learned much from these efforts, some of which quite successfully reduce incidents of mass killings and promote thriving. But often they fail, with high costs in human lives and suffering. According to our assessment, the United Nations Organization and its affiliated bodies, after some reforms, can fulfill increasing parts of the required measures and prepare the ground for the required global regime. But no historic prototype or contemporary governance structure is able to impose globally measures essential for the security of humanity. Therefore, a global regime very different from all its antecedents is essential, constituting a break in human governance history not less radical than the break in human abilities to impact on its future provided by science and technology. Efforts to build global institutions according to analogues of national institutions (Suganami 1989) lack the creativity needed to craft a Humanity Constitution and to design effectively a global regime and institutions.

Unavoidably, the Humanity Constitution will be "artificial" for quite some time, not being based "organically" on a vivid social and political culture and widely accepted opinions, images, and values. It is also radically and revolutionarily novel, being legitimized in terms of raison d'humanité and based on principles very different from those of state constitutions. Its functions, structure, and instruments are in the main different from those of existing multinational and international organizations. Therefore, its drafting involves much more of an original "work of art" than the Renaissance states (Burckhardt 1990, 19-97) and also the Constitution of the United States of America (Slauter 2011).

All this will take time and requires a lot of creative constitutional design, going beyond available experience (Ginsburg 2012), while utilizing it as much as possible. Therefore, we call on outstanding constitutional and related thinkers to start working on alternative concepts for the Humanity Constitution and on different ways to draft and ratify it.

However, we wish to clarify one point, so as to reduce unrealistic expectations: despite many opinions to the contrary (e.g., Wouters et al., eds. 2013), the Humanity Constitution, at least in its initial versions, will be neither democratic in the usual meanings of that term, nor mainly "bottom-up," though maximum global public support for it must be mobilized. Also, unavoidably the Humanity Constitution will be influenced by the actual features of catastrophes and novel forms of violence, as wars in the past have shaped governance (Bobbitt 2003). All the more important are therefore amendment procedures to be included in the Humanity Constitution, so as to enable adjustment to changing conditions and values while preserving basic norms and core principles.

We also studied carefully the literature dealing with the rise and decline of states, societies, and civilizations, seeking lessons for the future of humanity. Some of their lessons seem somewhat relevant. These include, for instance, the need, when facing recognized existential dangers, for top quality diverse thinkers to withdraw and consider creatively effective countermeasures, as our think tank tries to do. The role of civil society and various elites is important, as are features of societies, such as coherence and resilience, and of culture, such as innovativeness. However, political leaders are often a critical factor in efforts to cope with a novel and complex situation, or failing to do so. We think that without a much-improved political leadership our recommendations will be ignored or not implementable, and the future of humanity will be at serious risk. Therefore, we hope to present recommendations on upgrading political leadership, such as setting up a Global Political Leadership Academy, very different in participants, curricula and learning methods from existing attempts, such as most public policy schools, though much can perhaps be learned from pioneering efforts such as the Forum Academy set up in 2014 by the World Economic Forum, however much in need of partial redesign. But this is a subject for another Report.

The proposed Humanity Constitution, global law and related regime and institutions require and depend on supportive changes in political and social cultures and revaluation of values. Thus, essential is becoming of humanity as a whole a real community, in addition to an imagined one (Anderson 2006).

Having made the case for a novel Humanity Constitution and global regime, including a powerful Global Authority, we tentatively specified its essential features, as a basis for in-depth consideration. The Global Authority needs the legal right to promulgate global laws and issue directives which all states, organizations, and individuals are obliged to follow. It will maintain a global surveillance system and engage in inspections relevant to its tasks. The Global Authority needs the power to enforce its laws and directives, including effective and overwhelming instruments of force, to be used when necessary to compel states and other actors to comply with its directives or to enforce them directly. Also required is the authority to impose taxes and other payments on states, corporations, and individuals as needed for its activities. Essential are top quality staffs and suitable central as well as dispersed physical facilities.

The Global Authority will also deal with major global or regional crises endangering humanity or large parts of it, in cooperation with states or other actors or on its own if others cannot do so adequately. Accordingly, it needs the right to declare a "global state of humanity emergency," which abrogates usual legal norms and enables it to use all instruments and resources necessary for reducing damage and providing emergency help.

Relevant is the definition of Carl Schmitt (2006) that "sovereign is whoever decides on emergencies," in the double sense of declaring a state of emergency and deciding on what to do about the emergency. Having the authority to declare a state of emergency, on a global or local scale, with all that is involved (Agamben 2005), constitutes a transfer of crucial parts of sovereignty from states to the Global Authority. All the more so, rules for imposing "emergency regimes" by the Global Authority have to be subjected to strict safeguards, set down in the Humanity Constitution.

The composition of the new global institutions raises difficult and controversial issues. Global democracy, in one sense or another, is not feasible in the foreseeable future and the fiction of state equality cannot serve as a basis for the required global regime and the Global Authority. Instead, the following preliminary proposals serve to indicate major issues and possibilities: the Global Authority should include three main organs. The first is the Directorate which has the main legislative, decision-making and executive powers. It should be composed on the basis of three principles: (1) reflecting the majority of humanity, though in the foreseeable future not by universal global elections; (2) outstanding personal quality; and (3) complete independence. The number of proposed members is 16, appointed for a period of six years, with eight being selected by the most important or populated countries reflecting also different civilizations, such as (in alphabetic order) Brazil, China, European Union, India, Indonesia, Republic of South Africa, Russia, and the United States. Eight more members should be appointed by other countries to be selected periodically by lot from all members of the United Nations, subject to veto by a majority of two-thirds of the member states. Selection of the directorate members by the countries can be by special elections, a decision by the legislature, or appointment by the government, as each country may decide. The Secretary-General of the United Nations, before perhaps being amalgamated with the global authority, will be an additional ex *officio* non-voting member of the Directorate.

Once appointed, the members of the directorate must detach themselves from their countries, acting according to their best personal judgment in the interest of humanity as a whole. Members can be reselected once. After finishing their term of office they should receive a generous pension, but are not eligible for any political position in their countries and may not accept any other payments or other material benefits for a cooling-off period to be decided upon.

The Directorship legislates and makes decisions by a majority vote, with the exception of some extraordinary decisions as mentioned below and stipulated in its statutes, which require a two-thirds vote.

The second main body of the Global Authority is a Council serving also as checks and balances. Composed of outstanding thinkers and scientists, it functions in part as a science court, in charge of evaluating the dangers posed by science and technology developments. Its opinions on such issues have to be accepted by the Directorate and serve as a basis for its measures, unless rejected by a two-thirds majority vote.

A two-thirds majority of the Council has veto power over decisions by the Global Authority to use force to impose its decisions. However, the Global Authority can override such a veto by a special majority of 12 of its members.

We suggest that the Council should be composed of 16 members, half of them recipients of the Nobel Prize, one each in physics, chemistry, physiology or medicine, and economics; and two each in literature and peace, to be selected for 10 years by lot from the living recipients of those prizes below the age of 60. The other 8 members should include outstanding philosophers, theologians, social scientists, and jurists selected by the highest bodies of 8 universities located in countries with different civilizations to be chosen by the 8 Nobel Prize members.

The third part is a Global Constitutional Court, deciding all cases brought before it concerning global laws, regulations and decisions by the Global Authority. It will also give binding opinions on the validity of proposed global laws if asked to do so by the Global Authority or Council. Only governments of states and heads of United Nations and related organizations can submit cases for consideration. Judgments will be based on interpretations of the Humanity Constitution supplemented by principles of equity. Procedures will provide for appeals to a larger forum of judges and issuance of temporary orders, but assure rapid decisions.

All the more important is the composition of the Global Constitutional Court. We tentatively suggest the following principles: Appointments till retirement age of 65, after a probation period; judges to include top quality legal scholars, experienced lawyers, outstanding social science scholars, and persons with high level political experience. Candidates can be submitted by heads of governments and chief justices and presidents of universities worldwide. Appointment will be by a three-quarter majority of joint sessions of the Global Authority and the Council.

However all this is very tentative and needs further deliberation. It is too early to go into further details, such as adjustment of existing global governance and rules to the new ones. Indeed, we may well err in going so far into details as we did, but this is essential for clarifying our main rational and principle recommendations and to stimulate discussion on what are quite iconoclastic ideas compared to prevailing ones.

But we would like to emphasize four requirements concerning the Global Authority: (1) the quality of the advisory, implementation, and supporting staffs and their complete independence from states and other actors are of paramount importance; (2) additional checks and balances should be set down in the Humanity Constitution, such as an Comptrollership; (3) consultation and seeking of broad global consensus are essential, but the Global Authority should be decisive also in the face of opposition; (4) as already mentioned, but requiring reemphasis, the Global Authority must have the means and the will to enforce its decisions, including severe coercive measures when lesser ones prove inadequate.

Having devoted most of our work to the dangers facing humanity and the institutions needed for coping with them, we changed direction. The proposed Humanity Constitution is not primarily designed to promote some kind of "utopia" or to facilitate human rights, justice, pacification of non-bloody local conflicts, gender equality, animal rights, or any other values or ways of life that may be regarded as contributing to human thriving, including perhaps some that can be learned from traditional societies (Diamond 2013). These, for the foreseeable future, are matters to be handled by countries, non-governmental actors, and an enhanced United Nations system. Rather, the Global Authority should focus on coping with dangers to the very existence of the human species or large parts of it, main issues of human enhancement, and advancement of human thriving in selected respects as may be decided by it with a two-thirds majority from time to time. And the global regime should become involved in facilitating the pluralistic thriving of humanity in select domains, such as elimination of extreme poverty and reduction of large quality of life disparities, in cooperation with the United Nations and other international actors, when asked to do so by a two-thirds majority of all states. Imposing more on the proposed global regime cannot but dilute its main functions and make its establishment even more difficult.

The promulgation of a Humanity Constitution and establishment of a global regime depend on substantive value changes, which in turn are likely to cause with time further value innovations. But the Global Authority should not presume to engage in "value architecture," other than those essential for its core tasks. Thus, values endanger the existence of humanity or large parts of it should be prohibited and inhibited, in line with laws and action against genocide. But value issues not closely related to assuring the existence of humanity or preventing undesirable enhancement are beyond the competence of the Global Authority.

However, the value issues involved in "human enhancement" do require consideration and in part regulation. This may require additions to the Humanity Constitution depending on actual human enhancement possibilities, to be considered when the need arises.

There remain many additional problems, such as how the Humanity Constitution will be promulgated, how amendments will be decided upon, and how the Global Constitutional Court should be set up and operate. Some novel form of a Global Constitutional Assembly may be necessary, or perhaps imposition of a Humanity Constitution and global regime by an oligopoly of major powers will prove to be the only practical way. But it would be premature to go into such issues before there is broad agreement in principle on the need to move toward a strong global regime.

Essential, as important a value by itself and a precondition for advancing in the proposed directions, is a widely shared sense of human species commonality. We prefer this concept to the commonly used term "human solidarity." The latter is surely very desirable, but does not include all that is needed (Wilde 2013); realistically, not much can be expected from it in the foreseeable future (Chouliaraki 2013); and it tends to deal with marginal issues or serves as a rather empty slogan (Featherstone 2012).

Essential for assuring the future of humanity are, first of all, self-identities, commitments, imaginaries, and pervasive deep feelings best summed up in the proposed concept of "human species commonality." These values should be included in the Humanity Constitution for symbolic and educational reasons. However, advancing this sense is more a matter for cultural and spiritual leaders and a diverse global raison d'humanité avant-garde elite than subjects within our mandate.

We would like to conclude by emphasizing that the classical question posed by Max Weber (2004, 76) "what kind of a human being one must be to have the right to grasp the spokes of the wheels of history" is becoming more critical and also fateful than ever, especially with regard to qualities of mind required from political leaders. Without fitting political leaders our recommendations cannot be implemented, or may be misused—and all of the future of humanity will be in doubt.

AFTER STUDYING THE REPORT

Never mind if you like or dislike one part or another of the imagined Executive Report of the Omega-Alpha think tanks. Its presentation has one purpose only, but a crucial one: to dramatize and put starkly to avant-garde politicians, and to all others who can impact on the future, the revolutionary changes in global regimes, with all the associated changes in values, needed in order to meet the dangers to humanity posed by the self-produced capacities to terminate and change itself provided by science and technology.

Emphasizing the need for a fitting radically novel global regime is all the more necessary because most of the available literature, such as on "global public goods" (Brousseau, Dedeurwaerdere, and Siebenhüner, eds. 2012), global issues (e.g., CQ Researcher 2013; Payne 2012), global agency (Ypi 2012), and so on, tends to ignore the fateful "to be, what to be, not to be?" problematic facing humanity and the global structures required for coping with it.

Similarly, "the multitude" (Hardt and Negri 2005), global networks based on complexity theory (Root 2013), big city mayors (Barber 2013) and so on can deal with some issues. But they cannot cope with the really fatal challenges facing humanity. No such actors can compensate for the absence of strong global governance institutions coping with the fateful issues posed by dangerous and perhaps fatal misuses of the capacities supplied to humanity by science and technology.

Thus, all in all, the Executive Report presented above offers a provisional and indicative foundational frame for building essential global governance and for pondering, choice and action critical for the future of humanity, recommended to avant-garde politicians.

The Report also provides a horizon and basis for considering the raison d'humanité and a proposed value compass in the next two chapters, which in turn present the normative basis for a Humanity Constitution and global regime.

CHAPTER 3
RAISON D'HUMANITÉ

EXISTENTIAL IMPERATIVES

The basic norms, on which the Humanity Constitution is grounded and which it serves, which also serve as the main normative basis for the extraordinary mission of avant-garde politicians, include three existential imperatives:

1. Survival imperative: Absolute priority should be given to assuring the long-term survival of the human species and to preventing serious harm to large parts of it. This implies preventing human actions and non-action and counteracting natural events which can terminate the human species or grievously harm it or large parts of it.

2. Species changing inhibition imperative: Production, diffusion, and use of species changing knowledge and technologies and human enhancement should be rigorously controlled on a global scale. Minor species changing technologies, such as marginal human enhancement, should be strictly regulated. Studies leading to creation of life, construction of highly intelligent robots, and radical human enhancement should be limited to classified and supervised facilities. The design and production of self-reproducing organic or inorganic entities, attempts at human cloning, and work on similar technologies, as may be decided from time to time, should be prohibited or at least strictly compartmentalized and supervised. Concomitantly, informed discourse in public space, among value thinkers, and in professional forums on advisable grand-policies on such possibilities should be encouraged and ways to decide on them when necessary, with as broad a consensual basis as possible, should be designed.

3. Human flourishing imperative: Subject to the survival and species changing inhibition imperatives, strenuous efforts should be made to advance long-term pluralistic flourishing of the human species and its parts, while also taking care of the pressing short-term human needs. Free choice should be given to different societies in choosing their ways of flourishing, as long as they do not impair the free choice of others and respect universal human rights and other global higher-order values and Hypergoods (Taylor 1992), as decided upon by global forums representing or at least reflecting humanity.

These imperatives will for clarity be referred to collectively as "existential imperatives", and, separately, as the survival, species changing inhibiting, and flourishing imperatives, respectively.

PRIORITY TO RAISON D'HUMANITÉ

The survival and species changing inhibition imperatives constitute the core of raison d'humanité, radically distancing it from raison d'état. It should receive absolute priority when issues of importance for the future of humanity are at stake. To use another terminology, though I usually avoid it because of misleading connotations, "cosmopolitism" has priority over localism in all its forms when the future of humanity is at stake, in contrast to "statism," in the sense of states being the decisive actors and loyalty to them, or "state patriotism," being a supreme and unconditional value and obligation—which are forms of "tribalism" not acceptable any longer.

The survival and species changing inhibiting imperatives add crucial missing elements to global value discourse and goal setting. Examples of important documents which omit much of what is essential for the future of humanity include, for instance, the *United Nations Millennium Declaration* of 2000 and its follow-ups; the 2012 Report of the United Nations Secretary-General's High-level Panel on Global Sustainability 2012: *Resilient People, Resilient Planet: A Future Worth Choosing;* and the 2013 *Report of the High-Level Panel of Eminent Persons on the Post-2015 Development Agenda*: *A New Global Partnership: Eradicate Poverty and Transform Economies Through Sustainable Development;* and the *United Nations Global Compact.* Similarly serious omissions are also widespread in most global elite meetings, such as the "Davos" meetings of the World Economic Forum, and not less so in academic books dealing with global values (e.g., Widdows 2011).

What is grossly neglected in thought, declarations and actions alike and what the existential imperatives emphasize is the striking 1954 statement by Dag Hammarskjold, at that time Secretary-General of the United Nations: "The United Nations was not created to bring us to heaven, but to save us from hell."

The proposed existential imperatives avoid the fashionable term "sustainability." This is done for a number of related reasons. While "sustainability" includes some important principles which are included in the existential imperatives, it often has rather conservative and backward looking connotations, covers many domains which are not really important for human survival, and is frequently misused to prevent dynamic development by overemphasizing costs and being too risk averse. Also, the term has become a slogan and often serves as a cover for various vested interests and "green" establishments.

Furthermore, without disparaging the importance of secondary values widely advocated, such as "animal rights," they are not of cardinal importance for the future of humanity. Therefore, while some such values may guide ordinary tasks of political leaders and may become components of the flourishing imperative if so decided, they are not integrally a part of the existential imperatives.

CONSEQUENTIALISM

Values of others are "facts" to be known, understood, and influenced by an avant-garde politician as far as necessary and possible. But the values of an avant-garde politician are a fundamental quality of the mind, conditioning and shaping all of it, consciously and unconsciously. They serve as a normative basis for the extraordinary mission and related processes, including pondering, choice, and action. As many other qualities of the mind, they are in part plastic and subject to change, by external influences, ponderings, and also some bodily processes. Therefore, the values in one's mind should be considered, evaluated, and reshaped introspectively as an internal fact, similar to considering "coldly" one's moods and emotions.

The existential imperatives, as well as the value compass presented in the next chapter, also serve as guides for soulcraft (in the sense of Will 1983, but with different contents), aimed at having them accepted by increasing parts of humanity, as urgently necessary for effective measures against looming dangers, such as humanity-caused climate change, and as a basis for the Humanity Constitution.

A major distinction between two approaches to values applies to the existential imperatives. One approach, advocated strenuously by Immanuel Kant and his followers, and having religious roots, is deontological. It regards main values as absolute moral obligations that have to be followed without regard to consequences. The contrary school is "consequentialism," with the morality of acts depending on the normative standing of the consequences. It is the consequential approach, going back to utilitarianism as developed by Jeremy Bentham, which fits most of the missions of an avant-garde politician who is normatively obliged to look out after the future of the human species. This does not mean that the morality of means is unimportant, but the morality of consequences comes first.

Consequentialism too is inherently based on values to be realized. Therefore the distinction between the deontic and consequentialist approaches to values is not absolute. However, there is a significant difference: Consequentialism, as a "meta-ethics," in the sense of a higher-order ethical principle serving as a basis for substantive ethical norms, permits and sometimes makes obligatory acts which are "evil" by themselves, but are necessary for preventing a greater evil or realizing a more important "good."

Thus, the survival imperative justifies in principle evil means if the existence of humanity is at stake, such as torturing children to get information necessary to prevent activation of a doomsday device. The 2010 film *Unthinkable*, directed by Gregor Jordan, well presents such a situation on a local but catastrophic scale, as do some episodes of the UK television series *Nikita*. I hope you will never confront such terrible choices, but the very tragic may and from time to time does happen, all the more so in an epoch of metamorphosis.

DIRE NECESSITY

The discourse above leads to the doctrine of "dire necessity" which should guide an avant-garde politician in using force and other unsavory means to advance the extraordinary mission. The consequentialist meta-ethics justifies and also obligates an avant-garde politician to do all that is possible to advance raison d'humanité. This includes using force, dissimulation, breaking agreements, and so on, as well as engaging in necessary revolutionary action, however illegal—but all these should be strictly limited to the minimum essential for advancing core components of raison d'humanité, as implied in the term "dire necessity."

Machiavelli puts it very clearly in Book III, Chapter 41 of the *Discourses:*

> ...where the ultimate decision concerning the safety of one's country is to be taken, no consideration of what is just or unjust, merciful or cruel, praiseworthy or shameful, should be permitted; on the contrary, putting aside every other reservation, one should follow in its entirety the policy that saves its life and preserves its liberty (Machiavelli 2003, 350; for pertinent discussion, see Bobbitt 2013, 29-58).

Substitute "humanity" for "one's country" and you have a clear guideline for acting according to "dire necessity," as may be required by the existential imperatives. Let me add that the principle of "necessity" is well recognized in many jurisdictions, and also in international law with the addition of "proportionality" (Gardam 2011). In the context of raison d'humanité, "limited to what is necessary" should be substituted for "proportionality", which often does not apply or may be inadequate.

The doctrine of dire necessity throws sharp light on the moral duty of an avant-garde politician to be ready if necessary to dirty his hands and also have blood on them; and to ponder and decide on using violence, sometimes in large doses. This raises difficult psychological and ethical issues on maintaining moral integrity while using brute force, all the more aggravated by the terrible experiences of the twentieth century. Related dilemmas and ways for coping with them while doing what is necessary but keeping immorality of means to an essential minimum are discussed in chapter 17.

Three main dangers include getting used to it, in line with the "banality of evil" thesis of Hannah Arendt (2006b); even worse, starting to enjoy it; and, morally honorable but destroying an avant-garde politician, to get the Lady Macbeth syndrome, as put insightfully by Shakespeare in his play *Macbeth*:

> Lady Macbeth: "Here's the smell of the blood still:
> all the perfumes of Arabia will not sweeten this little
> hand. Oh, oh, oh!" (Act 5, scene 1).

Instead, an avant-garde politician must feel deep pain when using lethal violence and make sure that this is indeed a "dire necessity," with the help of trusty spiritual and security advisors. But when essential, an avant-garde politician has to act with determination, perhaps weeping in privacy, but without a disabling crisis of conscience. This is difficult, but is required as well as justified by raison d'humanité.

GROUNDINGS

There is a fundamental difference between the causes of a person holding a particular set of values as a fact, and the justifications which that person gives for the validity of those values.

The causes include genetic propensities, habitus (in the sense of Pierre Bourdieu of "the way society becomes deposited in persons in the form of lasting dispositions, or trained capacities and structured propensities to think, feel and act in determinant ways, which then guide them" (Wacquant 2005, 316), personal history, individual features such as "taste," and—very differently—inwardly mental processes which are partly autonomous from external causal factors, including for instance deliberation and "leaps of faith" (what Søren Kierkegaard called "leaps to faith").

An extreme illustration of such factors in action is the acceptance of Nazi values by many Germans looked at from the outside, which can be explained by some German traditions, traumatization of the First World War and economic crisis, the charisma of Hitler (which, in turn, needs explanation), systematic Nazi propaganda, social pressures, and so on (as dramatized in the 2012 BBC 2 series *The Dark Charisma of Adolf Hitler*).

Quite different are the justifications offered by various truly believing Nazis for their faith, which may include a comprehensive worldview on the mission of Germany, "proofs" that Jews are vermin, having read *Mein Kampf* by Hitler and being convinced by it, consciously viewing Hitler as a personification of history, and so on (Koonz 2005).

The problematic is exposed by a simple mental exercise: Please spend half an hour or so trying to image what your values would be if you were born and raised in the home of a senior commander of Iran's Revolutionary Guard Corps with a devout and educated Moslem mother also fully committed to the cause of the Revolutionary Guard. For sure your values are radically different from those of a person born and growing up in the home of a senior Israeli Mossad agent killed in action, a conservative Swiss banker, a Chinese coal miner, a prosperous slave-ship captain three hundred years ago, and so on. Then try to think about the justifications these persona would give for their beliefs. These would be very different from the socio-psychological causes of their beliefs, being instead explicitly normative, such as the commandments of the Koran, Zionist ideology, and so on.

All this has very serious implications for already mentioned "meta-ethics" defined by the *Stanford Encyclopedia of Philosophy* as "the attempt to understand the metaphysical, epistemological, semantic, and psychological presuppositions and commitments of moral thought, talk, and practice." Thus, the facts that one's values are largely shaped by an evolutionary imprinting and specific social habitus, and that persons of comparable intelligence and knowledge believe throughout history in very diverse and also contradictory values and provide very different justifications for their beliefs, cannot but lead to a good measure of moral relativism.

The ultimate personal answer to the question why one accepts a value is "because I believe in it." There are interim answers, such as "because God commands so," but this leads to the further probing "why should one do what God commands?" A utilitarian answer that "otherwise I go to Hell" too leads to further questions, such as "why is it bad to go to Hell?" Justifications of moral beliefs as "inherent in nature," or rooted in a "human moral sense," leave open the question, why should we accept what is inherent in nature or in a human moral sense, assuming there are such fixed phenomena, which is only partly true, if at all. All these lead unavoidably to the final statement: "This is what I believe because I believe in it." *Finito!*

Therefore, from the perspective of justification (as distinguished from causal explanations, such as psychological ones), human beings have the responsibility to decide what to believe in. This is essential for constituting moral entities. If the validity of values could be proven "scientifically" or "rationally," there would be no space for human moral choice. But this is inherently impossible, despite some claims to the contrary, ultimate values being extra-rational and extra-scientific by their very nature.

You may believe that your dearest held values are God-given, sanctified by tradition, inherent in the very idea of "good," or expressing the meaning of history. But, unless you are a fanatic ignoramus or not troubled by questions concerning the validity of the values by which you live and for which you may be ready to die and kill, even a minimum understanding of what is at stake must plant a seed of doubt in your mind, as well as make you more understanding of the values of others, however opposed to yours.

It is not my intention to lead you toward a fully relativistic, or cynical, or nihilistic view of values. But, still, in some corner of the mind doubts concerning one's values should find a home, even when being fully committed to them and laboring hard to realize them. This fully applies to avant-garde politicians, who may have to engage in activities carrying a heavy moral burden.

This is but a first illustration of a main overall recommendation of this book, namely to have in the mind at least some doubts about nearly everything. But at the same time it is necessary to compartmentalize doubts while making up the mind and acting for the missions wholeheartedly. This is not easy but essential for being an avant-garde politician.

Concerning the survival imperative, for instance, as already argued there is no absolute necessity and totally convincing justification for regarding the survival of the human species as desirable. I recommend this imperative as basic to the Humanity Constitution and to avant-garde politicians, but recognize that this involves an axiomatic assumption or transcendental belief, and/or a species-survival instinct imprinted into human minds, and/or an existential choice with or without a "leap of faith."

It follows that in our context the ultimate justification of the three existential imperatives is in their acceptance by you as avant-garde politicians, preferably as a result of deliberate value choice based on conscious justifications. But no absolute this-worldly basis exists for regarding the three existential imperatives (and other basic values in which one believes) as "obviously true and eternal."

VALUE DIMENSIONS

Values relate not only to substantive domains, such as "bread or guns." They include two additional dimensions, namely time preferences and values regarding uncertainty, called "lottery values," which overlap emotional attitudes toward various forms and measures of risk. The following hypothetical but not unrealistic cases illustrate these dimensions and the dilemmas associated with them.

To start with lottery values, let us take the realistic case of a bioscience laboratory working on viruses and developing a method to change them, which is very likely to help treat a serious disease which otherwise is lethal. But this method can perhaps also be used for engineering mass killing viruses. Shall this study be permitted to proceed?

This illustration brings out the need for a value choice between different substantive outcomes, one leaving for sure persons succumbing to the disease, the other healing them but perhaps resulting in mass killing, with additional substantive values being added to the consideration, such as freedom of research. The choice depends in part on lottery values, namely what weight to give to "perhaps" causing mass killings.

The survival imperative postulates the principle of "prudence" with risks to the survival of humanity to be avoided. This does not mean that all risks should be avoided, because the other existential imperatives have also to be taken into account. Thus, to achieve flourishing some risks have to be accepted, all the more so when "flourishing" includes seeking to understand reality through science and improving conditions of life through technology—the advancement of which involves risks. Thus, humanity may become unavoidably dependent on nuclear energy, with even the best of nuclear energy facilities carrying some risks of causing a catastrophe.

The climate issue constitutes a concrete example. As reflected in the *IPCC Fifth Assessment Report Climate Change 2013* (IPCC 2013), the vast majority of climate scientists are sure that human action results in a warmer climate with very serious consequences for humanity, though probably not endangering its survival. But there are distinguished scientists who disagree, and in science there is no basis for assuming that the majority is right. Furthermore, adopting the measures recommended for limiting the warming effects of human activities is very costly in terms of hardship and standards of living. And adopting small bits of measures may be useless.

Given all these considerations, applying the principle of prudence seems to lead to the recommendation to accept the high costs of avoiding further human contributions to the warming of climate, and my tendency is to recommend such a grand-policy to avant-garde politicians. But this is not a compelling recommendation and there is no justification for branding those who reject it after full and serious consideration as necessarily being sleepwalkers.

To move on to the time value dimension, an example will illustrate it as well as other dimensions in dynamic interaction. Building a dam which will provide much irrigation and clean energy for at least one hundred years and probably more is under consideration. But about 10,000 persons of an indigenous population will be displaced. Also, there is a small but indefinable risk that the dam may cause in an unpredictable future large flooding of downstream towns. Here all three value dimensions are relevant for the choice whether to build the dam or not: short-term suffering of displaced persons, long-term benefits of irrigation and energy, and the uncertainty of possible flooding in the future.

In concrete contexts, many additional complexities are added, turning such issues into both tragic choices (discussed below) and bounded fuzzy gambles (taken up in Chapter 16). Also, like all political leaders, an avant-garde politician is exposed to interest groups fighting for their values and interests, such as the tribe which may be displaced, potential beneficiaries of irrigation and energy, representatives of towns that may be endangered, builders who stand to make a lot of money, mass media looking for "sensations," and politicians who tie their career to one position or another. All these add to the convolutions of pondering and making up the mind.

To move from the examples to a general guideline on time preferences, the survival imperative aims at "the long-term survival" of humanity. "Eternity" is beyond human thinking and all the more so beyond human action. But the imperative requires avant-garde politicians to adopt long-term perspectives as may fit different domains. But the maximum recommended time frame is limited to, say, 100–150 years, and often much less—depending on the outlook possibilities. Beyond such time horizons, and also within it, metamorphosis will very likely produce radically novel realities largely beyond present conceivability, which in the main cannot be taken into consideration. These, in turn, shorten maximally advisable time horizons and require periodic adjustments of decisions and actions to unexpected developments.

The conclusion is that complex and also many seemingly simple issues require processing of multidimensional value dimensions. This usually involves, after explication of the various considerations, a kind of Gestalt value judgment. Efforts to reduce multidimensional value outcomes to a single metric denominator, such as monetary value, are in nearly all cases more misleading than enlightening. And sophisticated models of multidimensional scaling, however elegant and also impressive to those who do not know better, are quite useless and often misleading. An avant-garde politician should take care not to be blinded by them.

TRAGIC CHOICES

The concept "tragic choice" (Calabresi and Bobbitt 1978) refers to the need to give up important values in order to realize more important ones, with painful judgments in applying values to concrete situations. An example, based on a discourse with Herman Kahn, brings out in dramatized form the involved dilemmas.

Let us assume that in commanding a war an avant-garde politician has three options with assured equal victory as the outcome (thus putting into brackets the thick uncertainties of all wars and the impermanence of their outcomes). As a further simplification, let us assume that all other costs than those included in the analysis below are more or less equal for both sides, such as the number of soldiers killed and wounded and material damage. But in each option a known number of civilians are killed:

Option A: 5000 civilians of one's society killed, 4000 enemy civilians killed.

Option B: 100 civilians of one's society killed, 50,000 enemy civilians killed.

Option C: 1000 civilians of one's society killed, 50,000 enemy civilians killed.

Which option should the avant-garde politician choose? This is a tragic choice which depends on values and their relative intensity in the given situation: if the decisive value is the minimal number of total civilians killed, the avant-garde politician should pick option A. If the decisive value is a minimum of civilians of one's society killed, option B should be preferred. If the decisive values include both a minimal number of civilians of one's society killed but avoiding one's country being regarded as barbarian, option C should be picked.

This hypothetical case demonstrates the dependence of choice on values and their relative weights (or, to be more exact in terms of abstract theory, but less relevant to real choices, what hypothetically counts is the relative marginal weight of bits of value realization). It also illustrates an additional moral dilemma of an avant-garde politician elected by a given society. In terms of raison d'humanité, the minimal number of total civilians killed should be aimed at as a high priority value and option A chosen. But this may well result in the avant-garde politician being found guilty of high treason in his society, raising the fundamental value issue facing the extraordinary mission of avant-garde politicians of raison d'humanité versus constituency.

RAISON D'HUMANITÉ VERSUS CONSTITUENCY

Acceptance of the existential imperatives, with their emphasis on the future of humanity as a whole, is not a simple moral choice for an avant-garde politician, even if political difficulties are put into brackets, as often it is impossible. With the exception of the relatively few leaders of emerging global governance institutions, the vast majority of avant-garde politicians are elected or selected in order primarily to look out after the welfare and values of their "tribes." They have no mandate to advance raison d'humanité at the cost of the current and long-term needs and demands of their constituencies.

One hypothetical way out of the dilemma is to convince the relevant public to support the existential imperatives. But changing the basic public attitudes and deeply ingrained tribal feelings is a task for generations. Even if political needs can be satisfied by hiding the raison d'humanité values shaping choices, as discussed in Chapter 17, there still remains a tragic choice in terms of multiple loyalties. Relying only on personal conscience is fine when making decisions concerning oneself. But it is problematic and involves a lot of "moral hazard" (imposing risks on others to satisfy one's desires and values) when serving as the basis for choices having an impact on the future of many. Therefore, an avant-garde politician has to make a critical moral decision on whether and when to give much weight to raison d'humanité despite not having a mandate to do so, or to give a higher weight to tribal values and thus impair the extraordinary mission.

No formulae can provide an answer and relief to a decision maker from the moral burden of tragic choices. When the survival of humanity is at stake, the survival imperative dictates that avant-garde politicians should give it absolute priority, never mind other values. But this is a rare situation. The usual choice is between "perhaps more or perhaps less," leaving the onus of some kind of proportionality between values on the conscience of the avant-garde politician, who must be aware of such choice dilemmas, ponder them carefully, and accept moral and, if necessary, also public responsibility for value priorities and choices.

Very desirable, therefore, is some kind of forum where avant-garde politicians, together with philosophers, theologians, spiritual advisors, literati, and so on, who share commitment to raison d'humanité, engage in contemplation, cogitation and frank off-the-record discourse on value issues, dilemmas, and applications. Personal high-quality spiritual advisors too can be very helpful for maintaining the moral integrity of an avant-garde politician, in line with classical traditions of "keepers of the conscience" of rulers, such as religious and philosophical ones.

RADICAL REVALUATION

Radical revaluation of many widely accepted values, as discussed by Friedrich Nietzsche though in other directions, is essential for the survival of humanity and its flourishing. Facilitation of values conducive to human survival and pluralistic flourishing is one of the responsibilities of avant-garde politicians, together with their crucial role in the sensitive, dangerous but essential task of containing and if necessary neutralizing fanatic "prophets" and "crazy states" (Dror 1980), especially when becoming armed with mass-killing instruments.

To provide some feel for the radicalism of required revaluation of widely cherished values, here are some tentative examples of painful value changes likely to be essential for effective humanity-craft in the service of raison d'humanité:

- Values of state sovereignty and "equality" have to be partly abandoned, together with dreamy values, however attractive, of foreseeable "global democracy."

- The value of freedom of research and diffusion of its findings as well as some parts of "academic freedom" needs subjugation to selective regulation, so as to prevent production and diffusion of potentially dangerous knowledge.

- Freedom of expression has to be limited to prevent mobilization of support for predatory fanaticism and transfer of dangerous knowledge. This includes supervision of the Internet and its derivations, and reduced web privacy as far as necessary, subject to strict limitations and safeguards.

- Free markets have to be strictly regulated so as to prevent "black markets" of dangerous knowledge, instruments, and materials.

- Free personal choice has to be curtailed to prevent prohibited or suspended "human enhancements."

- Some rights to privacy have to give place to intrusive surveillance.

- Court procedures, rules of evidence, burdens of proof, methods of interrogation, and uses of preventive detention have to be changed to permit prevention and punishing of behavior contradicting substantively the survival and species changing inhibition imperatives.

- Global overview of school textbooks is necessary to prevent tribal hate inculcation and to advance human communality values.

- As mentioned, periods of global, or regional, emergency regimes may be necessary to prevent catastrophes and cope with them, involving various levels of temporary suspension of private rights and other values.

- Harsh punishments may be necessary to deter actions posing serious dangers to humanity, as may be non-proportional uses of violence for deterrence of dangerous behavior.

Additional major revaluations will be necessary to advance the flourishing imperative, such as on limiting income disparities. But enough has been said to demonstrate the radically innovative and in part revolutionary measures that may be necessary for assuring the future of humanity, with all the involved painful revaluations of important values. Such revaluations should be based as much as possible on wide consensus, will take time, and should be advanced in bits. Avant-garde politicians have to be very careful in promoting and advancing them, with spiritual, cultural and value leaders serving as the cutting edge. But catastrophes, hopefully relatively limited ones, may make necessary and also feasible accelerated adjustment of some critical values to the requirements of evolving raison d'humanité.

CHAPTER 4
VALUE COMPASS

VALIDITY AND RELEVANCE

The idea of raison d'humanité has been criticized as lacking an empiric basis in presently accepted values, which are particular to specific communities. But claims that raison d'humanité is an invalid value because it is not widely accepted are normatively irrelevant, because the validity of values does not depend on the extent of their acceptance and cannot be judged by empirical arguments.

A related claim that raison d'humanité is irrelevant because it lacks public support and therefore cannot serve as a guideline for action is also mistaken, for three reasons: (1) as a matter of fact elements of raison d'humanité, without using that term, are in part increasingly supported, though inadequately so; (2) throughout history elites and also individuals have accepted and acted according to values rejected or ignored by majorities; and (3) the claim ignores the historicity of values and their changeability. Thus, widespread acceptance in the past of slavery and subordination of women does not prove the impracticality of contrary values opposing slavery and subjugation of women, which did in fact become relatively rapidly widely accepted and implemented (nor, to return to the first claim, does wide acceptance of slavery and subjugation of women justify them as "proven").

There is much scope for disagreements on the particulars of raison d'humanité, but this does not invalidate the normative standing and action relevance of the concept and the values derived from it, as based on the three imperatives.

OPERATIONALIZATION

Values are on different levels of generality or specificity. "Following the commandments of God" is a fundamental value, but empty without operational values which are fundamental too, such as the Ten Commandments. The existential imperatives are basic norms on a high level of abstractness. To serve as guides for concrete choices they have to be transformed into more operational values, which includes a range of subvalues, such as goals, objectives, targets, and choice criteria—which add up to an operational value compass, at the service of avant-garde politicians for application to concrete choices within specific contexts.

Yehezkel Dror

The following components illustrate a value compass for avant-garde politicians. But, in contrast to the three existential imperatives, which I regard as definitive, the examples are tentative, leaving scope for quite different ones as long as they fit a reasonable conception of raison d'humanité.

SPECIES ENHANCEMENT VALUES

Especially vexing issues are faced in operationalizing the species changing inhibition imperative, in a broad sense, such as concerning human enhancement, human cloning, development of intelligent machines, and creation of self-reproducing multicellular life. The lack of experience and the rather hypothetical nature of future possibilities add to the difficulties of formulating operational values, as does the scarcity of high-quality literature (More and Vita-More, eds. 2013 serves partly as an example of what is needed). Thus, when it will be possible to buy publicly on a free health market additional years of high quality life expectancy for a large amount of money, as to a rather limited and hidden extent is already the case, havoc is likely to follow, all the more because of lack of fitting value discourse. And this is just a minor issue compared to those likely to follow increasing human enhancement and similar capacities.

These are extremely problematic in terms of human values and beliefs and social implications, as well as the future of the human species, all the more so as long-term outcomes are rather inconceivable. Even the relatively simple question of how a human society composed of individuals nearly all of whom have an intelligence quotient (IQ) of over 150 would behave cannot be answered. To leave the handling of this domain to free markets, self-regulation of scientists and engineers, and sovereign states acting on their own means in effect to abandon the future of humanity to side effects of choices motivated by tribal values, narrow interests and limited perspectives.

Doing so might well lead to unimaginable disasters. But the present thinking on such contingencies is necessarily speculative and opinions contradict one another. There exists no global decision process for making choices on issues posed by the species changing inhibition imperative. And state decision processes, such as Parliamentary legislation, are unequipped for coping with such novel and very divisive issues.

Therefore, in the following list of proposed components of the raison d'humanité compass, values relevant to the species changing inhibition imperative are not adequately represented, as their elaboration awaits study, thought, and choice dealing with actual enhancement capacities emerging in the near and longer term future, the more radical of which are at present hypothetical.

COMPONENTS

Moving on to the tentative value compass, as based on the existential imperatives and raison d'humanité, the following components are suggested as important:

Humanity is the measure

Protagoras postulated, "Man is the measure of all things." This includes what humanity needs or chooses to regard as important, such as limiting pain caused to other species to what is necessary for advancing humanity; and preserving fauna and flora as pleasant or useful to humans. But animals are not regarded as having "rights" on their own; and "nature" is viewed as material to be used for the benefits of humanity as decided by it, including enjoyment of wild nature if this is desired, but without preservation of nature being accepted as a value on its own. Thus, most of the values supported by "deep green" believers are not included.

Accordingly, quasi-mystical uses of the term "Gaia," as if the earth is a living entity with rights of its own, should be rejected. But serious versions of the Gaia theory, recognizing the necessity to maintain the conditions of the planet essential for humanity, as discussed next, are in accord with the survival imperative.

Protecting physical conditions of the planet essential or helpful for human life

This value in its vague formulation will be agreed on easily. The devil is in two questions which have only partly answers: What physical features of the planet are really essential for maintenance of human life, or helpful for a good human life as variously defined? And what can and should be done to preserve these features or compensate for whatever damage is done to them?

I leave detailed discussion of these and related questions to the proliferating literature devoted to them, directly or indirectly (e.g., Marchetti and Moyle 2010; Raven et al. 2012). But, despite contradictory views on crucial issues, such as the warming effects of human activities, it is at least very likely and perhaps certain that human activities do endanger conditions essential or at least helpful for human thriving and may damage conditions essential for the long-term existence of the human species. Therefore, extensive countermeasures are required which go far beyond what is being done or seriously considered by political leaders. This is an important challenge awaiting avant-garde politicians and a major component of the proposed value compass.

Panhuman communality

Without widely accepted values, feelings and emotions of panhuman communality, as already briefly mentioned, the survival imperative, with all its costs and pains, lacks an adequate social basis and cannot be realized. But panhuman communality is also a value in itself as a part of maturing humanity and advancing its thriving.

This value includes many prohibitions, such as against aggressive aspects of tribalism, fanaticism, and group egotism. It also requires large transfers of resources from the rich to the really needy, in and between countries; readiness to take personal risks and to endanger the lives of we-group members to help others; making education and textbooks more global; and personal distance reducing measures, such as a global youth corps mixing participants from different cultures, initially voluntarily and then obligatorily.

To put it positively, the proposed value comes to "embrace and to celebrate the common humanity that has always bound us together" (Cannadine 2013, 264), while trying to contain and reduce what separates humans, which is becoming increasingly dangerous for the future of the species and narrows the minds of individuals.

Belonging to a group, clan, society, and civilization is a necessary part of being the social animal called human and of having a full life. But this is different from seeking of national glory, discriminating against "others," violent competition, and many additional features of "tribalism," which not only contradict the panhuman communality value, but increasingly endanger the future of humanity. Therefore, panhuman communality is a critical component of the value compass. However, it contradicts in some respects widely accepted values related to extreme individualism which regards humans as largely autonomous agencies separate from their habitus. Not only is this an incorrect understanding of humans, but it inhibits essential human solidarity and all efforts to propagate and realize the value of human communality.

Therefore, even if "disembedded individualism is a necessary fiction for …liberal democracy" (Ezrahi 2012, 34), which is not clearly the case, then some parts of extreme liberal democracy have to give way to a more holistic view of humanity of which partly autonomous individuals are the constitutive parts, leading to more communality of humanity as a whole.

Eradication of absolute evil

Elimination of absolute evil, such as enslavement and mass killing, is a basic value serving all three existential imperatives. It is also a main value by itself, the validity of which does not depend on the imperatives. It includes acting against "toxic leaders" who inspire and do absolute evil, as illustrated by Adolf Hitler, in contrast to "disastrous" leaders, of which there are many, who cause much pain and damage but not absolute evil in the full sense of that term, however ambiguous.

Eradication of absolute evil justifies and requires the use of all necessary measures, including drastic punishment and lethal force. However, a major difficulty is posed by the lack of a universal definition of "absolute evil." Thus, the Nazis regarded the systematic killing of masses of Jews, Romans, captive Polish officers, and others as a moral duty fully justified by "higher values," and therefore not at all an evil. This is also the case with ethnic cleansing, mass-killing terror, and other deeds which are regarded by what regards itself "enlightened humanity" as absolute evil, but not by the perpetuators and their supporters.

It is inherently impossible to foresee what future generations will regard as absolute evil, as values change with time as illustrated by the already mentioned history of slavery. Thus, one can easily imagine that extreme quality of life differences between the very rich and the destitute will be regarded as an absolute evil. But we can only act by our present values as resulting from centuries of cultural evolution, hoping they will be further developed by future generations and perhaps by a Second Axial Age. However, there is no "law of history postulating moral developments" which guarantees that some possible futures, such as after a major global catastrophe but perhaps also without it, will not adopt value regarded by us as "barbaric" and approximating "absolute evil."

Subject to a measure of self-doubt in a corner of our mind, as noted, absolute evil has to be defined operationally in terms of main values accepted by the vast majority of humanity, such as reflected in United Nations declarations and resolutions. All the more so it is very disturbing that nearly all political leaders worldwide are paying lip service to these values, but usually take action to realize them only when this fits their raison d'état and political convenience. Therefore, quite a lot of contemporary reality includes "absolute evil" which is not effectively eradicated. Such de facto toleration of absolute evil, despite effective countermeasures being available, constitutes nothing less than being an accessory to absolute evil by non-action and a cardinal sin in a secular or religious sense. It must be strictly avoided, loudly condemned, and actively counteracted by avant-garde politicians.

Elimination of large-scale warfare and violent conflicts, in broad meanings of those terms fitting their changing forms.

It would be nice to postulate elimination of all warfare and violent conflicts as an important raison d'humanité value, but this would be utopian in the foreseeable future, and also contradicts legitimate and even necessary limited warfare and uses of violence. Therefore, with some hesitation, I formulate the value as above. But I expand it to include changing forms of warfare and violent conflicts, such as large-scale cyber-attacks, mega-terror, and credible threats of mass killings, with more innovative ones sure to come before long utilizing novel killing capacities supplied by science and technology.

This value illustrates components of the value compass the enforcement of which may require violent action. Talk, declaration, and "diplomacy" not backed up by a willingness and ability to use overwhelming though limited force are often inadequate and also futile. The next value is devoted to this crucial point.

Use of measured violence when essential for realizing the survival and species changing inhibition imperatives and other main values.

Many measures necessary for assuring the future of humanity will be met with much resistance, the overcoming of which is regretfully likely to require quite some violence. But the mood and measure in which such violence is used should be very different from enthusiasm all too often accompanying warfare throughout history. What is needed is strikingly put in a few sections from the Hindu Bhagavad-Gītā, Book Two, detailing what Lord Krishna said to Prince Arjun before a battle that the prince is reluctant to begin because he would have to kill relatives:

> Considering also your duty as a warrior, you should not waver. Because there is nothing more auspicious for a warrior than a righteous war. (2.31) Only the fortunate warriors, O Arjun, get such an opportunity for an unsought war that is like an open door to heaven. (2.32) If you will not fight this righteous war, then you will fail in your duty, lose your reputation, and incur sin. (2.33) …therefore, get up with a determination to fight, O Arjun. (2.37) Treating pleasure and pain, gain and loss, and victory and defeat alike, engage yourself in your duty. By doing your duty this way, you will not incur sin (2.38).

The use of violence is a last resort and should be measured. But using it in adequate critical masses when necessary for the realization of the imperatives and other main parts of the value compass is a duty for avant-garde politicians.

Responsibilities and duties added to human rights

All three existential imperatives require some changes in conceptions of human rights widely accepted at present, by adding duties and responsibilities. Fundamental human and civil rights will continue to have special status (Joas 2013), but so will fundamental responsibilities and duties, without which rights are morally and educationally undermined and do not meet adequately the requirements of raison d'humanité.

It is striking, though understandable in view of conditions at that time, that the *Universal Declaration of Human Rights*, adopted by the United Nations General Assembly on December 10, 1948, emphasizes rightly many human rights, but fails to relate them to human responsibilities and duties. Of the 30 articles of the Declaration, only number 29 makes a vague reference to what are "tribal" and not humanity-wide duties, stating "(1) Everyone has duties to the community in which alone the free and full development of his personality is possible," in sharp contrast to the detailed lists of rights in the Declaration as a whole.

Especially important is a personal duty not to harm others without overriding moral and legal reasons and to make an effort to help those in danger and need. This is a minimal version of the moral duty to respond to requesting "eyes," as postulated by Emmanuel Levinas in his writings emphasizing the responsibility and hospitality imposed by and in the face-to-face encounter (e.g., Levinas 2006), expanded to include virtually all of humanity and future generations. Feeling ashamed of belonging to a humanity guilty of many grave crimes (Morgan 2008) adds a necessary related feeling and mood.

The proposed approach differs from "communitarianism" in emphasizing duties and responsibilities towards other human beings, living now and in the future, and humanity as a whole, rather than toward one's society (Etzioni 1994; 1997; Selznick 2002). The proposed partly Levinas-type emphasis reduces the dangers of tribalism with its dismal consequences, serving instead raison d'humanité in its true human communality pan-humanistic meanings.

Human responsibilities and duties that should be added to human rights are illustrated by the duty to do one's best to help human beings in danger and dire needs, and to educate one's children in a spirit of human communality. A few years of obligatory humanity service, as already proposed, illustrates concrete duties that should be added to human rights.

Sanctions for breaking this value can include temporary suspensions of some rights proportional to the contravened human duties, accompanied by humanistic reeducation efforts. Harsher measures may be required against extreme egotism harming others, such as large scale "unjust enrichment."

Balance between individualism and social and humanity belonging

Tendencies in Western-type modernity and postmodernity, increasingly diffusing worldwide, adopt an extremely individualistic view of human persons with much legitimation of egotism. This misbalances the nature of human beings as in many respects a social animal, which cannot but cause in the longer run psychological and societal problems. More important from a normative point of view, extreme individualism encourages antisocial behavior and puts a barrier to feelings of belonging to humanity and a sense of human communality.

The contrary extreme of belonging to a tribe overriding individual autonomy and related personal responsibility must also be avoided. But the present trend in postmodern societies is more in the direction of too much extreme individualism. A striking expression is the 1957 book by Ayn Rand *Atlas Shrugged* (Rand 1999) and her "objectivism" philosophy (Peikoff 2012).

Achieving a balance between partly autonomous individualism and social belonging with emphasis on also feeling identity with humanity as a whole is an important value by itself and an essential one as a basis for advancing raison d'humanité.

Right to live and die

The right to life is a nearly universal value. But there are limits. Human beings are required to endanger their lives for protecting their country, doing military service when enemies approach the gates, and as proposed to fights against mass atrocities. And humans are entitled to risk their lives if they so decide, such as engaging in dangerous mountain climbing, becoming astronauts, and trying out on themselves new medicines. But what about participating in bloody sports? And the question what evil deeds abrogate the right to life and justify a death sentence is open to debate.

A hard issue is posed by the right to die: Does the right to life entail a duty to try and continue living as long as possible, or is suicide in one form or another normatively acceptable and entitled to help? Contrary to widely accepted views and many legal stipulations, I suggest to avant-garde politicians to include in their value compass a human right to terminate their lives, and to receive professional help to do so without pain, subject to a number of conditions. These include, for instance, deciding on termination of one's life after due deliberation and while being fully aware of what is at stake, and not making such a decision for financial benefits to one's family. But "being tired of life," for instance, may well be a fully acceptable reason for the elderly. And the case for a right to refuse painful life-prolonging treatments with a low probability of regaining good quality health seems compelling.

Making suicide a conditional right does not prevent religious prohibitions against it with sanctions, such as refusal of church burial. But, in terms of obligatory public values, deliberate termination of one's life after meeting some conditions deserves to be a right, with continuing living as long as possible being a right but not necessarily a duty. This may well be a value judgment fitting an advanced version of the thriving imperative applied to human individuals, however counter-conventional.

Increasing elimination of extreme poverty

I do not include in the value compass "global justice." This concept is inadequately theorized, very vague, full of contradictions, and depends on cultures and belief systems. Also, even if a definition could be agreed upon, which is a counterfactual assumption, given the critical existential imperatives and pressing problems, "global justice" is not necessarily a top priority value, despite quite some views to the contrary (e.g., Ypi 2012).

Instead, in line with the flourishing imperative, I propose for the value compass what can be called "sufficientarian justice," in the sense of remedying absolute deprivation on an evolving scale, in combination with other components of local and global social justice and human development (as discussed in the annual United Nations Development Program reports), depending on conditions.

I do so in line with the priorities proposed by Theodor W. Adorno:

> It would be advisable...to think of progress in the crudest, most basic terms: that no one should go hungry anymore, that there should be no more torture, no more Auschwitz. Only then will the idea of progress be free from lies (Quoted in Claussen 2008, 338).

There are more or less objective criteria of poverty such as are used by the multidimensional poverty index (MPI) of the Oxford Poverty and Human Development Initiative (OPHI) launched in July 2010. These can serve as a concrete baseline for realizing the proposed value in stages. But doing so is complex, a large-scale transfer of resources being necessary but inadequate. Thus, an essential first step is establishment of law and order, large-scale misery being unavoidable when warlords ravage countries.

Maturing humanity

"Maturing humanity" illustrates a recommended core value providing substance to the idea of "flourishing." But it is counter-conventional, many will disagree with it in principle or details, and it involves quite a radical revaluation. "Maturing humanity" is hinted at in cultural critique literature and movements, and has some affinity with Kant's views on "enlightenment," though not being identical with it and its later versions. But "maturation" is not recognized in the agendas of the United Nations, UNESCO, and other global organizations, nor in national education and related policies. Reasons include rejection of the notion that humanity is still immature; dependence of conceptions of "maturity" on diverse belief systems; and real difficulties in making humans more mature, as demonstrated by the costly failures of all endeavor to produce a "new human" as advocated in utopias and tried in radically revolutionary societies.

Most of humanity, including political leaders and senior professors and scientists, is juvenile if not childish in crucial respects. The dangers of such immaturity will increase with the expected expansion of leisure time of the vast majority of humans, thanks to 3D printing, partly intelligent robots, and so on, as already mentioned. Given the immaturity, having much free time can easily have harsh consequences. Thus, in addition to escape into hedonistic virtual realities and drugs, very likely are seeking of high-technology "bread and circus," such as in virtual realities. Not to be excluded are more alarming possibilities, on line with the "Hunger Games" (as depicted in the 2012 movie directed by Garry Ross, based on a 2008 novel by Suzanne Collins), and also "clockwork orange" violence (as presented in a 1962 dystopia by Anthony Burgess and a 1971 film produced by Stanley Kubrick), all to keep boredom and fear of death at bay.

"Maturity" is not a matter of more or less IQ, or the "Flynn Hypothesis" on intelligence increasing from generation to generation (Flynn, J. 2012), which in any case is very doubtful, inter alia because of reliance on the concept of "intelligence" as if it is a homogenous entity and as if it can be measured reliably. It involves deeper levels of the mind, as was the case with the First Axial Age and will be central in a Second Axial Age, if humanity reaches it. Maturation is also not identical with "enlightenment." Thus, in addition to parts of "enlightenment," "maturation" includes seeking of content-rich leisure time activities, engaging in some contemplation on basic issues of human existence, being curious about the nature of reality, serving instead of feeling all the time "deserving," and returning to some of the self-cultivation ideas of the "Bildung" as developed by Wilhelm von Humboldt—with emphasis on a reflexive attitude toward oneself and humanity as a whole.

Also critical are ways of life worthy of mature humans, such as emphasis on "being" and less on "having," as discussed by Erich Fromm (2005), and personal autonomy combined with identification with humankind. Qualities of thinking too belong to maturation, so as overcoming the finding by Howard Gardner that "except for individuals who become experts in specific domains and actually come to think in a fundamentally different way about the world, most adults continue to theorize much as they did when they were young children" (Gardner, with Laskin 2011, xii). Included in "maturity" are also esthetic tastes, worlds of feelings, and handicraft and personal creativity, as further discussed below.

First of all, human maturity requires avoidance of a number of vices, mainly related to rather childish animalistic pleasures, such as:

- Getting excited and often crazy about "celebrities" who have no substantive merits;
- Regarding simplistic hedonistic versions of "happiness" as worthy goals, as also advocated by some schools of populist psychologists;
- Fetishism, expressed in collecting and often paying a lot for mundane items used by famous persons;
- Extreme consumerism, with aggregation of material possessions beyond any possible use or esthetic enjoyment;
- High rates of viewing clearly stupid television programs, such as most of the "reality" shows;
- Following blindly fashions in clothing, music, and readings;
- Getting addicted to drugs, alcohol, and gambling, while being fully aware of their dangers;

- Accepting primitive stereotypes showing "the other" as evil, barbaric, or stupid;

- Being easily influenced by silly arguments and empty demagogy; and

- Enjoying blood sports, such as hunting, boxing, and also killing of human beings and even wars.

Nothing said above implies that being more mature involves lack of joy, avoidance of bodily enjoyments, withdrawal from friendly contacts, refusing to gossip as a human bonding activity analogous to grooming among higher apes, enjoying saga movies such as *Harry Potter*, looking for and identifying real "heroes," and so on. But there is a world of difference between mature gratifications and virtue-based happiness on one side and the instinctive-animalistic pleasures of a cow eating good-tasting grass on the other.

Spontaneous developments toward maturity are very unlikely outside small parts of humanity. Instead, education has to be reformed, amusement industries encouraged to provide more mature contents, good uses of leisure time taught (Leitner and Leitner 2004), and dramatic personal examples provided. But care must be taken to avoid utopian hopes for a "new human." This may have to wait for enhancement technologies, however problematic, and for a Second Axial Age. Taking some steps in the direction of moving away from what is clearly "childish" and toward what may be regarded as "more mature" is the maximum that avant-garde politicians can realistically aim at, as part of their pastoral and educational tasks, with most of the maturation efforts being up to spiritual leaders.

Creativity, subject to minimal censorship

Cave paintings, going back more than 35 thousand years, are evidence of impressive artistic abilities, probably developing together with quasi-religious mythology, starting human cultural creativity in earnest after a long period of primitive and slowly advancing tool making with some esthetic or proto-religious ornaments. Creativity goes to the core of what it means to be human in a trans-animalistic sense. Being creative also gives much pleasure despite being very demanding. And creativity, together with passing on of its products from generation to generation, is at the center of social learning and the accelerating Lamarckian evolution of human culture. It is no exaggeration to claim that creativity is a main part of what is best about the human species, though often misused.

Creativity is important in itself and of critical instrumental utility. It serves all three imperatives and is related to maturation. Facilitation of creativity in nearly all its forms therefore constitutes a major value to be advanced by avant-garde politicians.

It is unknown what makes the minds of some persons very creative. But it seems that nearly all humans have a potential for at least some creativity. Possibilities to facilitate, though not "produce," creativity, though its nature is not really understood (despite Csikszentmihalyi 2013), include encouragement, tutelage, nearly full freedom from censorship, availability of resources, material incentives, and social recognition. Special efforts should be made to identify potentially very creative children and young persons who lack encouraging environments and to provide them with a chance to fully realize their promises, thus more fully bringing to fruition the stock of potential human creativity. Peak creativity should be identified and provided with maximum support, including releasing it from the distorting effects of markets.

Interesting issues are posed by creativity based on various psychological deviations. All forms of geniality are in some ill understood psychological and not only statistics sense "abnormal." Therefore, for instance, proposals to abort fetuses with signs of the Asperger syndrome, or, when this becomes possible, healing persons suffering from this syndrome, but showing signs of special creativity, is problematic pending further research and pondering.

Also vexing are possibilities to enhance creativity with the help of drugs, as indicated by some studies. Minor effects may be beneficial. But if it should become possible to produce peak creativity with the help of drugs or other technologies, then the species changing inhibition imperative applies. Dr. Faustus by Thomas Mann (1999) illuminates such issues.

This value includes encouragement of personal creativity on a small scale, as part of the individual, family, and community quality of life, maturation, and leisure time uses. At the other extreme, it includes support of "big science" with all its costs. Thus, space exploration is an important form of creativity, in addition to expressing desirable adventurism, recommended as a value on its own and of possible major importance for the future of the human species.

However, the survival imperative requires limitation, supervision, and also prevention of forms of creativity, which may endanger the future of humanity, as distinct from endangering accepted views and vested interests. This applies mainly to science and technology creativity, as well as to poisonous spiritual, ideological, and pseudo-religious creativity which encourages beliefs and actions dangerous to humanity, all the more so as terrible historic examples are not lacking.

Counter-hegemonic expanded pluralism

"Pluralism" in the abstract is favored in liberal societies, but actually only within quite narrow boundaries set by hegemonic culture. The proposed value of pluralism is anti-hegemonic.

The justification of suggesting an enlarged version of pluralism is twofold: It is based on an expanded conception of the right of individuals and groups to freedom, as long as it does not cause real harm to others. And it gives much weight to social learning based on diverse pluralism, as demonstrated throughout history but endangered by increasing homogenization of global humanity. Thus, expanded pluralism serves the flourishing and also the survival imperatives, while also encouraging creativity.

Let me give some examples, however in part controversial: decriminalization of use of soft drugs; legitimation and formal recognition of polygamy and polyandry engaged in by consent of mature partners; permission of home schooling, as long as demanding educational standards are met; division of functions according to gender if freely accepted and not imposed forcefully; and legitimation of non-democratic and also theological regimes as long as they are supported by a majority of the population and not dangerously repressive to minorities or aggressive towards others.

Social experiments initiated in civic societies should also be encouraged, such as various forms of communal living illustrated by the Kibbutz movement in Israel, the Christiana alternative community in Denmark, and the Amish communities in the USA. Uncontacted people, such as "lost tribes" in the depth of the Amazon forest, should be protected against contacts which they do not desire. Local and historical languages should be preserved, folklore encouraged, indigenous schooling financed, cultural autonomy of minorities protected, and forced assimilation prohibited.

Compassion

The existential imperatives and the proposed raison d'humanité value compass involve some harsh measures. It is therefore essential to balance it with a good dose of compassion. It is not within the capabilities of humanity to eliminate a lot of human suffering as built into the very fabric of life, however often undeserved in terms of human justice. Mourning over the loss of loved ones, disappointed hopes, sudden disabilities, melancholy, and so on are part of being human and of maturation. *Weltschmerz*, in the sense of a feeling of sadness and pain at the limits of life and humanity, is an important source of philosophic and literary creativity and personal contemplation. And so is a tragic sense of life, related to doubts about the meaning of life and the certainty of death when not accompanied by unconditional belief in individual survival (Unamuno 1978).

Therefore, universal or wide elimination of subjective feelings of suffering and substituting for them feelings and moods of well-being and happiness, as may become possible with the help of drugs combined with virtual realities, should be regulated as hindering maturation of humanity and much of its creativity. All the more necessary is a good measure of compassion.

Compassion involves the understanding of others and empathy with them, also if blameworthy for their sufferings. But compassion should not be mixed up with sentimentality, which distorts pondering and contaminates deserved mercy.

Counteracting moral hazard

Moral hazard, as mentioned, refers to accepting risks the consequences of which are borne by others. Examples include polluting activities without bearing responsibility for their consequences, sending others on suicide missions, and causing a ship which one commands to sink with many persons killed but being among the first to escape on a lifeboat. Starting unessential wars without bearing personal risks may be unavoidable, but it involves a lot of moral hazard. There was an element of justice in the classical warfare tradition where the king rode into battle at the head of his troops.

Reducing moral hazards by imposing personal responsibility on those causing avoidable damage is therefore a value relevant to all three existential imperatives, also closely associated with the important but often neglected principle of retributive justice.

PUTTING INTO PRAXIS

The three existential imperatives, the concept of raison d'humanité and the value compass characterize the mind of avant-garde politicians and clarify their extraordinary mission. But their main purpose is not only to enrich the mind, but to be put into practice, with pondering and applying reinforcing one another.

This is not easy. Application of values to concrete situations is always problematic and often requires doubtful moral judgments (Sandel 2009a). Furthermore, many of the proposed values contradict presently accepted ones, requiring much revaluation adding up to a significant transition in human beliefs. Such a transition is likely only after some serious calamities serve as the Nietzschean hammer needed to change deeply ingrained human values and institutions. However, the saying of the Chinese philosopher Lao-tzu, best translated as "the journey of a thousand miles begins beneath one's feet," fits well an avant-garde politician: You should do all that is possible to realize the value compass as adjusted to your beliefs, even if often these efforts will have to remain in part hidden in your mind because of their counter-conventional nature.

PART TWO

BEING AN
AVANT-GARDE POLITICIAN

CHAPTER 5
TOTAL CALLING

EXTRAORDINARY "DELTA" MISSION

In order to deepen the idea of avant-garde politicians as an introduction to discussion of their calling, let me reformulate it with the help of the concept of "Delta", as used in mathematics and the sciences. Going back to "delta" as the initial letter of the Greek term *diaphorá*, which meant "change," the upper-case letter Δ is used to denote change (more exactly, the difference operator).

Using this term the extraordinary mission of avant-garde politicians is to bring about significant Deltas for the better in the modes of existence of humanity in an era of metamorphosis, with the meanings of "better" being supplied by the concept of raison d'humanité and its value compass. This concept also applies to the ordinary missions of avant-garde politicians, but in their case the difference is less significant for humanity and therefore denoted by the term "delta" without capital letter.

Given the idea of Delta, a further statement serves to present and bring out the crucial importance of the extraordinary mission of avant-garde politicians: With radical evolving changes (large measures of various forms of Deltas) in the emerging opportunities and dangers facing the human species, proportional changes (Deltas) in human pondering, choice and action abilities are required. These, in turn, require a Delta elite with evolving moral, cognitive and volitional qualities adequate for coping with rapidly changing challenges. In such an elite Delta-politicians constitute a leading component. But I will use the terms "avant-garde elite" and "avant-garde politicians," which are thicker and clearer in contents and meanings.

Let me add in a more technical vein that the mathematics of differential calculus (as not too demandingly presented, for instance, in Vrabie 2011) can provide very useful concept packages for describing and analyzing historic change modalities and also for pondering on them and coping with them. This book does not take up such advanced professional matters. But the concept of Delta is an important key to all of it and should be kept in mind. I will return to it from time to time.

"AVANT-GARDE"

The proposed concept and model of an avant-garde politician are in part radically novel, as required by the radically new features of the era of metamorphosis. The concept "avant-garde" is nowadays mainly applied to the arts (Calinescu 1987, 95-148; Cottington 2013), but it initially applied to the military. It became revolutionary-political after the French revolution (Calinescu 1987, 101). It assumed a central role in Lenin's revolutionary writings, especially *What is to Be Done*, first published in Russian in 1902 (Lenin 2005).

Leaving aside the Marxist, communist, terror and conspiracy sides of Lenin, despite their central importance in his thinking and policies, and the tragedy of terrible results following, perhaps inevitably so, his utopian vision, some of his comments on leadership are relevant for avant-garde politicians (all quotations are from Lenin 2005): leadership should be guided by a genuine "theory" (p. 105), instead of "bowing to spontaneity" (p. 46); long-range perspectives and holistic plans are essential, with "tactics-as-process" (p. 168) to be rejected; leadership is a kind of "profession" which has to be learned (p. 97) and requires self-training (p. 122); leaders should get rid of "wretched" (p. 124) "amateurism" (p. 98); leaders should be a "vanguard" and not "rearguard" (p. 84), avoiding "tail-ism, in the sense of following public from behind. Instead, leaders should lead the multitude while enlightening and educating the public; essential is holistic understanding, aiming to "transform radically the conditions of life of the whole of mankind" (p. 171); while flexibility is necessary (p. 171), "primitivism" (p. 162) and "opportunism, with "subservience to spontaneity" (p. 74) should be avoided; "forward march of the drab everyday struggle" (p. 150), "actual concern with trivialities" (p. 145), and so on are counterproductive. Instead, essential is coordinated large-scale action which can bring about massive results; leaders should also learn and teach "how to live and how to die" (p. 88), and lack of such leaders causes crises (p. 119).

The following statement succinctly sums up relevant lessons which Lenin's text provides: it is "the duty of the leaders to gain ever clearer insights into all theoretic questions, to free themselves more and more from the influence of traditional phrases inherited from the old world outlook" (p. 28).

In modern thinking, Lea Ypi's book *Global Justice and Avant-Garde Political Agency* (Ypi 2012) pioneers application of the concept of avant-garde to the global political agency, discussing an avant-garde being "aware of his contribution to conceptual innovation and political change in a normatively mediated way (Ypi 2012, 5, see also 61-66). But she does not take up the critical needs for a humanity constitution and for avant-garde politicians, and ignores many issues cardinal for the future of humanity.

Avant-gardism is central to the very being of the needed novel types of political leaders, in the sense of moving ahead morally, cognitively, and volitionally before the vast majority of contemporary political leaders, and also of global humanity, in recognizing, pondering, and acting on all that concerns the long-term survival and pluralistic thriving of the human species.

CALLING

The idea of "calling" is central to the proposed conception of an avant-garde politician and to his being. This is not the place to go into its history and development by various thinkers, such as Max Weber with respect to the development of the capitalist ethos as shaped by Calvinism (Weber 2001), and later on in the context of science and politics, and by Thomas Mann with regard to art (Weber 2004; Goldman 1988, 13-112). But a few quotes well present the idea of engaging in a calling (all are from Goldman 1988):

"For both Weber and Mann…it is work as a form of selfless service and submission or devotion to a higher ideal, goal, or object…a calling, the submission to which and the discipline of which provide a source of self-justification and meaning to…who feels himself called" (p. 35), leading to a "self built on the calling" (p. 15), the effect of whom "on the world about them was dramatic. Their 'unusual firm character,' 'ethical qualities,' and 'temperate self-control'…enabled them to 'win confidence,' gave them 'vigor' for overcoming 'opposition,' and showed their 'rigor' while they remained 'devoted to their object'" (p. 29). "It sets" them off "from others who only seem to be engaged in the same enterprise but who in fact lack qualities crucial to the calling" (p. 52).

As elaborated in the classical conceptions of political leadership presented in Max Weber's 1919 lecture on "Politics as a Vocation" (Weber 2004, 32-94), being an avant-garde politician (a term not used by Weber) is not a profession, vocation, employment, job, career, and so on. One does not live from it, but for it. It is a calling, encompassing most of you, in which the soul's passions resides, partaking in the classical meanings of "noble," "elevated," and "aristocratic." It carries obligations and commitments, and does not provide unearned privileges. The "calling" of an avant-garde politician constitutes a large part of the meaning of life and forms and remakes the personality, enlarging, deepening, and also in some respects limiting it.

Moving beyond Max Weber, the idea of "calling" and related concepts is not unproblematic. Thus, it can "isolate its adherents and make the self a prison" (Goldman 1992, IX), unless great care is taken. Coping with the challenges and problems of accepting and living the calling of an avant-garde politician raises a troubling dilemma of "more or less." And much depends on personal attributes and situations which in part vary between avant-garde politicians.

Whatever the specifics of a particular avant-garde politician may be, all engage in laying foundations for the future of the human species and of one's society. This makes an avant-garde politician somewhat a partner in the genesis of the future of humanity, at least by taking care of the existence of the species till a Second Axial Age or some other breakthrough epoch emerges.

This critical role provides the being of an avant-garde politician with a profound self-transcending aspect, which is both a heavy burden and a great privilege. An avant-garde politician must be aware of them and prove worthy, accepting an unconditional duty to make a maximal effort to acquire the qualities needed for fulfilling the missions as fully as possible for a human being.

The profit motive, however important as a driving force of the economy, is for an avant-garde politician a sordid one in comparison with serving unselfishly generations to come. Seeking power for its own sake or for personal benefits is a cardinal sin. Being addicted to fame is foul as compared with impacting for the better on the future. As put by Thomas Mann "death is imposed only on created beings, not on works of art" (quoted in Claussen 2008, 126). Impact on the future is the work of art of an avant-garde politician, his mission, destiny, and source of meaning, whether his authorship is remembered or not.

An event in the second season, episode 21, of the TV science fiction TV series *Babylon 5* well makes the point. An inquisitor from outer space interrogates the heroes if they are willing to die anonymously with their names soon forgotten if this helps to fulfill their mission. Unless they can truthfully answer with a clear "yes," verified by a reliable truth detector, they will be killed on the spot. But they pass the test and become the rulers of the federation of stars. As the Roman Emperor Marcus Aurelius puts it in Chapter 7 of *Meditations*: "How many after being celebrated by fame have been given up to oblivion; and how many who have celebrated the fame of others have long been dead".

VIRTÙ

I am using the term in its Italian form "virtù" as did Machiavelli, to emphasize that in this book its meanings are quite different from discourse in terms of moral philosophy of virtues, such as discussions of the classical ones of faith, hope, love, prudence, justice, courage and self-control, though there are some overlaps. Machiavelli used it to refer to "a congeries of manly traits: courage, fortitude, admiration of craft, competence, ingenuity, and above all the resolute exercise of one's talents" (Bobbitt 2013, 77). I include these in my meaning of virtù, with the exclusion of the gender implications of the term "manly," but add important qualities as follows, with more to come in later chapters:

Total commitment

I had the experience of being present at two occasions when top level military commanders, comparable in many respects to political leaders, were in charge of very serious and bloody military operations. In both cases, while air and ground battles directed by them were raging, they were informed that a son of them was seriously wounded while bravely fighting. One commander asked his deputy to take over and rushed to be at the side of his son in hospital; the second commander said "all our soldiers are today my sons and many of them are at the edge of death," and continued to direct the battle till victory came after 24 hours, when he joined his son at the hospital ward.

The first commander, however capable, is neither fit to be a senior officer nor an avant-garde politician. The second should be promoted to an even higher leadership position. This is the meaning of a "total" calling. An avant-garde politician has to give it total priority, happens what may. This does not preclude a happy family life, friendship, and going to museums and theatre. But not when duty calls. This must be fully accepted and supported by family and friends.

Praxis-directed solitary contemplation

An avant-garde politician has to combine *vita activa* with *vita contemplativa* by engaging periodically in solitary contemplation, considering deeply and without disruptions serious issues, consciously and subconsciously. But doing so should be praxis-directing, preparing the ground for making up one's mind.

This required virtù quality conflicts with the pressures to which an avant-garde politician is subjected. Studies on the time used by political leaders show that most of them prefer the comfort zone of their office and staffs and dislike solitude, want to be surrounded by people, and spend much time on trivial activities. Also a lot of time is wasted on travels which are not really necessary. Therefore quite an effort is required from an avant-garde politician to reserve adequate opportunities for being with oneself, preferable in a private contemplation-facilitating sanctum.

Gravitas

A distasteful habit of contemporary politics is the constant smiling of politicians in public, never mind the nature of issues on the agenda and their real feelings. Even if it is only a mask, it reinforces juvenile traits of the public. Also, such public demeanor of political leaders contributes to growing public skepticism and also cynicism on politics. Reality-distorting impacts on the politicians themselves are also likely, because constantly worn masks tend to influence habits and moods of the wearer. All these add up to a damaging effect of the "smile, smile, smile" political culture.

This "smile-smile" culture goes together with the more pernicious tendency to discuss politics, including tragic episodes such as warfare, as a kind of "game," in line with the Homo Ludens ("Man the Player") theory proposed in 1938 by Johan Huizinga (Huizinga 1971). Please note the irony of history in presenting such a theory a year before the Second World War broke out!

The frequent use of "game" terms for bloody conflicts is both psychologically revealing and damaging, leading to a subconscious feeling "after all, this is only a game," whatever the stakes may be. A classic example is the reference to the conflict between the British and the Russian Empires for supremacy in Central Asia as the "great game," as popularized in the 1901 novel *Kim* by Joseph Rudyard Kipling. The standard term "war gaming" for war simulation exercises is a further illustration of this bad verbal practice, which cannot but impact on subconscious images inside the mind.

In contrast to such modern language games, classical Rome regarded gravitas of politicians as a virtù widely lauded by political thinkers and writers, such as Cicero. It implied and demonstrated taking public responsibilities seriously and realizing their importance. Even when gravitas served as a mask its central place in the visible demeanor of political leaders compares favorably with the "smile optimistically" facades of modern ones. Avant-garde politicians should have the virtù of gravitas, first of all in their mind and also in their appearances.

Mental hygiene

Being an avant-garde politician requires a lot of physical stamina. The mind is embodied and good physical health is conductive to its high-level performance, though not always essential for it. An avant-garde politician should also look handsome, fit, and trim, so as to attract support which often has a quasi-erotic basis, though exaggerations, such as childish plastic surgery and hair coloring, should be avoided.

But the required virtù is different, namely maintaining essential mental hygiene. It involves giving the mind periods of rest from arduous tasks, otherwise mental processes will deteriorate, at least temporarily. Therefore, for instance, an avant-garde politician needs interests distinct from his calling, however total, to recuperate from pressures and let the mind engage in subconscious processes essential for creativity. Good examples include music, whether as a listener or a player, painting (remember Churchill), repairing old watches, reading literature, going to exhibitions, and cooking. It is preferable to develop such interests before becoming an acting avant-garde politician, when it will be hard though not impossible to start from zero (Marcus 2012).

Select physical activities can also help, such as long walks in a forest. Golf, a favorite of many political leaders in some countries, as hunting was one or two generations ago, is useful as long as it does not involve a lot of politicking or social contacts only with the very privileged ones.

Wakefulness

Wakefulness belongs to mental hygiene but its importance requires focused discussion. Adequate quality sleep is absolutely necessary for high-quality performance, also of an avant-garde politician. This is so obvious as seemingly not deserving to be mentioned as a part of virtù. But my work with high level political leaders taught me that often they suffer from sleep deprivation, also when engaging in importance activities. Furthermore, they are usually unaware of their situation and therefore neglecting required precautions, such as not making important decisions while drowsy.

"The reasons why we sleep remain frustratingly unresolved" (Lockley and Foster 2012, 40; the following quotations are from this book, with explanation added by me in parentheses). It is known that "sleep helps our brains find creative solutions" (p.1). And "In humans, procedural learning (which, often unconsciously, includes ways of performance, such as driving a car), declarative learning (which includes facts and knowledge that can be consciously recalled), and even higher-level "insights" – the process of mental restructuring in the brain, that leads to a sudden gain of understanding or explicit knowledge – have been shown to depend on sleep.(p. 52). "While there are individual differences in how sleep deficiency affects alertness and performance, no-one is immune….Unfortunately, our sleepy brain cannot judge our own abilities, and as a result we are sometimes blissfully, and dangerously, unaware of our impaired performance" (p. 91).

Jet-lags add to all the negative impacts of sleep deprivation and disturbances – a fact all the more dangerous because of the bad habit of many senior politicians to rush by fast planes through several time zones to participate in important decisions without opportunities to adjust to the time differences.

The vice of lack of wakefulness is especially pronounced in crisis situations, when high-quality choices are all the more essential. I will return to this serious error-propensity and ways to deal with it in later chapters.

Responsibility, shame, regret

An article by Peter Baker in the New York Times on May 27, 2010, dealing with the Mexican Gulf oil spill, started with the following words "President Obama uttered three words on Thursday that many of his 43 predecessors twisted themselves into knots trying with varying degrees of success to avoid: 'I was wrong.'"

This pinpoints a contemptible vice of political leaders throughout history, which is very pronounced in modern times because of the mass media. With very few exceptions, neither while acting as senior politicians nor in writings after leaving office, do they accept more than formal responsibility, express sincere shame and show real regret for dismal failures, even after very serious mistakes, including criminal acts. And, if they do express shame and regret, this is often a purely tactical move to enable staying in office or to improve their image.

It is worthwhile to study such cases and find out if the guilty political leaders are psychologically unable to admit to themselves that they are at fault, or in their inner self know the truth but are unwilling to admit it in public. In those few cases where I had access to relevant material, which is nearly never in the public domain, it seems that both explanations operate in one and the same person, reinforcing one another, with the additional feelings that "after all, this is a small matter if considered against sacrificing myself for the public" and "I will surely get away with it." There are exceptions, such as Robert McNamara (McNamara 1996), but they are very scarce.

This is a clear pathology of power. Instead, accepting the responsibility for errors of action and inaction, feeling deep pain about them, showing sincere shame, and expressing authentic regret, together with demonstrating true learning from errors, are an essential virtù of an avant-garde politician.

Hara-kiri is not in fashion any more in Japan and nearly never had been practiced by politician leaders elsewhere, even after making glaring errors causing untold slaughters and injuries, as harshly illustrated by the generals in charge of the West front in World War One. I may be in a minority of one, but I am not sure that the norm of not "falling on one's sword", or at least doing repentance in a monastery or some equivalent, after being at fault for human tragedies, is a sign of "human progress." However I limit myself to recommending to a grossly failing avant-garde politician to publicly admitting fault and then get out of the public arena and never return to it.

Aware of being a human, nearly like most

Preoccupation with all that is special about an avant-garde politician can easily make one forget that an avant-garde politician is fundamentally like all other human beings. There are significant differences between humans, biologically, mentally, and culturally. But much more is common to all, quantitatively and qualitatively. An avant-garde politician, with all that is really special about her, should avoid regarding herself as-if significantly "above ordinary humans."

A good way to assimilate this cardinal virtù is to visit a rehabilitation center for patients after a stroke. There it becomes emotionally obvious what all should know but usually ignore: only a small clot of blood makes the difference between a powerful avant-garde politician and a paralyzed and half-witted patient. Never mind if doctors give you aspirin as a prophylaxis and statins to lower cholesterol. Any moment the best of avant-garde politicians regarded as a paragon of health can become a mentally invalid on a ventilator.

I provide this unpleasant image not to frighten, but to try and make sure that when an avant-garde politician asks himself "what am I?" his first answer is not "I am a partner in making the future," but "I am a human being." This is basic for the required identification with humanity, the commitment to try and take care of the future of humanity, and for making maximum efforts to help other humans and not to hurt them without compelling reasons.

Preparing for death, without being depressed

I suggested to a top-level political leader an important future-impacting idea, which he immediately endorsed and instructed his aids to implement. But that night he had a massive brain hemorrhage and never regained consciousness. Of course, his decision became naught. Neither were his grand policies continued, no successor having been cultivated, nor were up-to-date transition documents prepared.

An avant-garde politician should prepare for sudden death or disability by constant endeavor to make his major policies and projects go on also without him. This is a virtù of utmost importance for extraordinary missions, where a good measure of continuity is essential for achieving long-term impacts.

However, this virtù is psychologically very burdening. It requires resilience of the mind enabling functioning sturdily without being disturbed by awareness of the possibility of death and disablement. Politically too the matter is sensitive, because if others are aware that you are preparing for the possibility of sudden exit they will start to prepare for it too and thus destabilize the power which you need. And depression stimulated by personally preparing for the worst may paralyze the will power.

Thus this virtù may entail high costs. Therefore, needed are an appropriate philosophic stance and long-term attitudes to exit, as discussed in Chapters 19 and 20.

Joy

Real "joy" can stem from the sense of having a meaningful life, the excitement of coping with very difficult challenges, and the elation at achieving high qualities of mind and putting them into action. This is not the pleasure of a gourmet meal, of passionate love, and of victory over an adversary—none of which is prohibited to avant-garde politicians if enjoyed in measure at appropriate occasions. But the main joy of an avant-garde politician is similar to the joy of a composer creating a symphony, or a scientist making a discovery. It is the joy of a creator partaking in shaping the future of humanity, even if it is in small bits. Therefore, feeling deep joy while struggling with demanding tasks is a virtù combining being enjoyable, necessary, and possible.

VICES TO AVOID

Parallel to virtù there are vices which an avant-garde politician must avoid. Relevant are classical vices, such as pride, anger, envy and jealousy, greed, sloth, lust, and gluttony. But let me start with the most vicious ones of humans with power, including political leaders, all of which are related to Idolatry of power.

The Roman historian and Senator Tacitus coined the term *furor principum*, that is "ruler's craze," referring to a range of mental malaises of emperors, such as the loss of contact with reality, highly exaggerated self-esteem up to a delusion of grandeur and infallibility, and paranoid suspicion of others. Being tragically experienced with powerful political leaders easily developing such corruption of the mind, one of the countermeasures invented by the Romans was the presence of a slave in the carriage of a victor during his triumph parade, who constantly whispered into the ears of the hero "look behind you and remember that you are a human being." But obviously this did not help.

Lord Acton famously stated "power tends to corrupt, and absolute power corrupts absolutely." History provides plenty of examples of glaring corruption caused by possessing power. This applies to all types of power holders, including in business and mass media. But our concern is with politicians, serious vices of whom can cause grave damage to societies and all of humanity.

To present the scope of this morbidity of power, regarded in the French literature as belonging to *maladie professionnelle* (diseases caused by an occupation), let me move through some related vices that can ruin the very being of an avant-garde politician, which therefore must be avoided and counteracted.

Red shoe syndrome: In one of his fairy tales Christian Andersen describes a dancer who buys red shoes which make her dance till she falls down dead. This applies to political leaders who lose control over themselves and cling to their position in spite of illness and failures and do everything they can to maintain their power irrespective of law and morality.

Extreme narcissism: This vice includes getting increasingly in love and full with oneself, engaging in self-adoration, becoming overstuffed with "me", losing the ability to engage in self-criticism, and increasingly demanding and expecting that others too should love and admire the narcissistic politician.

But this is a matter of degree. A good dose of self-appreciation is needed by an avant-garde politician in order to have the courage and determination to take up difficult tasks and make risky choices. But too much self-appreciation is poisonous (Maccoby 2007). This is the nature of quite a number of psychological accompaniments of power which is well expressed by the Greek term "pharmacon," which refers to a drug which in correct measure heals, but in incorrect measure kills.

King Lear Syndrome: Believing flatterers, surrounding oneself with sycophants, and rejecting those who "speak truth to power"—these are among the more insidious vices of political leaders. This syndrome prevents serious staff work, biases discourse, and chokes the inputs necessary for critical thinking and self-improvement.

"I appear on TV—ergo sum": A widespread vice of political leaders, which can easily infect an avant-garde politician too, is a revision of the famous statement of René Descartes *"Cogito ergo sum"* (I think, therefore I am) into "I appear a lot on television; therefore I exist and do my job well."

This vice is associated with an overall fixation on images, "spins," branding, marketing, and other forms of what is whitewashed under the name "communication." Paying much attention to image manipulation is unavoidable for mobilizing and maintaining power. Previous forms of doing so characterize rulers from the early history on, as evidenced by monumental buildings designed to demonstrate "greatness." An avant-garde politician too has to engage in image architecture, as discussed in Chapter 17. But the vice takes three mutually aggravating forms: enjoying marketing oneself, believing slanted images one projects, and, worst of all, slowly but surely giving priority to images over impacting for the better on the future.

"Othello Syndrome": Seeing enemies everywhere—this vice operates on multiple levels. At a minimum, it regards all criticism as resulting from hostility; the mass media are regarded as "an enemy;" and also as seeing oneself surrounded by foes . True, an avant-garde politician will have a lot of competitors, adversaries, and also real enemies. Trusting others too much can also become a vice, even though a "nice" one. But the Othello Syndrome is insidious and hard to resist.

I am fail-safe: Relying on one's judgment is important for an avant-garde politician, otherwise it becomes very hard to make up the mind and harmful procrastination is the result. However, feeling too sure about one's judgments and lacking a good dose of self-doubt and also self-criticism is a serious vice, easily resulting in dismal failures.

The trouble is that successes and achievements easily produce hypertrophy of self-assurance, leading to the downfall also of outstanding political leaders, as illustrated throughout history. Thus, success easily breeds failure, though failure usually does not breed success. This dynamics calls for much caution by avant-garde politicians to avoid the "I am fail-safe" vice.

All the goodies I can get I fully deserve: A feeling of deserving all that one can get is widespread among political leaders (and their families), closely associated with a sense of being above the law, which is for "ordinary people," a delusion of "sacrificing oneself for the common good," and an assumed identity between what is good for oneself and what is good for the country. Modern culture, which emphasized "you deserve it" and concentrates on rights rather than duties, contributes to this vice, as does public tolerance of many extravagances of political leaders.

The Willow Tree Syndrome: *The Willow Tree* is an impressive 2005 Iranian film directed by Majid Majidi, telling the story of a blind man whose eyesight was restored by what was regarded as a "miracle," following his ardent payers and vows to do good if regaining sight. But, once "normal," he spends all his energy looking for bodily pleasures till blindness strikes him again.

This applies to an avant-garde politician, having spent years to acquire necessary qualities and climbing up the ladders of power, all the time promising to oneself to be totally devoted to the mission given an opportunity. But, once reaching dreamed-about standing, the politician succumbs to temptations, forgets good intentions, and becomes addicted to power games and seeking of pleasure.

Faustian delusion: The delusion of Faust, as presented by Goethe in Act V towards the end of the second part of the poem, illustrates in a dramatic form the tendency of political leaders to distort and falsify the images of their achievements. They tend to view ambiguous results as great successes, minor successes as tremendous achievements, and glaring failures as heroic endeavor ruined by others.

The scene from Faust is worth recapitulation: it presents the noise of preparing the grave for Faust being mistaken by him for the labor bringing to successful conclusion his great swamp reclamation project, till he says the magic formula wishing this moment to continue forever, which delivers his soul to Mephistopheles (though it is saved by the grace of heaven).

As put by Goethe:

> Clattering of shovels cheers me!
> It's the crews still laboring on (lines 11539–11540)
> A swamp lies there below the hill,
> Infecting everything I've done:
> My last and greatest act of will
> Succeeds when that foul pool is gone.
> Let me make room for many a million (11559–11563)
> Then, to the Moment I'd dare say:
> 'Stay a while! You are so lovely!' (11581–11582)

This fully presents the vice in action.

Losing trust in main facets of one's mission

A very difficult personal problem is illustrated in extreme form by clergy who no longer believe the creed (Dennett and LaScola 2013). This can also happen to political leaders, who may support policies, including very costly ones in terms of human lives, for political convenience though not really essential for their justified power needs (as discussed in Chapter 17), or because of lack of nerves which prevents them from cutting costs and stopping an ongoing policy with which they do not really identify. Even worse, an avant-garde politician can abandon the extraordinary mission, despairing of it or losing the energy needed for it.

Once an avant-garde politician does not fully identify with the extraordinary mission and its main policies, but stays in office, she is guilty of the cardinal vice of betrayal She should resign immediately, or be widely condemned and dismissed as soon as possible.

SELF-REFASHIONING

No-one is born as an avant-garde politician, nor becomes one by accident. Genetic endowment, environments, and mentors can help. But strenuous and well-chosen self-refashioning by a would-be avant-garde politician is essential. A prior requirement is a strong will to become an avant-garde politician. Shakespeare put it well in *Henry IV* (Part Two, Act 5, Scene 5):

> Presume not that I am the thing I was,
> For God doth know, so shall the world perceive,
> That I have turn'd away my former self;
> So will I those that kept me company.

The last line points at an important task of an avant-garde politician, namely the duty to motivate and help others to become avant-garde politicians, as will be discussed in Chapter 20 and the Epilogue.

However, being an avant-garde politician requires a lot of power. This leads to an internal contradiction, because having power easily corrupts the mind, as already emphasized. As put by Nietzsche:

> It is a costly affair to come to power: Power *makes us stupid*...Politics devours all seriousness for actually intellectual things...(Babich 2007, 35, emphasis in original).

This is only one of the many corruptive influences of power, which make all the more necessary constant self-monitoring and remaking by an avant-garde politician, as will be elaborated in following chapters.

CODE OF PERSONAL ETHICS

All the more necessary is a code of ethics for avant-garde politicians, which serves to sum up and conclude this chapter. Despite some conceptual ambiguities and important overlaps, I present the code as dealing with your personal virtue ethics (Athanassoulis 2013), as partly distinct from the raison d'humanité guiding your ex officio pondering, choices and actions, as discussed in Chapters 3 and 4, and as radically distinguished from the requirements of public interest Machiavellianism, as discussed in Chapter 17.

CODE OF PERSONAL ETHICS FOR AVANT-GARDE POLITICIANS

1. Regard being an avant-garde politician as a calling, destiny, mission, and engagement of central importance for all of your life and personality. The elements of being consequential and making a significant difference (Delta) in creating a better future make your mission into an exalted endeavor of profound significance. It is far better to resign or lose your position than betray your being.

2. Your missions require outstanding qualities. Their constant development, evaluation, and upgrading is an absolute duty of yours.

3. An avant-garde politician is exposed to many corruptive influences, such as those stemming from possessing power. All the more so, you must engage in constant self-monitoring and self-improvement, however demanding and also painful.

4. In all activities relating to your missions do not let personal considerations intrude.

5. Behave in your personal life in ways fitting the being of an avant-garde politician and in accordance with the higher standards of private morality accepted in your society, without claiming "privacy" rights and privileges.

6. Strictly avoid misusing your position for benefits and pleasures to which you are not formally entitled. This applies also to your family.

7. Your mind is what makes you into an avant-garde politician. You should focus on it and its upgrading so as to acquire and constantly improve its core qualities essential for your missions. Remember, the prime responsibility for being an avant-garde politician and developing its necessary qualities is yours, not that of your genes and environments.

8. Pondering, deciding and acting are at the core of your being an avant-garde politician. You must constantly improve them.

9. A critical facet of your mind is your conscience, including your values with special attention to raison d'humanité, the existential imperatives, and the value compass, as adjusted by you to fit your preferences and concrete situations. They should operate as a kind of "second self" in your mind, what Socrates called his *daimon*, whom you constantly consult.

10. You must not let your personal morality dominate your acts as an avant-garde

politician, which often involve extra-moral and also immoral choices essential for your main tasks and justified in terms of high-value consequences.

11. To acquire and maintain the power essential for your missions you have no choice but to behave according to a public interest version of Machiavellianism. But you have to keep such behavior to the essential minimum and take great care not to enjoy it.

12. You are a social animal largely shaped by your location in time-space. But you can and should strive for maximum autonomy of your mind, as needed for thinking and acting as an innovative avant-garde politician.

13. You are duty-bound to engage in your extraordinary and ordinary missions to the best of your ability and on your responsibility. You should take public opinions into account only on their merits, or if absolutely necessary for maintaining the power you need for your tasks without ruining them.

14. Have the courage of your convictions, willingly risking your position and also your life if this becomes essential for your missions. *"Here I stand, I cannot do otherwise"* is the principle which should guide you in your mind and behavior when critical issues are at stake.

15. If illness or other causes impair your qualities as an avant-garde politician, as judged by your physicians, you have to leave your position, temporarily or permanently as the case may be.

16. If for political reasons you cannot implement critical parts of your missions you should resign rather than cling to power empty of worthy contents.

17. Do not let your family, friends, and acquaintances interfered with your missions. Resist and reject any emotional pressure they may put on you.

18. Be very careful while selecting knowledgeable and reliable advisors and encourage them to remonstrate with you. But insist on confidentiality and get rid of all busy with ego-promotion.

19. Be on constant alert against the vices caused by power and avoid them, with the help of spiritual advisors, however called.

20. Accept full responsibility for your errors and failures, by feeling and showing shame, and making a maximum effort to learn lessons from them.

21. Learn from criticism directed at you, without hostility towards the critics.

22. You should do all you can to influence other political leaders to become avant-garde politicians.

23. It is your absolute duty to act against evil politicians and get rid of them.

24. Cultivating avant-garde politicians for the future is an important task of yours, both while you are in office and afterwards.

25. Remember that you can die or be incapacitated without advance notice, so readying worthy successors should not be delayed.

CHAPTER 6
THE MIND IS YOUR "I"

MIND AT YOUR CORE

Goethe stated in 1771 "I, that I am all to me, as I know everything only through me!" (Goethe 1998, 87. My translation). This expresses well the proposition that the mind is the core of the "I" of an avant-garde politician and the location of the needed qualities. Accordingly, this book concentrates on the mind of avant-garde politicians, regarding behavior relevant to the missions as produced by it. But I take into account relevant ideas from the philosophy of action (Mele, ed. 1997; O'Connor and Sandis, eds. 2013), which partly overlaps the philosophy of the mind.

In focusing on the mind, my approach differs from most discourse on rulers, politicians, leaders, and so on, as well as the majority of training and mentoring activities. These deal mainly with behavior, with the exception of discussions of "character," "personality," and similar vague concepts, which are not very useful.

A person can exert an influence on others only through behavior, including speech acts and bodily movements. Only behavior can be directly studied, including material processes within the brain, which have become much more accessible thanks to modern imaging instruments. But concentrating on the mind is justified by the fact that nearly all behavior specific to an avant-garde politician is caused by the mind, however embodied, including both its conscious and unconscious levels. Many processes of the mind which are not immediately and often not at all translated into overt behavior are also of cardinal importance, such as pondering, contemplation, and fantasizing leading to mental images and conclusions. Therefore, it is the mind which is put at the center of understanding, describing and trying to develop avant-garde politicians.

The mind constitutes a holistic entity, the most complex one on the earth. Analytically one can and must distinguish between "reasoning," "feeling," "moods," "imagining," "conscious and tacit processes," and additional "tunes" of the mind, some of which are beyond conceptualization and many of which are not really understood. However, all of them are aspects of the mind as a whole and operate as integrated facets, despite some specialization of different parts of the brain. A fitting term, which has already been used in earlier chapters, may be "imaginaries," as proposed by Yaron Ezrahi in respect of "political imaginaries" (Ezrahi 2012, 3-7). As he puts it "The very division between the imaginary and the real is in itself a product of the creative, transcendent imagination as an all-encompassing human meta-faculty. The still widely held separation in our culture between reason and imagination, including the Cartesian or Kantian versions of the autonomy of rational reasoning and the subordination of the imagination to reason are in themselves products of the imagination understood as a composing, decomposing, and recomposing faculty" (Ezrahi 2012, 5).

There is progress in understanding important aspects of the brain, but not of the mind (and the brain) as a whole. Its full comprehension probably requires a super-mind and super-brain, being beyond the innate capacities of the human mind and brain. The view that humanity with its present brain can "create a mind" (Kurzweil 2013) and "reverse-engineer the cerebral neocortex" (Kurzweil 2013, 9) is extremely doubtful.

The Human Brain Project (HBP), inaugurated in 2013 and co-funded by the European Union, aims to develop the technology needed to create a computer simulation of the brain. Its multi-year vision is to "build a completely new information computing technology infrastructure for neuroscience and for brain-related research in medicine and computing, catalyzing a global collaborative effort to understand the human brain and its diseases and ultimately to emulate its computational capabilities" (https://www.humanbrainproject.eu/). It would be presumptuous to predict its results, but even ardent supporters of the project do not expect a complete understanding of how the brain works, which in turn is much less than understanding the mind.

Thus, creativity is built into human action (Joas 1996) and values are fundamental to the nature of humans. But the processes related to them are radically different from "reasoning" and beyond conceivable algorithms (a step-by-step procedure or program). Therefore at present no conceivable model of the brain can encompass some of the most fundamental processes of the mind.

However, subject to the caveats above, enough is known in the philosophy of the mind and cognitive sciences to support plausible working assumptions adequate for discussing some salient features of the mind of an avant-garde politician and their upgrading.

Central for doing so is the idea of consciousness as embedded in the mind, which in turn is embodied. While the nature of consciousness is not understood, it is aware of itself and engages in self-reflection. Sentience of being an avant-garde politician, with all that this entails, depends on the self-reflective ability of consciousness which somehow is a product of the mind as a whole and central to its very nature.

"GREATNESS"

It would be convenient if a metrics of mind quality would be available and a range fitting avant-garde politicians could be defined. But no such metrics is available, and none is theoretically possible. The concept of "intelligence" is complex and not clear (Hunt 2010). The intelligence quotient (IQ) concept and its measurements do not fit our needs, even if multidimensional and multicultural, as usually they are not. And the complexity of "greatness" (Simonton 1944; Kaufman, ed. 2013) makes the very idea of a single definition of mind quality unsustainable. An avant-garde politician needs a "high-quality" mind with many required qualities being specifiable, as proposed in this book. But a person can be less or more of an avant-garde politician with different mixtures of various quantities of required qualities. Also, much depends on the specific context in which the missions should be fulfilled. Thus, the extraordinary missions of an avant-garde politician in the United States require in part different qualities from those needed in China.

Let me add a comment on "genius." The definitions and essence of being a "genius" vary and are ambiguous (Robinson 2011), but it is agreed that their number is extremely small and their genesis and nature is not understood. Among the political leaders who were in the same domain "geniuses" only a few made their people thrive and many had a bad end, however dramatic their impacts may have been. Reasons include the pathologies of power, which are especially vicious when a political leader regards himself as a "genius", and the limits of the range of domains in which a given genius excels. Cases of nearly "universal geniuses" of the kind of Leonardo de Vinci are extremely scarce. And even he, in the opinion of some scholars (Masters 1999), was involved with Machiavelli in a failed river diversion project which was part of a military venture of Florence. Furthermore, assuming one has a statecraft genius heading a country and he does not make serious mistakes caused by overrating himself, still the danger looms that no genius-successor will take over and that lesser politicians following a statecraft-genius will ruin what the latter accomplished, with possible catastrophic results. Otto von Bismarck and the long-term calamitous results of his large achievements are a dramatic case in point (Steinberg 2011).

It follows that avant-garde politicians have to be between good and outstanding in many qualities, but they are not expected to have the minds of "geniuses." And "geniuses" can be quite dangerous when serving as political leaders.

BRAIN AND MIND

The performance of the human brain, which is in ill understood ways somehow the material basis of the mind, is in evolutionary terms outstanding. Its energy use reflects this fact: in humans the brain uses 20%–25% of basal metabolism, while its weight is about 2%

of the body, consuming energy per gram at 10 times the rate of the rest of the body. But the human brain has many limitations, which too are not well understood, and many error propensities, an increasing number of which are known but many remain unrecognized.

Simple-looking but complex examples are optical or visual illusions, in which our mind sees a number of geometric and color forms wrongly (Scientific American Mind 2013). Knowing that we are looking at such a geometric and color form and "willing" to see it as it really is does not help: our mind processes the input of the eyes so as to produce a wrong mental image. What we can do is to learn optical illusions and use a ruler and other instruments to identify and measure the geometric and color forms which form them, instead of relying on their appearance in the mind. In some cases looking at them from a different angle or distance can also help. But such easy remedies are not available for the vast majority of the distortions built into the human brain and, somewhat differently, into human minds.

The relationships between the brain and the mind are not known. Philosophers of the mind and neuroscientists hotly debate whether the mind and in particular consciousness can be explained in terms of material processes of the brain or not, and there exists no known way to resolve this issue, which may be beyond human understanding. To get at least some understanding of consciousness, for example, some basic assumptions on which contemporary natural sciences are based may need revisions and additions, as strongly argued by Thomas Nagel (2012), but as just as strongly denied by other scholars and scientists.

Without going into debates over the philosophy of the mind and neurosciences, the subjective consciousness of the vast majority of humans seems to tell us that we have in the minds much scope for choice, however constrained by external circumstances, though there is much debate on this issue (Pereboom ed. 2009; Harris 2012). Even if genetic propensities, life history, and habitus exert much influence on what appears to be "free choice", often unconsciously so, believing in a good measure of "free will" seems justified. In any case this is an essential working assumption for an avant-garde politician. Furthermore, avant-garde politicians (and, as part of becoming more mature, all human beings) should strive to enlarge and deepen the scope of their free or relatively free will, by decreasing the dependence of the mind on inheritance, life history, and environments as far as possible.

There are attempts to distinguish between the brain as "hardware" and the mind as "software" which operates within the hardware but is not fully determined by it. Alternatively, quantum physics is called upon to show that non-deterministic processes can take place within the laws of physics. But such explanatory attempts, none of which is very convincing, have no practical implications for an avant-garde politician, who should assume that human beings have in their mind quite some scope for "free will" and that deliberate efforts can further expand it.

Q&A

Some additional issues concerning the mind relevant to an avant-garde politician can be summed up in the form of questions with tentative answers, on some of which there are strong disagreements:

Is the mind, and consciousness as a whole, embedded in the brain and in the body as a whole?

Yes. Other parts of the nervous system than the cerebral ones, such as visceral, cortical, limbic, endocrine, and perhaps other systems too, take part in mental processes or influence them, in limited and partly unknown ways.

What is the relative importance of evolutionary hardwired innate features of the mind as compared with environmental and self-shaped ones?

The border between them is not known and is in part fluid. Innate features are very important, but they usually are propensities and potentials rather than prefixed specifics. This leaves much scope for environmental influences and self-shaping, including choosing the environments which influence one's mind.

Is the mind bound to fixed modules of the brain specializing in different tasks, such as language, executive functions, and memory, or are brain processes flexible and distributed over various parts of the brain, enabling substitutions between them?

Studies of the brain with the help of magnetic resonance imaging (MRI and fMRI) and of persons with brain injuries indicate that the brain has fixed structures but is also adjustable with a lot of elasticity. Furthermore, complex mind processes involve large networks distributed over different parts of the brain with quite some scope for substitutions within constrains. Major mental activities seem to involve large parts of the brain and probably most of the mind as a whole.

Do activities change the brain?

The brain can acquire new capabilities based on activities, which involve changes in brain structures. Thus, children who spend a lot of time with computer games improve the speed (though probably not the quality) of their multitasking capacities while losing some reading skills, together with related changes in their brains. And London taxi drivers develop in their brain a kind of topographic map of the city clearly identified by modern image technologies. However most changes of the mind, such as acquisition of new knowledge, different moods, new social contacts, improved thinking habits, and so on, are not reflected in known more or less permanent changes in the brain, though there may be some.

Are there significant differences between the brains of men and women which are likely to indicate differences in their minds?

Yes (Scientific American Mind 2012). The average brain size of men is 11%–12% bigger than that of women; men have about 4% more brain cells and 100 grams more brain tissue; there are differences in cellular connections, and more. Furthermore, fMRI studies show some differences in brain processes. And experiments, such as war simulations, show differences in perception and reasoning. However none of these indicate "higher" or "lesser" qualities, but rather diversity which adds to the capabilities of the human species. It is a matter for speculations and ideologies how far these differences are the result of division of labor throughout the evolution of humanity related to the child-bearing function of women. It is also unknown what the short-and long-term effects of more equal life narratives between males and females may be on brain and mind differences. My recommendation is to acknowledge the existence of differences, reject them as a justification for discrimination, and use them to benefit from pluralism and multiple perspectives.

How far should one rely on the various schools of depth psychology and psychoanalysis for understanding the mind and improving it?

Without going into the pointless debate if depth psychology is "scientific," it has much to contribute to the understanding of the mind and improving its performance, especially of persons with some kinds of psychological pathologies. The disregard of depth psychology in many modern approaches to psychology, which then are regarded as innovative in "discovering" by rather simplistic experiments that human beings are not fully "rational" in a rather thin meaning of that term, is but one example out of many of narrow knowledge impairing scientific work. I will discuss separately the possibility of avant-garde politicians trying to improve their minds with the help of psychotherapy and psychoanalysis.

What about experimental psychology?

It is interesting, but limited. Much of it depends on simple experiments on students in artificial situations. For examples, findings on "slow and fast" thinking and on "irrationality" when facing simple probabilistic questions (Kahneman 2011), while interesting and important in some domains, in the main do not apply to the complexities of real-life choices by political leaders, and they can be quite misleading when relied upon in the context of high level political judgment.

What about psychology and psychiatry in general?

Different schools provide quite some insights into the mind. But very much remains in doubt and is under debate. This is well illustrated by the disagreement among various schools of psychotherapy and even sharp disagreement among mental health professionals in the United States on the definition of some major mental disorders in preparing the new Diagnostic and Statistical Manual of Mental Disorders (DSM) number 5, published in 2013.

How far should one rely on studies of the brain with the help of modern imagining instruments, such as magnetic resonance imaging (MRI), functional magnetic resonance imaging (fMRI), and additional ones as continually being developed?

Such studies enable breakthroughs in understanding of the structures and functioning of the brain. However, with all their advantages, modern brain imagining instruments do not provide accurate images of the brain and its detailed functioning. The pictures as published, however impressive and in part enlightening, are not a kind of "photo" or "film." Rather, they are the product of complex computer processing of very much data provided by the instruments, leaving much scope for doubt on the finer aspects of the brain, which are very important. This is a cause for many reservations on what is often presented, mainly in the mass media but also in some professional literature, as "findings" presuming to explain aspects of the mind. However this may change in part with progress in large-scale projects on the brain in the United States and the European Union.

What about evolutionary psychology, which presumes to explain the main features of the mind, such as emotions, in terms of evolutionary processes?

Such explanations are interesting hypotheses, but not reliable findings. With a little ingenuity, if human emotions were different it would be quite easy to explain them too in terms of evolution. And there are many additional reasons for being doubtful about the "findings" of evolutionary psychology (Richardson 2007), without ignoring them.

So what do we know?

Quite a lot is known on the rough structures and main functions of the brain and, much less so, of the mind, providing a partial basis for understanding human beings and humanity. But the mind as a whole, consciousness, free will, and many functions and attributes are far from being understood, and may well be beyond full human understanding.

WILL

"Will" is a main feature of the mind, whether as "willpower" or "weakness of the will." In some views will is a basic ingredient of life as a kind of "vital force." It is clear that a person needs a strong will to become, be, ponder, decide, and act as an avant-garde politician. But issues of the will, as discussed both in philosophy and in psychology, leave much ambiguity and many question marks.

Aristotle discussed akrasia, which constitutes knowingly acting against one's will. A simple example is a person who knows that he should go every day for a brisk walk, is able and free to do so, and wills to take the daily walk but, somehow, day after day, "does not feel like doing it." This is not a case of inability to break an addiction, such as smoking, which is biologically entrenched, but a much harder to explain case of akrasia.

Explanations, none of which is fully satisfactory, include differences between explicit and hidden will, an overriding subconscious desire to harm oneself, irresistible impulse, and more. Important for an avant-garde politician are ways to overcome akrasia. It is easy to exhort oneself to "will harder", but this is more irritating than helpful. Instead, some strategies of "self-management" and "self-binding" may work.

A classic example is the episode of the Sirens in the Homeric poem *Odysseus*. On his arduous trip home Odysseus had to pass through the territory of the Sirens, dangerous mermaids whose seductive singing caused sailors to shipwreck and perish. The easy way to escape this danger would have been to plug the ears of all persons on the ship. But Odysseus, as a political leader who was a master of practical wisdom, was very curious and eager to learn, including hearing the Sirens. What he did was to have his sailors bind him to the mast, instructing them not to release him before the ship was out of reach of the Sirens, and to plug the ears of the sailors, but not his own. He thus bound himself against an inability of his will to resist the call of the Sirens.

Applied to an avant-garde politician, self-binding is illustrated by time use routines, checklists in decision-making processes, and remonstrating advisors whose opinions are not easy to ignore.

EMOTIONS

Let me start with a comment on "passion," as an extreme form of an emotion. An avant-garde politician, as all human beings, has passions. Furthermore, an avant-garde politician should be passionately committed to his missions. However, the Greek ideal of *Sophrosyne* fully applies. Without going here into scholastic discourse, for our purposes it is enough to understand it as "the harmonious product of intense passion under perfect control" (North 1966, X). This formulation can serve as motto for the present chapter.

Emotions, moods, and feelings are all-embracing states of the mind, with feelings tending to focus on particular matters. All three and related subjective phenomena are pervasive features of the mind. For our purposes they can be lumped together.

"It's not the event that determines our emotional state, but rather the way in which we make sense of that event" (Freeman and Freeman, 2012, 23). Still, emotion, including many outside deliberate control, influence the operations of the mind, often strongly so. Emotional storms are not always bad. When confronting absolute evil an avant-garde politician should be filled with abhorrence, strong emotions of empathy with the victims and determination to help them, and intense desire to punish the guilty. But when pondering how to act, such emotions are a serious hindrance. Hence the need for a self-imposed rule not to consider important issues when being in a "negative" mood or having "bad" feelings, such as anger, desire for revenge, depression, and so on, including bodily suffering which influences moods and feelings.

There are practical measures for getting into appropriate moods and evoke helpful feelings. Studies and experience show that physical environments, including music, colors, pictures, and the persons with whom one interacts, can influence moods and feelings. Thus, it seems that blue is associated with calmness and red with aggressiveness, though some cultural biases may be involved. However, other than mood-influencing drugs which should be used only in emergencies, it is music, if well chosen, which seems to affect moods best. An avant-garde politician should learn to use music to overcome emotions which distort judgment and, perhaps, to aid mission-directed contemplation. Select physical activities may also assist in regaining mental composure. And the carefully monitored use of tranquilizers should not be excluded in some situations, such as crises.

PLASTICITY

Crucial and difficult is the question how far one "owns" one's mind and can reshape it. Extreme views, as expressed in popular slogans of the type "sovereign self," are wrong. Our mind is partly predetermined and significantly shaped by inherited propensities, habitus, and also bodily features, such as hormone balances as interacting with the mind. Together these shape and also hardwire much but not all of the mind, its potential, and predispositions.

However a lot that seems fixed is elastic and can be changed by environments and also by deliberate efforts, with persons differing in the plasticity of their minds. Revolutions, emergence of new religions, and appearance of new schools of art—these are only some illustrations out of many demonstrating that some human minds, while not "radically free," are far from being fully bound by genetic inheritance, social habitus, and other constraints, with amazing creative freedom being within the potential of some minds.

Salient is the distinction between "crystalized intelligence" and "fluid intelligence." Crystalized parts of the mind include stocks of concepts, knowledge, and understanding which are used to cope with issues, including new ones which are processed in terms of the available stock. "Fluid" parts of the mind are able to consider new situations with the help of innovative concepts and understanding, subject to quite some bondage to the past as discussed in the next chapter.

The fluid parts can draw radically new lessons from experiences, both on conscious and subconscious levels. This should be compared with the danger of "more of the same" of the crystalizing experience, which in rapidly changing situations becomes trained incapacity and a Procrustean bed (to be discussed later). Therefore one of the main ways in which the mind works, namely apperception, in which old experiences assimilate and give meaning to new perceptions, is often misleading in an epoch of metamorphosis.

Accordingly, one of the major required qualities of the mind of an avant-garde politician is the ability and propensity to adopt and develop innovative perceptions, concepts, understanding, values, and options, instead of having the mind frozen in the past, as is the habit of many mainstream political leaders.

Findings in neuroscience research seem to show that the brain changes in some of its physical properties as a response to specific demands made on it, up to rewiring significant parts of the cortex, as already indicated. This has been clearly demonstrated, for instance, in the brains of professional violinists. It follows that an avant-garde politician who earnestly and consistently practices some ways of pondering, such as recommended in Part Four, may adjust the brain and thus make them a stable quality of the mind, while partly "dissolving" earlier ones.

PSYCHOLOGICAL INTERVENTIONS

Related is the question if psychoanalysis, psychotherapy and related forms of psychological interventions can upgrade select qualities of the mind. To put you on warning, let me present an episode described to me by a very well-known psychiatrist, now deceased, who was in charge of psychological services in the British Royal Air Force (RAF) during the World War Two, which according to him has never been made public (he agreed to me citing it in my writings after he dies, without mentioning his name).

RAF pilots suffered from battle shock after a number of missions. The well-working standard treatment was to give them two weeks of rest and recuperation, with a lot of amusements, good food, and plenty of drinks, after which they returned to battle volunteering as before for dangerous missions.

After some time it was decided to try out another approach, namely giving the battle-shocked pilots a week of intensive psychotherapy. The pilots indeed felt well and returned to their duties, but none of them volunteered again for dangerous missions. The experiment was stopped immediately and nothing on it was published.

Applied tentatively to avant-garde politicians, some forms of psychoanalysis or psychotherapy may "help" get rid of the very drives which cause some troubles but which turn them into avant-garde politicians. To be added are well-established findings on some personality disturbances facilitating creativity and other mental abilities. Therefore I do not recommend psychotherapy as a routine in the making of an avant-garde politician, though it may help self-knowledge. Even more am I wary of the effects of depth analysis, unless needed as a treatment for some kind of psychosis which otherwise disqualifies an avant-garde politician.

A light neurosis is often not an impediment and may in some respects be helpful in making one "extraordinary," as required from an avant-garde politician. Lincoln's melancholy was probably essential for making him into what he became (Shenk 2005). And this is only one case out of many (Moran L 1966; Post 1995), most of which never reach public knowledge.

To sharpen the problems of specifying the "mental health" required from an avant-garde politician, let me present the puzzling and disturbing case of Lyon Mackenzie King. He was the longest-serving prime minister of Canada, for a total of 22 years, which included the critical World War Two period. Despite a number of achievements, he was not an impressive ruler but became prime minister again and again. The shock came after his death when his private diaries were published. They revealed, far beyond all earlier rumors, that he consulted fortune tellers, adjusted his actions to "lucky" and "unlucky" timings, pursued psychic research, communicated with deceased relatives in séances, based political actions on the imagined advice of his dead mother and his dogs, and so on.

The fact that he had a good academic background, including a Ph.D. from Harvard University, only aggravates the riddle which he poses. Had the facts become known while King was alive he would have been diagnosed as a border case of a certifiable lunatic. Instead he served as prime minister for a long time.

The few biographies who take up in earnest the challenge posed by this case tend to adopt one of two positions: that King's mental derangement influenced badly his behavior as the prime minister, or that he led a kind of "divided life," keeping apart his political choices and his occult believes and behavior. I tend to the first view, as supported in a book review (Woodcock 1976, 4):

> ...there is no such thing in reality as a 'double life'. All lives are unities, and Mackenzie King's private superstitions permeated his public life as surely as Hitler's mania shaped the collective life of all Europe in his time and in ours too.

This holistic view of personality has broader implications. In particular, it refutes the view that the private behavior of a political leader has nothing to do with the ways in which she fulfills her mission and is, therefore, entitled to protection from public gaze. Such a separation has no psychological base. This is an additional reason for the required virtue of avant-garde politicians to lead an impeccable private life.

Quite a number of senior politicians, including impressive ones, had and have some "magic" believes, such as in lucky and unlucky numbers, fortune tellers, astrology, and so on. To mention one minor example, U.S. President Woodrow Wilson regarded "thirteen" as his lucky number and adjusted state activities to fit that date.

I hesitate to disqualify a political leader with marginal strange beliefs that do not influence substantively the performance. Mackenzie King should have been barred from public offices. But Woodrow Wilson was a great president (Cooper Jr. 2011) who was in many respects a proto-avant-garde leader (as discussed in Chapter 8). He should not have been disallowed because of his belief in a lucky number, though this may perhaps have been a warning sign of failures to come.

AUTONOMY

The qualities of an avant-garde politician depend a lot on the mind achieving significant autonomy from given traits and external pressures. Relevant for an avant-garde politician, with adjustments, is an intriguing feature of the Ignatian spirituality, namely the use of spiritual exercises to ensure that the mind of the exercitant achieves increasing autonomy from moods, feelings, drives, and passions, so that decisions are not influenced by mental processes irrelevant to the merits of the issue under consideration. But I am not qualified to provide guidance on such exercises.

A mind can be more or less "fallen", as Martin Heidegger puts it, or "in bad faith," as Jean-Paul Sartre entitles it, or "inauthentic", in the sense of not thinking one's own thoughts and not living one's own life, being instead dominated by external influences. But this again is a matter of "more or less." Unavoidably, the main aspects of any "I" are shaped by genetic endowments and social and physical environments. The very languages which one acquires impact significantly on the mind. No human person can be "radically free." Even limited measures of inner autarchy are difficult to achieve in a world of interdependence and communication overflows.

But humans can to some extent break out from their chains, enlarge the autonomy of their minds, and also achieve some detachment from prevailing "common sense" and imaginaries. Maximizing such possibilities is a required critical quality of an avant-garde politician. It is essential for understanding radically novel realities and coping well with their unprecedented challenges with the help of openness to creativity and much personal innovativeness.

What is discussed here is the autonomy of the mind, not freedom of action. The latter is shaped by features of reality which constrain what is "possible." Parts of that reality are elastic and can be overcome, gone around, or changed by human efforts.

Avant-garde politicians have to increase the domains of their freedom of action far beyond the slogan "politics is the art of the possible," using a variety of ways to do so, as discussed in other chapters. But internal autonomy comes first. No avant-garde politician can consider and try to do what does not first occur in the mind.

Most human beings are very aware of external constraints, but not of internal lack of autonomy. Accepting common opinions, being one of "the people," following fashion, and so on, come naturally. This is true also for the many who want to "stand out." In fact they want to excel according to socially accepted criteria, such as making money, acquiring power, and being what is regarded as "beautiful" as changing with time. Liberal modern societies provide individuals with many more options than traditional ones, but within limits of dominant ideologies, amusement industries, and so on—all misperceived by the vast majority as "obvious" and even "empowering" and "enriching," not as an imposition on the mind, which they largely are.

No society can exist without many shared contents of minds. The very survival of the human species requires many widely and also globally shared values, reality understandings, and so on. But the cultural evolution of humanity depends mainly on a few exceptional individuals who move beyond what is widely accepted and serve as creators of new values, knowledge, ideas, art, and so on—often for the better, but also for the worse.

An avant-garde politician must be one of the exceptions, seeking maximum internal autonomy in many domains. This requires a lot of detachment from parts of what was implanted in the mind since before being born. Also needed is expansion of the fluidity of the mind to the maximum, so as to enlarge autonomy up to the rigid limits of hardwiring of the brain, while becoming aware of such limits and trying to compensate for them.

The first essential steps in augmenting internal autonomy is recognition of the shackles put on the mind by inheritance and environments and a strong will to overcome them, including readiness to engage in iconoclasm of what is held dear and is deeply rooted in the mind. This does not imply giving up basic values after reconsideration, and certainly not moving towards a kind of mental anarchism or nihilism. On the contrary, an avant-garde politician has a demanding set of values and a strict personal moral code, as discussed. But these are for the mind of each and every avant-garde politician to adopt after careful consideration, and not because of wide acceptance or pressure by others.

An initial step is to expose oneself to a variety of cultures and thus reduce the hold of any one of them on the mind. Diversified studies, readings, discourse, and personal experiences are helpful. Living from time to time for at least one year in a different civilization, not in an enclave of expatriates but fully mixing with the "natives," is very important. Studying at least two different disciplines can be mind-opening. Acquiring fluency in additional languages can enrich significantly the modalities of the mind. Moving virtually in the past and in imagined alternative futures, with efforts to enter the mind of historic political leaders and imagining those of future avant-garde politicians can be mind-stretching.

More is needed, including dreaming, wild thinking, counterfactual contemplation, and some fantasy-fed imaginaries. This is one of the reasons why time-off from current pressures is essential. But most important is a constant awareness of the mind as being the real "I" of an avant-garde politician, and persistent truth-seeking evaluation of its qualities, while working hard to improve them.

CHAPTER 7
CORE QUALITIES

MULTIPLE PERSONAS

The required qualities of the mind of an avant-garde politician constitute bundles, pictorially presented as multiple "personas," with overlaps and interactions.

The persona which most fully expresses the required core qualities is that of a foundational leader. Laying foundations for a novel future ensuring the long-term flourishing of the human species, while preventing serious damage to humanity, is in many respects the essence of the extraordinary mission. This is qualitatively different and much more than "transformational leadership" (Bass and Riggio 2006), which is more limited in scope, radicalness, aspiration, and historic impacts.

Similarly of prime importance is the persona of composer, especially in "composing" humanity-craft and its grand-policies, as discussed in Part Four. This involved innovating and also creating new ideas, within constraints, and putting them into various forms of "notations," such as grand-policies, serving as guides for different players using various instruments.

Related are the overlapping personas of a visionary, institution builder, social architect, pedagogue, gardener, and entrepreneur: visionary, in drawing in the mind images of alternative futures, involving imagination and design fitting values and taking into account the potentials and limitations of available materials and also aesthetic considerations; institution builder, in preparing plans, preparing the ground, and initiating institutional innovations, especially global ones; social architecture realizing desired features of societies top down, such as elimination of poverty; pedagogue, in trying to impact on mentalities, such as advancing maturation; gardener, in facilitating desired action bottom up, seeding ideas, providing fertilizers, and plucking out weeds; and entrepreneur, in initiating novel ventures and advancing them against inertia, conservatism, and active resistance.

An additional set of personas of an avant-garde politician includes conductor, and leading player in an orchestra. Conductor, who inspires, motivates, mentors, and coordinates the players. And leading player, engaging personally in crucial actions.

An avant-garde politician also has various measures of the persona of a revolutionary, advancing radical changes strongly resisted by widely accepted ideologies, deeply rooted habits, venerated traditions, and powerful vested interests. Often elements of a commander and warrior persona are also needed (Kaplan 2003), using enforcement measures.

Related to all other personas is that of an explorer, seeking new knowledge, novel ideas, innovative understandings, and going with the help of a team "where no human has gone before." The mind of an avant-garde politician has also to include the persona of a labyrinth-sophisticated puzzle solver, trying to understand and orient oneself in vexing and also in seemingly mysterious situations and seeking ways through them.

Crises are a permanent part of human history, constituting sometimes important turning points. All the more so are frequent and in part critical crises built into metamorphosis. Therefore the persona of the crisis direction (Carrel 2010), and also sometimes crisis instigator, constitutes an important quality to be exercised and developed in the mind of an avant-garde politician.

Most personas of an avant-garde politician need a lot of support and involve diverse publics. This requires the persona of a story teller: communicating stories to relevant publics which make sense of what is happening and needs to be done, with efforts to relate to all of humanity, is part of the roles of all political leaders, in which some excel for better or worse. The extraordinary tasks of an avant-garde politician require more, including the reshaping of important parts of political and social culture, self-images, common sense, imaginaries and feeling of identity, and encouraging the change-over of public perspectives from "tribal" to human species ones. All the more so is being a story composer and presenter an important persona required in the mind and acted out in public.

Related are the personas of physicians of humanity and stress managers, and a kind of "pastor" of the public. The persona of a "physician" applies with clinical concern evidence-based professional knowledge together with experience-based personal knowledge and skills to public predicaments. Interestingly, classical Portuguese writings on statecraft used this metaphor a lot. Closely related is the persona of a stress manager. An era of metamorphosis produces a lot of trauma and much stress hitting many persons, societies and humanity as a whole. These entail high costs in terms of human welfare and raise the danger of destructive behavior. Therefore the mind of an avant-garde politician has to engage a lot in trauma treating and stress managing. Even more demanding is the persona of a pastor, not in a religious sense but including taking care of the morals and spirituality of societies and humanity, such as the already mentioned soulcraft.

Much depends on what Machiavelli called "Fortuna," in the sense of contingencies and what appear to be chance events. This is all the more so the case in an era of metamorphosis, when many processes relatively stable in the past become "wild." Therefore, even if an avant-garde politician could achieve full knowledge of what can in principle be known, which is not and never can be the case, still the prevalence of thick uncertainty would make all choices into "fuzzy gambles," which cannot be reduced to probabilities or other scales leading to "optimal" or at least clearly "preferable" options.

Otto von Bismarck put it clearly: "My entire life was spent gambling for high stakes with other people's money. I could never foresee exactly whether my plans would succeed…everything depends on chance and conjecture. One has to reckon with a series of probabilities and improbabilities and base one's plans upon this reckoning." (Steinberg 2011, 130). This applies to nearly all the extraordinary mission of an avant-garde politician. It follows that the mind of an avant-garde politician must include a central persona of a maestro gambler, as elaborated in Chapter 16.

To balance the emerging impression let me add and emphasize that in many respects an avant-garde politician is a "caretaker," in the sense of taking care of the existence of humanity and parts of its welfare, but not a ""Master of the Future." It is up to value creators, cultural processes and humanity as a whole to shape the future contents of human existence, as far as depending on humanity, such as moving towards a Second Axial Age with unforeseeable and largely inconceivable contents, as already mentioned. Such "future making" is far beyond the mandate and capacities of even the most outstanding avant-garde politicians. It is important that you keep this limitation in mind, as an antidote to dangerous tendencies towards megalomania.

All the personas in the mind of an avant-garde politician have to cognize, imagine, ponder, decide and act in terms of grand-policies and grand-projects directed at realizing the existential imperatives and the value compass by swerving history so as to move towards desirable futures. This requires in the mind of an avant-garde politician a "grand-strategic" persona, dominating much of humanity-craft composing, as discussed in Part Four.

HYBRID HEDGEHOG-FOX

In 1953 Isaiah Berlin published his famous essay "The Hedgehog and the Fox" (Berlin 2013). Going back to a fragment attributed to the ancient Greek poet Archilochus "the fox knows many things, but the hedgehog knows one big thing", Berlin applied the distinction to the difference between having a single defining idea versus having multiple perspectives. Berlin admitted that he never regarded this dichotomy as very serious. Nevertheless, famous as it became, it can serve to characterize significant required qualities of the mind of an avant-garde politician as a kind of hybrid hedgehog–fox, including the better parts of both while bringing to the foreground more of one or the other as may fit particular issues and situations.

The overriding idea of an avant-garde politician is ensuring a thriving future for the human species. This requires broad perspectives, accepting parts of an adage of the

Roman playwright Terence "I am a human being, I consider nothing that is human alien to me," within practical limits and as supporting rather than hindering required focusing of the mind on concrete issues and tasks. Involved are both particulars and broad views, hence the need for a hybrid hedgehog–fox mind.

BONDAGE TO THE PAST

All the required mental richness discussed above is subject to a major difficulty in facing novel challenges as posed by the metamorphosis, namely much bondage to the past. This is all the more problematic, however inevitable, because of the distorted images of the past dominating our mind (MacMillan, 2010) and unavoidable hermeneutical gaps biasing cognition and understanding of situations radically different from what was.

Bondage to the past is not a total hindrance, because in metamorphosis too there is much continuity making the past partly into a helpful guide for the future, though a risky one requiring handling with constant doubts. But, still, unavoidable bondage of most and perhaps nearly the entire mind to the past is a very serious impediment to comprehending and dealing with radically novel issues.

An impressive 2013 book on thinking by Douglas Hofstadter and Emmanuel Sander includes a number of statements on the dependence of our thinking on the past, such as "the past we have lived through is all we have for thinking about the future" (Hofstadter and Sander 2013, 331), and "thanks to categorization through analogy-making, we have the ability to spot similarities in order to deal with the new and strange" (Hofstadter and Sander 2013, 20).

However, the mind must have additional meta-images and meta-dimensions of thinking not considered in that book, which are essential for choosing analogs and deciding on their relevance. This does not weaken the proposition that thinking about the future is very much in bondage to the past, with grave consequences when facing really unprecedented issues, which are surely to multiply and become increasingly critical. But the existence of meta-levels in the mind hints at the likelihood that humans have some mental equipment for comprehending and coping with the radically novel, such as imagination which is not necessarily fully in bondage to the past, as proven by many radical innovations characterizing the history of humanity.

To return to a relatively simple example, let us assume that the overall IQ of most humans is augmented to an average of 150. There is no applicable analogue in the past on which an outlook on such a world can be based. Even less can be foreseen on the effects of human cloning and on the nature of consciousness, if any, of "intelligent" robots. No appropriate concepts are available from human experiences in the past. But this does not prevent imaginative thinking which at least alerts the mind to some attributes of what might come. So does the ability of the mind to conceive the concept of "inconceivability," which can stimulate imaginative ideas which prepare us somewhat for what will happen, even if the future turns out to be very different from what was imagined.

On mass-killing terror with synthesized viruses some guesstimate is possible, by analogy with more conventional mass-killing in the past and large epidemics. However the consequences of world-wide lack of employment because of large scale transfer of human jobs to 3M printing, molecular level engineering, and quasi-intelligent robots are shrouded in thick uncertainty, convincing analogy with the past not being available. Still, there are somewhat analogous situations in the past which can serve as bases for imaginative pondering that can indicate some likely features of such a situation, such as social disruptions and search for "time-killing" amusements. And partial past analogy can also help in designing some modes of coping, such as ensured minimum income and facilitation of edifying leisure time use. Still, the bondage of our minds to the past is very extensive and poses harsh difficulties for comprehension of radically new situations sure to face humanity and coping with them without very high learning costs.

This bondage also applies to most social science theories. Thus, when the dynamics of economic phenomena changes radically no reliable theories are available as a basis for coping. This is in part demonstrated by the relatively minor case, in comparison with what is likely to come, of the global economic downturns during the early twenty-first century.

Given such situations pondering will be speculative and choices will be quite wild fuzzy gambles. Moving forward with eyes glues to rear mirrors will lead to disasters, trying to do more of the same will fail dismally, and incremental renovations will not work. Instead, essential are radical innovations based on peak imaginative creativity and accompanied by multiple safeguards against failures. But no amount of creativity and no precautions can fully compensate for the lack of salient analogues and relyable theories. And these do not exist when radically novel issues arise, as they increasingly do. Consequently antifragility strategies (Taleb 2012) and accelerated learning, together with a maximum of long-term pattern recognition efforts which reduces some of the surprise elements of novel developments, become crucially needed qualities in the mind of avant-garde politicians. Also needed is "foresight intuition," as discussed later, but it is not clear if and how far it exists, what its groundings might be, and how it can be recognized before the future hits humanity.

INTUITION

This brings us to "intuition" as a quality, or a set of qualities of the mind. A symptom of the populist bias of modern Western culture is the proliferation of literature extolling the merits of "blink" (Gladwell 2005), "gut feelings" (Gigerenzer 2007), and so on. Such ideas may have some validity for routine choices, but when complex issues are at stake they hardly apply and are likely to mislead. This is also true with the so-called "strategic intuition" (Duggan 2013) and similar propositions when going beyond seeking of creativity. But there is no escape from the importance of intuition neither from its somewhat enigmatic nature.

Most of the processes of the mind, including thinking, take place on subconscious levels. Large parts of them cannot be made conscious, neither by acts of will nor with the help of presently available instruments or methods, with the partly exception of psychoanalysis which is not relevant for our present concerns. All reservations and requirements concerning bondage to the past fully apply to intuition, with the important but not clear exception of not understood "leaps of insight," which can be very helpful or fatal.

To survive, humanoids and later *Homo sapiens* had to develop "intuition" enabling navigation in their environment and utilize and start to shape it, before developing concepts and explicit knowledge. Such intuition, as further developing with cultural evolution, is based largely on pattern recognition, which catches the form or *Gestalt* of coherent parts of reality and copes with them accordingly. Pattern recognition is crucial for comprehending and handling reality clusters, connecting dots, giving meaning to multifarious raw facts and enabling dealing with "systems," such as a forest understood as different from a collection of disparate trees.

Good intuition on slowly changing domains is widely available, including among political leaders. It may enable "seeing what others don't" (Klein 2013). Taking mainly the form of tacit knowledge, it can be acquired by personal experience, cultural socialization and systematic study and practice, but additional unknown processes seem also to take part. It includes inter-alia skills becoming largely automatic, such as "procedural memory," which cannot be fully explicated, such as riding a bicycle.

More complex are the clinical skills of a surgeon which seem as if located in the hands, though residing largely in the mind. This applies to "primed choices," which are made subconsciously and instantly, as demonstrated by studies of decision making in real situations, such as by fire fighters (Klein 1999).

An advanced basis of intuition is "professionalism," which is based on much experience and study. Good examples are master chess players and also experienced political apparatchiks who know how to operate in the arena of gaining influence and acquiring goodies as long as the rules of conventional politics, as developed in different cultures, prevail.

Professionalism includes plenty of tacit knowledge and pattern recognition, but also a lot of reasoning based both on experience and abstract knowledge. An interesting example are professional poker players who apply a mix of "reading of the minds" of other players and probabilistic calculus to relieve non-professional players from their money (fascinating is Hilger and Taylor 2007). I discuss the cardinal importance of a special type of generalist-professionalism quality in the mind of avant-garde politicians below.

Whatever its bases may be, intuition is a crucial quality of the mind. However, at least most of it is in bondage to the past. Therefore, intuition too is more likely to be misleading than helpful on novel issues as increasingly facing humanity. It follows that an avant-garde politician should regard upgraded intuition as an essential quality of the mind, but one that cannot be relied upon and which may mislead pondering on novel issues that are significantly different from the past, but which sometimes produces striking insights. Updating of intuition by constant, deliberate and conscious exposure to new situations, including virtual "games" in the mind, is therefore required from avant-garde politicians. But on complex novel issues intuition should always be regarded with much doubt and subjected to critical reasoning, without being ignored.

Let me reemphasize: The tacit knowledge of a physician may have dismal results when guiding treatment of a radically new disease. The intuition of an experienced fire fighter will result in his death when relied upon, probably unconsciously and automatically, in coping with novel incendiary materials. This is also the case with the "feel" experienced military officers have for "reading" a battlefield, as discussed by Carl von Clausewitz in his classic book *On War*. It combines outstanding pattern recognition with tacit knowledge based largely on experience, augmented by a good knowledge of military history and theory. But when the nature of conflicts changes radically, thanks to novel technologies and tactics and new political, social, and legal contexts, then the insights of the victorious generals of yesterday become the debacles of today, as amply proven already by the Battle of Verdun in the First World War. Therefore, "forgetting much of Clausewitz" may be a good advice for the military commanders of the future. Similarly, ignoring obsolete "wisdom" of great politicians of the past, after drawing from it selectively useful lessons, is a good advice for avant-garde politicians.

EUREKA EFFECTS

There can be sudden insights, conveniently called "Eureka effects." These are important and sometimes critical in scientific discoveries, artistic creativity, and occasionally in statecraft. However, "breakthrough" mental events are scarce and do not occur in a vacuum. They are the result of much knowledge, brooding, and hard work. And, if dealing with more than trivial matters, they are the preserve of few persons and happen to them very seldom. Also, they can be very misleading, though much less is written about serious intuition errors than about much fewer cases of impressive success. Therefore, while some kind of sudden insights may help with difficult novel issues, and should be nurtured, they are not a mental phenomenon sure to come when needed or always reliable. All this may easily leave an avant-garde politician at a loss on what to do.

Not acting is often the worst of all options. Therefore, making up the mind on the relatively better or least bad option, together with recognizing its fuzzy gambling nature and acting accordingly, may often be the only reasonable choice. But it may be inadequate and also dangerous. Therefore seeking persons who have creative minds, outstanding pattern recognition abilities, and unusual intuition that may produce at least minor "Eureka" occasions is mandatory for avant-garde politicians. Relying on oneself is essential, but often risky and never enough. This recommendation has practical implications for building and working with advisory staffs and other helpmates, as discussed in Chapter 18.

I realize that all this leaves you somewhat bewildered. But this is unavoidable when confronting hardly understandable surprises which metamorphosis suddenly throws at you. Luckily, as noted and further discussed in Chapter 15, invariances and slow change processes provide a scaffold for some learning from the past and also partly reliable intuition. Recognizing and accepting being bewildered is therefore an essential quality of the mind of an avant-garde politician, together with ways to cope with bewilderment as far as possible.

READING MINDS

Of utmost importance is the ability of a mind to "read" the mind of other persons, based on basic similarities of all human minds, social learning, experience, and evolutionary imprinted pattern recognition. In this matter bondage to the past is not a disadvantage, as core features of human beings are among the invariances remaining stable during metamorphosis, with the possible future exception of radical enhancement.

Human beings have in their mind a tacit "theory of the mind" and "mirror images" of other (as apparently have higher apes and some other animals), otherwise social life would be impossible. But some people are better at "feeling" others and some are worse, as is the case with all forms of intuition. Biases and prejudices are widespread and cause serious misapprehensions. Also, some persons are very adept at hiding their true nature from others, intuitively or by deliberate masking.

Therefore deciding whom to trust and how far carries many risks. This raises serious problems when "personal chemistry" fulfills important roles, requiring much caution and quite some skepticism, together with seeking of relevant information, including psycho-profiles despite being often unreliable. However, a lot of trust in others is essential for all human cooperation, including by avant-garde politicians. Therefore, tuning the quality of comprehension of the minds of others is cardinal for the quality of an avant-garde politician.

GENERALIST-PROFESSIONALISM

An essential core quality of the mind of an avant-garde politician, important for all mind processes, is generalist–professionalism. This concept sounds like an oxymoron, because of the apparent contradiction between "generalist" and "professionalism." A generalist has wide knowledge and a macroscopic view of broad domains, while a professional, often overlapping an "expert," knows a lot about a defined domain, returning us to the hybrid hedgehog–fox and to earlier comments on the intuition of professionals, but now quite differently so. Generalist–professionalism is a special quality required of the mind of an avant-garde politician, namely being a professional in the general fundamentals of the extraordinary and also ordinary missions.

This critical requirement contradicts much of the folklore and also habits of politics. Thus, according to many political traditions "experts should be on tap but not on top," as succinctly put by Harold Laski (in line with Laski 1931). Politics often suffers from the cult of the amateur, and, indeed, many senior politicians, with important exceptions, are amateurs on crucial issues, lacking even the minimum knowledge essential for benefitting from the inputs of professionals and often not really desiring it, relying instead on their political instincts and what they call "common sense," which may help with common issues, but not with the uncommon really important ones.

Let me correct myself somewhat: many political leaders are experts in "politicking," that is gaining and holding on to power. Avant-garde politicians too have to gain and maintain power and have something to learn from politicking on doing so, and a lot on what not to do. But in much of modern politics the findings of Henry Fayol, a French business executive, who developed important theories of management, apply: persons rise on the career ladder on the basis of success in former positions and not the qualities needed for the new positions, which are often radically different (Fayol 1949). A modern satiric formulation is the well-known Peter's Principle that "every employee tends to rise to his level of incompetence" (Peter and Hull 2011, 15).

The history of medical practitioners is partly relevant to the professionalism of avant-garde politicians. Up to the seventeenth and eighteenth centuries Western medical practice was dominated by Hippocrates and Galen. Bleeding was often the main treatment, causing much pain and grievous harm. Training in medicine took the form of apprenticeship with some incorrect theoretical lectures, passing on ignorance with quite some bits of insight from generation to generation. Only in the nineteenth century did medical training become a rigorous university study based on growing scientific knowledge, first in Europe and after some delay in the United States, with quite some emphasis on training of the mind (Groopman 2007).

Politics is very different from medical practice. It can be based only in part on more or less valid knowledge and evidence, depending instead a lot on world views, tacit knowledge, conjectures, guesstimates, creativity, and intuition. But the needed new version of political leaders also requires what I call "generalist–professionalism," including its ethical dimensions. All these have to be of much higher quality and fit better the challenges of metamorphosis than hunches, obsolete experiences, simplistic dogmas, wrong analogues, mistaken reasoning, inappropriate frames of appreciation, personal idiosyncrasies, egocentric power seeking, political convenience, mass media impacts, quite some ignorance, and many thinking fallacies, which dominate the minds of the vast majority of contemporary political leaders, together with much "chatter," making even the better ones largely into "amateurs" in dealing with the challenges of metamorphosis. Therefore needed are generalist–professional avant-garde politicians.

Let me sharpen the question whether being an avant-garde politician is a "profession"? The correct answer is "largely but not fully yes, but of a special generalist–professional type." The essence of professionalism is "knowledge in action," consisting of three main components: (1) a body of defined and reasonably validated knowledge, (2) good familiarity with particular issues and domains to which that knowledge is to be applied, and (3) the skill actually to apply the knowledge to the issues on hand. The first two components can be learned, both by explicit studies and by gaining experience-based tacit knowledge. The third component requires mainly on-the-job learning, with a lot of feedbacks and, when possible, the guidance of qualified mentors.

It is not difficult to identify standard knowledge which a twenty-first century avant-garde politician should possess as a quality of his mind, such as science and technology literacy, principles of economics, some public law, introduction to social sciences including also psychology, theories of history, moral philosophy, policy planning, and so on. To be added are familiarity with the world and its main civilizations on one hand and rather technical skills, such as in public image shaping, on the other. It is not very difficult to design a graduate or post-graduate university program, or a personal study program, which provides this knowledge. This can also be done with the help of books written with senior political leaders in mind, but only very few texts meeting requirements are available (honorable exceptions are illustrated by Muller 2009; 2013).

However more is needed for the extraordinary mission, such as frames of thinking on humanity as a species, approaches to humanity-craft design, abilities to upgrade fuzzy gambling in the face of bounded thick uncertainty, action-oriented thinking-in-history, and a deep understanding of emerging metamorphosis processes.

Much of the essential knowledge is not available. Thus, a 2013 text trying to sum up "behavioral foundations of public policy" (Shafir, ed. 2013) is comprehensive and interesting as far as it goes. But this collection fully reflects the scarcity of knowledge on basic issues of human metamorphosis, humanity-craft and other domains which is sorely needed for the extraordinary mission of avant-garde politicians.

Contemporary "normal" sciences are unlikely to supply that knowledge without a paradigm shift. Therefore, you should encourage relevant research and teaching, while realizing that large parts of the knowledge needed for the extraordinary mission, parts of which can in principle be generated given a sustained effort, are unavailable or hard to find, while being also disliked by most mainstream scholars. Thus, important insights into antifragility (Taleb 2012) received less attention by the community of scholars than interesting, but rather narrow findings in experimental decision psychology of limited importance and applicability, as already mentioned. And many economists cling to sophisticated but clearly no longer correct theories, stubbornly trying to peddle them to political leaders instead of frankly recognizing their inadequacies.

Therefore, take care! Relying on obsolete, inapplicable and misleading knowledge ensures failure. Instead, the mind of an avant-garde politician has to be aware of the lacunae of mainstream professionalism and try to compensate for them by seeking reliable advisors and appropriate ways to compose humanity-craft in the face of much ignorance and thick uncertainty, as discussed in Part Four.

EXECUTIVE FUNCTION

Also required as an essential quality in the mind of an avant-garde politician is a very good executive function, together with metacognition involving images and thoughts about one's thinking. Probably located largely in the frontal lobe (Goldberg 2001), it activates the various qualities and processes of the mind salient to particular issues in appropriate forms, while also monitoring and mentoring them. The executive function is also in charge of time and attention allocation and pondering scheduling, as discussed separately.

Theses executive and metacognition functions are all the more important because of the subjection of the mind of an avant-garde politician to plenty of multiple overwhelmings (Ford 2013, 7-10, though dealing with another context).

SELF-EVALUATION AND IMPROVEMENT

Carved onto the temple of Delphi in Greece was the commandment "know thyself." But for an avant-garde politician more relevant is the recommendation of Epictetus: "First say to yourself what you would be; and then do what you have to do." This is the task of the quality of self-evaluation and self-improvement, reemphasized here though already discussed in parts. Some of your deficits will be rather obvious. But studies of self-knowledge (Butler, 2005; Vaziere and Wilson, eds. 2012) as well as pronouncements and writings by political leaders, including subjectively frank ones, clearly demonstrate that knowing the mind of oneself, its qualities and deficiencies, is very difficult and in part impossible. Usually you are very likely to appear to yourself as being of much higher quality than your mind really is.

Therefore, the mind of an avant-garde politician needs help in the form of a "hall of mirrors," but not distorting ones showing all the time how very smart one is. Instead, needed is a kind of virtual "meta-mind" or internal "alter ago" that serve as an "inner eye" observing the mind and evaluating it in terms of required qualities, but without distracting or otherwise disturbing pondering and choice.

Public self-criticism was in the Soviet Union an instrument of brain-washing and public humiliation. However, there is something to learn from more educational uses of self-criticism in modern China (Vogel 2011, 147, 723), in a more private form. Much can also be learned from "self-examination" in the form of adjusted "spirituality for decision makers," initiated by Ignatius of Loyola and practiced in the Society of Jesus. It includes periodic meditation on oneself, keeping frank diaries, and getting candid evaluations by trusted and discrete spiritual advisors and mentors. But an avant-garde politician must exercise a lot of discretion in sharing self-critical thoughts with someone else. Today's confidant can become tomorrow's enemy.

An open mind, as required from avant-garde politicians, can also learn a lot on what needs improvement from public criticism if carefully sifted for elements of truth. And learning from the results of decisions, if correctly done with fully taking into account the nature of choices as bounded fuzzy gambles, is very important for self-evaluation and improvement. All these require time for critical reflection, as part of the solitary contemplation which, as noted, is a must for an avant-garde politician.

The self-assessment should be strict but not over-demanding. Avant-garde politicians, as all humans, differ in quality. Meeting the demanding qualities of the mind of a "good" avant-garde politician satisfies the requirement, though one should work hard to be "very good." Achieving a level of overall "excellence" may well be beyond human capacities. No human mind can be outstanding in all of the core qualities. Being good in most of them, very good in one or two, fair in some, and not "bad" in any one is fully adequate, while also being very demanding.

CHAPTER 8
HISTORIC PROTOTYPES

REALISTIC TEMPLATES

The time has come to check whether the proposed construct of avant-garde politicians is a utopian (or, in some opinions, "dystopian") impossibility or it can be approximated by human beings and is therefore fit to serve as a guiding model. To try and respond one could delve into psychology and show that the qualities of mind required from an avant-garde politician do not surpass what is achievable by an adequate number of humans (e.g., Martinez 2013, though overoptimistic), all the more so as no single avant-garde politician is expected to be outstanding in all the necessary qualities. But I prefer to proceed by way of examples of the relatively few but very illuminated historic political leaders who did achieve significant influence on history, thanks to impressive qualities of the mind which justify regarding them as prototypes of avant-garde politicians. Such Delta "proto-avant-garde politicians" serve as empirical proof that the model proposed in this book can and should serve as a template for radically upgrading political leadership.

HISTORIC EXAMPLES

To go back before the beginning of the twentieth century, some striking examples of political leaders who significantly influenced the shape of large parts of the world include, in temporal order, Emperor Qin Shi Huang (259–210 BCE), who laid the foundations for unified China; Emperor Ashoka Maurya (304–232 BCE), ruler of the Mauryan Empire, who underwent a personal conversion becoming a devoted Buddhist, adopted non-violence, protected animals, and made Buddhism into a major religion; Alexander III of Macedonia The Great (356–323 BCE), who reshaped large parts of the Euro-Asia and North Africa geopolitically and culturally; Augustus Caesar (27 BCE–14 CE), who, on the basis provided by Julius Caesar (100–44 BCE), founded the Principate and laid the foundations for the Roman Empire and thus for the future or Europe; Constantine the Great (c. 272–337), who made Christianity into the dominant religion of the West; Saladin (full name Salah Ad-din Yusuf Ibn Ayyub, 1137–1193), together with Mehmet II the Conqueror (1432–1481), who conquered Jerusalem from the Crusaders, and Constantinople from the Byzantine Empire, thus establishing Arab and Ottoman empires standing up to the West and competing with it for centuries; Peter the Great (1672–1725), following in some respects Ivan IV Vasilyevich the Terrible (1530–1589) in pushing the Westernization of Russia and making it into an empire; Napoleon Bonaparte (1769–1821), who, despite being defeated at the end, irreversibly exported crucial enlightenment elements of the French Revolution all over Europe and beyond; Abraham Lincoln (1809–1865) who, following George Washington (1732–1799), stabilized the existence and overall structure of the United States of America and its basic values, which in turn exert profound and sometimes dominant influence on the world; Simón Bolívar (1783–1830), the leader of the struggle for the independence of Latin America; Otto von Bismarck (1815–1898), the unifier of Germany, but who had no equally prudent successors, with unexpected dismal impacts on the future of Europe and the world, as already pointed out; Emperor Mutsuhito Meiji Tennō, (1852–1912), a major modernizer of Japan; and Sun Yat-sen (1866–1925), the founding father of the Republic of China leading to the emergence of modern China.

Moving on to examples of proto-avant-garde politicians in the twentieth and twenty-first centuries, who are more relevant as direct predecessors of modern avant-garde politicians, I proceed alphabetically with 22 political leaders, mainly but not only heads of states or governments. I selected them somewhat arbitrarily according to two criteria: (1) importance of their impact on modern history and (2) significance as prototypes from which noteworthy lessons can be drawn for avant-garde politicians. With a few exceptions I have not included political leaders who were still alive when I finished proofreading.

When appropriate, I discuss concisely the main achievements and hint at lessons than can be drawn, which are enlarged upon in the last part of this chapter.

Konrad Hermann Joseph Adenauer (1876–1967). After Germany was occupied and divided by the victors of the Second World War, Adenauer became the first chancellor of the Federal Republic of Germany, rehabilitated West Germany and ensuring its democratic nature. Also noteworthy is his success in establishing good relationships with France and the United States, accepting the responsibility of Germany for the *Shoah*, paying large reparations to Jewish survivors and Israel and reaching a kind of reconciliation with it. These were unusual future-shaping achievements after the crimes of the Nazi Regime and the total defeat of Germany.

Mustafa Kemal Atatürk (1881–1939). Founder of the modern Republic of Turkey after the First World War, on the ruins of the defeated Ottoman Empire. He instituted a unique cultural revolution transforming Turkey from an Islamic religious state to a rather secular one, including changing the script and westernizing large parts of the public space. He did so as a revolutionary political leader leaning on the army, but without significant resort to terror.

Defeat, disintegration, and crisis throughout history have provided opportunities for radical changes, if outstanding leadership was available, as illustrated by Atatürk. This is put into sharp relief when compared with Mohammad Rezā Shāh Pahlavi (1919–1980) and his father, whose reforms of Iran were a failure and laid the ground for the Islamic Republic of Iran and its founder, Ayatollah Khomeini, discussed below.

In Turkey there is a reaction against some of the transformations made by Atatürk, but the new foundations laid by Atatürk remained strong. One reason for his unusual success is the large scale of his reforms which include enforced transformation of the culture, even if mainly effective in urban elites. These reached a critical mass of intervention in historic processes adequate for resetting their trajectory, which was not achieved by the much shallower efforts of the Pahlavi dynasty in Iran.

David Ben-Gurion (1886–1973). A major leader of the Zionist Movement and the Jewish state-in-the-making in mandatory Palestine, and then the first Prime Minister of Israel, Ben-Gurion combined philosophic interests and contemplation in solitude with tough decisiveness, however accompanied by physical signs of stress. He took a fateful gamble with history in declaring establishment of the State of Israel following the UN General Assembly decision in 1947, in full awareness of a pending large-scale attack by Arab states and irregulars, the outcome of which was in no way preordained. After the success of Israel's War of Independence, Ben-Gurion laid foundations for the main features of Israel, including Israeli defense doctrines. However he got entangled in party political quarrels and retired rather frustrated.

Osama bin Laden (1957–2011). Bin Laden illustrates a different type of political leader, namely non-state religious fanatic ones acting regionally and in part globally, in this case by founding the Islamist terrorist organization Al-Qaeda with the aim to bring about an extreme form of religious regime in Islamic and especially Arabic countries and expelling the Western and especially U.S. influence. His most extreme act was the September 11, 2001 attacks on New York and Washington DC, leading to the U.S.-led attack on Taliban in Afghanistan, and, in May 2011, the killing of bin Laden.

While bin Laden pursued an impossible goal, he achieved significant global geostrategic and large regional ideological impacts and his influence continues. But it is unclear what his traces in long-term history may be.

Fidel Castro (b. 1926). There are differences of opinion on his policies, but without doubt Fidel Castro is an impressive prototype avant-garde revolutionary leader, who relived Cuba from the rule of the military junta headed by Fulgencio Batista and significantly improved the life of most of the population, even though he could have done better.

Castro also distinguished himself by providing humanitarian help to African and Latin American countries sharing his semi-Marxist ideology and supporting revolutionary movements, in cooperation with Comandante Ernesto "Che" Guevara (1928–1967), who can also be regarded as a revolutionary prototype avant-garde politician. Both were true believers, ready to give their lives for the revolution. Che did so, but Fidel Castro went much further.

During the Cuba Missile Crisis he asked the Soviet Ambassador in Havana Aleksander Alekseev to convey to Khrushchev an amazing message, the gist of which was repeated in less explicit terms in a letter from Castro to Khrushchev dated October 26, 1962. As reconstructed from oral history studies and released archival material, the message was as follows:

> …fundamentally I want to say to Comrade Nikita that he must be prepared to destroy the United States. If, in his judgment, Cuba must be also destroyed in the war, then so be it. Cuba is ready to martyr itself for the cause of global socialism and the destruction of America's imperial empire. (Blight and Lang 2012, 116)

This demonstrates the fatal dangers of mass-killing instruments available to political leaders with fanatic values, posing a major challenge to humanity.

Winston Churchill (1874–1965). It seems superfluous to discuss Churchill as a prototype avant-garde politician, but his case if far from simple. He was much of an adventurer and for many years failed in politics. Also, he adhered to the idea of "British Empire," such as on India, after it should have been clear that this is a lost cause. But he had an early insight into the dangers posed by Hitler and opposed appeasement while supporting rearmament.

When the hour of truth stroke, he reached the apex of power, refusing any compromises with Hitler and leading Great Britain in a bitter war to victory, thanks largely to slow but increasing U.S. involvement which Churchill carefully nurtured and which became total after the Japanese attack on Pearl Harbor.

In directing the war, he supported science and technology efforts which, however controversial, made an important contribution. He was far from being a grand-strategic genius, but he read the mind of Stalin more realistically than Roosevelt. After the war he lost elections, showing that being a widely popular heroic war leader does not ensure success as a political leader in peace time.

There are a number of striking features about Churchill, from which much can be learned. Without the Second Word War he would not have appeared in any list of outstanding political leaders. As revealed by well-documented studies (Lukas 2001), it was not preordained in May 1940 whether the United Kingdom would negotiate with Hitler or continue the war against Nazi Germany, but Churchill made sure of the latter. He was outstandingly successful in maintaining the morale of the UK after devastating defeats. And he painted and had significant literary talents.

Ziaoping Deng (1904–1997) On the foundations laid by the maker of Communist China, Mao Zedong (1893–1976), Deng is the founder of modern China as a global superpower in-the-making, combining state capitalism, free markets, opening to the world and an authoritarian, somewhat repressive, and on the local level often corrupt, single party ideological regime.

To understand what was involved one must take into account that China is the world's most populous country, reaching during his rule a population of about 900 million (and in 2013 about 1.35 billion), with a long history of tensions between local and central authorities leading from time to time to breakups of the state. This makes governing of China one of the most difficult tasks for any political leader, second only to the difficulties of ruling India, with a slightly smaller population (about 1.22 billion in 2013), but much more heterogeneous in terms of religions, languages, ethnicity, and more.

Deng radically changed the main policies of Mao, reversing the disastrous Cultural Revolution and ruinous economic policies, as well as reshaping foreign relationships. Thus, he not only was an outstanding proto-avant-garde politician, but also illustrates that it often takes two or three successive political leaders to stabilize a revolution and put it on a successful trajectory.

Mahatma Gandhi (1869–1948). Gandhi was much more than a "political leader." He was the leader of the main Indian independence movement and also an outstanding Indian and global spiritual leader, espousing, among other ideals, nonviolent resistance.

India would in any case have achieved independence after the Second World War and Gandhi failed in his efforts to prevent the partition between India and Pakistan and large-scale religious killings and refugee movements. He himself was assassinated by a Hindu extremist. Building the Indian state was the task of Jawaharlal Nehru (1889–1964), illustrating again the division of labor between leaders struggling for independence and political leaders of the independent state once established (though some, such as Ben-Gurion combine both tasks). But Gandhi achieved a global impact by propagating the use of non-violence passive resistance, which influenced strongly the African-American Civil Rights Movement lead by Martin Luther King, Jr. (1929–1968).

Charles De Gaulle (1890–1970). This is another fascinating case of an outstanding proto-avant-garde politician who reached power thanks to a very unlikely mixture of historic accidents and personal qualities. Till World War Two he was an officer sponsored by Marshal Philippe Pétain (1856–1951), the hero of World War One, who later became the Chief of the State of Vichy France, was condemned in free France to death for treason with the sentence changed to life imprisonment by de Gaulle, his former protégé (this being just one example out of many of the strangeness of life reflected in the fate of political leaders).

Before the French defeat by Nazi Germany De Gaulle was not especially appreciated in France, but his pioneering books on the use of large armor formations were eagerly studied by the German General Staff and put in successful practice by them. De Gaulle also wrote a book on leadership, presaging some of his own performance.

With the defeat of France he began his new life as an outstanding political leader, illustrating like Churchill the contingency theory of leadership in action, according to which dissimilar types of persons can serve as successful leaders in different circumstances. They both also illustrate the critical importance of Fortuna in the path of some outstanding leaders. Interesting is the impact of years without power in preparing some persons for becoming outstanding proto-avant-garde politicians.

De Gaulle first heading the Free French Forces, and then founded the French Fifth Republic, introduced a new presidential constitution and served as President. Foundational activities as President included reassertion of the standing of France as a great power, developing nuclear weapons, and withdrawing from Algiers at the risk of his own life. It is worth noting that De Gaulle was a practicing Roman Catholic, austere in his personal habits, with an exemplary private life.

Despite partly controversial evaluations De Gaulle played a crucial role in founding modern France and is regarded widely in France and elsewhere as the greatest French political leader since Napoleon Bonaparte, without the ultimate failure of the latter.

Mikhail Gorbachev (b. 1931). Gorbachev became a proto-avant-garde political leader after gaining power as Secretary General of the Communist Party, surprising his colleagues, who appointed him without expecting what was to come. He instigated a revolutionary transition to elements of a market economy and brought about the dissolution of the Soviet Union, operating as a "revolutionary from within" the centers of power. A distinguishing feature of his founding activities was his reliance on professional advisors and think tanks.

While the USSR was due in any case to change profoundly, the results of Gorbachev's radical reform, as pushed further by Boris Yeltsin (1931–2007) after a failed coup against Gorbachev and a break between the two, were not as intended and surely not over-determined. It is quite possible that the USSR could have changed in other directions, such as maintaining the federation and combining a market economy with an authoritarian regime somewhat on line with China, perhaps avoiding some of the social and geopolitical costs of the abrupt breakup of the Soviet Union.

Leaving aside such and other speculations, Gorbachev impacted strongly on the future of the USSR with profound global implications. He continues activities as a respected world figure but exercises no real power.

Dag Hjalmar Agne Carl Hammarskjöld (1905–1961). Hammarskjöld was a distinguished senior Swedish civil servant, when appointed as Secretary-General of the United Nations in 1953. In many respects he can serve as a model of a global avant-garde leading politician. Despite being constrained by the structure of the United Nations and the dependence on the main powers, he acted independently in trying to cope with main issues and crises, making strenuous efforts to settle conflicts, reduce bloodshed and help the needy. He died in a still not explained airplane crash while fulfilling his duty and trying to deal with one of the many bloody African conflicts. Hammarskjöld is one of the three persons awarded a posthumous Nobel Peace Prize.

Paul Kennedy points out the ability of Hammarskjöld to shape events (Kennedy 2007, 61). John F. Kennedy said after the death of Hammarskjöld, in relation to the actions of Hammerskjöld: "I realize now that in comparison to him, I am a small man. He was the greatest statesman of our century." (Linnér and Åström 2008, 28).

This is only half the story making him one of the most unusual proto-avant-garde politicians. He never married. After his death his diary was published, revealing a lonely spiritual life and longings which served as a basis for his total commitments to what he accepted as his mission. Symptomatic is the fact that while on his last trip to Africa he worked on translating some of the writings of Martin Buber, whom he met several times at his initiative, into Swedish.

Adolf Hitler (1889–1945). Hitler is the most extreme case of a poisonous future-impacting politician in modern history and also one of the biggest success stories ending in total failure and destruction. Leaving aside his biographic details, the following facts are important for understanding this most dangerous form of political leaders. He was very consistent from early on, presenting his main ideas in the two volumes of *Mein Kampf* published in 1925 and 1926. Extreme anti-Semitism was one of his deepest beliefs, leading to the "final solution." He combined fanatic intensions with high quality tactical and some statecraft skills, enabling him to gain power and lead Germany to some great achievements till the invasion of the USSR. "Everthing or nothing" seems to have been one of his main beliefs, accompanied by growing extreme self-confidence, leading to his downfall after amazing successes.

Most astonishing of all was his success in mobilizing the support of the vast majority of Germans, including the educated strata. Terror was a secondary factor, compared with his outstanding charismatic effects, which continue to defy understanding. But his success would have been impossible without the defeat of Germany in World War One, some of the harsh conditions of the Versailles peace dictate, extreme inflation, weaknesses of the Weimar Republic, and popular fear of a Communist takeover. To be added is that Hitler avoided personal risks, never visiting troops on the front, but he is credible to have used a doomsday weapon if available rather than accept defeat, being apparently in thrall of Wagner's Nibelungen Ring (Kohler 2001), and reputedly stating several times that a Germany which lets itself be defeated does not deserve to exist.

To be added is the disturbing fact that very few statesmen worldwide realized the dangerous nature of Hitler, though his pronouncements made them quite clear. Churchill, as mentioned, was one of the few exceptions. All in all, Hitler is an extreme example of the dangers of a highly capable murderously fanatic charismatic political leader, raising the specter of a murderous fanatic faith engaging in mass-slaughter using novel mass-killing instruments. Prevention of such a contingency is a major duty of avant-garde politicians.

Ayatullah Ruholla Khomeini (1902–1989). He established the Islamic Republic of Iran, serving as its Supreme Leader after overthrowing the Shah following 15 years in exile. Being both a religious and political leader, he installed an authoritarian regime unique in important respects, such as a combination between supremacy of religious bodies and elections, strict Islamic laws and impressive activities of women, and more. Under his rule Iran became a dramatic global actor, taking the U.S. Embassy staff as hostages and fighting Iraq in a bloody war.

Ayatullah Khomeini serves as a clear illustration of an "armed prophet" who was very successful in terms of his values, but long-term implications for the future of Iran and the region are uncertain.

Juscelino Kubitschek de Oliveira (1902–1976). Kubitschek, a medical doctor by profession, illustrates a political leader who can in part be regarded as a proto-avant-garde politician for implementing a single important project having much impact on the future, namely moving in 1960 the Capital of Brazil from Rio de Janeiro to the new city of Brasilia. Discussed for many years, it was only during his presidency, 1956–1961, that Brasilia was built as an effort to reduce the central roles of Rio de Janeiro and Sao Paulo and encourage development of the country as a whole. A military takeover ended his political career and caused him some suffering, but he remained very popular in Brazil.

Opinions differ on the success of his vision, but it seems that establishment of the new capital located in the mid-west of the vast Brazilian territory had positive impacts on the country as a whole, including moving the government out from the culture of Rio de Janeiro. This justified viewing Kubitschek as a "single foundational project" future-impacting political leader.

Findings by an investigative commission in Brazil of evidence that the ex-president Kubitschek was murdered by the 1970s military regime further testify to his importance also after leaving office.

Lee Kuan Yew (b. 1923). Kuan, who served as Prime Minister from 1959 to 1990, transformed Singapore, which was a part of Indonesia and ridden by racial conflicts, into one of the most thriving small states in the world. He did so by combining an authoritarian regime with well-considered social policies and facilitation of a global competitive market economy. Singapore is one of the greatest success stories of the twentieth and first part of the twenty-first century, due to the personality, qualities, and policies of Kuan, and some lucky circumstances, such as the push which the Korean War provided to the development of Singapore. The authoritarian but not very repressive regime was in my evaluation essential for the achievements.

Kuan institutionalized a high-quality and well remunerated merit civil service and groomed worthy successors, to whom power was passed on. He continues to serve as a kind of senior mentor to the government.

Vladimir Lenin (1870–1924). Lenin was crucial for creating the Communist Soviet Union by revolutionary violent action and rebuilding of the state and main feature of society according to Communist revolutionary theory, as in part developed by him. He was one of the few history-shaping political leaders engaged in original theoretical thinking (Lukács, 2009), however mistaken in critical parts, which is still regarded by some impressive thinkers as valid in revised forms (Budgen et al. 2007). But his comprehension of reality was often wrong.

Terror was for Lenin a legitimate and necessary instrument, but did not reach the dimensions of Stalinist mass-killing measures. It is impossible to know how the Soviet Union would have developed if a person other than Stalin had inherited

Lenin's position, as Lenin recommended in his political testament. Another successor might have avoided the great terror, but most probably would not have changed the fundamental antinomies and wrong assumption on which the USSR was constructed.

To be noted are Lenin's insights into revolutionary leadership parts of which are relevant to avant-garde politicians, as detailed in Chapter 5.

Nelson Rolihlahla Mandela (1918-2013). Mandela stands out as probably the most impressive prototype avant-garde politician of the twentieth century. He achieved by the strength of personality what was universally regarded as nearly impossible: Peaceful transition from the South African apartheid regime to democracy, without retribution against the white minority which for many years denied political rights of the black majority, discriminated harshly against it, and subjected non-whites to repressive measures.

Parts of the credit belong to Frederik Willem de Klerk (b. 1936), the last white president of the Republic of South Africa, who understood that the apartheid regime was not only unjust but also unsustainable. However it was Mandela who brought about the "miracle" of a peaceful revolutionary change with quite some reconciliation. However he could not solve stubborn problems of poverty, violence, disparities, and more, which continue to plague the country.

Born to a royal tribal family and designated to become a political leader, his life passed through three very different phases: serving as a leader in the African National Congress, he directed terror attacks against government targets. Sentenced to life imprisonment, he served 27 years in prison. Then he became the President of South Africa, making great efforts to overcome the legacy of hate, such as establishing a Truth and Reconciliation Commission, the first of its kind.

It seems that the many years in prison had a critical influence on this thinking, making him into a unique reconciliatory successful political leader. In 1993 he received the Nobel Peace Prize. After refusing to run for a second term, he devoted himself to combating poverty, but continues to be acclaimed as "father of the nation." However, he failed to control his family, which caused him a lot of trouble.

Jean Monnet (1888–1979). Monnet illustrates a non-politician with high political achievements, operating largely behind-the-scenes but well-recognized by those in-the-know. Never elected to any public office and not personally conspicuous, this French economist and diplomat fulfilled a central foundational role in rebuilding the economy of France after World War Two and, even more importantly, laying the foundations for the European Union. He had an exciting romantic life which did not disturb his public performance.

He received the American Presidential Medal of Freedom with Special Distinction by President Lyndon Johnson; and, after dying at the age of 90, his remains were transferred to the Panthéon of Paris, by order of the French president François Mitterrand.

Pope John Paul II (born Karol Józef Wojtyła, 1920–2005). There are a number of founders of religions who also qualify as proto-avant-garde politicians, including primarily Moses as described in the Jewish Bible, on the leadership of whom a number of interesting books have been written (especially Wildavsky

2005) despite the scarcity of reliable historical data, and Muhammad about whom much is known (Hazleton 2013), and whose achievements were amazing.

But the Roman Catholic popes are a category of their own; in the past because of their religious leadership, their importance in making and unmaking kings, and their activities as political leaders of states in Italy. And nowadays as rulers of a unique type of religious community with global geopolitical, geo-cultural, and global spiritual significance.

The doctrine of the infallibility of the pope in some of his pronouncements, adopted by the First Vatican Council of 1870, adds to the uniqueness of popes as spiritual but also in some respects earthly political leaders, accepted as such to various degrees by more than 17% of the global population who are baptized Catholics.

Among the popes of the twentieth and twenty-first centuries John Paul II was the most future-impacting one (I leave out of account the present Pope Francis). He fulfilled a significant role in the liberation of Poland from the Communist rule and thus the disintegration of the Communist Block, and changed radically for better relations between the Catholic Church and Catholic faith with Judaism and the State of Israel. He also strengthened the standing and prestige of the Catholic Church worldwide despite his conservative stance on matters of doctrine.

He studied and taught many years and received a Doctorate in Sacred Theology. Throughout his long life he was interested in Catholic ethics and phenomenological philosophy, writing a number of influential books. Many of them clearly show the influence of his experiences under Nazi and Communist rule.

Margaret Thatcher (1925-2013). Thatcher is one of the few women who can be regarded as a proto-avant-garde political leader. Her main foundational achievement was the rehabilitation of the British economy by strengthening its free market character and reducing the power of trade unions. Though condemned by many, it seems that her steps were in the main essential for the later economic achievements of the UK. In terms of global impact, her decision to use force to protect the British Falkland Islands against invasion by Argentine may have been important. And her tough stance against the USSR played some roles in the Cold War. But her main impact on the future was in the UK, for better and for worse.

Harry S. Truman (1884–1972). When deciding what US President to include in the list, both Woodrow Wilson and Franklin D. Roosevelt were obvious candidates. But I chose Truman because of his history-shaking decision to drop two nuclear bombs on Japan (Miscamble 2011), which started what I call the era of metamorphosis.

Truman became President of the United States when as vice president he took over after Roosevelt died. He performed much better than expected, both domestically and internationally. His fateful future-impacting act making him a prime example of a prototype-avant-garde politician was the decision to drop on August 6, 1945, a uranium-fueled atomic bomb on Hiroshima and two days later a plutonium implosion-type atomic bomb on Nagasaki, leading to total surrender of Japan at the cost of devastation of the two cities, more than 250 thousand dead, and many more maimed.

Global shock effects were huge. Thus began in earnest the nuclear age of humanity, inaugurating an era of human capacities to kill large parts of humanity and also to terminate the human species quite suddenly.

There is an ongoing debate whether the nuclear attacks on two Japanese cities were justified in military and moral terms and prevented later nuclear wars thanks to their shock effects, or perhaps they started a process likely to lead to catastrophes. In any case, the decision to drop the bomb makes Truman into one of the most important makers of the modern world.

He also decided, against much opposition, that the United States should vote at the UN General Assembly for the establishment of the State of Israel, which had drastic consequences for the Jewish People, the region and perhaps in some respects the world, all still in the making.

Zayed bin Sultan Al Nahyan (1918–2004) founder of the United Arab emirates and its developer. As far as can be learned from the best available biography (Emirates Center for Strategic Studies and Research 2005), he was clearly a prototype-avant-garde politician, all the more interesting and significant because of the special context in which he acted, which is very different from the usually known states.

GUIDING MODEL, NOT UTOPIA

The examples of political leaders who in many respects approximate qualities of avant-garde politicians demonstrate that the proposed model is a guiding, not a utopian, one. Suitable persons making a concerted effort and having luck can become avant-garde politicians, not perfect ones, but good enough to qualify as such.

The examples above, together with the biographies of about one hundred additional prototype avant-garde politicians which I processes, raise a number of questions and indicate a number of lessons on qualities necessary or helpful for being an avant-garde politician, or to be strictly avoided.

Let me start with the gender issue. Striking, though not surprising, is the fact that only few women can be categorized as prototype avant-garde politicians, out of a very small number of female political leaders throughout history. In large part this is a result of the status of women and their social roles till very recently, and in many ways continuously so. But personal qualities, hardwired or socially produced, may perhaps play a role.

Before the nineteenth century a number of impressive female political leaders, such as Queen Elizabeth I (1558–1603) and Catherine II the Great (1729–1796), may in part qualify as prototype-avant-garde politicians. In the nineteenth and twentieth centuries there were a number of significant female political leaders, such as Golda Meir (1898–1978) and Indira Gandhi (1917–1984), but with the exception of Thatcher none of them meet my criteria for being a prototype avant-garde politician.

Maria Theresia (1717–1780), ruler of the Habsburg Empire, and the few other female rulers before the twentieth century do not qualify. But it may be justifiable to add to the list of prototype avant-garde politicians Cleopatra VII Philopator (69 BCA–30 BCA), the last pharaoh of ancient Egypt. I do so not to have one more woman on my lists, nor because her fame and the abiding interest in her, but thanks to her career which illustrates some important points. According to what is known and increasingly emphasized in modern biographies (Schiff 2011; Tyldesley 2009), she apparently was not only extremely seductive to Julius Caesar and Antonius, but was a clever ruler. She stimulated drama and literature and acting quite optimally to maintain her rule and at least some independence for Egypt, but failed. She did not succeed because the forces shaping history were far stronger than the instruments at her disposal. Thus, her political leadership is one illustration out of many of the crucial interplay between historic processes and the virtù of political rulers, with female beauty being a significant factor.

To be added in this context are some wives and many concubines and lovers of male rulers who in fact exercised a lot of "borrowed power," as well illustrated by Madame de Pompadour (1721–1764) (Mitford 2001; Algrant 2002).

LESSONS

It would be convenient if historic and comparative studies of a variety of political leaders could provide significant lessons to avant-garde politicians. However, the number of such studies is small; a disproportionate number of those written in English deal with the U.S. Presidents (e.g., Barber 2009; Nye 2013; an important exception is Rotberg 2012); they usually limit themselves to heads of governments, who are only a part of political leadership and not always the most important one, and their findings are not always convincing.

Another problem is that the evaluation of political leaders often changes with time, so that the same leader can be regarded as making a significant impact on the future, and later as not doing so, or verse versa. Also different historians often disagree on given political leaders as having or not having a substantive impact on the future, and that impact being for the better or worse. The changing views on U.S. President Dwight D, Eisenhower (Smith 2012) serve as a striking example.

Nevertheless, on the basis of many biographies and other historic studies, some comparative studies, and partly applicable theories, a number or lessons emerge from the history of future-impacting political leaders which help in pinpointing qualities of the mind important, in part essential, in principle achievable, though not sufficient, for being an avant-garde politician.

To be noted, first of all, is the variety of proto-avant-garde politicians in many of their features. They come from different backgrounds. Having rich and powerful parents helps, but is neither essential nor ensuring success. Impressive proto-avant-garde politicians come from low social strata, though with single exceptions not the lowest ones. They differ in character, education, styles, and many other attributes. Some succeed thanks to a decisive and radical strategy, while others do a relatively good job quietly, and so on.

Given this diversity, widely shared attributes of proto-avant-garde politicians include the following, with individual exceptions and adjustments:

1. Devotion to the embraced mission.

2. A certain detachment from prevailing situations and a realistic vision of its substantive improvement.

3. Much pondering combined with high-quality improvisations.

4. Periods of contemplation.

5. Unconventional thinking, innovativeness, and creativity-friendliness.

6. Readiness to swim against the current and assume risks.

7. A good dose of self-confidence.

8. Toughness with quite some stubbornness and even rigidity.

9. Readiness to use human beings as materials, including causing them suffering and risking their lives.

10. Capacity to inspire people and gain support, also for what is very difficult and requires "blood, toil, tears, and sweat," as put by Winston Churchill in a speech to the UK Parliament on May 13, 1940.

11. Alternatively, also when lacking any charisma, having a major source of "borrowed" power, combined with inner "demonic power," can make up for what is in some respects personal political powerlessness (Steinberg 2011, 480).

12. Iron will and steely determination.

Given all these and additional qualities, luck fulfills an important role. Thus, to become a successful political leader, including an avant-garde politician, depends on fitting situations and also personal coincidences. Imponderables are also important. Therefore, it seems quite impossible to predict in advance who will become an avant-garde politician, and even less so who will achieve high leadership rank. And, most disturbing of all, it is sometimes hard to foresee who will be a beneficial avant-garde politician or a toxic political leader effective because of sharing many qualities with avant-garde politicians, but not their values and personal ethics.

PAST AND FUTURE

I cannot say who if any of the proto-avant-garde politicians of the past might have developed and become a full-blown avant-garde politician if facing the new challenges of the later parts of the twenty-first century and beyond, though I think that some may well have qualified. In any case, there is a double relationship between what was and what is needed in the new era of metamorphosis: on one hand, avant-garde politicians require qualities in part above and beyond those of historic proto-avant-garde politicians, as shown in the following chapters. But there are important overlaps. Therefore, on the other hand, there is much that can be learned from carefully selected biographies of historic political leaders. Engaging in such readings is therefore recommended to acting or wishing to become avant-garde politicians.

PART THREE

WORLDS IN THE MIND

CHAPTER 9
COMPREHENDING REALITY

"REALITY"

"Reality" seems to be a simple concept, but it is ambiguous and complex, as are related concepts such as "facticity." Cutting through philosophical, psychological, and physical debates, for our purpose relatively simple differentiation between three types of "reality" are adequate: (1) historic reality, which refers to all that existed, whether known or not, including what was just a moment ago, which melts instantly into the past; (2) future possible realities, which are imagined in one way or another; (3) virtual realities, which include fictional situations which are not assumed to present the past or possible future, such as surrealistic paintings, some types of novels, images of counterfactual worlds, and computer-simulated fantastic worlds.

These distinctions are fuzzy, with many "mixed" or "in-between" realities, such as utopias and science fiction. Also, what some regard as possible future realities others may view as counter-factual ones, and so on. But for our purposes the rough division is adequate, with border cases to be designated as such if necessary. To simplify discourse I use the terms: "reality" to refer to images of historic realities, adding for clarity the term "current" when helpful; "futures" to refer to what are regarded as possible future realities, with or without discussion of their plausibility; "virtual realities" to refer to images of reality knowingly regarded as fiction, perhaps mistakenly so.

All forms of reality share a cardinal feature of utmost importance, namely that for humans they exist as "worlds in the mind," that is images of the different types of realities as cognized by the mind and mapped in it. The mind does so in different "languages," such as narratives, mathematical and other symbolic languages, models, metaphors, and analogues. Furthermore, the worlds in the mind necessarily include only a minute part of the various realities and their diverse aspects, selected by various processes and criteria, such as accessibility, interests, salience, personal experience, and dramatic effects.

A consequent cardinal problem is the degree of fit between worlds in the mind and the parts and aspects of reality important for human pondering and action. This fit is never complete and often tends to be vague and also incorrect. Thus even with the best of intelligence services an avant-garde leader can never accurately know essential facts about an adversary and even less on its intentions, as changing somewhat or radically with time. Sometimes it is possible to know more or less the degree of reliability of various images of reality, but often we are left with many doubts on the confidence with which to regard them, especially when dealing with ambiguous phenomena, such as intentions of others, or images of the future.

Often what really matters in not "knowing" parts of reality as "facts," but understanding them, including having at least some notions on their causes, dynamics, and effects. I call this "comprehension." Furthermore, for an avant-garde politician comprehension of past and current realities is mainly important in order to arrive at somewhat reliable images of possible future realities and ways to influence them. Doing so requires at least some understanding of causal connections leading from the past to the future, which are often contingent, complex, convoluted, hard to understand and at least in part unknown and often unknowable, all the more so in an era of metamorphosis.

It should be emphasized that the future cannot be "researched" as it does not exist. Those who claim to engage in "researching the future" are not more than a modern version of soothsayers. There are methods for moving from the reality of the past to images of possible futures, some of which are based on research. But their validity in an epoch of metamorphosis is often low, especially when longer time horizons are considered. In any case, preparing an outlook is not "research."

I leave these and related issues for later. The present chapter deals with realities of the past and present, which are very important for dealing with contemporary challenges and for constructing images of the future at which the endeavors of an avant-garde politician are directed. Relying on the past for trying to foresee and influence the future is inadequate. But efforts to impact on the future without comprehending salient realities of the past are doomed.

SEMINAL REQUIREMENT

Comprehending reality is essential for survival and thriving, including adjusting to reality, utilizing it and changing salient parts of relevant environments. The required comprehension can be instinctive, as embodies in different ways by evolution in nearly all living entities, including viruses and plants. But for the survival and thriving of humanity more is needed, including highly developed intuitions and conscious constantly improving comprehension of important aspects of reality, which are accumulatively passed on to future generations via "culture." This seems to be true to a limited extent for Chimpanzees and perhaps some other animals, but nothing on the Earth comes near to human abilities to increasingly comprehend complex reality and imagine future and virtual realities.

The ability to engage in mental "time travel" to the past and future and mental space travel to imagined worlds is a critical human ability, of special importance for the future-impacting extraordinary mission of avant-garde politicians. Constantly expanding and deepening this ability, with care taken to differentiate between different levels of veracity and realism of various realities, is essential for upgrading this core quality of the mind.

Images and comprehensions of realities are stored, used and developed in the mind, constituting "worlds in the mind". But they are always partial and distorted imaginaries, serving "as-if" they reflect reality, but never reliably representing "reality" and its dynamics as it is—as far as at all accessible to human senses and minds. Thus a brief glance at recent history shows on one side increasing as-ifs comprehension of reality, for instance in quantum field theory and neurosciences. And, on the other side, persistent misleading as-ifs, despite strenuous efforts to avoid them, as illustrated by repetitive grave security intelligence failures.

The benefits of increasing comprehension, as largely supplied by science and parts of philosophy, are large. And the costs of lacking or mistaken comprehensions can be, but not always, very high. The balance between valid and invalid comprehension of reality as salient to human concerns, which too change with time, is a paramount factor in shaping the future of humanity between thriving and decline and perhaps demise. The looming danger is that complexities of an era of metamorphosis will tilt the balance in the negative direction, seriously endangering the human future.

One of the qualities required from the mind of an avant-garde politician is good comprehension of metamorphosing realities which strongly impact on the future of the human species. To do so, an understanding of the problem of comprehending reality and the ability to use tools for overcoming them as far as possible, with special attention to comprehending an era of metamorphosis, are essential.

INACCESSIBLE "REAL" REALITY

The very existence of the human species and its achievements prove that our minds are well able to arrive at quite valid images of much of reality relevant to human survival and advancement. These images also include creation myths and magical believes, which help humans to cope with demanding situations. However, on a deeper level the very concept of "valid" images of reality is not tenantable if presuming to refer to the world as it "really" is. Reality is accessible to us only in part, and the very meaning of "real" reality is not clear. As claimed by Meinard Kuhlmann "Physicists speak of the world as being made of particles and force fields, but it is not at all clear what particles and force fields actually are in the quantum realm. The world may instead consist of bundles of properties, such as color and shape" (Kuhlmann 2013). Or, to take a fascinating more extreme view, Max Tegmark (2014) suggests that the universe is "mathematical" in a complex and imaginative sense.

Thomas Nagel puts it well: "The world is an astonishing place, and the idea that we have in our possession the basic tools to understand it is no more credible now than it was in Aristotle's days" (Nagel 2012, 7). Though partly overstated in downgrading the understandings supplied by modern sciences, this statement is reinforced, for instance, by quantum physics experiments, which "tell us rather emphatically that we can never perceive reality 'as it really is'. We can only reveal aspects of an empirical reality that depend on the nature of the instruments we use and the questions we ask" (Baggott 2011, xvii).

The insights into the fundamental reality supplied by quantum physics are improved interpretations of the reality, which build better bridges between images in our mind and "reality." They also help to "expand the vistas of the mind" including the very meaning of "reality" (Deutsch and Ekert 2013), and do supply concept packages of broad heuristic applicability. But they do not provide "factual" information on real "reality." We can enlarge and deepen comprehension, but this usually raises further questions requiring new comprehensions, which raise further questions, ad infinitum.

Basic frames of apprehending and explaining the reality shape much of comprehension, including on subconscious levels of imaginaries. Kant was clear about the human dependence on a priori concepts. But more is involved. Thus civilizations seem to differ in tendencies to view realities more in terms of parts or more as "wholes," patterns and gestalt. Western ones often tend more towards focusing on components while Asian ones tend to see more "fields." Never mind if this is explained in terms of relations between the right and left hemispheres of the brain, as influenced by civilizations while shaping them (McGilchrist 2012) or otherwise, an avant-garde politician should strive to comprehend "wholes" rather than being captive to narrow focusing on particulars.

A table can be perceived and comprehended as a platform for putting things on it, a piece of wood or metal as the case may be, parts of the furnishing of a room making it esthetically satisfactory, a complex quantum phenomena, and so on. Asking what the table "really" is can on a very abstract level be in part answered in terms of relativity and quantum theories. But we know that these are "interpretations" which are very likely to be revised with further accumulation of knowledge and advancement of theories.

Leaving further discourse on "reality" as it really is to philosophy, science, and ontology, for avant-garde politicians a "praxis" and utilitarian approach to comprehending reality is recommended, which focuses on what is needed for the missions. But awareness of the ontological and epistemological difficulties is essential for recognizing the pitfalls of such comprehension too. The trouble is that levels of comprehension needed for the missions also are accessible to our minds only in part and full with distortions. One of the basic reasons for such limits of comprehension is embodiment of the mind.

EMBODIMENT

An illuminating way to approach the embodiment of comprehension, as part of the embodiment of the mind, is the short 1904 story by Herbert George "H.G." Wells, "The Country of the Blind." It describes an isolated community which for generations has been composed of blind people who are not aware that "seeing" exists. Their culture and behavior is fully adjusted to being blind and they manage well on their own terms.

By chance a normally seeing person from the outside world reaches them and tries to explain what seeing is and to restructure the world views of the blind community so as to fit reality as he knows it thanks to his eye-sight. He fails completely, is regarded as sick, and offered an operation removing his eyes so as to make him "normal." He escapes, leaving the community happy in its blindness.

Humanity survived and developed with many embodied blinders on comprehension. But, to continue to exist and thrive, better "seeing" is required. Avant-garde politicians need a kind of multi-dimensional super-stereo vision and augmented abilities to process its inputs in the mind, so as to constantly improve comprehension of salient reality. But the limits of embodiment cannot be escaped, though it is possible to partly overcome them and compensate for them.

Try to image how the world would appear to you if you were a dog. You are small so you pay much attention to what is on the floor and near it, and humans appear as very big; your eyesight is weak, but your smelling senses are excellent—beyond present understanding and much superior to humans, and also to presently available instruments trying to imitate the bomb detection abilities of suitably trained dogs. Accordingly, much of your subjective world consists of scents, such as smells of urine of dogs, including yours, demarking territories. All breeds of dogs are dogs to you, good for playing, fighting, and mating. Human masters are at the center of your life; you are good at sensing their feelings and empathize with them. In short, your world is the unique world of dogs. It can be partly influenced by interacting with humans, training and selective breeding, but still remains the world of dogs only in part accessible to human comprehension (Horowitz 2009).

This is true for all animals and plants too, which perceive the world uniquely, depending on their perceptive apparatus and neural system, that is embodiments, which selects and processes sensory inputs and interacts with them.

Humans have 10 critical advantages over other animals which upgrade the worlds in their minds and neutralize partly the limits imposed by embodiment: (1) augmentation of sensory perception with the help of instrumentation transforming phenomena beyond our natural five senses (sight, hearing, touch, smell, and taste) into images accessible to them, as illustrated by microscopes, infrared photography, and gas chromatography; (2) humans not only perceive aspects of reality but try and partly succeed to make sense of them, such as comprehending in terms of causes and effects, or as the results of magic, or in terms of a tentative and very abstract "Theory of Everything" (Hawking and Mlodinow 2011, 85-120); (3) human minds can operate on the level of "meta-comprehension," that is comprehension of the mind's ways of comprehending, leading to improvements; (4) the human mind can think on ways to learn more of reality, this being the domain of epistemology and cognitive sciences, laying foundations for science as a main modality for improving comprehension; (5) human images of reality depend a lot on belief systems, such as viewing history as an interaction between humans and God, which provide sometimes pragmatically useful "meanings," however often incorrect; (6) symbolic models and abstract concepts serve to present realities and to deepen, broaden, and sharpen human comprehension; (7) thanks to imagination and model construction the world in the mind expands, including now all of the cosmos since the Big Bang till its ultimate end, and also alternative universes; (8) physical realities are integrated into our culture, including artistic images of reality which diversify and deepen our comprehension, as illustrated by abstract painting; (9) reality is consciously transgressed and also overcome with virtual realities, such as alternative futures and fantastic worlds, which can serve as a kind of reflection upgrading comprehension of reality itself; and (10) as mentioned, the human mind can engage in time and space travel to supposedly real, possible, or fantastic realities in the past or future, in our universe and beyond.

Despite such impressive and enlargeable abilities of the mind, humans cannot achieve a "detached" and "objective" view of reality as-if from a location outside and beyond the reality itself. "The View from Nowhere" (Nagel 1989) is not for us. Whatever we do and however we think and intuit we live within our subjective world, the world of imaginaries in our mind. Our comprehensions of reality are "as-ifs." They are often, though far from always, adequate for our needs, as ensured by evolution and cultural learning. But they fit "real reality" only in part, if at all. "We can never perceive reality 'as it really is.' We can only reveal aspects of an empirical reality that depend on the nature of the instruments we use and the questions we ask" (Baggott 2011, xvii). This is a critical feature of the world in the mind which has an important implication for humanity, including especially avant-garde politicians: you must constantly be aware, cognitively and emotionally, that you ponder and act on the basis of limited and error-prone comprehension of reality, which constantly require doubt and correction.

PERCEIVING TIME

An important dimension of the world in the mind reflecting a rather obscure dimension of reality of profound importance for humans, which often does not receive adequate attention, is time. In terms of relativity and other theories "time" and "space" are a unity, but this is not how humans perceive them. The "objective" time was measured for eons by the sun, moon, stars, and yearly seasons. Nowadays it is measured by exact physical processes, such as atomic clocks. But for the world in the mind the "subjective time" is central, which sometimes seems to move slower and sometimes faster.

The perception, or sense, of time in the mind changes with the life expectancy. It is different if one has a terminal disease, or if one just had his twenty-first birthday and is full with vigor and health. Therefore, the constantly expanding life expectancy of humans is likely to influence the subjective time and related images of reality, though it is not clear what the impacts on human minds and behavior will and should be.

Human time scales are different from those of long-term physical processes, such as tectonic movements on the earth, cooling of the sun, and expansion of the cosmos. Still, there are links, such as earthquakes and climate changes. Therefore, awareness of select long-term physical processes is in part necessary for dealing with humanity-relevant stretches of time.

Social processes, such as rise and decline of states and civilizations, are much quicker than geological and astrological processes, but also take generations. However they accelerate from time to time and condense in fast turning points, as illustrated by decolonization and the modern rise of China. Paying much attention to them is a main required quality of avant-garde politician distinguishing them from the vast majority of political leaders, for whom electoral cycles often constitute the most important time scales.

An overall distinguishing quality of the world in the mind of an avant-garde politician is the importance of longer stretches of time, as relevant for taking care of the long-term future of humanity. But current pressures are strong and reach a peak during serious crises. Maintaining a balance in the mind between such different time dimensions is difficult but required.

Various "clocks" can serve as metaphors for different time rhythm images of reality needed in the mind of an avant-garde politician for comprehending and dealing with various domains. A chess clock dictates time frames for responding to acts or events by others, including forcing human events and nature. Some of these are predictable and are part of an annual or multi-annual schedule, but many come unexpectedly and are in part unexpected.

Countdown timers are another important image of time. All of the life of an avant-garde politician should be considered as-if contained in a sand clock representing vividly the passing of time and the need to use it well while still available. However the countdown timer in the mind needs different calibrations to fit diverse processes. Thus, one scale reflects the time till election; some scales reflect the time of major projects; and in crisis situations the calibration may have to be in bits between days and 5–10 minutes and sometimes less.

Interesting is the use of a kind of metronome in the mind, to reflect the rhythm of activities, with units of time to be carefully allocated and punctuality kept, subject to needed elasticity.

All these "timings" merge in the mind into a symphony of time tunes. But an avant-garde politician has to act as a conductor, making sure that different timings and actions are in harmony, as may be required in different situations and for dissimilar issues.

HABITUS

As already noted, habitus informs, shapes, and limits the mind, including comprehension of reality. An avant-garde politician must be aware of the existential situation of constituting a speck in a minuscule bubble of time-space, created, growing up, and living at a particular place and time. While localities can be changed and living in other times can be imagined, a human being is inexorably bound between the womb and the tomb to a very thin slice in time-space.

This slice is expanding, largely thanks to science and technology, which partly unbind humans from the chains of a particular time and locality. With a computer connected to Internet one can chat with colleagues all over the world, view exhibitions far away, and store folders in the "clouds." A jet plane can bring one quickly to another continent and culture. On digital television events far away can be viewed in real time. All these can be put into a pocket, and soon before your eyes, with iPhones and visual display glasses. And more is sure to come. Therefore avant-garde politicians can and should live and act in "expanded time-space," but still they remain caged in a thin though growing slice of reality.

This minute time-space bubble, however expanded, shapes much of the world in the mind and its comprehensions. But genetic endowment, personal history and individual beliefs also significantly shape and usually limit and bias comprehension. To vary the examples, image the radically different worlds in the mind of a Harvard professor of theoretical physics, a practitioner of Freudian psychoanalysis, a child fighter in the army of an African warlord, and a business executive in Singapore.

An avant-garde politician has to achieve in the mind as much mental detachment from habitats as possible, also with respect to comprehension of reality and imaginaries. But an avant-garde politician, as every human being, depends on doubtful worlds in his mind. You should constantly be aware of the limits of your comprehensions, regarding the world in your mind as a provisional, partly and biased interpretation of unreachable realities, and therefore in need of constant testing and improvement accompanied by constant doubts and hedging against errors.

IDEOLOGIES

Of all the caves in which you unavoidably are living, the most influential, insidious, unavoidable, but also necessary and sometimes ennobling, are "ideologies," including all systematic belief systems, such as religions, Marxism, and Liberalism. Some ideologies paint also scientific findings, such as rejecting evolution or what the Nazis called "Jewish physics."

Whatever their sources may be, such as indoctrination, habitus, or thinking on your own, ideologies color most of what mental eyes see and influence large parts of the world in the mind. But they are unavoidable and also fundamental to meanings of life, including the missions and values of avant-garde politicians.

A human being unavoidable has, needs and should have value systems for orientation in the world, self-identity, guidance, and life significance. Thus, an avant-garde politician is committed to the pluralistic future of humanity; and the three existential imperatives also constituting a kind of ideology. However, the mind of an avant-garde politician needs a good measure of distance from its own ideologies in order to reduce biases in perceiving and comprehending reality. This leaves you somewhat, so to speak, "in the air," all the more so as mental caves not only limit the mind but also provide it with protection and a sense of security. Therefore, avant-garde politicians are in some respects "strangers" in the world, while being denizens devoted to improving it. Learning to live with these tensions and contradictions is incumbent upon you. It should also deepen your spiritually—a term from which you should not try and escape, though you are free to give it a meaning which you like as long as it fits your calling.

THEORIES

"Comprehension" includes knowing and understanding dynamic relations and causal nets. Doing so necessitates theories. Single concepts presuming to present reality, such as "being unemployed" or "gross national product," are also based on theories. Theories may be tacit or explicit, based on personal experience, scientific experiments, contemplation, and other sources of insight. But, never mind how much a person may regard oneself as "practical" and dislike "bookish theories," still nearly all of thinking and practice is based on theories of one type or another, usually tacit but sometimes explicit ones.

Moving from "knowing" to "understanding," as parts of "comprehension" involves a leap in the mind from images of reality as "facts" to images of the causes of reality, views on the susceptibility of realities to deliberate change, consideration of alternatives including counterfactual worlds, and so on. These outstanding acrobatics of the mind take place on both explicit and tacit levels. Its quality depends on the capacities of a particular person and on inputs stimulating higher levels of comprehension.

"Folk wisdom" and its tacit pre-theories are not a reliable basis for comprehending intricate domains. Instead, an avant-garde politician needs the best available inputs and bases that can improve comprehension. To put it otherwise, the imaginaries in the mind of an avant-garde politician have to be significantly superior to commonly accepted ones, especially as far as relevant to the missions.

Relevant inputs include a lot of explicit theories, supplied by studies, advisors, readings, and so on. Also important are tacit theories based largely on experiences. The trouble is that many of the theories dealing with metamorphosis are of doubtful validity, being at best conjectures to be considered as such. But often obsolete theories are misrepresented to you as "proven and valid," also far beyond their domains of applicability. Be on guard and maintain a good dose of doubts also when being lectures by famous "authorities." They may be among the most obsolete ones. Listening a lot to young, original and "daring" thinkers is recommended. They can serve as a counterweight to "establishments" and will at least stimulate your mind even if their ideas may be speculative.

To all theories some caveats and suggestions apply, some of which have already been touched upon but are included here so as to provide a comprehensive view:

1. Explicit theories are either based on empirical data on the past or imaginative conjectures. If derived from the past with the help of accepted scientific methods and if the issues are relatively stable, then the theories can supply adequately reliable comprehensions, subject to critical evaluation. However if realities change significantly then past-based theories often do not apply and easily become very misleading.

2. Theories that are the product of imaginative thinking lack solid empirical basis and do not meet the criteria of "positivism." But positivism is not necessarily the only or best approach to comprehension. For instance, hermeneutics, in the sense of humanistic and impressionistic interpretations, often provide better comprehension, however limited, of important domains.

3. Literary and artistic works can provide insights equivalent in utility to formal theories and sometimes superior to them, especially on comprehending humans and getting a better feel for the importance of chance. But the principle of constant doubt applies to them with full strength.

4. Tacit theories, as expressed in professionalism, are important. But they also suffer from bondage to the past, with the additions of accidental bases, little openness to critical thinking, and not being subjected to peer review. Therefore efforts to explicate them when important matters are at stake and then subject them to critical evaluation are required.

5. Many explanations take the form of quasi-theories, such as analogues, mathematic models which may catch some elements of a situation but often not the most pertinent ones, projections from personal experience, enlightening but also misleading metaphors, and so on. All these can be helpful if used with discrimination, but require much caution and a good deal of doubt.

6. Abduction, in the sense of partly fact-based but not "proven" conjectures, is often the best available approach for constructing theories on many of the convoluted issues with which avant-garde politicians have to cope. This is fine as long as such conjectures are consistently viewed as tentative and conclusions drawn from them are handled with much caution, multiple hedging, and diverse safeguards.

7. On many issues there are competing theories, all of which are of part-validity or less. When facing such a situation it is a mistake to pick one of the competing theories as the working assumption. Instead, all that seem plausible should be used as multiple perspectives helping comprehension while emphasizing the uncertainty and need for caution up to skepticism.

8. With the exception of those dealing with fundamental physical or biological phenomena, all theories are limited to more or less defined situations. Careful checking of the degree of match between faced situations and the domains of validity of a theory is required.

9. Many theories are probabilistic stating causal effects in terms of likelihood, explicitly or hidden. This must be fully understood and conclusions drawn from them adjusted to the forms and extent of uncertainty.

10. Theories on random factors, accidents, mutations, inconceivability, very low likelihood, and so on are in part missing. Furthermore their correct use requires high qualities of abstract thinking, in addition to at least some literacy in special languages, such as modal logic, both of which are a "must" for avant-garde politicians. Moreover, realization of the often major role of random, within an overall view of reality as contingent, is essential but demanding. It requires a lot of uncertainty sophistication together with emotional acceptance, which too are qualities essential for avant-garde politicians.

11. Some critical features of reality are beyond reasonably reliable comprehension. Thus, the real intentions of others are often not clear to those acting themselves and cannot be plausibly comprehended by others.

12. It is much better to recognize limits of comprehension than to fool oneself that one understands more than one really does.

13. "Command decisions" on "how to comprehend" bits of reality that are not really known or understood are a gross error with dismal results.

14. Transcendental, magic, and other supernatural images of realities and their dynamics should be strictly avoided by avant-garde politicians. Religions and similar belief systems are legitimate sources of values, private practices and rituals, contemplation of other-worldly meanings of life, and so on. But they should not influence efforts to comprehend this-worldly reality. Similarly, prayers have their place for believers as long as they do not sway images of realities and decisions. This is well recognized by most high-level theologies.

CAVEAT

Some specific warnings must be added:

- While "big data" can be helpful, it can also be very misleading. This danger is especially acute if you are not literate in statistics and other big-date handling disciplines, which help you not to be taken in by wrong uses.

- The concepts used to describe reality are often fuzzy and also misleading. Thus, "unemployed" can mean: lacking employment but looking for it actively; unemployed but not looking for employment, either having despaired of finding suitable jobs or not interested to work, or not able to work; having registered for unemployment benefits; having declared oneself to be unemployed, though in fact employed on a gray market; and more. Similarly, commonly used statistics of national productivity, gross national product, and so on depend on doubtful definitions. This does not imply that such statistics are useless. If definitions are kept constant they can indicate trends. But avant-garde politicians must understand what they are describing and their limits.

- The situation is much worse with surveys and polls when cheaply done and dealing with inherently vague subjects, such as "happiness," all the more so when based on simple responses to telephone surveys. Avant-garde politicians should be very skeptical about such information.

- The same is double true for security intelligence data and analyses, all the more so when ambiguous issues, such as intentions, are at stake, and when realities are hidden or camouflaged and disinformation is likely.

- Related is a misleading tendency towards over-interpretation. A striking illustration is the mental tendency to misperceive stupid errors of others as super-wisdom camouflaging smart plans. Similarly, regarding accidents and random events as having hidden significance and looking for complex subtext in the simplest of messages constitute over-interpretation, in the sense of reading more subtexts into events, signals, speech acts, and behavior than is warranted.

- Suppliers of information often have interests of their own which influence the data and theories which they present, even if they are not lying on purpose—which too is not a rare event. Therefore, when briefings are important, they should be carefully checked for reliability, the briefers should be cross-examined, and on crucial matters the opinions of multiple persons and bodies should be sought.

- Trips, inspections, and so on by an avant-garde politician are an important source of comprehension on a tacit level. But all who are concerned will do their best to prepare a show. Nevertheless, if you are on guard against attempts to mislead, personally seeing important bits of reality can provide insights that no written or oral source can supply.

- Internet, with its search engines and social networks, makes the access to information and opinions easy. It is enough to put a term into a search engine and pose a question to a chat room or web list and plenty of answers will arrive. But there is a big catch: in order to separate the little wheat from the plenty of chaff a lot of knowledge is needed.

- The observation above also applies to the so-called "milking," namely trying to get ideas from many Internet users. One can easily get swamped with responses many of which are in-between ignorant and stupid.

CONCEPT PACKAGES

The quality of the world in the mind depends on the adequacy of the concept packages used to categorize and comprehend realities. This adequacy is always problematic, but especially so in the era of metamorphosis. Comprehension of metamorphosis and coping with it require more advanced concepts than available in folk language-games, in usual public and political discourse, and also in a lot of professional and scientific thinking. On many aspects of metamorphosis adequate concept packages as still missing. This is related to the already discussed dependence of concepts and also analogues on the past, which makes them often inadequate and in part also misleading when applied to novel realities.

To take a crucial example, of utmost importance is the concept of "contingency," which is often used but without real understanding. Ilya Prigogine contends in *The End of Certainty* (Prigogine 1997) that determinism is no longer a viable scientific belief. This insight has many precedents, but partial and less sophisticated ones. The images of Fortuna and the "wheel of fate" played a large role in Middle Ages discourse, Machiavelli paid much attention to coping with Fortune, probabilistic calculus was developed by Pierre-Simon Laplace at the beginning of the nineteenth century, and so on. But Prigogine helps to emphasize and clarify a crucial required quality of the mind of avant-garde politicians, namely comprehending fully and deeply that reality includes a lot of what seems as-if "random" events and processes. This requires thinking and intuiting in terms of novel concepts, such as bound thick uncertainty, alternative worlds, and so on, as discussed in Part Four.

To be added are concepts such as "nonlinearity," "quantum leaps," "invariances," "known unknowns", "unknown unknowns," "inconceivability," and more. Widely used scales of "risk" and "probability" are to be put aside, because of the fallacy of inappropriate exactness, in favor of concepts from modal logic, such as "possible," "likely," "very likely," "unlikely," "very unlikely" and "impossible," with additional ones such as "surprise prone" and "counter-expected." Selective borrowing from advanced scientific concepts, however counterintuitive and paradoxical, such as "entanglement" and "superposition" from quantum theory, to be used metaphorically for considering contradictory features of metamorphosis, illustrates possibilities to upgrade comprehension of reality, and pondering as a whole, by enriching the concept packages of the mind. And novel concepts developed by individual thinkers, such as "antifragility" (Taleb 2012), can also be very helpful.

But many lacunae remain, hopefully to be filled by study, thinking and creativity focused on the uniqueness of an era of metamorphosis driven by science and technology together with value transformations. Therefore an avant-garde politician should learn and absorb in the mind novel concepts that may be useful, while being aware that many features of the realities with which he must deal cannot be adequately comprehended, in part because of lack of fitting concept packages. This will put you on guard, which is much better than being misled by relying on inappropriate concepts.

BETWEEN PHASE JUMPS AND INVARIANCE

The era of metamorphosis, as discussed in Chapter 1, is characterized by a mix between radical change, up to phase jumps, producing much bound thick uncertainty in which the very shapes of emerging situations cannot be foreseen and in part are inconceivable, with a lot of "invariance," in the sense of stable or relatively stable features. Thus, as mentioned, while some parts of the human mind and behavior are changing significantly, for instance as a result of the Internet and globalization as well as value innovations, most of the features of humanity are very stable, being hardwired into the embodied mind.

Understanding this contradictory mix and comprehending different dimensions of metamorphosis accordingly are essential, but are difficult for most human minds, which dislike the dissonance caused by seeing reality simultaneously in mutually contradicting images. The minds of avant-garde politicians must be able to cope with such inconsistencies and integrate them into overall comprehension adjusted to the particularities of different domains as changing with time.

All these apply fully to the most important domain requiring maximal comprehension by avant-garde politicians, namely "humans," as taken up in the next chapter.

CHAPTER 10
HUMANS

FOREPLAY

Let us engage together in a thought experiment, serving as an intellectual foreplay that serves to put you into the mood of this chapter. Assume that the human species is put on trial in a cosmic court before judges fully informed about all of human history, while having minds similar in intelligence to ours, but with a much higher morality. My surmise is that in some ways the court would pity humanity. Bound to animalist nature but having much curiosity and quite some intelligence and creativity, humans created for themselves a very painful history full with avoidable suffering and premature death, but also much cultural development and impressive creativity. Because of perverted but not preordained thinking and feelings, the miseries of warfare and fanaticism fulfilled paradoxically a major role in driving the advancement of knowledge, including science and technology, and stimulated much abstract thinking and artistic achievements.

Such pity and sympathetic understanding is unlikely to prevent a verdict finding humanity guilty of misusing its talents and engaging in contemptible immoral behavior. Examples likely to be discussed at length in the verdict include mass-killings and repression, aggressive tribalism and fanaticism, coexistence of a booming luxury market with large-scale dismal poverty, much unearned super-wealth concentrated in less than 1% of humanity, lack of action by powerful nations to stop mass killings and other atrocities because of narrow selfish interests, economic activities based largely on greed, and much more.

A special section in the verdict is devoted to dismal personal behavior, such as in their families, by philosophers expounding demanding moral systems. But the harshest findings are reserved for many political leaders throughout history who misused their power for personal benefits and to do evil, instead of promoting what is right.

Taking into account that human behavior also includes some altruism up to self-sacrifice, much curiosity, and impressive esthetic as well as scientific achievements, the court decided not to eliminate immediately the human species as not worthy to exist, but to put it on probation. A strict regime is imposed on humanity for three generations including, inter alia, intense moral and humanistic education; need for permission to have children, based on the educating abilities of prospective parents; three years of obligatory humanity service between the ages 18 to 21 by all without any exceptions, in units mixing participants from different social strata and cultures; restrains on material standards of living, with disparities depending on personal merits; encouragement of literary and artistic creativity, but some parts of scientific research and technology development are prohibited; mass-killing and heavy weapons are destroyed; possession of firearms is forbidden unless essential for public safety; greenhouse effects are rationed, and so on.

The vast majority of political leaders receive special treatment. The court regards the levels of hell and purgatory reserved for them in the *Divine Comedy* of Dante as appropriate, but decides to exercise mercy for those who did not commit evil. Instead most political leaders are immediately dismissed as under-qualified morally and cognitively and prohibited from even fulfilling any public office. More culpable ones are condemned for many years of purgatory community service in poor neighborhoods, depending on the measure of their turpitude. And the few promising ones are sent, together with other carefully selected candidates, to an intensive residential three-year leadership academy to develop required qualities of the mind, so as to be prepared for meaningful missions if successful in remaking themselves into worthy political leaders.

COMPREHENDING HUMANS

Given an appropriate mood, as hopefully stimulated by the thought experiment above, let us embark on the winding path of trying to comprehend humans. They are at the core of the activities of avant-garde politicians, being the masters, constituting the target, and serving as the most important material for weaving the future. Therefore high quality comprehension of humans, as individuals and collectives, is an essential quality of the mind of avant-garde politicians.

This sounds obvious and simple. All political leaders must acquire some understanding of humans, otherwise they would not survive in politics. And some political leaders are outstanding in sensing the mood of the masses and excel in manipulating them. However history is full with political leaders who failed dismally because of misunderstanding humans with all their mix between childish simplicity and extreme complexity, half saints and raving murderers, and other contradictory propensities coming to the fore in various moods and situations. Acquiring the necessary comprehension of humans is therefore a demanding task.

It would be easy to recommend a few texts in psychology, neurosciences and sociology. You should do some readings in these and related disciplines, but this will provide you only with parts of the required comprehension while also misleading you quite a lot. However impressive the progress in some fields of study of humans, they do not penetrate many of the layers of human beings. Furthermore, the study of humans is divided between different disciplines and schools, which present radically different and also contradictory images of what and how humans are.

For example neurosciences contribute much to the understanding of the brain and some mental processes, but cannot be integrated with depth psychology. Psychology is divided between depth psychology, behavioral psychology, evolutionary psychology and more. Sociology is divided between schools that detest each other. And, to make matters worth, there is more than a kernel of truth in the aphorism of Taleb that "Social science means inventing a certain brand of human we can understand" (2010, 95), as illustrated by the model of the "economic man" which helps to make economics into a sophisticated science of the artificial.

Luckily there are many additional sources from which one can gain some comprehension of humanity. Most important is your own brain, which, as already discussed, has hardwired "theories of the other," without which humanity could not exist. Also there are "mirror structures" in the brain, which permit empathy and its accompanying comprehension. And, as you are a human being, introspective understanding provides much insight into other humans, though this can be very misleading.

To do better, your inner resources should be expanded by exposure to diverse human realities. Living in other cultures, meeting persons from different social strata, and sharing time with people in hard or exhilarating situations—these can be very enlightening if your mind is open, as it should be. Also important is learning from others who have deep insights into humans. *Macbeth* by William Shakespeare, the "The Frieze of Life" paintings by Edvard Munch (presented in Skira Rizzoli 2013, 102-127, discussed in Guleng 2013), *Ecco Homo: How One Becomes What One Is* by Friedrich Nietzsche, *Crime and Punishment* by Fyodor Dostoyevsky, the *Animal Farm* by George Orwell, and Cao Xueqin's classical Chinese novel *Dream of the Red Chamber* —these are just a few illustrations of the richness of artistic and literary works providing insights into humans essential for an avant-garde politician, beyond scientific investigation. Not less rich a source are better biographies and books in history, which should be a central dish on your plate of readings.

I do not go so far as to insist that artistic and literary works together with readings in history can provide more comprehension of humans, as individuals, collectives, and a species, than some professional texts. But such a statement has much to recommend itself. There are many relevant findings and theories in sociology, anthropology, psychology, history, neurosciences, and so on. But, avant-garde politicians have to be aware of the underdeveloped state of scientific comprehension of humans. You should be wary about advice given by certified "experts" on humans, unless having on your staffs some of the very few professionals and thinkers who somehow arrived at good comprehensive comprehension of humans, on the levels of explicit and tacit knowledge, while being aware of blind spots and doubtful assumptions and ready to admit them. Finding such knowledgeable and insightful connoisseurs of humans and working with them is difficult, but very much worth the trouble.

To try and provide more help on comprehending humans I focus on what is most important for the extraordinary mission without trying to supply an overall overview of humans. I start with some enlightening icons, however unconventional this approach of mine may be.

ICONS

Four icons serve our purposes in addition to already mentioned ones: the bronze sculptures *The Thinker* by Auguste Rodin; the *Scream* paintings by Edvard Munch; an about 11,000 years old Ain Sakhri lovers figurine, found in the Judean desert and now at the British Museum, which is the oldest known sculpture of love making; and the 1935 movie directed by "Leni" Riefenstahl *Triumph of the Will* on the 1934 Nazi Party Congress in Nuremberg.

As all artistic creations, these four are open to many interpretations, which are not bound to what their makers may have had in mind: the interpretation of *The Thinker* which I suggest is one of contemplation, creativity, puzzlement, and also worry; *the Scream* is a cry of despair about the certainty of suffering and death, which have no clear meaning, and about the predicaments of humanity as a whole; the *Ain Sakhri* love figurine represents the animalistic nature of humanity raised to a higher level of mentality by becoming a subject of art and receiving ritualistic and spiritual significance; and the *Triumph of the Will* movie shows in technologically superb form the fascinating and horrible human syndrome of being mesmerized by leaders, accepting fanatic ideologies, readiness to regard "others" as vermin, and behaving as a vile half-robot eager to engage in mass killing.

Together they reflect the multiple natures of humanity and its contradictory potential and propensities. Humans are very problematic. Thus, they are:

- torn between individualistic subjectivity and being part of packs;
- burdened by the inevitability of death, which pushes them into pursuing Dionysian escapes into various forms of ecstasy and seeking some kind of immortality;
- capable of heroic self-sacrifice, which all too often takes the form of willingness to sacrifice one's life in order to kill others "for a higher cause";
- reaching sublime peaks of art and awe-inspiring achievements in science and technology, while tending towards simplistic thinking and barbarism;
- fluctuating between animalistic drives and sainthood;
- seeking enemies, capable of deep love, and in need of self-abrogating solidarity;
- cooperating, but brimming with envy;
- able to penetrate into the secrets of the cosmos and atoms, but easily clinging to the most absurd beliefs;
- unequal and equal, with constant tensions between these two.

SPECIAL ANIMAL

Whatever may be the views on the nearness or chasm between humans and other animals, such as Chimpanzees which do share about 96 percent of the same genetic material with us (showing that it may perhaps not take very much genomic engineering to produce a new species), what seems correct is the "Hauser's hypothesis" on "humaniqueness" (Gross 2012, 100-126). In this view, which supports what is called the "deep chasm" theory, humans are unique as compared to all other animals in four main abilities: generative computations, enabling a practically infinite variety of expressions; multiple and open-ended combination of ideas; a variety of mental symbols; and abstract though. As put by Hauser (2009, published before doubts were cast on other works of his), in contrast to all animals, including Chimpanzees, humans can combine and recombine different types of information and knowledge in order to gain new understandings; apply a "rule" or solution to one problem in a different and new situation; create and easily understand symbolic representations of computation and sensory input; and detach modes of thought from raw sensory and perceptual input.

Animals have what is called sometimes "laser beam" intelligence, in which a specific solution is used to solve a specific problem. But these solutions cannot be applied to new situations or to solve different kinds of problems. In contrast, humans have "floodlight" cognition, allowing the use of thought processes in new ways and transfer of the solution of one problem to another.

Leaving aside novel and not always fully convincing findings on animal "intelligence," in any case humans are animals, though very special and unique ones. Thus, what is called "animal spirit" explains important economic phenomena better than the "economic man" rationalistic model (Akerlof and Shiller 2010). There is at least a kernel of truth in the statement by Minotaur in the opera *The Minotaur*, towards the end of the libretto by David Harsent: "Between most and least, between man and beast, ...next to nothing." The paintings by the South African Jane Alexander depicting humans with animal heads (Subirós 2011) can be understood as making the same point, as do quite a number of old and also recent myths. Keep this in mind so that you are not surprised by "beastly" behavior and are ready to contain it, while welcoming and facilitating altruistic values, motives, and actions.

With all the differences between cultures, throughout history all humans share the same animal bodies with all the drives and instincts that come with them. Food, protection against heat and cold, sex, parenthood, and companionship are animalistic features of humanity. These go together with egotism, greed, envy, aggression and kill-instincts, Machiavellian skills, and hierarchies with leaders. All these are shared to some extent with our closest living animal relatives, the

Chimpanzees, who belong to the Hominidae family, together with gorillas and orangutans, and in part with other animals.

But human beings have many dimensions of mind of critical importance not shared with any other being on earth, which can perhaps be summed up in part under the term "mentality." It is the uneasy cohabitation between the animalist and the mentality sides of humans, their overlaps and their conflicts, which are the basis of "civilizations." As discussed, among others, by Sigmund Freud in his 1929 book *Civilization and Its Discontents*, all civilizations have to cope with the dilemma between giving more freedom to animalistic aspects of humans, or repressing, redirecting, and sublimating much of them in favor of "civilization" in one form or another, with resulting discontent, personality disorders, social tensions, and other problems, but also many advantages. Such tensions are endemic to the human condition, but take different forms in various cultures, including so-called primitive, pre-modern, modern and post-modern ones.

Without going into a comparative survey of civilizations and their evaluation, Western civilization moved since the advent of modernity in the direction of secularization, liberalism, individualism, and human rights, all of which, perhaps paradoxically though inevitably so, also increase the freedom of expressions of animalistic desires. Thus, capitalism legitimizes a good dose of greed, and contemporary Western values provide and also encourage much sexual freedom.

A crucial question for avant-garde politicians is what degrees and forms of balance, separation and integration between freedoms and restraints are more conductive to realization of the existential imperatives and related values. And what can be done to influence the dynamics of civilizations so as to prevent self-destructive tendencies and humanity-endangering cultural evolution, while facilitating maturation and trying to prepare the ground for a Second Axial Age.

My own tentative conjecture is that pluralistic thriving can go together with different civilizational balances between instinct gratification and restraint, and with different mentalities, as long as destructive potentials are contained. Furthermore, much civilizational and individual pluralism is conductive to creativity and cultural learning. But dangerous propensities and the ease with which humans can often be prompted to engage in evil deeds require selective restraints. And so do mental attributes which can lead to mass killings, such as aggressive fanatic beliefs.

COLLECTIVES

It is illuminating to consider an organismic view of human collectives, as-if they were a kind of organism with individuals being like cells with very limited independence. While incorrect in critical respects, such as ignoring the subjective individuality of consciousness and creativity, an organismic view, if not taken too seriously, is a good counterbalance to extreme reductionist views, which regard collectives as aggregates of autonomous individuals. Both do provide important but limited insights.

The type of life called "superorganism" (Hölldobler and Wilson 2008) is best represented by social insects, especially ants, bees, wasps, and termites. These form highly complex colonies based on cooperation, communication, and division of labor. But each individual is a rather simple semi-automata operating according to a limited program imprinted by evolution, as far as known without conscious discretion. The aggregation of simple algorithms within a swarm into one of the most successful and complex forms of collective life is a miracle of nature, demonstrating the capacity of systems to produce intricate emergent properties which go far beyond a simple additive sum of the properties of each component.

What about us humans? Aggregates of humans form collectives, which also reach levels of complexity and learning much larger than a simple additive sum of the capacities of its individual components and above the capacity of the vast majority of human individuals. Also, less obviously but still true, the subjective worlds, motives, feelings, thinking, and actions of human individuals are largely shaped by a synthesis between innate programs, shared environments, and collective cultures, with only relatively few humans exercising "free choice" beyond options existing a priori in the mind or supplied by society. Thus, one can reduce the main leitmotifs of life or of literature to a rather limited set of master-themes. This is also true for politics, but must change because of the radically novel issues posed by metamorphosis.

All these do not make human collectives into superorganisms. Small variations between humans make a large difference, as illustrated by poems or paintings dealing with the same leitmotif, such as love, in very different ways. And, most importantly, some individuals exit readymade patterns, become radical innovators, and serve as the main change agents of humanity. Thus, human collectives are in-between superorganisms and collections of self-shaping, self-expressing, and radically creative individuals, with variations between different types of collectives and cultures.

This brings us to mass psychology, which is unpopular in modern culture, which believes in "subjectivity" and autonomy of individuals. But the Roman *panem et circenses*, "bread and circuses", had it largely right. Having a good time, including food, company, sex, and excitement, to feel pleasure and to keep boredom and thinking about death at bay are main contents of individual, group, and mass behavior, together with shared worship of gods, celebrities, and hero-leaders if available, clinging to ideologies, and seeking "enemies."

Technology is making an increasing difference, with the emergence of social networks and "netizen," who constitute novel types of "collectives" with unforeseeable characteristics and consequences. It is not clear if social networking will make more of a difference for the better or worse in terms of the existential imperatives. Optimism on the "liberating," "democratization," and "equalizing" effects of social networks may be more of an illusion produced by optimistic cultural biases than a reliable outlook, though this is not certain.

Internet makes it much easier to mobilize mass street action that can destabilize regimes and provides opportunities to private "action entrepreneurs". Results include reduction of capacities to govern in democratic as well as non-democratic regimes, all the more so as governmental control of Internet is in debate and difficult though not impossible. But widespread views that the potentials of Internet are all for the better have no basis, neither in facts nor in theories.

Interesting is the following statement by the U.S. Secretary of State John Kerry in February 2013, though it may well be far too optimistic: "For the first time in human history, young people around the world act as a global cohort [...] they are more open-minded, and more proficient with the technology that keeps them connected in a way no generation has ever been before." Internet, ease of traveling, and globalization facilitate development of new global communities, including elites. This may provide avant-garde politicians with opportunities to mobilize support and crystallize influential global actors for advancing raison d'humanité. However efforts to do so for coping with global warming show that much more is needed to implement costly humanity-craft measures facing strong opposition.

TRIBALISM, FUNDAMENTALISM, FANATICISM

A simple test for tribalism is asking "who or what are you?" The usual answer is "a French woman, a Catholic, mother, and engineer" and so on, with the nationality, religion, or gender often coming first. Very seldom is the first answer "a human," or "an inhabitant of the world." This may be just a way of speaking, with self-identity as belonging to the human species being so obvious that one neither thinks about it nor mention it. But this also indicates the strength of various forms of tribalism and the weakness of a sense of human communality. For ensuring the future of humanity it is essential that more and more responses put "I am a human being" first. Certainly an avant-garde politician should answer the question to himself in this way, though it may often be inadvisable to do so in public.

When a President of an important country says in public "I do what is good for my country," he should try and add "and for humanity." This is important for strengthening his personal commitment to the human species and its future and for educating the public to feel more human communality. But very few political leaders do so, with good reasons in terms of maintaining public support in most countries in which tribalism is strong.

Pluralism and diversity are important for human cultural learning and survival. They should be facilitated as long as they are not dangerous. But this also opens a Pandora box. Diversity is closely associated with "tribalism." "Tribalism" is different from "in-group."

A feeling of in-group involves familiarity, small social distance, personal solidarity, sometimes love, and usually mutual assistance, and sometimes but not necessarily a sense of superiority to "other groups." In contrast, tribalism usually involves, in addition to some of the features of in-groups, a feeling of being in some ways superior to other tribes, of being "select" or "selected." Also, under some conditions, tribalism leads to fundamentalism and fanaticism, causing in many cases large-scale bloodshed.

Tribalism characterizes many types of real or virtual communities, ranging from tribes in the anthropological sense to classes, elites, societies, states, religions and civilizations. It plays an important role in furthering cooperation inside the tribe, and often motivates peaceful competition and also cooperation with other tribes. But tribalism also stimulates "we–they" distinctions, "survival of the fittest" competition, search for enemies, and bloody wars.

Fundamentalism and especially fanaticism are militant forms, or offshoots, of tribalism, which have complex and not fully understood causes, probably including some hardwired human propensities. They are not necessarily always "bad" (Toscano 2010), while providing meanings of life for humans. They also fulfilled major roles in the cultural development of humanity, often serving religions and belief systems nowadays evaluated as "good," such as liberalism. And wars caused by fundamentalism and fanaticism advanced science and technology and were important for the evolution of modernity. However there is more than a kernel of truth in Samuel P. Huntington's thesis on *The Clash of Civilizations and the Remaking of World Order* (Huntington 2011), despite quite some misperceptions. Fundamentalism and especially fanaticism easily cause merciless slaughters, subjugation, and enslavement. And they hinder and also prevent human species communality as increasingly essential.

Tribalism, fundamentalism, and fanaticism cannot be fully evaluated in the abstract as inherently "good" or "bad." It depends on their contents and impacts. However, in some prevalent forms they pose dangers to the future of humanity. The pressures of metamorphosis may well stimulate malignant forms. Thus, a fatal possibility is a fanatic cult convinced that salvation can only come from humanity committing suicide, which synthesizing a mass-killing airborne virus that has no known antidote. Such cults, which are prone to sprout during spiritual and social crises accompanying metamorphosis, are not a figure of imagination, having precedents in history.

What Kautilya calls in the *Arthashastra* the "law of fish", with the big fish eating the little fish, cannot be permitted to continue when the "teeth," also of small fish, include nuclear weapons and mass-killing viruses. If "making love, not war" would work, this would be fine. But this is not the case. The terrible reality of devoted SS members who are engaged in mass butchery and happy to have an opportunity to exterminate what they regarded as sub-humans, while loving their families and taking good care of the family dog, must be taken into account. Publication in January 2014 in Germany and Israel of family letters, diaries and other personal papers by Heinrich Himmler, Head of the SS and the person in charge of the mass-killing of Jews and many others regarded as "non-human" clearly document the awful combination between being a good family father and a chief of slaughterers of which human beings are capable, with all this implies for the future of the human species when becoming supplied with easily available mass-killing instruments if not brought under strict control.

Less extreme scenarios too justify determined preventative and counter actions. Raison d'humanité requires limiting forms of fundamentalism and fanaticism having dangerous potential. And most forms of tribalism tend to hinder human communality and global action. Therefore containing, reducing and counteracting tribalism and, especially, many forms of fundamentalism and fanaticism, is a difficult but crucial task of avant-garde politicians and, even more so, of sorely lacking but urgently needed caring global spiritual leadership.

Emphasizing the shared inheritance and fate of humanity may help and should be part of maturing efforts. But decisive global governance with overwhelming enforcement instruments, as suggested, is essential for restraining tribalism, fundamentalism, fanaticism, and related human propensies when they endanger the existential imperatives.

Fine-tuning of civilizations and their evolution is beyond human understanding and abilities, luckily so. But an avant-garde politician has to try and intervene with both animalistic and mentality features of humanity in order to realize the imperatives by maturation, education, and various ways of soulcraft on one hand, and forceful restrain on the other. Cooperation with other future-impacting elites and, as mentioned, especially spiritual leaders, is essential, as is mobilizing of as much public support as possible. But, first of all, essential is full awareness of human propensies to do evil, while often regarding it as "good."

INDIVIDUAL AUTONOMY

As pointed out, humans are largely shaped by inheritance and environment and limited to options provided by societies. This is not a state of "fall," "bad faith," and "inauthenticity," as claimed by Martin Heidegger, Jean-Paul Sartre, and other existentialist philosophers and by various other thinkers and critics of culture, but rather the natural situation of humans as very highly developed social animals. Sartre warns that the "vertiginous" experience of absolute freedom is very unpleasant. And "escape from freedom" (Fromm 1994) is a powerful motif.

Individual autonomy is increasing in many societies, which provide growing varieties of life options. This trend is likely to accelerate with globalization together with improved subjective choice abilities, thanks to education and easy access to more information. Nevertheless, despite given "objectively" more options, as already discussed the world in the mind of the vast majority of humans includes only a limited range of life options, nearly all of which are provided by their society and legitimized by it.

This reality in no way impinges on human happiness. Happiness is not increased by lonely choices going against social conventions, as an avant-garde politician finds out early in the calling. In contrast, for the vast majority of humans to be "one of the crowds," while fooling themselves that they are "special," provides reassurance, a sense of belonging, friendship and other sources of "happiness." There is nothing inherently bad about all these as long as select individuals can and do break out of most of social bondage. The utopia of humanity as consisting of "sovereign" individuals, whether hedonists or philosophers, may well be a dystopia.

What is extraordinary, as already pointed out, is the advent of some individuals who detach themselves from given alternatives and create new ones, for themselves, for others, and sometimes for all of humanity. These relatively very few radically creative and often daring innovators are main drivers of the future of the many, for better or worse. An avant-garde politician must be one of them impacting for the better on the long-range future of humanity and its subparts and nurturing and helping others who can do so. However, to reemphasize a critical prerequisite, first an avant-garde politician must achieve high levels of personal autonomy from external influences and accepted imaginaries, despite more than a little feeling of disorientation and mental dizziness following doing so.

BETWEEN GOOD AND EVIL

The concepts of "good" and "evil" have changed throughout history and differ between civilizations. True, nearly no human tribe supports murder, but what is called "murder" depends on specific and mutable value systems. Thus, killing children by sacrificing them to some kind of "god" has in some relatively highly developed societies been regarded as very virtuous.

Throughout history much of what contemporary global values regard as evil has been and continues to be regarded by some groups as "good." And what is regarded as "noble" behavior often stems from base motives. Therefore the question whether humans are "good" or "bad" has two different meanings: Do humans deliberately do what they themselves regard as "evil?" And do humans do what "we," whoever we may be, regard now as evil? The answer to the first question seems to be that doing what one regards as evil is unusual and often accompanied by extenuating explanations. The second question depends on who "we" are and therefore has only local answers which are often positive: humans do what we regard as evil but is regarded by them as good, justified, or value-neutral.

As already discussed, attempts to provide "scientific proof" of the validity of values, so that we could rely on them in evaluating humans as "good" or "bad," are based on a serious category errors expecting from science what is beyond its domain. We are left with the moral responsibility to choose what is "good" or "bad," before choosing whether to do good or bad. It follows that the question where humanity stands between good and evil is meaningful only within specified contexts and conditions. Furthermore, given history, and all the more so an era of turbulence, only extreme hubris can presume that "our" values are eternal and sure to prevail in the future.

This does not lead to value nihilism, but, as already discussed, to an unavoidable measure of value relativism recognizing as a fact the plurality of values held by individuals, societies, and civilization throughout history, nowadays, and very likely in the future. Given this insight there exists no reliable basis for evaluating the human species as more "good" or "evil" in absolute terms. But, as we are not a Cosmic Court of Justice where humanity is being tried, we do not need an overall verdict. Rather, our need is for moral terms of reference that guide out actions, recognizing that from a human perspective they are ours in this period of history and that any claim of ours that they are of universal and eternal validity is itself a temporary value judgment of ours.

Given the existential imperatives as the normative basis, avant-garde politicians can adopt a more optimistic view of human beings or a more pessimistic one. If the view is more optimistic, they should engage largely in "gardening," helping humans to accept raison d'humanité as their main hypergood or metaethics. However if the view is more pessimistic, then avant-garde politicians have to engage a lot in containing human propensities and regulating human behavior, so as to prevent realization of what are their evil potential in terms of raison d'humanité, as itself changing with time.

As I read human realities throughout history, prevailing at present and likely to continue in the foreseeable future, my recommendation to avant-garde politicians is to base actions on quite some pessimism regarding human nature between good and evil, while trying to nurture its potential for the better and adhering to the Principle Hope.

CAUSES FOR PESSIMISM

The Strange Case of Dr. Jekyll and Mr. Hyde by Robert Louis Stevenson well presents the contradictory nature of human beings. Good insights into evil propensities are also provided by the novels *Lord of the Flies* by William Golding and *Heart of Darkness* by Joseph Conrad. And *Moby-Dick* by Herman Melville perfectly presents a total fanatic: just imagine Captain Ahab armed with a mass killing virus seeking revenge on humanity!

What may well be the most dangerous forms of extreme evil are genocide, mass killings and enslavements perpetuated by persons who sincerely believed that they are doing what is morally justified and often also regarded as morally mandatory. No "banality of evil" (Arendt 2006b), psychological conjectures (e.g. Fromm 1973), theory of "true believers," (Hoffer 1951), Fundamentalism Project (Marty and Appleby 2004), and similar efforts at understanding do provide full comprehension of malignant belief systems and frames of mind leading to murderous behavior. This is a phenomenon rooted deeply in human history which is becoming extremely dangerous and potentially fatal for the future of humanity, thanks both to intensification of extreme fanaticism in parts of the world which is likely to accompany metamorphosis crises, and the increasing ease of access to mass-killing instruments sure to become more deadly in the foreseeable future.

Available explanations, such as psychoanalytical, evolutionary, and cultural ones, are partial. This is all the more a serious lacuna as coping with extreme evil, which is regarded by its practitioners as highly moral, is essential for realization of the existential survival imperative, and thus a top priority for avant-garde politicians. As it is, trying to comprehend as much as possible mass-killing propensities and actors within your domains, and re-educating, containing, incapacitating, repressing, and destroying them, whether you comprehend them in depth or not, is your duty.

OPTIMISTIC VIEWS

As a counterweight, let me mention the work of Steven Pinker (2011), which claims that there is a historic decline of violence. Brutality is reduced, empathy increases and killing is decreasing when measured as a proportion of total human population. He explains this trend as resulting from a variety of factors, including increasingly accepted human rights and anti-killing values.

This is not the place for a detailed evaluation of this important study. For our purposes it is enough to recognize that even if main conjectures of the book and similar hopeful views about humanity are more or less correct, which is open to debate, they are of limited relevance to the fateful problems with which avant-garde politicians have to deal. Even if a smaller proportion of humans than in the past is likely to try and engage in mass killings, it has much larger damaging potential thanks to the tools provided by science and technology, up to endangering the species. And nothing claimed by Pinker and similar thinkers confronts the tragic fact of ferocious fanaticism and similar belief systems resulting in mass killings which the perpetuators regard as morally necessary. Nor do they confront the likelihood of upsurges of large scale bloodshed following social disruptions brought about by likely crises, such as mass unemployment of the destitute youth. Statistic trends of the past, however mapped and understood, are therefore an unreliable basis for outlook into the future.

It is quite amazing that reputable thinkers view humanity as clearly on the way to benevolence. This contradicts the lessons of history, including the shocking cases of highly educated modern societies engaging in the twentieth century in unprecedented factory-like genocide, with the willing cooperation of both highly cultured elites and "ordinary citizen" (Goldhagen 1997), and of the twenty-first century "assaults on humanity" (Goldhagen 2009). It also contradicts a variety of social experiments and studies, such as by Stanley Milgram (2009) and Philip George Zimbardo (2007), which demonstrate—though in artificial laboratory settings—how easily human beings can be goaded to cause pain to others.

I find it hard not to explain Western cultural optimism on humans and their improvement in part as a reaction to and escape from the memories of Western barbarism as demonstrated in much of colonialism (still relevant is Mark Twain's 1905 pamphlet on Belgian rule of Congo, Twain 2012), and in the long war from 1914 to 1945, which continued the religious wars tradition. But optimism on human beings is not a responsible working assumption for an avant-garde politician. Instead, prudence requires regarding humans with quite some suspicion. They cannot be relied upon to do "good." Under many conditions they are quite likely to do the "bad," including recklessly and also deliberately causing much harm to others—often with the best of subjective moral justifications.

Avant-garde politicians should not ignore strong propensities towards benevolence, human solidarity, love, and also willingness to sacrifice oneself for others. But being on guard against dismal human propensities is mandatory, all the more so in the era of metamorphoses and increasing availability of very effective mass-killing instruments.

HUMANS AS MATERIALS

Martin Buber made the distinction between relating to others as "I–you" or as "I–it." I–you is the morally correct form which accepts the other as equal to me in an open interaction ("dialogue" in Buber's terminology). However, the missions of avant-garde politicians often require relating to many human beings as "it", that is a material to be used for the sake of the long-term survival and thriving of humanity.

This is a bitter necessity, which can easily damage seriously the moral integrity of an avant-garde politician. Only by keeping the I–you relation active in the mind and reducing the I–it relation to an essential minimum, however large this may be, while constantly regretting this necessity built into the missions, can an avant-garde politician limit moral harm to oneself. And only by trying to do a maximum of good for fellow humans, with much empathy and also compassion, as long as it does not unduly endanger the existential imperatives, can an avant-garde politician make somewhat up morally for using human beings as materials.

PROSPECTS

Christian de Duve, a recipient of the Nobel Prize for physiology or medicine, who is a Roman Catholic and was educated by the Jesuits, argues that natural selection favored human traits which were immediately useful, but became increasingly dysfunctional and thus constituted "original sin". Therefore humanity as a species is doomed unless it achieved "redemption" by using its unique reason to counteract the results of natural selection. But in his view "the prospects are not encouraging" (Duve 2010, 210).

I prefer to leave the evaluation of prospects open, because we cannot know what may be possible and will happen in the future, and because a good dose of optimism in the mind of avant-garde politicians is necessary to help them engage in very difficult tasks. Also, overall human optimism may serve as a self-fulfilling prophesy, on the condition that an avant-garde global elite committed to raison d'humanité (to be discussed in Chapter 18) with a core of avant-garde politicians does not let optimism hide the real dangers and hinder the necessary tough countermeasures.

There are good reasons to hope that a mix between maturing efforts and a restraining Circumscribed Global Authority can prevent extreme forms of evil and strengthen desirable human propensities so as to reduce the probability of bad future and increase the likelihood of thriving ones, as discussed in the next chapter. But this is an optimistic view contradicted by not less plausible pessimistic ones. However, as the future in not predetermined and depends largely on human deeds, both more optimistic and more pessimistic views converge in the requirement to do our very best to increase the likelihood of desirable futures. Therefore the relative confidence we have in either a more optimistic or more pessimistic view does not really matter for praxis, though philosophically and psychologically I recommend, as noted, the Principle Hope.

BENEFICIAL MYTHS?

There remains the difficult problem whether beneficial myths about humans, in the sense of widely held but false beliefs which help to maintain peace and advance desirable values and behavior, can be justified in moral and long-term utilitarian terms, and should therefore be propagated by avant-garde politicians. Certainly, they themselves should try to arrive in their minds at valid images of humanity. But is this good for the majority of humanity?

A clear example is provided by the foundational U.S. Declaration of Independence as adopted on July 4, 1776 and serving since then as an inspiration for humanity. It famously states in the key passage "We hold these truths to be self-evident, that all men are created equal, that they are endowed by their Creator with certain unalienable Rights, that among these are Life, Liberty and the pursuit of Happiness." This statement does express highly moral values, but these are not self-evident truths in any meaningful sense of those terms, with other views being regarded as "self-evident" at various times by different civilizations, including Western ones. Therefore the Declaration is in part based on a myth, however ethically worthy and in many ways also useful.

Consequently, the question must be faced whether such imaginary conductive for peace, liberty and other situations regarded widely as desirable should be exposed as myths. Or whether they should be propagated as "obviously true" because of the desirability of their consequences. For instance, Yaron Ezrahi in an important book explicitly supports "choosing the imaginaries we want to live by" (Ezrahi 2012, 299–320), independent of their truth value. Thus, he supports "disembedded individualism" as "a necessary fiction for the evolution of liberal democracy" and regards "its correspondence to or deviation from a particular conception of the 'essence' of humanity" as "either secondary or utterly irrelevant." (Ezrahi 2012, 34).

With due respect to a much appreciated colleague, I regard this view as unacceptable in principle and contradiction efforts to mature humanity (in addition to other problems, nor relevant in the present context). Certainly, avant-garde politicians must free themselves as much as possible from such and other myths, as distinct from values and transcendental views clearly recognized by them as based on personal choice and subjective convictions, in part shaped by habitus.

However, from a consequentialist perspective, as the meta-ethics recommended to avant-garde politicians in all matters involving their missions, I do agree that as long as most of humanity is juvenile and evil propensities are not contained, avant-garde politicians should propagate raison d'humanité serving myths as part of public interest Machiavellianism, this being a case of falsehood justified because of weightier high-value consequences.

LIKELY DELTAS

Let me conclude this chapter by adopting a different perspective, namely a provisional outlook into main Deltas likely to characterize humanity in the foreseeable future.

Overall, basic characteristics of humans will not change rapidly, unless altered by human enhancement technologies, regulation of which is a main part of the extraordinary mission of avant-garde politicians as postulated in the species changing inhibiting imperative. But many images, world views, social habits, patterns of living and so on are likely to change radically, constituting major Deltas.

These may well include, at least within the 21st century, the following main ones, in the absence of humanity-craft grand-policies swerving historic processes:

- Population: Global population is likely to stabilize between 8 to10 billion, unless a global catastrophe reduces it significantly. Life expectancy will increase. Families are likely to become smaller, with the ratio of older to younger adults (OY ratio) changing with aging of the population, raising difficult problems of taking care of the elderly and the role of grandparents.

- Family: The proportion of single parent families and same gender families, with or without children, is likely to grow till reaching a plateau and perhaps leveling off. Most education is likely to be institutionalized, with impacts of parents on children probably diminishing.

- Standards of living and work patterns: Standards of living are likely to increase, with large disparities. However, human labor is likely to be largely taken over by robots and computers, together with new manufacturing technologies. Human services and leisure time industries are unlikely to make up for the decrease in employment opportunities, resulting in a major crisis leading to unforeseeable forms of large non-working populations, entitlements, leisure time activities and so on, together with political turbulence, outbreaks of violence, and perhaps novel New-Age type belief systems – including malevolent ones.

- Maturity: Unless radically novel maturation grand-policies are adopted and globally implemented, humanity must be expected to remain in the main immature, as discussed.

- Tribalism: While globalization will deepen and reach larger parts of humanity, tribalism is quite sure to continue as a main feature of humanity, with parts of it radicalizing and becoming more deadly as a reaction against globalization and its correlatives, such as immigration of "others."

- Sociability: Globalization and Internet are likely to change radically sociability, such as increasing the proportion of humans combining loneliness and multiple modes of interactions with stranger-friends in virtual worlds and chat groups. Psychological impacts are likely to be profound but unpredictable.

- Trauma: Most of humanity will move through a variety of traumas, including harsh ones, caused by the transition crises built into metamorphosis.

All these Deltas and the challenges they pose to avant-garde politicians are in-between possible, likely and very likely, based as they are on a mixture of estimate and guesstimate. This applies to all discourse on alternative futures, as taken up in the next chapter.

CHAPTER 11
ALTERNATIVE FUTURES

MENTAL TRIP INTO FUTURES

As discussed, only humans have the amazing capacity and interest to think, imagine, feel, and plan in terms of alternative future. This is part of the ability of the mind to engage in thought experiments, which is of profound importance for cultural evolution of the species. A special type of such mental activity is virtual time travel, namely imagining the world, or parts of it, at different points in the past or in the future. But there is a big difference between imagining the past on the basis of the study of history, with the aim of arriving at more valid knowledge and understanding of what was, why it was, and what its impacts are on what is now and will be, and imagining alternative states of the future, which by definition cannot be based on "reality," but only on conjectures based on some mixtures between professional outlook methods and creative imagination.

The human mind produces and considers images of futures for amusement and contemplation, such as in science fiction. In construction of some types of alternative futures values are paramount, such as in utopias and dystopias aiming at influencing human endeavor by presenting models to be approximated or escaped. But distinctions between "possible" and "fantastic" futures are fuzzy, because rapid advancement of science and technology has realized many images regarded as fanciful when presented in science fictions, such as by Jules Verne and Hans Dominik.

For avant-garde politicians the main aim of mental time-traveling into imagined futures is preparing for what may come and influencing what will be. An example, though amiss in important respects, is the U.S. National Intelligence Council Report *Global Trends 2030: Alternative Worlds* (National Intelligence Council 1212). It is this type of alternative futures that has to be developed and retained in the mind of avant-garde politicians to serve as a basis for endeavor to impact on the future in the directions set by raison d'humanité.

This requires distinguishing between images of alternative futures assuming there are no major changes in human efforts to impact on them, and images of futures contingent upon alternative human efforts to influence them. A major rule for composing humanity-craft derives from this distinction: if it is very likely that main alternative futures meet human needs without innovative interventions with historic processes shaping them then "more or less the same," with only incremental innovations, is an appropriate principle for humanity-craft composing. But if there is a significant likelihood that the range of possible alternative futures includes both very undesirable and/or very desirable ones, then radical efforts to impact on the future for the better are required.

Many outlooks favored by political leaders tend to view historic processes as preordained to bring about, after some ups and downs, desirable futures, as if humanity can rely on some "hidden hand," or "cunning of history," or "progress built into the dynamics of human history." Thus, despite current events which provide quite some ground for pessimistic views on the future, many Western political leaders speak about the "right side of history," assuming ensured progress towards what they regard as desirable, such as global peace, democracy, liberalism, and thriving free markets. But this is a hallucination given the nature of metamorphosis which has much potential for bad future, or at least very painful transition periods into unpredictable and also partly inconceivable futures. In view of such dangerous potentials of future-shaping historic processes, massive interventions constitute a fateful task of avant-garde politicians, as discussed in Chapter 15.

DESIRED AND DISMAL ALTERNATIVE FUTURES

Outlines of one desired and one moderately dismal alternative future of humanity towards the end of the twenty-first century will illustrate the nature and importance of such constructs for the extraordinary mission of avant-garde politicians and provide a basis for the following chapters.

	Desired Alternative Future of Humanity 2100
Ideologies and Values	Supporting raison d'humanité. Possibilities of human enhancement up to approaching homo superior and creating multicellular life held in abeyance, for further pondering and consensus building
Fundamentalism and Fanaticism	No mass-killing fanaticism
Mass Culture	Slowly improving
Leisure Time	Increasing with changes in labor market. In the main put to good use
Literary, Artistic and Philosophical Creativity	Increasing both qualitatively and quantitatively
Signs of a Second Axial Age	Some clear precursors
Science and Technology	Developing human welfare serving knowledge and tools, but very little that enables mass-killing, which is kept under strict control. Selective regulated work on highly intelligent robots, human enhancement and creation of multicellular life. Many contributions to the understanding of the material world and the universe
Cultures	Pluralistic with many shared basic human values, much mutual learning and creativity

	Desired Alternative Future of Humanity 2100
Violence	Restrained, without mass killing
Markets	Overall free, but well balanced and avoiding serious economic crises. Effective limitations on selling harmful services and goods
Quality of Life	Near worldwide elimination of dismal quality of life, overall rising human development with reduced disparities
Earth Carrying Capacity and Demography Balance	Thanks to science and technology the earth carrying capacity is increased and does not impose limitations on the human population size, which is globally stable
Natural Large-Scale Catastrophes	Good global defense systems and crisis preparations avoid large-scale catastrophes, including global mass-killing pandemics
Human Communality	Increasing, without eliminating tribal identities providing feelings of belongingness
Global Elites and Networks	Highly developed, pluralistic, reflecting most segments of global populations
Thinking on Human Species Alternative Futures	Highly developed in think tanks, academia, parts of global elites, and global governance
Global governance	Improving, increasingly decisive, operating largely by consensus, enjoying much global support, increasingly able to overrule national sovereignty when essential for welfare of humanity as a whole
Global Political Leadership	Much improved, thanks in part to well-designed global leadership development programs and improved electoral judgment
Random events	A number of limited natural disasters and one local war help bring about desirable future, as described above

	Moderately Dismal Alternative Future of Humanity 2100
Ideologies and Values	Constant "clashes of civilizations" with conflictive ideologies and values. Little concern for the welfare of humanity as a whole. Some countries and groups experiment with radical human enhancement and creation of multicellular life, while others oppose such efforts
Fundamentalism and Fanaticism	Quite a lot of mass-killing fanaticism, by some states and non-state actors, and also martyrdom-seeking sects—all with access to mass-killing tools and some seeking doomsday devices
Mass Culture	Becoming more sordid
Leisure Time	Increasing with changes in labor market. Mostly used for drugs, virtual reality machines and mass amusements lacking cultural contents
Literary, Artistic and Philosophical Creativity	More or less stable, with ups and downs
Signs of a Second Axial Age	None
Science and Technology	Completely free, developing a lot of both very useful and very dangerous knowledge and technologies, party inadvertently and party on purpose. Efforts to impose controls failed
Cultures	Pluralistic with much mutual hostility. Some tend towards aggressive mysticism

	Moderately Dismal Alternative Future of Humanity 2100
Violence	Quite some mass killings. Efforts to restrain them are only partly successful
Markets	Overall free, eager to sell whatever is in demand, including harmful services and goods. Efforts to limit markets largely fail. Unrestrained competition and short-time speculations cause repetitive serious global economic crises
Quality of Life	Average quality of life is increasing, but disparities are very large with significant parts of humanity suffering from relative deprivation and periodically from lack of essentials of life
Earth Carrying Capacity and Dem. Balance	The situation if out of balance, with ecological degradation and uncontrolled increases in global population creating an unsustainable dynamics
Natural Large-Scale Catastrophes	A large meteor hit the earth causing vast destruction. A pandemic killed 5% of the global population. Inadequate allocation of resources prevents setting up effective global defenses and sufficient crisis preparations
Human Communality	Not pronounced, other than on declarative levels. Much tribalism, including aggressive forms
Global Elites and Networks	Highly developed but limited to a small part of global populations
Thinking on Human Species Alt. Fut.	Neglected and of low quality
Global governance	Some upgrading of the United Nations, but very inadequate for required action
Global Pol. Leadership	More of the same inadequacies
Random events	Some serious natural catastrophes, but without resulting in real learning on taking care of the human species

CONSTRUCTING ALTERNATIVE FUTURES

The very term "alternative futures" expresses the view that the future is not fully determined by the past, but can take different forms. This view is fundamental to human thinking and action, all the more so of avant-garde politicians. Alternative futures can deal with various subjects and be of different scales, ranging from a single domain or locality to the world as a whole. They can be explicitly marked with degrees of possibility, impossibility, likelihood, or necessity. The time to which they relate can be more or less defined, or left open. And they can be graded with the help of postulated values according to more or less desirability or undesirability.

Constructing alternative futures involves both a lot of comprehension of the processes of history and the ranges of what may be possible, with much horizon scanning and full alertness to novel futures becoming possible thanks to science and technology, and changes in other drivers of future, including values. A lot of imagination is also required, together with mixtures of more or less structured outlook methods used with care.

Humans can design in their mind and present in various forms purely fantastic and also counterfactual futures (for instance inhabited by wizards and witches), expected futures, visions of desired and realistic futures, and more. Authors of utopias imagine different and in their views happier humanity in better worlds. But all futures that humans can imagine are limited by what is conceivable to the mind as largely based on the past, which imposes limits on even the most creative thinkers.

An avant-garde politician can get quite some inspiration and stimuli for creativity from such and similar writings, for instance *A Modern Utopia* (1905) by Herbert George Wells, and *Walden Two* (1948) by "B. F." Skinner. But avant-garde politicians are not utopians. They try to impact for the better on the short- and long-term futures of humanity, as well as of their societies, through political action in a broad sense of that term, with emphasis on avoiding, as noted, "hell on earth." While their eyes should look at the sky, their feet must remain on the ground, with both being integrated in the mind.

Once we go beyond naïve approaches, construction of alternative future worlds involves a lot of important methodological issues, such as distinctions between possible, likely, unlikely, and impossible futures; the idea of futures with "alien" properties; reduction of the infinite number of possible futures to a few "pure type" models around which other possibilities cluster, and more (Divers 2002, which uses the term "possible worlds" within a rather philosophic approach). These are mainly issues for professionals, though avant-garde politicians should be literate in relevant knowledge and efforts.

Here again a warning is necessary, concerning the widespread illusion of the mind that the more detailed and specified an alternative future is the more it appears convincing and reliable. The opposite it true: a more general alternative future is more likely to fit future reality than a more detailed one. Thus an image of the future postulating much violence covers a broader range of possible events than that which postulates a war between two specified states. However, very general futures often do not meet the needs of humanity-craft composing. Thus the tendency of various outlook units, such as intelligence analysis staffs, to present very general alternative futures so as to protect themselves against making errors, makes their products less useful.

DIMENSIONS

Alternative futures can take various forms, by combining five main dimensions, with various overlaps: predictive–prescriptive; large-limited scope; short-long time horizons, with special attention to outlook possibilities and socio-political constrains; low-high realization likelihood; and fitting available concepts—inconceivability.

Predictive–prescriptive

Predictive alternative futures serve as bases for trying to influence for the better the futures and for coping with those that cannot be influenced significantly. The range of possible futures is mapped in a clinical-realistic mood, with or without the likelihood of realization notations. While all alternative futures are selective and deal with what is relevant to the values and time horizons under consideration, predictive outlooks try to avoid biases caused by value preferences, such as overemphasizing what is very much wanted or feared.

Prescriptive alternative futures start with values and try to design alternative possible futures which maximally realize them, with priority given to futures which provide more of desired values and which are more achievable. These serve as realistic visions, construction of which is a main task of avant-garde politicians as they serve as important guides for pondering and action. In contrast, what I call "realistic nightmares" present possible futures that are catastrophic or very bad in terms of cardinal values, the prevention of which is a top priority. They are essential a tool for realizing the survival imperative.

Large-limited scope

A world system began developing around the fifteenth or sixteenth century, but it is only since the ninetieth century that political leaders have to act within increasingly encompassing and deep globalization, with all important issues requiring at least some measures of a global perspective. While not all regions are of equal global significance, the fully globalized core is expanding, with most of the world becoming increasingly integrated. Therefore, while many alternative futures are necessarily mainly local and regional so as to be relevant for the normal mission of an avant-garde politician, even when acting very locally pondering in global terms is also necessary in order to take into account local-global interactions and to serve the extraordinary mission.

Cyberspace needs attention in nearly all alternative futures, however local. And for some issues various layers above the planet earth and parts of outer space also have increasingly to be included.

Short-long time horizons

Alternative futures should have different time horizons, to be decided upon in light of four criteria:

Values: As already explained, the importance given to different times in the future is not a matter of rational choice, or of economic discounting, but of values. It is a matter of time stream preferences.

Domain maturation time: Different domains of action need various critical stretches of time to ripen and produce results. Thus, when considering a big dam which has significant consequences for at least 100 years, it is appropriate to consider it within such a time frame. To try and achieve human settlement on other planets of our solar system or their moons, persistent efforts for two or three generations may well be needed. Building new institutions, such as decisive global governance, probably depends on some catastrophes serving as "forcing events," so that an open-ended time horizon, which covers repetitive efforts and progress in stages, is needed. Coping with a global mass-killing epidemic is an urgent crisis to be dealt with immediately, though increasingly gearing up for such emergencies is an ongoing activity not divided into predefined slices of time other than phased action plans.

Outlook possibilities

The two criteria above lead mainly to long-term perspectives, but the opposite is often true for outlook possibilities. When no relatively reliable chain of causes and results can be established between actions now and in the near future and results at a stipulated time in the future then that time is irrelevant for making choice now. Outlook possibilities are often negatively correlated with the length of time. This is a major consideration compelling shortening of time horizons also when other considerations require longer ones. However in such cases too some tentative thinking on longer-term alternative futures is recommended, to serve as perspective and background in the mind.

In some important domains longer time frames enable plausible outlooks more than shorter ones. Thus, it is impossible to say when some scientific and technological development which is highly likely in the longer run will in fact take place. Therefore, if an important possible development in an unknown time has to be coped with, as a matter of prudence some action should be taken, or at least prepared, as if it is likely to occur soon, even when there is no strong basis for such an expectation.

In all cases outlook possibilities are a critical consideration in designing and using alternative futures. Therefore they are considered below in more detail.

Socio-political constraints

Even the best of avant-garde politicians is constrained by social and political conditions in the length of time that can be taken into account. It is often practically impossible, and also morally doubtful, to pay much attention to the welfare of future generations when the here and now is suffering harshly and crying for help. And when elections or reappointments are near an avant-garde politician too has no choice but to engage in some short-term support mobilizing acts.

Low-High realization likelihood

Estimation, or guesstimation, or at least informed guessing of the realization likelihood of alternative futures is very difficult. As exposed by the soon discussed outlook approaches, all of them are limited and become increasingly unreliable the more future-shaping historic processes are changing, deviate from past patterns, become non-linear and unstable, and include phase jumps, as is very much the case in the era of metamorphosis.

Therefore, it is necessary (1) to use a fitting language for denotation of likelihood, the widely used risk terminology with quantitative probabilities being often misleading, as already explained; (2) to include inconceivability in alternative futures; and (3) to adopt various approaches for coping with irreducible thick uncertainty.

The main distinctions in modal logic, as mentioned, are between possibility, impossibility, necessity, and contingency—in the sense of maybe and maybe not. This applies not only to quantitative likelihood of a defined event happening in the future, but usually to qualitative features of the future. This qualitative uncertainty is an important feature of thick uncertainty which standard probability scales completely ignore and which modal logic does not adequately handle.

Therefore, to recapitulate, the categories of modal logic need supplementation with concepts applied explicitly to quantitative or qualitative uncertainty, such as "known unknowns," "unknown unknowns," "unknowable unknowns," and "inconceivability"— which is the most extreme form of "not even imaginable," to which I turn next.

Fitting available concepts-Inconceivability

"Inconceivable" implies being beyond the reach of available concepts and explicable imagination. As already discussed at length concept packages with which the mind operates stem largely from past experiences as processed by the abstraction and language abilities of the mind. Some concepts are also supplied by creative imagination, which is a main source of radical innovation, as illustrated by the emergence of new forms of music. Novel theoretical thinking is an additional important source of concept enrichment, as illustrated by quantum theory and the idea of "antifragility."

Thus the qualified human mind is more or less equipped for conceptualizing known and also imagined realities. But it is inherently unable to conceptualize the complete unknown, even if it is a known unknown, such as the values accepted in a society of super-humans. Rather, these are the domains of inconceivability.

Given the rapid rate of nonlinear change and many phase jumps, a lot of inconceivability is sure to happen, much more radically than "black swans" (Taleb 2007). This by now very popular metaphor does not really do justice to the sure-to-come inconceivable. A green or violet swan is still a swan. But the impacts of raising life expectancy to 150 years, and all the more so cloning humans and perhaps creating life are not in the same mental space as a swan with a surprising color. They are largely "inconceivable."

This is what avant-garde politicians have to gear up for and cope with. Therefore, the inconceivable must be taken into account in all but the simples of alternative futures. In the mind, this implies adding to all alternative futures question marks and open spaces to signify and leave place for what cannot be imagined, and also for what can in principle be conceived but was not taken into account.

SCENARIOS

Alternative futures can be presented as maps of the possible situations of a select set of attributes at some more or less defined time in the future, or explicitly at an undefined point in the future. In contrast to such defined future history, alternative futures can be presented as scenarios, which include a series of slices of futures evolving over time. The first form shows a kind of static picture and the second a kind of movie composed of consecutive pictures.

All observations on alternative futures apply, with some adjustments, also to scenarios. Thus, the more detailed a scenario is the more it is regarded as trustworthy by the uninitiated, but the less likely it is to fit future development.

Scenarios should present the consecutive snapshots of alternative futures and the processes leading from one to the next within a sequential framework, such as stage t_1 leading perhaps, for sure, or with unknown likelihood to stage t_2 and so on. Therefore, scenario construction and interpretation is not as easy as often presented.

Contrary to some opinions, scenarios are not an outlook method, neither is scenario writing. Scenarios are the product of outlook approaches. Their preparation can stimulate better use of outlook approaches, such as thanks to posing questions on underlying temporal logic. But outlook approaches are the grounding of alternative futures in all their forms. Therefore, suitable computer programs can on the basis of adequately developed scenarios and alternative futures move from one to another, helping thinking on the future by presenting alternative panoramas.

OUTLOOK APPROACHES

Outlooks into alternative futures are based on some mixtures of four approaches: extrapolation, theories, tacit knowledge of experts, and imagination. But let me start with an additional approach in the making, namely big data analysis (Siege 2013; Mayer-Schönberger and Cukier 2013). A concrete example is the "Data to Decisions" program run by the U.S. Defense Advanced Research Projects Agency (DARPA), which inter alia tries to analyze a large quantity of diverse data in order to predict instabilities. In fact, such efforts started before "big data" milking, and were not very successful. It remains to be seen what big data analysis can supply. This depends on the availability of reliable theories on relevant variables, on which data is collected. Data, including a lot of data, does not easily speak for itself.

Therefore I tend to the views that most of the novel issues faced by humanity are not susceptible to the presently conceived quantitative algorithms of big data processing, which therefore can provide only limited help to the extraordinary mission of avant-garde politicians. But keeping updated with the potentials of big data collection and processing for humanity-craft issues is recommended, together with a good measure of doubts.

Moving on to the four well-established outlook approaches, let us start with extrapolation. Extrapolation is conditioned on the assumption that what was will be. When dealing with invariant facts extrapolation is quite reliable. Extrapolation is also useful when patterns of change are stable, or instability is within a stable range. Thus, given stable changes in life expectancy without significant migration, the age composition of populations can be predicted with high reliability. Similarly, given stable life cycles of pandemics their length and periodicity can be quite reliably predicted probabilistically. This also applies to classical economic cycles, but not to novel forms of "jumpy" economic crises.

When long-term processes are considered, adequate knowledge of the past is a necessary condition for extrapolation. Thus, predicting climate changes and assessing impacts of human activities on them require much knowledge on climate cycles over very long periods, which is only partly unavailable. Therefore the debate on what climate changes are part of a natural cycle or the result of human activities is hard to resolve.

In some opinions long-term cycles of historic changes can be identified, such as the so-called Kondratiev waves dealing with economic cycles of 40 to 60 years, and some rise and decline cycle speculations. But, even if valid in the past, which is not sure at all, they lack validity for the future because of radical changes in the very nature of historic processes.

The next outlook approach relies on theories which deal with change over time. Some of the famous philosophers proposed such theories, such as Hegel's views on "the cunning of history" leading humanity to a predetermined future; Marxist views on proletarian revolutions, withering of the state, and a future global classless just society; and more recent claims on "the end of history." But these are at best stimulating speculations, not plausible theories on which reliable outlooks can be based.

For shorter time spans less ambitious but still broad theories of social change can provide some outlooks, as illustrated by theories of voting behavior. But the rapid obsolescence of many social theories, which are necessarily based on the past, makes them into doubtful bases for outlooks. A striking illustration is provided by various theories on the stages of economic growth (e.g., Rostow 1960) none of which stood the test of time.

Still, the importance of invariances, such as core features of the human nature, does enable some rather reliable outlooks based both on extrapolation and theories, such as on the likelihood of fanaticism increasing in periods of social turmoil and of new mass-killing instruments being used at least occasionally.

To illustrate the problem of theories, let me take up the fate of the unfortunate people of Melos exterminated by the Athenians, as described by Thucydides. It illustrates military strength ratios as determining outcomes of violent confrontation. Given the military technologies of that time the small population of Melos had no chance against the might of Athens. But nowadays a relatively poor and underdeveloped country can acquire nuclear weapons keeping at bay strong powers who would love to teach it a lesson, as illustrated by North Korea. Alternatively, a small number of hackers can cause much damage with a large-scale cyber-attack without requiring many resources.

Global security and international relationship theories as well as statecraft practices are just beginning to adjust to this novel reality, ignoring even more so the likelihood of poor countries and non-state actors developing or acquiring mass-killing biological weapons. Therefore, as mentioned, my recommendation is to "forget Clausewitz!" and not to base geostrategic policies on obsolete theories and experiences. Military history is in the main irrelevant for future conflicts.

Socioeconomic theories provide additional important examples of increasing obsolescence, disqualifying more and more of them as bases for outlooks. Thus, the expectation that better education necessarily increasing significantly the chances of finding a job, and a well-paying one, is increasingly doubtful when the total number of jobs may decrease radically thanks to new technologies, as already discussed. The still wide acceptance of clearly obsolete economic theories testified to the stubbornness of scholars too in clinging to what is no more relevant, and the reliance of political leaders on them is an act of both ignorance and desperate clinging to straws however rotten.

The outlook approach which is likely to be used most often by avant-garde politicians and their advisors is tacit knowledge of experts, based on long engagement with a subject. But, as already discussed, such tacit knowledge shares a major weakness with extrapolation and theories: the more radical change processes are the less can expertize, which is based on the past, supply reliable outlooks.

IMAGINATION

A different approach altogether is "imagination." This is a hard nut to crack, because its nature is not understood. The functions of imagination are multiple and in part very important, including in creativity. It has an important role in inventing utopias and designing social experiments, wilder or more realistic. Constrained imagination is important for designing prescriptive alternative futures. But its role in mapping alternative possible futures is both fascinating and problematic.

Let us assume we go to one of the more serious "futurism" conferences (I have a lot of experience with them). Not a meeting in Honolulu on humanity in the year 3000, which is only good for enjoying the beach, but one in Pisa on the shape of the European Union in 30 years. Participants include well-known futurists who mainly rely on their imagination, even if some of them call it otherwise, together with experts on the EU. As usual at such conferences, there will be quite some mix-up between predictive outlooks trying to foresee the future as it is likely or may be, and prescriptive outlooks, proposing futures as they should be according to one or another view. Altogether a large number of alternative futures for the European Union will emerge, let us say 15 major ones, some of them rather mundane and others very imaginative.

Assuming we meet again 30 years later and happen to speak about the conference. It is likely that 14 of the alternative futures mapped there bear no or very little resemblance to the actual shape of the European Union after 30 years. But one of the more imaginative outlooks, not taken very seriously by most conference participants, hit the nail, describing quite accurately what the EU has become. We are now faced with the questions how to explain this successful prediction, and whether to rely on other predictions for the next 30 years by its originator.

There are two possible answers to the first question, which determine the answer to the second: The successful prediction may have been a random accident, or it was the result of some outstanding foresight intuition probably based on superior capacity to grasp subconsciously long-term patterns of history invisible to others. If the first explanation is the correct one, we will not give any special credibility to other outlooks by the same person. If the second explanation is more likely, we will take other outlooks by the same futurist rather seriously. But there is no way to decide which one of the explanations is more correct, in the absence of a series of long-term outlooks by the same person which have been proven more or less true or false so as to permit statistical evaluation of the role of chance or tacit knowledge—and this is nearly never available when serious longer-range issues are at stake.

SO WHAT?

Extrapolation, theories, and expertize are all based on the past. In an era of metamorphosis, their ability to supply valid images of the future is limited, but there are many important exceptions due to the many invariables and slow change processes. And imagination, however sometimes stimulating, is not a reliable outlook approach. Little wonder that studies of outlooks of many pundits demonstrate that most of them are proven wrong with the passage of time (Tetlock 2005). My advice is not to be taken in by various claims of celebrities and teams that they are "proven" reliable predictors.

This recommendation is fully supported by evaluation of outlooks by intelligence units which are staffed with high-quality professionals, have plenty of supercomputers, and enjoy access to much information not available in the public domain. Their outlooks are either rather obvious, or present a large range of contradictory possibilities making them hard to use, and altogether are of low to mixed validity when complex issues and longer futures are at stake. Even worse, often they are very misleading, as demonstrated by plenty of intelligence analysis fiascos. This is inherent in the nature of historic metamorphosis processes, but aggravated by the lack of uncertainty sophistication by most outlook professionals, and even more so by political leaders who expect from professionals the impossible and press them to provide it.

Sophisticated outlooks are important in indicating some possibilities and stimulating thinking. They can also point out some crucial mega-trend and future developments clearly stemming from present dynamics or invariances, some of which are discussed in this book. But, unless distinguished by much uncertainty sophistication, including avoidance of probabilistic predictions, providing illustration of "surprises," and considering inconceivability, they should be taken with a pound, not with a grain of salt.

The overall conclusion is not total skepticism on alternative futures. Many features of the world, such as much of human behavior, together with rather stable mega-trends, such as some main directions of science and technology, do permit construction of quite plausible predictive outlooks for the short and longer range future. Addition of relatively stable, or predictable, or postulated values enables construction of quite plausible alternative prescriptive futures. These, if accompanied by question marks and rapid learning, can help meet the needs for alternative futures in the mind of avant-garde politicians as an essential basis for composing humanity-craft, if suitable pondering approaches fitting bounded thick uncertainty are used. This challenge is taken up in the following chapters.

PART FOUR

COMPOSING
HUMANITY-CRAFT

CHAPTER 12
PONDERING

HUMANITY-CRAFT

The most important activity of an avant-garde politician is composing humanity-craft realizing the extraordinary missions and, in particular, the three existential imperatives. I prefer the term "composing" to other possible and often used ones, such as forging, making, crafting, forming, and so on. I do so to emphasize critical creativity and other essential inputs into humanity craft, that go beyond most practices of statecraft and policy making by main stream political leaders. However, as noted, this does not mean that an avant-garde politician himself supplies most of the inputs, which are often provided by partners, staffs and advisors, who also supervise the not less important implementation, as discussed in Chapter 18.

The term "humanity-craft" is based on "statecraft," but is transformed so as to apply to taking care of the long-term future of the human species and its main parts. Humanity-craft is expressed in a series of grand policies that are further translated into more specific policies, plans, projects, operational directives, and so on.

The central process in the mind engaged in composing humanity-craft is "pondering." The mind engages in many additional processes, such as esthetic and emotional ones, which can be paramount at various times. However all mind processes interact and overlap, with pondering, for instance, including also esthetic and emotional facets, though these should not dominate it. Therefore, upgrading the quality of pondering, as required for being an avant-garde politician, can be approached from different perspectives and involves diverse dimension of the mind, and in some respects all of it.

Dictionaries define "pondering" more or less as "reflecting, considering and weighing carefully and thoroughly in one's mind." Pondering includes both "thinking" as a set of mainly conscious processes and "intuiting" as a set of largely unconscious processes, with shifting boundaries between the two. Will, moods, emotions, and feelings also participate, mainly unconsciously, requiring as far as possible monitoring by conscious processes, so as not to spoil humanity-craft composing.

Composing humanity-craft depends on clarified values to be realized within comprehended images of future reality, as changing with time, so as to move in the direction of the most desirable world among alternative possible ones, but with top priority to avoiding the worst ones. Presentation of some conjectural examples of humanity-craft grand-policies, followed by a few "pondering exercises," will serve as a substantive background to discourse on some of the main required qualities of pondering in the mind of an avant-garde politician.

GRAND-POLICY CONJECTURES

Some conjectural examples of humanity-craft grand-policy conjectures, in part already touched upon, related to the existential imperatives and the value compass, include the following:

- Innovative global laws dealing with critical humanitarian issues, including limitations on novel forms of aggression, such as cyber-attacks and use of killer-robots; prohibition of hate propagation; and so on.

- Strict control over all mass-killing weapons and prevention of their proliferation and use, together with firm measures to eliminate in stages all forms of war and large-scale violence.

- Cutting through the lengthy socio-psychological dynamics of "intractable conflicts" (Bar-Tal 2013) and imposing a solution, to prevent festering conflict from becoming dangerous wildfires using mass-killing weapons.

- Selective and carefully focused monitoring, inhibition, and prohibition of research and technology developments that may enable mass killing.

- Special restrictions on research in synthetic biology and diffusion of its findings if they can pose serious dangers to humanity, in line with the principles of prudence, even if significant benefits may stem from such research and widespread knowledge of its results. This grand-policy requires special emphasis because contrary policies have been adopted (Garrett 2013), which may cause much damage and will be difficult to revise.

- In line with the grand-policy above, strict restrictions and confinement of life-creating and radical human enhancement research and technology to closed and supervised facilities.

- Prevention of diffusion of knowledge which may enable production and use of mass-killing tools or uncontrolled human enhancement.

- Expanded and strictly enforced "responsibility to protect (R2P or RtoP)," preventing all forms of mass atrocities. This idea has a long history (Orford 2011), but achievements are very limited compared with needs (Power 2002). Required measures go far beyond the *Report of the International Commission on Intervention and State Sovereignty,* 2001. Thus, besides prevention and protection, harsh punishment of all responsible for such crimes is required, according to the principle of retributive justice and as essential for deterrence.

- Help to prevent states from failing, including economic, social and military means as may be required, up to setting up temporary "protectorates" managed under the control of the Global Authority or a revamped United Nations organ.

- Inhibition of ferocious fanaticism, its prophets, and leaders. Their containment, isolation and also destruction if they may acquire mass-killing capabilities and murderous followings.

- Careful non-violent biopolitics to assure a sustainable balance between the number of humans and the carrying capacity of the planet, as changing with advances in science and technology, variations in human consumption patterns, and ecological situations.

- Protection of features of the earth important for human existence and thriving, such as containing greenhouse effects, preserving important natural resources, and protecting useful biological diversity, unless and until substitutes are made available by science and technology.

- A global forest policy, balancing biodiversity habitat and ecological value with sequestering CO_2, which require novel forest management principles.

- Geoengineering, to ward off or compensate for planetary changes that are dangerous to humanity, such as erecting an artificial sun shield for the planet, as may become feasible, though with quite some risks (Hamilton 2013).

- Preparations for avoiding or containing large natural disasters, including erection of an effective global defense system against large asteroids and large meteors.

- Protection of major artistic work and archeological findings and assured public access to most of them.

- Large-scale measures to prevent dangerous global pandemics and preparations for coping with them, including compulsive ones such as obligatory vaccination.

- When necessary, radical revamping of concepts and policies in respect to "employment" and "unemployment," probably combined with some form of assured minimum income (somewhat in line with Murray 2006).

- Gearing for massive increases of leisure time, preparing the next generation for using it well, improving the cultural qualities of leisure time industries by providing incentives, and investments in many and diverse facilities for educational–cultural leisure time activities.

- A global refugee policy, including strict definition of "refugee," protected travel arrangements for authentic refugees, obligatory quotas setting down the minimum number of refugees that countries have to accept fitting their economic and cultural absorption capacities, global regulations on treatment of legally entering refugees, and forced repatriation of illegal immigrants not meeting the definition of refugees.

- Reduction in phase of disparities in human development, as defined by the United Nations Development Program in its *Annual Human Development Reports* and redefined from time to time, together with obligatory progressive transfer payments by states as may be necessary for this purpose.

- Introduction of a novel form of obligatory contributions to public causes, in between voluntary philanthropy and obligatory taxes: Globally persons with very high incomes or very much capital have to contribute a fixed proportion to a public cause of their choosing from a menu of options, such as education, research, public health and social welfare, in whatever location they prefer but without deriving any personal benefit from doing so, publicizing their contributions or not as they wish. Not doing so will be a criminal offense, comparable to not paying obligatory taxes.

- Elimination of all tax havens, anonymous bank accounts and other *mala fide* ("bad faith") ways to escape payments of taxes as legally imposed.

- Restrain of the moral hazard of polluting countries not compensating less polluting ones that are harshly damaged by consequences of global warming, with obligatory compensatory payments.

- Imposition of personal responsibility on heads of corporations transgressing against directives of the Global Authority, with penalties and imprisonment as may be decided by courts.

- Global enforcement in stages of a minimum list of basic human rights, such as availability of essentials of life, prohibition of slavery, and basic human equality.

- Preparing, adopting, and enforcing in stages of a Universal Declaration of Human Responsibilities and Duties, to supplement the Universal Declaration of Human Rights.

- Limitations of markets and private choices in respect to services and products dangerous for the future of humanity, such as addictive types of pleasure machines, presetting of the gender of embryo at conception, and uncontrolled human enhancement.

- Allocation of large resources to select "big science" projects and space exploration.

- Promotion of educational programs, symbols, mass media programs, and other efforts to strengthen human communality and restrain aggressive tribalism.

- Shared efforts to restructure education systems, such as in ways of combining the experiences of Singapore, which focuses on nurturing elites (Tan and Tee 2005; Birger, Lee, and Goh 2008), and Finland, which concentrates on the weak and average pupils assuming that the very gifted ones will manage on their own (Sahlberg 2011), but based on human–computer–Internet-based learning. However unwarranted hopes that formal education, however improved, will produce "new humans" should be avoided.

- Setting up of a "humanity corps," initially on a voluntary basis, but moving toward universal obligatory two years of service advancing the welfare and maturation of humanity.

- Systematic efforts to develop globally humanity-committed leadership, elites, and grass-root movements.

- As already discussed, advancement of decisive global governance, with reduction of sovereignty, imposition of human-craft policies globally, and taxation to finance global policies.

EXERCISES

To provide you with more of a concrete sense of what is involved in pondering on humanity-craft, please consider a number of exercises: Imagine that you are a senior political leader of a major power, which has much influence on the decisions and actions of an enhanced United Nations Organization with some global enforcement capabilities. Given the possibilities and dilemmas below, what will be your recommendations and how will you reach them in your mind?

1) A novel technology prolonging life expectancy to 120 years of good health has been developed. The chemicals achieving this effect have to be given to babies in their first year of life. There are no known risks and the treatment is very likely to succeed, but unavoidably it will take at least 150 years before the results can be evaluated. The costs of the treatment are around 500 thousand US dollars per person and are not expected to become less so in the foreseeable future. Technically, it is possible to prevent or ration this treatment because only very few laboratories can produce the chemicals. (You may like to read first a relevant public opinion survey in the United States [Pew Research Center 2013a], but consider what weight, if any, to give to it, and why).

2) A "crazy" country with fanatic rulers is in the final stages of producing thermonuclear bombs and perhaps also mass-killing biological materials. Diplomatic pressures and economic sanctions have failed. The only way to stop production of the bombs and biological materials is a surgical nuclear strike with relatively "clean" nuclear warheads on the production facilities, but "collateral damage" is expected to reach between five hundred thousand and one million civilians killed or seriously maimed. Two other countries with nuclear ambitions are closely monitoring developments and are expected to produce nuclear and other mass-killing weapons if the first country does so.

3) Very important experiments in synthetic biology approach a breakthrough in the treatment of all viruses, including emerging very dangerous ones. But the same technology can be used in easily available "kitchen laboratories" to synthesize mass-killing viruses against which there is no protection. There is still time to prevent the technology from being developed, but once available it will be very difficult to keep it secret for long.

4) In a very religious underdeveloped country, a large majority of women supported in a referendum supervised by the United Nations female circumcision at young age as obligatory for all citizens and permanent residents, unless belonging to another religion.

5) A cheap drug is developed which provides prolonged feelings of ecstatic happiness without direct health damage, but is habit forming.

6) A novel type of brain imaging enables fully reliable findings on whether a person is speaking what he regards to be true or is lying. It is proposed to introduce this technology into the legal system, changing the laws of evidence and rules concerning self-incriminations so as to speed up court procedures and make verdicts more truth-based.

7) In a failed state, systematic mass atrocities take place. The war lords engaging in them possess very dangerous chemical weapons and threaten to use them against any international or other intervention against what they regard as religiously required "ethnic cleansing."

Aided by such conjectural examples of the issues and substance of humanity-craft, we are ready to move on to required qualities of pondering.

APPOSITE BANISTER

Hanna Arendt coined the term "thinking without a banister" ("Denken Ohne Geländer," Arendt 2006a), applied by Tracy B. Strong to select thinkers of the twentieth century (Stong 2012). Expanding on Arendt's view, apposite banisters, such as a clear worldview and appropriate principles for coping with bounded thick uncertainty, provide groundings for pondering, choice, and action, though they needs periodic updating and care must be taken to prevent them from becoming barriers to creativity.

Thinking without a banister is both an advantage and a disadvantage. It is an advantage because pondering is not constrained and therefore may be more creative. However, lacking a banister is often a disadvantage, because pondering lacks overall directions and guidelines and therefore easily gets lost in mental labyrinths. But worst of all are misleading banisters, which misdirect and ruin pondering.

Applying these concepts to the challenges posed by metamorphosis, two contrasting modes of coping emerge. One moves along the banisters of the past, however corroded, with some small repairs which do not change the path that they mark. This works well in relatively stable domains, but is misleading when faced by radically novel challenges. Continuing to rely on obsolete banisters is a main form of bondage to the past. But most political leaders follow outdated banisters, with the result of getting lost in novel terrains.

Instead, an avant-garde politician has to check carefully whether banisters built in the past lead to dead ends. If so, as is often the case because of metamorphosis, construction of new banisters leading in preferable directions is required, even though the topographic features though which they should lead are largely unknown and the banisters are unstable. However, the imperatives and raison d'humanité values indicate directions and enable, together with some understanding of the nature of metamorphosis, construction of at least tentative and experimental apposite banisters guiding pondering, subject to constant adjustments. They are far from fully reliable and do carry significant risks, but are much better than leaning on misleading banisters, which are leftovers from a different past.

RISE AND DECLINE PARADIGM

A potentially encompassing perspective for pondering on humanity-craft, which could serve as a strong banister, would be an at least partly validated paradigm on the future rise or decline of the human species. But it is available only in bits and pieces which do not add up to what is needed.

There is plenty of literature on the rise and decline of organizations, states, and civilizations, classic and modern, such as the classical *The History of the Decline and Fall of the Roman Empire* by Edward Gibbon, published in six volumes from 1776 to 1789; and *A Study of History* by Arnold J. Toynbee, published in 12 volumes over 1934 to 1961, with various later additions and corrections. More recent and much shorter ones include, among others, Fagan (2009), Diamond (1999; 2011); Ferguson (2012); and Wald (2014) which is in some respects the most comprehensive of all.

Such studies, however in part doubtful, do provide parts of a general theory on the rise and decline of states and civilizations, but not on the quite different issues of the rise and decline of the human species. Some deal with specific factors, such as technology, ecology, demography, and warfare. But all together supply only some conjectural ideas applicable to the rise and decline of humanity which can serve as a rudimentary and provisional bannister for composing some of the needed humanity-craft grand-policies.

It is not the purpose of this book to try to provide a humanity rise and decline paradigm which can serve as a main banister. But a few inklings based on available studies can indicate why it is urgently needed and what some of its components may be. To start with an overall observation, there is no basis for assuming that the long-term future of humanity is somehow assured by deterministic historic processes, but neither are there any convincing reasons for accepting an opposite assumption. Rather, the future of humanity should be viewed as not predetermined, partly contingent and partly open and increasingly shaped by freely chosen human action.

To be more specific, fragments of a theory of the rise and decline of humanity might well include, among many others, the following conjectures and components, in part already mentioned but integrated here into two clusters, one more pessimistic and the second more optimistic. I start with the most pessimistic one:

- There is no necessary overall positive correlation between the progress in science and technology and the future thriving of humanity. It is also possible and perhaps likely that future progress in science and technology will seriously endanger the existence of the human species.

- There is no necessary positive correlation between the spread of democracy and a thriving human future. It is also possible that given hedonistic and short-term public opinions, conventional mass democracy may prevent timely measures essential for the future thriving and perhaps also for the long-term existence of humanity.

- Tribal thinking, patriotism, and related values and emotions clearly endanger the long-term future of humanity.

- Unrestrained state sovereignty is sure to become a clear and serious danger to the future of humanity.

- Religious and secular belief systems can facilitate thriving or decline, depending on their contents. In particular, fanatic believers are increasingly likely to endanger the future of humanity because of their growing kill potentials.

- Freedom of opinion, right to privacy and other human rights and humanistic values can in part endanger the future of humanity, if they hinder the measures needed to contain and counteract serious dangers, such as those posed by human enhancement and increasingly lethal and easily available instruments of mass-killing.

- The multiplicity of possible and in part likely catastrophes caused by humans will probably cause much harm and may endanger the very existence of the human species, unless counteracted well in time, at the latest after one or two hopefully limited catastrophes.

Turning around the pessimistic conjectures leads to some of the optimistic ones of a theory of humanity rise and decline, such as control of dangerous technologies, restrain of fanatic movements, and values emphasizing human commonality. To these I add sample of relatively optimistic conjectures on requirements of assuring a thriving future of humanity, in part already mentioned but adding to the cluster:

- Achieving a consensual balance between the number of humans and the carrying capacity of the earth, as evolving over time.

- New scientific knowledge and technologies providing necessities of life, such as sweet water, energy, and food, together with geoengineering taking care of necessary conditions of life.

- Desired enhancement of humans, decided upon by a suitable global forum and subject to constant monitoring.

- Much space exploration and establishment of human settlements in the solar system, with suitable enhancement of explorers and settlers to make them fit conditions different from earth, up to perhaps advancing with time towards human-machine-merging Cyborgs.

- Enlarged search for signs of life beyond earth, together with efforts to develop theories and then technologies perhaps permitting faster than light exploration of the cosmos, if possible.

- Spiritual leaders and cultural creators who inaugurate a Second Axial Age leading inter alia to human maturing.

- Global governance containing dangers to the future of humanity and facilitating its thriving.

- High-quality political leaders and elites who design and implement measures that assures, as far as it depends on human action, a pluralistic open-ended thriving future for humanity.

All these together fall far short of an adequate paradigm of the rise and decline of the human species, but indicate parts of what is needed. Avant-garde politicians should facilitate work on such a paradigm, which require top-quality interdisciplinary teams, follow it, and use it when adequately developed.

OPTIONS INNOVATION

The historian Christian Meier wrote a short fascinating book in German the title of which, translated by me into English, is *The Powerlessness of the Almighty Dictator Caesar* (Meier 1980). Regretfully, this book is not available in English, so let me sum up its main thesis: Julius Caesar had the power to do with Rome more or less what he wanted, but lacked ideas how to reform the regime so as to fit the new situation of Rome becoming an empire. Only his successor, Augustus Caesar, developed in his mind an innovative option and laid the foundations for the Roman Imperial system and *Pax Romana*, becoming one of the most important future-impacting political leaders. This case well illustrated that power without creative ideas what to do with it is inconsequential for the future, but having ideas without power to try to implement them too makes a political leader impotent, unless his ideas are later taken up by powerful actors.

It is important for avant-garde politicians to understand how Augustus overcame formidable constraints, including the resistance of the Senate and the ruling elite as a whole. It was not enough to command legions able to impose his will. In order to found a stable regime legitimation and at least some support of the power elites is necessary, unless all of them are sent to a Gulag. Augustus maintained the outward façade, honors and formal structure of the Roman Republic, but added to it some features changing over time radically its basic nature.

But much more important is the lesson that without options power is futile. True, good options without power are fine for writing books and giving advice, but not for being an avant-garde politician. You need both options and power, leading to public interest Machiavellianism, as discussed in Chapter 17. But having good, or at least reasonable options is absolutely necessary for your extraordinary mission. And having such options requires a lot of innovativeness, based on creativity.

I distinguish between "innovativeness" and "creativity." Innovativeness refers to a desire and ability to adopt novel ideas, encourage them, and search for them. But it does not necessarily imply the ability to invent new ideas, which is "creativity." Innovativeness is a required quality of the mind of avant-garde politicians, while creativity, and especially needed peak creativity, is a quality of very few persons, the vast majority of whom neither desire to become political leaders not fit most of its requirements.

In this context, it is relevant to consider the difference between creative findings in the sciences and creativity in art. In the sciences, creativity is in essence a combination between discoveries on the regularities of nature, including also humans and societies, and imagining-inventing various symbolic systems in which to express the discovered regularities, such as mathematical formulations and abstract models. In the arts, creativity is more de novo. It may imitate nature and surely is influenced by what exists, but a symphony by Ludwig van Beethoven or the architecture of Oscar Niemeyer is more a "free" creation of the mind than the vast majority of scientific theories related in principle to reality and empiric findings. More freedom of the mind from empiricism also characterizes many literary and contemplative creations, however much influenced by reality, such as some dialogs of Plato or the dramas of Shakespeare. Technological creativity may be in-between, with "open" design elements but based on science.

Composing of humanity-craft requires both kinds of creativity and synergetic interactions between them, involving quite some multi-perspective efforts. Therefore avant-garde politicians should be open to and search for different types of creativity as bases for composing humanity-craft.

For most issues related to the extraordinary mission, good options are sorely lacking. And without promising options even otherwise high-quality minds lack raw material essential for fruitful pondering, choice, and action. Therefore, creative humanity-craft option invention is critical for avant-garde politicians. Such creativity is above and beyond all the more structured approaches to composing humanity-craft, as discussed in this and the following chapters. No amount of "analysis" can identify a good idea if it is not available for consideration.

Though essential, it is not enough for avant-garde politicians to be personally innovative, in the sense of willing and eager to consider and adopt novel ideas. They must constantly search for new options developed by others, while doing all they can to encourage and facilitate humanity-craft option creativity. Furthermore, the integration of various inputs into composing novel humanity-craft, grand-policies and so on involves itself some elements of synthesis creativity. There are needed as qualities in the mind of avant-garde politicians.

A word on "flow" (Csikszentmihalyi 2008) is required here. Mainly related to "happiness," it may also be a mental state of intense creativity leading to "eureka" experiences. It can occasionally provide useful inputs into pondering, but ideas emerging from "flow" need careful screening, as they can be very mistaken and the feeling of "flow" may misbalance the mind.

GUIDELINES

To fashion well humanity-craft, grand-policies, policies, laws, organizations, and implementation tool boxes, the mind of an avant-garde politician requires a number of approaches, schemata, frames, and other semi-structured but open-ended pondering templates. Some of the most important ones are presented in the next chapter, to be supplemented by approaches to swerving history in Chapter 15, and coping with thick uncertainty in Chapter 16. A converse approach to improve pondering by reducing error propensities is presented in Chapter 14. Techniques and methodologies, such as decision trees, theory of games, cost–benefit–risk analysis, simulation, model building, and more, are left to policy professionals — though an avant-garde politician should acquire some familiarity with them, for his personal use and in order to check the quality of the staff work done for him.

But be aware that many professionals, books and teaching programs in policy analysis, policy planning, strategy design, and so on, however very useful for more or less "normal" problems, lag far behind the requirements of humanity-craft composing. Some of them are good in rational choice theories, "cost–benefit–risk analysis, political feasibility mapping, expected value estimation, classical forecasting, and so on. But all these do not adequately meet the essential features of metamorphosis, such as stressors and shock effects, bounded thick uncertainty, inconceivability, value shifts, rapidly evolving science and technology, deep globalization, and more.

Some business and corporate leaders do sense what is happening and adopt partly appropriate entrepreneurial strategies, often failing but sometimes amazingly successful— in some views thanks to ignoring classical "strategic planning" (Mintzberg 1994). But political leaders, with their advisors and staffs, are much less innovative. There are exceptions, usually after serious crises, such as the founders of the European Union and the innovative leaders in China leading to very rapid economic growth. But most of high-level policy pondering is entrapped in a past, which is less and less relevant for the future.

All the more required are appropriate guidelines for pondering on domains undergoing metamorphosis. The following guidelines illustrate what is needed. Some have already been discussed and others are detailed in the following chapters. But together they serve all of pondering on vexing issues posed by metamorphosis.

1. Needed is not "thinking outside the box," but thinking in "novel dimensions." This required imagining alternative worlds and considering issues and options in their context with a lot of detachment from "what was" and also from "what is."

2. Real "zero-thinking" is required, on images of reality, historic processes, expectations for the future, widely accepted values, existing policies and institutions, and so on.

3. "Rationality" in the strict sense of that term, as further discussed later in this Part, does not apply to critical components of humanity-craft pondering, such as value judgments and option creativity. Nor do "masses" of date and other panacea reommended by various pseudo-experts.

4. Much attention must be given to current and expected scientific and technological innovations and their likely impacts, within both optimistic and pessimistic perspectives. This required personally science and technology literacy, and excellent science and technology advisors.

5. Value changes are much less conspicuous, but sometimes even more important than science and technology innovations. They need careful monitoring, in order to take them into account and to try and influence them if necessary. But care should be taken not to be blinded by baseless assumptions on predestinated "directions" of value evolution, as widely accepted in the West, such as toward Western versions of liberal democracy and free markets. The opposite may happen in parts of the world. Inconceivable value innovations are also likely in an era of metamorphosis, all the more so if developments lead towards a Second Axial Age.

6. Constant awareness of the likelihood of unforeseen and partly unforeseeable surprise events, including more undesirable than desirable ones, and also of the inconceivable happening, should accompany all pondering on issues undergoing metamorphosis. This requires recognition of early signs of what is coming, building antifragility into main options, and developing top-quality crisis coping and utilization capabilities.

7. Accepted theories should be regarded with much doubt. Alternative theories, including esoteric ones, as long as proposed by credible persons and also some "strange" ones, but not "mystics," should be explored for possible use in dealing with novel situations.

8. Impacting significantly on the future in the direction of *raison d'humanité*, in one version or another, necessitates a large-scale critical mass of interventions in relevant historic processes (Schulman 1981). Required interventions are often also radical and sometimes revolutionary. Pondering in such terms is a needed quality of the mind of avant-garde politicians, however disliked in many societies and political cultures and therefore not to be carelessly presented.

9. The slogan of "politics is the art of the possible" should be rejected. Instead, extraordinary missions often require doing what is regarded as politically impossible. This implied making what is necessary maximally feasible, keeping some pondering and action secret or camouflaged, and assuming political risks.

10. To assure and advance the long-term future and thriving of humanity, as far as humanly possible, including necessary radical interventions in historic processes, force may have to be used. An avant-garde politician should dislike doing so, but not hesitate to apply as much strength as may be necessary.

11. However outstanding the quality of pondering, all of humanity-craft, with their grand-policies and other derivatives, are in their essence "fuzzy gambles," including quite a few half-wild and also very-wild ones. However bad a feeling necessarily accompanies pondering which results in fuzzy gambles, often for very high stakes, an avant-garde politician has to recognize and accept morally, emotionally, and cognitively this inherent nature of decisions. This understanding should not impair the decisiveness required for making up the mind and directing actions.

12. Serious pondering and humanity-craft composing require a lot of mind work, consume much attention, and use many personal resources. Therefore, it is not possible to deal in earnest with many issues and domains simultaneously. Concentration of pondering (and action) on issues carefully selected according to orders of importance within an open-ended schedule is, therefore, essential – this being a main task of the already discussed executive function of the mind.

13. High-quality pondering requires a synthesis between lonely contemplation and intense interaction with diverse knowledgeable or otherwise relevant persons, together with a lot of reading. All these require careful but elastic allocation of scarce time and energy.

14. The nature of choice as fuzzy gambling, with unforeseen and partly unforeseeable consequences, and the unavoidable roles of Fortuna in shaping outcomes, require steep learning curves, constant ability to change the mind and much antifragility.

15. Pondering requires a mix between disciplined thinking, quite some fantasy, and "eureka"-seeking inspiration. Neither hemisphere of the brain nor structured schemata, however important, should dominate it.

16. All of pondering has to be iterative, so as to move in stages to the best possible choice.

17. No single perspective or "frame of thinking," disciplinary, cultural, ideological or personal, can do justice to complex issues. Therefore application of multiple perspectives (Linstone 1984) and frames of thinking (Vickers 1995) is essential.

Additional guidelines can and should be added. But the suggested above should suffice to provide a "taste" of what is involved. As a cluster they apply with adjustments to all of the pondering of an avant-garde politician on major humanity-craft issues, and in part also to more ordinary ones.

META-PONDERING

One of the important theories in organization theory is the so-called "garbage can model of choice" (Cohen, March, and Olsen 1972; Lomi and Harrison 2012). In contrast to viewing decision making as proceeding through consecutive phases or as an iterative process, the garbage can model views decisions as the outcome of a disparate mix between problem points, potential solutions, participants, and choice opportunities, within a rather anarchic setting.

Something similar can easily happen to the pondering of an avant-garde politician (and his staffs), with mix-ups between various approaches, schemata, and so on. The consequences are mainly dysfunctional, with pondering on solutions for problems which do not really exist; problems persisting without being seriously confronted; and pondering which does not lead to making up of the mind.

This phenomenon is related to what I call "cluttered mind," which may be good at creativity but not at coping with complex issues. Still, quite some "anarchic" and "wild" thinking is important in pondering on complex issues, if kept under control. Therefore, an essential controller of pondering is needed in the mind of an avant-garde politician, engaging in "meta-pondering," that is pondering on pondering, so as to structure the pondering processes, including open-ended and also messy ones as needed for innovativeness and creativity, and guiding them all toward integration into making up the mind, deciding, and acting.

QUANTUM CONCEPTS

I do not wish to complicate matters, but would like to take up for a moment cutting-edge concepts and ideas stimulating pondering on complex issues. A glance at quantum models applied to cognition and decision (Busemeyer and Bruza 2012) is relevant, quite separate from the question whether quantum models can explain consciousness and free will.

A first relevant idea of quantum theory is that observation of some aspects of a phenomenon may change its other aspects, which is also known from quite some social science studies. Thus, the order of questions in a survey will often influence the responses. Applied to the mind, earlier pondering is likely to influence later pondering, sometimes for better but often for worse by prejudging what comes second and third in order. This also applies to moving from perspective to perspective, the conclusions from one perspective influencing and often prejudicing those from later ones.

A second main application is the importance of context, which unavoidably "paints" comprehension in various ways. "Context can be conceptualized as a mental representation (overall holistic picture) …in which items or events have occurred" (Busemeyer and Bruza 2012, 207). While context must be taken into account, it must not drive out of the mind specifics and focused attention.

However, this leads directly to the misleading effects of decomposition of issues into elements, as inherent in analytical thinking. Thus, when non-decomposable interaction systems are at stake, up to interrelations similar to "entanglement" in quantum theory, where changes to one component impact on other components without a discernible connection, then pondering faces harsh difficulties in understanding particular issues and tends to ignore so-called side effects of decisions, which can be very important. Therefore, a dynamic balance between more divergent and more convergent pondering, concentrating more on fields or systems and on components respectively, is necessary.

The next idea to be added from quantum theory to the mental lexicon of pondering (leaving aside a lot, such as quantum uncertainty calculus) is the concept of "indefinite states," which is more radical but often also more appropriate than "indeterminacy" for much of metamorphosis. Quantum theory allows certain forms of reality to be in an indefinite state (called "superposition state"). This is a recommended way to think on quite some "undefinable" but not necessarily inconceivable phenomena, including significant parts of alternative futures.

This concept also "allows one to model the cognitive system as if it was a *wave* moving across time …until a decision is made" (Busemeyer and Bruza 2012, 3). Applied to pondering, this way of thinking, combined with the earlier points, brings out the dangers of making up of the mind prematurely, or of working one's way to a final decision through a chain of tentative decisions, because the earlier phases of pondering and provisional choices unavoidably bias the later ones, as noted above. Instead, an avant-garde politician should keep his mind as far as humanly possible in a state of superposition (a "wave" in quantum terminology), before making up the mind ("collapsing the wave into a particle," in quantum terminology).

DEMANDING, BUT NOT IMPOSSIBLE

The requirements of good pondering, as presented in this and other chapters, look prohibitive. But these are essential core-qualities of the mind of an avant-garde politician (and many others), to serve at least as comprehensive perspectives and encompassing frames and to be applied, first exploratorily and then more definitely, in pondering on critical quagmires.

The relative nature of the qualities required in the mind of an avant-garde politician needs here reemphasis. As already explained, having a quality is not a matter of "yes or no," but of "more or less." There exists no clearly defined "optimum." Your mind should strive to use most of the guidelines, schema, approaches and so on, be very good in some of them, and be aware of what is lacking so as to compensate for it. This is demanding. But no "superhuman" pondering is expected. Being significantly superior to the thinking of typical political leaders is essential, but this is not asking for the impossible. It is within the potentials of avant-garde politicians having suitable abilities and making strenuous efforts. And good professional advisors, however hard to find, can help.

To sound somewhat paradoxically, let me add that if the actual pondering of most political leaders would be good in main respects, improving it significantly may be very difficult. But it is clearly inadequate for coping well with the challenges posed by metamorphosing. To put it more brutally but, in my experience, often correctly, much of the decision making processes of many political leaders are quite primitive, however presented to the public and often evaluated by the leaders themselves as based on profound wisdom. Therefore, achieving a significantly higher ponder quality is not prohibitive and is within the potentials of competent and hard-trying avant-garde politicians.

CHAPTER 13
SCHEMATA

ON "SCHEMATA"

"Schemata" include perspectives, schemes, frames, modalities, models, templates, structured heuristics, check lists, considerations, formalized principles, trains of thought, concept packages, procedures and formats to be applied in pondering. They partly overlap the guidelines presented above and additional pondering approaches taken up in the following chapters, and should be used in ways fitting them. But what distinguishes schemata is that they are more specific than theories, guidelines and approaches. Therefore, they require a disciplined mind which acquires habits, conscious and tacit, of using them systematically as may fit given issues. An avant-garde politician can acquire the necessary habits of pondering by gaining experience in applying them, if necessary with the help of mentors and professional staffs.

RECOMMENDATIONS

Without further ado, let me present some recommended schemata, with longer or shorter exposition as necessary. Many of them have already been touched upon or will be taken up again in later chapters. But here they are presented as a coherent set enabling selective choice of what may fit best specific issues and their contexts.

Realistic visions and nightmares

Needed in the mind, and often on one's computer, are realistic visions of the domains with which an avant-garde politician is seriously concerned. "Nightmare visions" should also be prepared, the preventing of which is top priority. The visions can deal with various points of time, with shorter-term visions being usually more detailed than longer-term ones and easier to use in pondering.

Realistic visions or nightmares are related to alternative futures, but are more operational. They are relatively detailed and of shorter time-span, providing concrete guidance for policies, plans, programs, and actions.

A major difficulty in constructing realistic visions and nightmares is balancing of values and wishes on the one hand with the limited potentials of reality and thick uncertainty on the other. This problem faces all of pondering. Therefore, it constitutes a fundamental schema of its own.

Balancing values with reality

Pondering involves seeking a balance, synthesis, and compromise between wishes, values, and hopes on the one hand, and images of the constraints and potentials of future realities on the other. But much depends also on images of capacities to shape the future: The more powerful one imagines them to be, the more one's values and visions will be regarded as realistic.

The issue is not about "yes" or "no," binary pondering usually being inappropriate. Rather, it concerns estimating, or guesstimating the likelihood of success in realizing parts of a bundle of values and visions as higher or lower, taking into account involved costs and risks, and willingness to be more or less "daring" and try to achieve what is difficult and even nearly impossible.

Karl Marx and Friedrich Engels wrote in Chapter Four of *The Manifesto of the Communist Party* "The proletarians have nothing to lose but their chains. They have a world to win." This expresses the mood and images of most revolutionaries. Efforts by an avant-garde politician to change partly some widely accepted human values and institutions so as to assure the survival of humanity and its long-term thriving fit somewhat into this frame of mind, trying to do what is quite likely to fail, and failing again—till success perhaps comes, or catastrophes transform what was impossible into possible or absolutely impossible.

Trying to realize as much as possible of values despite stubborn realities, on the combined metaphors of a sculptor working hard to impose his dream creation on a block of very hard and brittle marble and of a pastor trying to convince his congregation to do good, is at the center of pondering on humanity-craft.

Basic choice schema

Pondering aims at "making up one's mind," finally or provisionally. At the core of making up one's mind is the basic choice schema. It includes four core elements: (a) values, goals, and objectives, including avoidance of undesirable and realization of desirable alternative futures; (b) options; (c) outlooks, which provide images of possible and likely outcomes in terms of values, goals, and objectives, including desired and undesired ones in, with distribution of the expected outcomes in time and assessment of their likelihood, including uncertainty; and finally (d) integration of all the above in the mind of the avant-garde politician, expressing his preference for one of the outlook clusters, and choice of the salient option, often by a kind of partly conscious and partly subconscious Gestalt judgment constituting "making up one's mind."

Put in the form of an analytic matrix, the scheme looks as follows:

(a) <u>Values, goals, objectives</u>

(c) Assessment of outcomes of options

(b) <u>Options</u>

in terms of values etc. in time-stream, with likelihood and uncertainties

(d) <u>Integration in the mind of the avant-garde politician and choice: making up one's mind</u>

However simple this schema may seem at first look, it leads to demanding pondering requirements, while helping to expand and deepen it. Thus:

- The four elements involve conscious and subconscious dimensions of the mind, including thinking, intuition, and feeling.

- All the elements require constant development and improvement. Thus, continuous search for additional options and their creative design and invention are crucial for the quality of choice.

- Developing the elements involves a lot of iteration, which in complex domains requires time. As issues are often urgent, preparatory staff work anticipating needed choices, and time-compressed work processes, such as parallel teams, are often needed. This is especially so in crisis situations.

- Distinctions in part of decision psychology between "slow" and "fast" processes and similar classifications do not apply to more than secondary elements of pondering on complex issues, if at all.

- The schema clearly demonstrates the inadequacy of common notions of "rationality." Thus, value reasoning as required for the development of element (a) and option creativity as essential for element (b) are "extra-rational" (though not "irrational") processes, requiring approaches very different from "rationality."

- Appropriate concepts for pondering are "outlook" and "likelihood," not "prediction" and "probability." The latter two make a misleading impression of exactitude and reliability. Much of the assessments of expected outcome are "guesstimates," with more than a little speculation, because of the nature of thick uncertainty. This is an additional reason while many findings of quantitative experimental psychology based on posing before subjects, often students, probabilistic questions, are irrelevant for most of the pondering of an avant-garde politician.

- Most of the "likelihood" notations will be in terms of "possible but unlikely," "very likely," "unknown", "unknowable," and similar scales, with additional concepts such as "inconceivability" being added. These terms have to be clarified, but in the vast majority of cases they cannot be validly expressed in probabilities.

- Reliance on so-called "subjective probabilities," however often recommended and used as a basis for "expected utility" calculations and related quantitative techniques, is in most cases a dangerous delusion. Exceptions include the very few situations in which tacit knowledge can be relied upon to provide relatively valid subjective estimates of likelihood on probabilistic scales.

- Uncertainty sophistication, as discussed in Chapter 16, is crucial for making adequate choices, as is full cognitive understanding and emotional assimilation of the nature of humanity-craft choices as "fuzzy gambles."

- In some limited but occasionally important cases, all four elements can be fully or approximately developed in quantitative language. This is the domain of operational research. Also, in some interesting cases quantitative models can serve as helpful metaphors of complex situations, not supplying "solutions" but providing useful insights if carefully used. Thus, the theory of games can sometimes help to clarify qualitative issues in strategic interaction and economic behavior.

This schema does not stand by itself. All pondering takes place within multiple contexts, including cultural imaginaries and biases. But most directly related to pondering and in many respects parts of it are pre-schema processes, such as formulation of issues and allocation of resources to pondering; concurrent processes external to a specific choice, which may change the issue as a whole; and post-choice processes, including implementation, monitoring, and learning—sometimes resulting in changing one's mind on what was decided in the past. But, still, the basic choice schema is a main aid to pondering, to be applied heuristically for structuring core parts of pondering, raising issues, and stimulating pertinent questions.

Prioritization

As pointed out by Herbert Simon in his Nobel Prize speech in 1978, the scarcest decision-making resource is "attention." Other critical resources needed for pondering on serious issues, such as quality time, relatively reliable information, and high-quality staff work, are also scarce.

All the more disturbing are findings on the allocation of time by political leaders. As already mentioned but bearing reemphasize, a lot of time and energy goes to activities that lack real significance or at least political utility, such as banal rituals. Even worse, much of the time allocated to difficult issues is of low quality, constantly interrupted by trivial disturbances. Worst of all, most political leaders devote no time whatsoever, or far too little, to brooding on their own on critical issues, in solitude or with a few selected advisors.

Avant-garde politicians have to husband and allocate their time, energy, and attention differently, according to explicitly considered agendas with orders of priority and barriers against waste. This requires discernment between the important and the pressing and conspicuous. A good measure of self-discipline and a well-developed executive function in the mind are essential for doing so. But reserve pondering resources and allocation elasticity are needed to adjust priorities to changes in situations, which are frequent in an era of metamorphosis.

All these requirements also apply to the allocation of high-quality staff work, collection and analysis of data, and so on, as far as controlled by the avant-garde politician.

Extended time horizons

The necessity to take into account longer time horizons than is usual in "normal" politics has already been emphasized as central to the extraordinary mission of avant-garde politicians. But its importance justifies some further elaboration. A few outstanding political leaders are concerned with long-term effects of their action. But the vast majority is caught up in current affairs, with what Walter Benjamin called "now-time."

In his 1940 work *On the Concept of* History (also known as *These on the Philosophy of History*), Walter Benjamin used the term *Jetztzeit* ("now-time, "or "time of the now"), with some variations, as referring to a moment without history, a moment outside of time, with the "everlasting now" disengaged from history's causality (Thesis XVIII, A). Most political leaders tend to focus on this now-time which is regarded as if detached from the long-term streams of history, only paying lip service and offering slogans on the longer range, if at all. As a maximum they add a few odd years to their time horizons, which is much less than needed.

The blame does not lie on political leaders alone. Public pressures often demand giving priority to the now and here and many political leaders give in to such claims, either because of dependence on public support or thanks to their values giving priority to current sufferings and needs. Democracies are especially prone to this pathology. It is the duty of avant-garde politicians to stand up against this tendency, which is poisonous for large parts of pondering on humanity-craft.

But time-scale megalomania too must be avoided. "Eternity" is a term to be avoided in all but theological discourse, which is not the domain of avant-garde politicians. Given metamorphosis I suggest three main time horizons for pondering on humanity-craft, which are correlated with the time horizons of alternative futures but not necessarily identical, being in part shorter so as to fit the realism requirements of humanity-craft: the next five years for pressing issues; 10 to 20 years for most pondering; and up to about 100 years as the time frame for select critical choices and as background for pondering within shorter time frames.

Crises require much shorter time frames: minutes, hours, days, or a couple of weeks. But these should not push out of consideration longer time horizons, as background also in crisis coping—which often impacts on long stretches of time.

Holistic view

An important already mentioned difference between Asian and Western dominant ways of perceiving realities and coping with them is a more holistic field view in Asian philosophy and cultures and more of an analytic and also reductionist and analytic approach dividing fields into components and dealing with them separately in Western philosophy and cultures. When pressures to deal with issues "pragmatically," in the folk-sense of that term, are added, then the result is a clear tendency to deal more with particulars and very little with meaningful systems as a whole.

This is a grave error, as well recognized in systems theory (Wright and Meadows 2009). Systems have so-called "emergent" properties, with the whole being quite different in nature and effects from all the components added up. But many political leaders take the "straightforward" way of focusing on conspicuous particulars, neglecting and also ignoring systems, even when these are clearly the correct unit for considering an issue.

There are exonerating circumstances, such as the division of machineries of government into resorts and ministries, each one anxious over its turf; and the division of knowledge into disciplines, as if this is the structure of reality. Efforts to advance "holistic governance" (6, 2002), such as central staff units illustrated by the UK Strategy Unit and various forms of "national security councils", super-ministries, multi-departmental budgeting, and so on, have hardly made a dent in the "component"-focus" of most political leaders and machineries of government most of the time. This bodes ill for humanity-craft.

Instead, pondering by avant-garde politicians should seek to map and understand systems as "wholes," as far as possible and relevant, and cope with them as such, while also dealing with components as far as necessary. The encompassing systems, of which a system at stake is a component, also have to be taken into account—without going too far. Therefore, required is constant movement of pondering between different levels of systems.

Divergence and convergence

Pondering on complex issues influenced by metamorphosis requires not only movement between components and systems and between different levels of systems, but – as already mentioned -- an overall pendulum and then synthesis between divergence, in the sense of looking far, wide, and long for perhaps related phenomena, and convergence, in the sense of focusing on specific issues and directly relevant knowledge, as already touched upon. But in fact the required movement between divergence and convergence and their later integration is very scarce, most political leaders not being able to engage in such mental gymnastics, however healthy for pondering.

Avant-garde politicians have to learn and practice divergence–convergence calisthenics, till it becomes a habit of the mind. This also stimulates innovativeness and sometimes creativity and eases the strenuousness of pondering caused by monotonous and too formalized ways of thinking.

Abstractness

Closely related to systems and holistic schemata is lots of abstractness, such as abstract concepts and symbolic models, including mathematical ones, essential for structuring and processing complex processes. But care must be taken not to get lost in purely abstract mental constructs which lose contact with reality, as happens for instance in parts of economic theory.

Required abstract pondering involves the use of abstract languages, not only the natural ones. A good measure of pondering in numbers and mathematical symbols is often required, as are uses of modern logic and some qualitative model building, including multi-dimensional and dynamic ones. Also essential are abstract concept packages, as already suggested. But abstract pondering is not the favorite of political leaders, who like to stick to the "concrete" in the name of a misunderstood "pragmatism," in addition to many of them lacking mental abilities to think in abstract terms.

One of the distinctions of the mind of avant-garde politicians is the ability to engage in abstract pondering and also liking to do so, while understanding its potentials, being alert to its limitations, and keeping it linked to the requirements of praxis.

Process focused

Pondering on humanity-craft requires viewing reality as "processes" with attention concentrating on dynamics, rather than "situations" or "institutions" in a static sense. This involves more than being aware of change, as most political leaders are. Thinking in terms of processes requires pattern seeking and recognition, with special attention to non-linear, contingent, long-term and phase-jumping ones.

Such pondering goes a number of big steps beyond the pre-Socratic Greek philosopher Heraclitus of Ephesus, who made the famous statement "no man ever steps in the same river twice," put by later thinkers into the formula "everything flows." Some processes are very slow in terms of human time and can for many purposes be regarded as "invariant," as already explained. But in the era of metamorphosis irregular processes are critical and shape many of the challenges facing avant-garde politicians. Pondering largely in terms of various forms of discontinuities is, therefore, the rule—with important exceptions.

Multidimensional

In 1884, Edwin A. Abbott published his famous book *Flatland: A Romance of Many Dimensions* (Abbott 2009), dealing with sentinel creatures living in two-dimensional space and unable to understand that other dimensions can exist. This book was followed in 1965 by a novel by Dionys Burger (Burger 1983) entitled *Sphereland: A Fantasy About Curved Spaces and an Expanding Universe*, dealing with various multidimensional realities as contrasted with limited human capacities to comprehend them. These books pose well the requirements of multidimensional pondering by avant-garde politicians, as distinct from the strong tendency towards single dimensionality of most main stream political leaders.

Multidimensionality requires pondering with different perspectives, disciplines, languages, imaginary, value systems, and more. However, limits of the human mind prevent coping with more than a small number of dimensions. Symbolic models, visual aids, and computer graphics can help. But still it is necessary to be selective in choosing the dimensions which are most relevant for given issues within a multiple systems perspective and keep them within what human minds, however distinguished by high quality, can handle.

Depth

The related requirement of "depth," in contrast to surface thinking and intuiting, applies to all of pondering. But it is best illustrated in the context of "thinking-in-history," and also quite some "intuiting-in-history, as further discussed in Chapter 15.

The French historian Fernand Braudel distinguished between "events" that are conspicuous like bubbles on the surface of cascading water, but make no real difference to the future, and deeper currents shaping the topography for decades to come (Braudel 1982). The distinction between more or less "surface" or "deep" is a relative one. There is no ultimate depth accessible to us. Sometimes surface and deep processes overlap. But seeking to understand deeper processes is critical for high-quality pondering. This contrasts with the vast majority of discourse and deliberation on "current issues" and "pressing matters" in the hot corridors of power, as well as in the mass media and publics at large, which are between somewhat and completely superficial.

However, going deeper depends on theories, which as stated are often missing or problematic, leaving scope for apprehensions that some critical deep factors are ignored. Others are mistakenly regarded as important while being only conspicuous. Careful discernment between what is really important and what is eye-catching is therefore essential.

Radically innovative, with revolutionary portions

To enlarge on what has already been said on this critical quality, some comments on incrementalism are first required. Incrementalism is both an empiric model and a prescriptive approach. Empirically, it claims that most leaders and organizations tend to improve their choices by small increments rather than radically so. This is not always the case. Thus, in our epoch many organizations are increasingly forced by rapid changes in their environments to "remake" themselves quite radically. Still, there persists a strong tendency among political leaders to limit innovations to small bits, which reduces resistance and cost and is relatively easy to do.

Prescriptively, incrementalism was recommended by distinguished scholars, professionals, and practitioners as being more feasible and as reducing uncertainty on expected outcomes. But innovation is essential for coping with novel issues. And, when situations change, the results of doing more or less that same as in the past become uncertain instead of remaining stable. Consequently, a lot of radical innovativeness and some revolutionary qualities are required in pondering on humanity-craft issues which are undergoing radical change. This is demanding, but essential.

Dialectic

Pondering should be dialectic, in the sense of moving iteratively between opposing points of view and different considerations in order to come up with a preferable choice. This does not necessarily take the form of thesis, antithesis, and synthesis. Rather it is a matter of different ideas virtually confronting each other in the mind and in pondering discourse of teams, so as to arrive at superior comprehension and better making up the mind.

A lot of "internal dialogue," as well as "mental gaming with moves in the mind" (Gobet et. al. 2012) is involved, closely related with the already discussed need for iterative thinking. While "conversations in one's mind" come naturally, theory of games and decision trees can help in structuring it. And interactive computers add important possibilities for upgrading pondering, which an avant-garde politician should fully utilize.

Opportunity seeking

As emphasized by Machiavelli, seeking and utilizing opportunities are among the main features of the virtù of a worthy political leader. This fully applies to avant-garde politicians in an era of metamorphosis. They face great difficulties in advancing raison d'humanité and therefore are all the more in need of opportunities to do so, as both required and provided by the processes of metamorphosis, often unexpectedly so.

This returns us to crises, which often "soften" the rigidities of reality and thus provide unique opportunities to realize humanity-craft. Because of the time constraints characterizing crises, preparatory pondering on utilizing them and also readying of necessary action abilities are necessary, as already mentioned.

Crisis instigation may sometimes be necessary in order to create opportunities to realize essential humanity-craft measures. This is a sensitive action modality that requires strict secrecy. But the widespread view that "crises" are necessarily bad, that they should be maximally avoided and, if occurring, rapidly "solved" by a return to the pre-crisis situation, are often incorrect. An avant-garde politician should not be bound by such conventional thinking.

"Praxis" permeated

"Praxis" refers to constant synthesis between theory, abstract thinking, and feelings on one side with concrete images, ideas, materials, and experiences on the other, all aiming at arriving at operational humanity-craft recommendations and actions. It also involves integrating symbolic thinking with concrete images so as to make up of the mind on what to do.

"Praxis" emphasizes action-directed theory-guided reflective pondering and thus, in some senses, applied to all of pondering in the mind.

Constant but not paralyzing doubt

The last somewhat different required quality of the mind of an avant-garde politician, which fully applied to all pondering, is constant doubt, both on all inputs and considerations and on one's own pondering and pondering qualities, as repeatedly emphasized in this book. Involved are both a sense of fallibility and constant seeking of corrigibility. This hermeneutics of doubt should pervade the "atmosphere" of the entire mind, tacitly and explicitly.

Not skepticism and certainly not cynicism are recommended, but a constant "background melody" of doubt. It must be of due dosage, otherwise it causes undue dithering and even paralysis hindering essential decisiveness in making up the mind.

HIGH-QUALITY MIND

I avoid the term "wisdom," preferring instead to specify the required core qualities of pondering, and of the mind as a whole. The term "wisdom" is overloaded with various meanings and used differently in diverse context. Thus, speaking about the "wisdom" of an Asian sage is quite different from what I have in mind when considering avant-garde politicians.

Even relatively good definitions include ambiguities and tautologies. Typical is the following one: "Wisdom presupposes a passion for meaning, knowledge, and understanding, and also embraces such elements as discernment in complex matters, doing justice to many dimensions of reality, coping well with contingencies and difficulties, ethical responsibility, good judgment, combining theory and practice, and far-sighted decision making" (Ford 2013, 11). Inclusion of terms such as "discernment," "doing justice," "coping well," and "good judgment" begs the questions what is "wisdom," which assumes such traits, and what do they mean.

A more appropriate term is what Aristotle called "phronēsis," usually rendered in English as "practical wisdom," though I prefer the term "practical reasoning." Its main classical use to characterize Odyssey indicates "smartness" and "cunning," with meanings further mixed up by modern use of the term "smart" (Nye 2008).

Saying that an avant-garde politician should ponder in terms of "good practical reasoning" adds nothing, neither would reference to "wisdom," "sagacity," and so on be little more than slogans. Therefore, I avoid this terminology, discoursing instead on required qualities which add up to a "high-quality mind."

The qualities discussed in this and earlier chapters do not cover all of "high-quality pondering." Additional required qualities are presented in Chapters 15 and 16. And there is an important approach to improving pondering which is different from specifying required qualities, namely "debugging" in the sense of reducing pondering fallacies. This is taken up in the next chapter.

CHAPTER 14
DEBUGGING

INVERSE APPROACH

Given the human mind as it functions, a different and in essence inverse way to improve pondering is "debugging", in the sense of significantly reducing serious error propensities. Leaving aside cogitation errors of limited importance for the quality of pondering on complex issues, however interesting, which are discussed well in many publications (e.g., Kahneman 2011; Pohl, ed. 2012), I concentrate on 25 serious and widespread fallacies which are dangerous for composing humanity-craft, with additional ones presented in other chapters. All of them need careful diagnosis, maximal avoidance, and determined treatment by self-monitoring and openness to critical thinking, by oneself and others.

Some of them have already been mentioned, but need reiteration here for providing a coherent picture and implanting them in your mind.

TWENTY-FIVE CARDINAL FALLACIES

1) Exaggerated trust in "rationality"

This is not the place to engage in an extended philosophic discussion of the term "rationality" and its many misuses, especially by behavioral economists and public choice theorists, and even more so in public and also political discourse. Leaving aside the question whether "mathematics" in all its forms is at least in part a form of rational logics, for our purposes it is enough to present briefly five different meanings of the term, four of which are much too narrow for serving as a basis for pondering on complex issues, while the fifth "passes the buck" to the terms "reason."

The five main meanings can be summed up as follows: (1) Logical thinking in the strict sense of that term, usually according to classical rather than modern more loose logic. (2) Dealing with relations between means and ends, it being "rational" to pick the best means in terms of cost–benefit–risk from the available options. (3) Various choice models and procedures based on abstract models, such as theory of games or Bayesian inference for dealing with uncertainty, and other forms of probability calculus. (4) Being "reasonable" in the eyes of beholders, such as using magic if accepted culturally as valid. And (5) using "reason" as fully as possible, with the term "reason" usually being taken for granted and "as fully as possible" not being provided with clear meanings or criteria.

As already pointed out, all of the five meanings of rationality leave out of account values which pose goals for action and also constitute the implicit context of pondering, including the cultural infrastructure of the very term "rationality." Nor do they take up the essential roles of creativity and cultural stocks of knowledge in providing options from which choices must be made. Furthermore, usually ignores are the importance of intuition and other tacit processes in good pondering. Furthermore, forms of reasoning specific to different domains, such as aesthetics and law, are usually not considered as parts of "rationality."

"Rationality" in the first three meanings has its uses in pondering, including pinpointing clear "irrationality." But these are limited and secondary at most. The fourth meaning is subject to anthropological relativism and prima facie impressions. And the fifth meaning requires elaboration of what using of reason means and is therefore superfluous for consideration and upgrading of pondering, which can be better engaged in relying directly on the concept of "using reason," with "reason" including value judgment, creativity, selective use of intuition, and more.

Pertinent, among others, are the views of Pierre Bourdieu and Yaron Ezrahi. Bourdieu opposes accounts of practice "when, in the name of a narrow rationalism they consider irrational any action or representation which is not generated by the explicit posed reasons of an autonomous individual, fully conscious of his or her motivation" (Bourdieu 1998, viii). Ezrahi discusses what he calls "the fallacy of misplaced rationality," committed when one confines "one's approach to politics to the rational analysis of reasons, norms, or interests, while dismissing or ignoring imaginaries and other non-rational components of the fabric of politics" (Ezrahi 2012, 25). In my view both are valid criticism of exaggerated reliance on "rationality" in its usual meanings.

2) "Common sense," "pragmatism," "Occam's razor"

A dangerous set of fallacies in much of pondering, all the more misleading because supported by some philosophical, psychological, and political literature, includes misunderstanding and misuses of "common sense," "pragmatism," and "Occam's razor."

Concerning "common sense," a distinction must be made between two meanings of this term. One regards common sense as that "which is the sense of the in-common" (Badiou 2005, 19), covering widely accepted ways of thinking, images of the world, political imaginary, and so on, as historic and changing culture-dependent facts which make "political worlds" (Ezrahi 2012, 83-103). The second meaning regards "common sense" as an often recommended way of pondering.

Widely accepted opinions and views have to be taken into account as facts, which constrain pondering while also constituting targets for educational and imaginary-creating activities of avant-garde politicians. But here I am concerned with "common sense" in the second, prescriptive, meaning, rejecting it as a valid approach to pondering.

Dictionary definitions of "common sense" are either tautologies or void of contents. They range from "behaving sensibly" to acting in ways fitting the ordinary situations. However, the novel issues facing avant-garde politicians require "uncommon sense," which often deconstructs and debunks "common sense."

Pragmatism in its true meaning is an important philosophical approach, mainly developed by Charles Sanders Peirce, William James and John Dewey, and their modern followers. For our purposes, it can be summed up as emphasizing practical consequences as the main criterion of truth and validity of concepts and theories. This true meaning of pragmatism fits well with the requirements of humanity-craft composing which is consequentialists and praxis-directed.

Also very important is the already mentioned proposal of Pierce to add abduction to induction and deduction as a main "logical" (here, in the sense of "based on reason") way to arrive at conclusions. Abduction implies arriving at explanatory hypotheses, which are well based but not fully proven. It is of critical importance for pondering on nearly all issues dealt by avant-garde politicians, on which data are problematic and reliable theories are lacking. This applies with double force to novel issues; and, all the more so, to efforts to influence the future, on which by definition empirical material does not exist and theories based on the past often do not apply.

All this is completely different from the usual laudatory misuses of the term "pragmatic" for doing what is "practical," comes relatively easily, is politically convenient, and meets narrowly defined goals. Pragmatism in this common but misleading meaning is dangerous when applied to pondering on complex and novel issues which need systemic comprehension and root treatment.

More technical but important are wrong notions of "Occam's razor." This is a principle of thinking going back to the ideas of Franciscan friar William of Ockham, as expressed in his pronouncement "plurality must never be posited without necessity." Its main implication is to prefer simpler theories and explanations, if satisfactory, to more complex and multi-variable ones.

However, it is far from clear what is "simpler." What is simple for a trained mathematician is beyond understanding to the numeracy ignorant. Still, in the natural sciences Occam's razor has often, though not always, been used appropriately, though to call theories of evolution or quantum theories "simple" is not simple. However, in the social domains search for simple explanations and treatments is in most matters very misleading, because nearly all phenomena have multiple and complex causes and dynamics.

3) Planck effect

Max Planck, one of the founders of modern physics, made the following statement: "A new scientific truth does not triumph by convincing its opponents and making them see the light, but rather because its opponents eventually die, and a new generation grows up that is familiar with it" (Planck 1949, 33-34). This idea was developed by Thomas Kuhn, in his famous 1962 book *The Structure of Scientific Revolutions*, into the thesis that "paradigm shifts" in sciences occur with difficulties and after many efforts to accommodate new findings in older paradigms.

Planck's thesis, however doubtful for some parts of the sciences, is important for pondering by avant-garde politicians on issues involved in his extraordinary mission, which often require revolutionary paradigm shifts in understanding and coping. Therefore, the widespread conservative propensity of many minds, conscious and subconsciously alike, is a pernicious form of bondage by the past and malignant for pondering, which has to be overcome.

The observation by Planck also fully fits the frequent situations when avant-garde politicians face difficulties advancing their extraordinary mission before the demise or pushing aside of political leaders wedded to obsolete views.

4) Keynes' insight

It is hard to improve on a statement by John Maynard Keynes in his 1936 opus magnum *General Theory of Employment, Interest and Money*:

> ... the ideas of economists and political philosophers, both when they are right and when they are wrong, are more powerful than is commonly understood. Indeed the world is ruled by little else. Practical men, who believe themselves to be quite exempt from any intellectual influence, are usually the slaves of some defunct economist. Madmen in authority, who hear voices in the air, are distilling their frenzy from some academic scribbler of a few years back. I am sure that the power of vested interests is vastly exaggerated compared with the gradual encroachment of ideas. Not, indeed, immediately, but after a certain interval; for in the field of economic and political philosophy there are not many who are influenced by new theories after they are twenty-five or thirty years of age, so that the ideas which civil servants and politicians and even agitators apply to current events are not likely to be the newest. But, soon or late, it is ideas, not vested interests, which are dangerous for good or evil (Keynes 1965, 383).

As already postulated, the most extreme "doer" is inexorably bound to tacit theories in his mind on what makes the world go round, of which he is not aware, which he does not really understand, and which he is not able to subject to critical evaluation. Many of these theories are increasingly obsolete, because of the rapid and often radical changes in situations on which they were based.

Instead, theories on which important elements of pondering are based should be subjected to careful reexamination and often revised, with strenuous efforts to arrive at novel theories fitting radically new situations, even if initially as guesstimates or also "daring hypothesis". These are better than relying on obsolete theories, though they have to be used with much care.

Keynes, who had a lot of experience working on complex issues with political leaders, such as at the Versailles Peace Conference after World War One, expressed in essence the same view as Planck on the dependence of innovative thinking on a younger generation not committed to older views that have become obsolescence. This implies, inter alia, that the best years of an avant-garde politician are while being still relatively young. When becoming older, special personal efforts are needed to avoid misplaced allegiance to traditional reality images, theories, and policies. Therefore, whatever your age may be, and all the more so when you become older, surrounding yourself with a relatively young staff is a good idea.

These comments are subject to changing meanings of "young" and "old," as a result of constantly longer life expectancies, including high-quality years. But still they are in principle correct, with the border between "young" and "not so young" being probably somewhere around the age of 40 to 50, depending on the individual mental aging rates. But there are exceptions to these generalizations.

5) The Bed of Procrustes

This term, borrowed from Nassim Nicholas Taleb, presents an important idea: "We humans, facing limits of knowledge, and things we do not observe, the unseen and the unknown, resolve the tension by squeezing life and the world into crisp commoditized ideas, reductive categories, specific vocabularies, and prepackaged narratives…" (Taleb, 2010, xii; the following quotes are from this book). And "Because our minds need to reduce information, we are more likely to try to squeeze a phenomenon into the Procrustean bed of a crisp and know category (amputating the unknown)" (p.105), leading to what Taleb appropriately calls "epistemic arrogance….imagining the territory as fitting his map" (p. 106).

These are important insights on an insidious fallacy worthy of much attention, all the more so with humanity moving into an era of metamorphosis posing much that is unprecedented and also inconceivable.

6) Blindsight and agnosia

Blindsight is a neurological disease in which a person is perceptually blind to parts of the visual field, though his eyes see much more than his mind is aware off. This "mind-blindness" is closely related with agnosia, a disease in which a person can see the characteristics of an object but cannot recognize it or make sense of it. And integrative agnosia is the inability to put parts of which one is aware into a meaningful whole.

All imply inability to make sense of what is clearly happening, to combine dots into patterns, and to discern systems when knowing their components. These are major defects of pondering, to be reduced by cultivating broader and more divergent perspectives and deliberately trying to "see" and think in terms of wholes and systems.

7) Linear thinking and intuiting

Studies in the psychology of music deal with the expectations in our mind when hearing a melody. These tend to be linear, sudden jumps taking us by surprise—unless we know that the kind of music to which we listen is characterized by sudden changes, but even then they still surprise us.

This tendency to expect linearity seems to be inherent in much of the mind, being probably imprinted as a result of routine, including cyclic regularities and "normal" surprises, dominating much of life during the evolution of the human species. But pondering linearly has become an increasingly dangerous and insidious fallacy when applied to non-linear processes, all the more so in an era of metamorphosis. A direct consequence is the tendency to react to the failure of a policy with "more of the same," instead of recognizing that novel developments require non-linear responses.

8) Rashomon in action

The classical Japanese 1950 movie *Rashomon*, directed by Akira Kurosawa, shows the same events from the perspective of a number of participants who describe them very differently, each version being true in their minds, but none of them being "really true." This is the case of perception and memory of much of the past and contemporary events. Even if raw facts are clear, many different narratives and explanations are provided by different observers, participants, and historians.

Instead of drawing the correct conclusion that different narratives may be true and false to various and often unknowable degrees and act accordingly, many political leaders tend to select one version as "true," usually as a result of biases. This easily misdirects much of pondering. Required instead is awareness of ambiguity, uncertainty and the need to act on the basis of different versions of realities all of which are partly true and partly false, in often unknown measures.

9) Mistaken uses of history

Human beings are made by the past and depend on it for shaping their future. Not only is the human genome a product of evolution and our personal makeup largely shaped by individual and social history, but nearly all of our knowledge is based on the past. Therefore, the ways a mind learns from the past to understand the present and consider the future are critical for the quality of pondering. But correctly learning from the past is very difficult and human minds tend to use the past for imagining the future in much distorted ways.

Friedrich Wilhelm Nietzsche in his 1874 essay "On the Use and Abuse of History for Life" pointed out that we are selectively influenced by "monumental history" contrary to the needs of the future. But this is just one of the defects, to which must be added not knowing the past other than from superficial mass media, doubtful historic novels, and rudimentary memories from school days; focusing attention on what is most dramatic rather than on what is significant; giving undue weight to single events, including unusual ones; being too much influenced by necessarily narrow personal experiences; viewing past episodes as precedents rather than metaphors and analogs which often are irrelevant and also misleading; and drawing conclusions from history which fit one's interests and prejudices.

Learning from history is both necessary and unavoidable on conscious and subconscious levels of the mind, exerting much influence on pondering. But, being very error prone, this learning should not be left to spontaneous processes when important issues are at stake. Instead needed are explicit approaches, taken up in the next chapter.

10) Selective and biased evaluation of opinions

When hearing a discussion in which reputable participants express different views or reading documents presenting diverse opinions, listeners and readers tend to be more impressed by those which fit their own views and confirm their trust in what they thought before, or which are better presented, instead of taking fully into account the opposing arguments. This is known as "biased assimilation," closely related with what is called the "anchoring bias," with the mind tending to process and accept new information selectively—trusting more what supports initial thoughts and earlier presented or adopted positions. These misleading tendencies also apply to processing of experience.

Selective and biased evaluation of opinions is a serious fallacy ruining pondering, which is all the more dangerous in an epoch of metamorphosis. An overall stance of doubt as a main quality of the mind, together with deliberate seeking of contrary views and taking them seriously, are recommended countermeasures.

11) Wishful or terrified distortions

Leaving aside pathological states of the embodied mind, such as paranoia or extreme euphoria, wishful and terrified distortions are a prevalent propensity of "normal" pondering which ruins its quality. Sometimes wishful distortions serve as useful self-fulfilling prophesies, pushing peak efforts in situations which require radical action and in which there is not much to lose. But these are exceptions to the vast majority of issues where wishful thinking has damaging effects.

Less well known but not less significant are insidious effects of terrified or extremely fearful distortions. They produce incorrect images of reality and damage pondering and choice, such as causing panic decisions, action paralysis, or unjustified abandonment of important values.

A main way to avoid such distortions is to engage in pondering on serious issues in quality time and balanced mood, as already recommended. Critical decisions should not be made under the influence of strong feelings. If necessary, light tranquilizers taken in consultation with an experienced professional may help, especially in crisis situations.

12) Erroneous attribution

"Attribution theories" deal with the causes to which one attributes what happens, ranging from grand theories of everything to simple causal explanations of minor events. Their basis can be belief in magic and spirits or folk "wisdom", observation and experience, or scientific theories as far as understood and assimilated. They are fundamental to all pondering. Therefore, incorrect causal attributes ruin it.

Humans often rely on incorrect attributions when dealing with domains outside their professional expertise, and also in them. Especially insidious is simplistic thinking in terms of single deterministic chains of causes and effects. Not only is it necessary to distinguish between different types of "causes", as already proposed by Aristotle, such as necessary and sufficient ones, but many causal chains are probabilistic and, in social affairs and also some fields of science, contingent and partly random. Furthermore, with the exception of the artificial situations of controlled experiment, most of reality has multiple chains of diverse, multilevel, and interacting nets of causes and effects. And, worst of all, often causes are not known and also practically unknowable, without the pondering mind being aware of such ignorance.

Complex nets of causes and effects tend to overtax most minds. Mathematical models and computer programs can help, but can also mislead by oversimplification or by being taken too literary by unsophisticated users, including many professionals. Little wonder that much pondering on serious issues suffers from very dangerous attribution oversimplifications.

Strengthening the generalist-professionalism qualities of the minds of avant-garde politicians and selection of high-quality professional advisors, together with uncertainty sophistication and constant doubt, are the main ways of reducing the dangers of erroneous attribution.

13) Intolerance of ambiguity

Reality is ambiguous. Therefore, accepting ambiguity is essential for high-quality pondering, but does not come easily. Instead, most minds tend towards dichotomies, thinking and feeling in binary terms, "yes–no," "true–false," and so on, as well as other crude simplifications, driven in part by the need to make up one's mind, which is much easier with less ambiguity.

The history of logic is relevant. Classic logic as first developed by Aristotle is a formal system of valid inference and correct reasoning largely based on "true–false" categories. It continues in its Western version (different from some Asian ones) and legitimized simplistic binary thinking and intuiting, which seem to be in part programmed into our mind because of their usefulness during the evolutionary history of the human species. But it is a dangerous defect when applied to most of the issues increasingly challenging humanity.

Modern logic goes beyond the classical one, introducing categories expressing ambiguity in modal, temporal, and other types of logic. But these too are inadequate. And many scientists and professionals are not familiar with modern logic and nearly all political leaders never heard about it.

Many of the ways of pondering suggested in the preceding chapter help to adjust pondering to ambiguity. Literacy in modern logic can help and is not difficult to acquire by persons having the mind of an avant-garde politician.

14) "A rat in a maze"

Imagine a rat in a maze receiving a light electric shock. It rushes in different directions, getting increasingly agitated and then lethargic, unlikely to find the exit other than by chance. This is one of the defects of pondering under pressure, when the time is short and all options seem very bad.

 The result may be rushing into one of the bad options without innovative search, or dithering as discussed next, or escaping into groupthink, or abandoning a main goal and picking an easier one instead—all quite erroneous and sometimes disastrous. Innovativeness is the main therapy, as well as keeping the mind "cool" and making sure to ponder in quality time, all the more so when feeling that one is in an impasse.

15) Dithering

When there are good reasons to assume that an issue will become easier to handle in the future then delaying making up the mind is justified. But dithering and procrastination are serious defects when they are the result of value dilemmas, overloads, lethargy, political inconvenience, and other inappropriate tendencies of pondering on quandaries. An act of will is necessary to overcome this danger.

Dithering is especially prevalent in the face of long-term problems which get worse all the time but show no conspicuous symptoms in the short run, similar to a slowly growing cancer without immediate symptoms but sure to become much harder to treat if not excised promptly. Political leaders often prefer allocating scarce pondering resources to what seems pressing, even when this will increase future burdens and make successful coping less likely.

This propensity is especially harmful when delays in making up the mind are caused by harsh dilemmas, with an avant-garde politician himself being "a house divided against itself." But there is also a prevalent opposite error propensity of the mind to rush prematurely into making up one's mind, which will be discussed soon.

16) Dissonance reduction

But first dissonance reduction needs clarification. Leon Festinger developed the idea that the mind tries to reduce tensions caused by holding simultaneously conflicting "melodies," such as values, images, feelings, and so on. Such efforts cause quite a number of pondering defects, from which I select post-decisional dissonance reduction as a striking illustration. It goes back to the " Fox and the Grapes," fable of Aesop, with the fox declaring and making himself believe that the grapes beyond his reach are "sour."

In his book *When Prophecy Fails*, Festinger et al. (1956) present their study of a small sect of fundamentalist who were sure that the earth would end at a given day. When that time passed and nothing happened, nearly all of them believed that their God has decided not to destroy the earth thanks to the efforts of the sect.

Let me add an example from my experience. In a modernizing country a large dam was built for providing energy and irrigation. Because of inadequate geological studies, most of the water seeped into the ground. The senior political leader in charge of this expensive project explained to me that the dam was built to raise the level of ground water! My strong impression was that he indeed convinced himself that this was the real purpose of the dam, though the planning documents which I studied told a very different story.

This is the essence of dissonance reduction: You are sure that the cosmos changes rather that what you believed was wrong. Or, in more mundane cases, you adjust your bona fide image of your goals to what was achieved in fact, despite aiming at objectives that were not realized. This defect illustrates an overall error propensity of the mind which ruins much pondering, namely reading, remembering, and evaluating results of one's choices as successes, or as failures due to causes that could not be foreseen—as a part of the general need of most humans to try and "feel good" about themselves. This may be psychologically useful if not overdone, but prevents learning from mistakes by changing them mentally into illusions of successes.

Related is the widespread tendency of political leaders not to clarify goals, neither in public nor in their minds. This is both a deliberate stratagem and an instinctive way to prevent in advance dissonance, with all results instead being declared "a success." But this ruins pondering, spoils choices, and makes learning from mistakes impossible.

17) Decisionism and "Doism"

There are ideologies which support rush choices, because of trust in the excellence of mental flashes and the reliability of quick intuition of select leaders, as well as emphasis on "will" as contrasted with careful pondering and all its hesitations and doubts. "Decisionism" is the name given to it in German literature, before this approach was discredited by the history of the Nazi period. Related is a tendency, pushes in some cultures, to get on with "doing," without much energy and time "wasted" on "thinking." This can become a disastrous habit of "non-pondering" if not counteracted early and strongly.

Rushing into making up the mind before adequate pondering is also advocated by some popular literature on "gut feelings," and supported by unjustified feelings of infallibility prevalent among political leaders. These are prescriptions for failures. No "flow," strong feelings, "inspiration," and cultural–political pressures to "act" should be permitted to hinder pondering on complex issues, subject to real constraints.

18) Misplaced preference of a "golden mean."

The idea that some point between the two extremes is preferable is deeply ingrained in many cultures. But it applies to moral choices and virtues, not options. Thus, the virtue of courage according to classical Greek philosophy is in-between recklessness and cowardice. However, the idea of the golden mean is often misunderstood as an inherent advantage of compromises over clear-cut choices. This is convenient in political discourse when agreement is desired, and also inside the mind to reduce the necessity for tragic choices. But it is often a major pondering defect, as compromise options need evaluation anew. Being somewhere in-between more definite options does not assure that a compromise is substantively superior, the opposite being often the case.

19) Trusting in the magic of words

Magic believes in the power of incantations to shape realities is deeply rooted in human history and the human mind. It continues in the modern form of trusting that declarations, expressions of intensions, condemnations and so on have real effects on what is to come. As a result, much pondering efforts are wasted on formulations with careful selection of words which remain only declarations without any constitutive impacts.

20) Concentrating on what is easy to known

A well-known debate in research methodologies is reflected by the metaphoric question whether to look for a lost key where there is a lamp, or to try a random search in the dark places where it is more likely to have been dropped. Many researchers prefer the first option, seeking study subjects fitting well into easily available and widely accepted research methodologies, even when of trivial importance. This also fits many of the criteria of academic promotions, making what is bad into even worse. But most of the dramatic discoveries result from moving into the unknown, with all the associated risks.

Leaving aside the sciences, avant-garde politicians must not concentrate on pondering where there is a lamp, though many political leaders do so. Instead, pondering should be broad-gauged and seek good options wherever they may perhaps be found or created, before targeting sharply on making up the mind.

21) Following fashions

Fashions and their prevailing influence are not limited to what to wear and eat, what music to like, what physical features to find attractive, and so on—where they are harmless and perhaps somewhat useful for social cohesion, though they are a clear sign of the juvenile level of humanity. Fashions also have powerful influences on pondering, such as providing concept packages, theories, and readymade options which are "in fashion" in relevant communities, including political and also scientific and professional ones.

This causes much harm. Being in fashion does not certify validity and usefulness. And fashions cannot show the way to cope with rapidly emerging novel situations. Instead I suggest the following principle: The more fashionable concepts, theories, and opinions on complex issues are, the more in a period of metamorphosis should they be suspected of being wrong.

22) Relying on "miracles"

Philip II, the King of Spain, Portugal, and much more, sent in 1588 the Spanish Armada against England. His advisors were against it, warning him among other dangers that bad weather was expected. But he rejected their opinion and claimed that Heaven was sure to help his war against the infidel Queen Elizabeth I. As he put it on one of the many occasions when miracles were relied upon in Spain's strategic culture:

> If this were an unjust war one could indeed take this storm as a sign from
> Our Lord…but being as just as it is, one cannot believe that He will

disband it, but rather will grant it more favour than we could hope…I have dedicated this enterprise to God (Parker 2000, 107).

This reasoning was not unusual before what is called, somewhat misleadingly, the "enlightenment". It continues to shape choices, often taking the form of some kind of trust in "providentialism," which in substance is closely related to reliance on miracles. Quite some case studies, and also my experience at the highest levels of governments, clearly show that difficult issues are often coped with, after long discourse quite empty of deep understanding, by relying, at least implicitly, on some kind of *deus ex machina*, equivalent to a miracle, despite "modernity."

This applies all the more so to true believers of all types, and in particular religious fundamentalists. There is no use telling them that they are wrong also in terms of their faith and trying to prove it by quoting sophisticates theology. Unless you understand this serious fallacy of the mind of others you cannot comprehend much of past, current, and expected future reality, including so-called "crazy states" (Dror 1980).

23) Culturally biased reasoning

Unavoidably, ways of reasoning, including in so-called "hard sciences," are in part shaped by cultural imaginary, however partly corrected by reality testing. Policy pondering is especially susceptible to cultural biases introducing serious errors, as illustrated by differences between countries and cultures on sensitive bioscience issues important for humanity-craft (Jasanoff 2005), which have to be viewed in the context of broader policy-cultural differences (e.g., Kagan 2004). Raison d'humanité pondering requires unitary global policies on critical issues, subject to the subsidiarity principle. Therefore, pondering by avant-garde politicians and their staffs must, as far as humanly possible, arrive at "global culture" reasoning which is less constrained than presently practiced local public reasoning (Jasanoff 2013).

24) Forgetting Murphy's Law as expanded

As well known, Murphy's Law, as poignantly formulated, states that "if anything can go wrong, it will" (Bloch, Arthur 2003, 1). I suggest an addition, which applies with particular force to pondering on humanity-craft issues in an epoch of metamorphosis: "And many things that are regarded as fail-save which supposedly cannot go wrong— also go wrong, disappointing all expectations."

This expanded version is equivalent to postulating: "Everything can and much is very likely to go wrong," as a necessary pondering and action assumption which is very realistic in an epoch of metamorphosis. It is of profound importance as a counterweight to overdoses of optimism and inadequate gearing for failures. This fallacy easily infects also avant-garde politicians, the strong commitment of whom to their missions goes necessarily together with quite some enthusiasm, which easily produces optimism—necessary and beneficial in limited portions, but dangerous if not strictly limited and confined.

25) "Betrayal"

I would be guilty of gross negligence and also of being an accessory to sin if I would not conclude the list of pondering fallacies, however incomplete, with what cannot be called otherwise than one of the forms of "betrayal" of the missions. I refer to putting personal political interests above other considerations.

This is not to deny the necessity to take into explicit though often hidden account power considerations as far as essential for the missions as a whole, as discussed in Chapter 17. But compromising main parts of the extraordinary mission by following the adage "politics is the art of the possible," and even more so in order to advance one's personal ambitions and goals, is nothing less than betrayal of trust. Instead, the correct way of pondering is to consider issues first on their substantive merits and then to add political feasibility and essential power considerations as more or less elastic constraints.

COPING

These and additional fallacies add up to quite a depressing picture of the barriers and hindrances to high-quality pondering. Little wonder that "wisdom" has not built a strong house in the minds of the vast majority of political leaders (and also many academics and publics at large).

However, the picture must be balanced by emphasizing the amazing abilities of the human mind, including handling high levels of complexity. To do so, there is no need for a "science of complexity," however helpful in some limited ways. Nor do I have to rely on the often given example of "primitive" tribes managing very well in complex environments, such as Amazonia and the Papua-New Guinea rain-forests. The most striking proof of the high qualities of the human mind in managing complexity is the natural ease with which young children acquire language skills far beyond super computers. And many humans are able to acquire fluency and the ability to think in a number of languages and move freely between them.

One striking illustration, which I ran into while doing a student internship at the United Nations Headquarters in New York studying UN decision making patters, was a simultaneous translator who translated, or to use a better term "transculturated", a quote from Shakespeare in English into a Russian quote from Pushkin having the same mood and associations, more so than any rendering of Shakespeare in one of the

Russian translations. This is the human mind at its best, however limited and error-prone, handling easily and quickly some hyper-complex tasks.

There are significant differences between minds in qualities of pondering. But in principle the human mind, as based in one way or another on the brain, has many high-performance qualities and can develop and acquire some more, though there is an unknown and perhaps elastic ceiling. Therefore, improving the core qualities of pondering as essential for an avant-garde politician is not a real "mission impossible," though it is not easy.

A "perfect mind" engaging, inter alia, in "perfect" pondering is beyond the maximum potential of humans, in addition to the very idea of a "perfect human mind" being beyond human minds. But higher qualities of some main processes of the mind, including pondering, can be achieved, in part by debugging and mainly by deliberate efforts to approximate preferable models, as detailed in preceding and following chapters.

CHAPTER 15
SWERVING HISTORY

SWITCHING TRAJECTORIES

The possibility of both very desirable and totally dismal alternative futures, including termination of the human species, necessitates switching of the trajectories of history. The present trajectory makes it likely that novel human capacities to impact strongly on their futures will be used, at least in part, more for the worse, up to endangering the future of the human species. Therefore, needed is swerving of significant parts of the processes of history, so as to try and prevent history, as influence by humans, proceeding in the fashion of a "hit-and-run" driver abandoning by the side a killed humanity.

The rationale, reasoning, and "logic" of swerving historic processes making the future require exploration of alternative possible futures, evaluation of their desirability or undesirability, identification of main variables shaping their realization likelihood, selecting from those variables policy instruments that can be used to reduce the likelihood of undesired futures and increase the likelihood of desired futures; and integrating the selected policy instruments into grand-policies and their derivatives. All this is subject to bounded thick uncertainty and surprise events, up to unconceivable ones, which are sure to occur.

Therefore, trying to influence the trajectory of history is a demanding and in part speculative endeavor constituting inherently a fuzzy gamble. Because the stakes are often high, up to the very survival of the human species, this is a risky activity, but an essential one which is at the core of the extraordinary mission of avant-garde politicians, separating them from the vast majority of mainstream political leaders.

Not trying to swerve future history is also a choice, whether deliberate or by default. But this is probably one of the worst options, because of the serious dangers posed by letting critical historic trajectories continue more or less on trajectories posing serious dangers to humanity, together with non-utilization of great opportunities.

DIFFICULTIES

Comprehension of the processes shaping the future is always limited. They often differ from those which shaped the past and include much that is contingent and indeterminate. Their modality is some combination between necessity, possibility, likelihood, chance, and choice. Therefore, it is not surprising that many efforts to influence the future fail, with unanticipated results, whether desirable or miserable, often overriding anticipated and desired ones.

All historic developments are the results of a multitude of causes, which in turn are the result of further causes, permitting at best only vague understanding of major transformations. Thus, theories on the causes of the scientific and industrial revolutions in the West include impacts of the bubonic plague, reformation and counterreformation, reawakened inheritance from classical Greek and Rome, stimulations by warfare and commerce, and so on. Thus, even leaving aside the search for the causes behind these causes and the significant roles of not really understood chance and personal free choices, still the coming of the scientific and industrial revolution in the West is far from being fully understood. All the more so it is difficult and in part impossible to map in advance the main variables shaping the future, which themselves are in flux.

Little wonder that most revolutions had results very different from the intentions of their instigators. Therefore, there are advantages in keeping efforts to influence future history limited. But this is impossible, or useless, or dangerous when humans are very dissatisfied with their situation and want to change it significantly, or when likely alternative futures include ominous ones, or when it seems that very desirable futures are within reach. All these conditions prevail in the period of metamorphosis.

History does provide examples of significant successes of humanity in bringing about desirable futures which would not have realized without deliberate choices and efforts, in part led by proto-avant-garde politicians. To take recent examples, these include the establishment and thriving of Singapore and the State of Israel, setting up of the European Union, reforms in China, and substantive improvements of the health, education, and welfare of most of humanity. But counterexamples abound, such as the First World War. Even more disturbing and instructive are the failures of many efforts to help some underdeveloped countries, despite the investment of large material resources and quite some high-quality thinking. These show that successful redirecting of future-shaping historic processes is possible, but failures come frequently and easily.

Swerving history is one of the most ambitious, and also risky, efforts of humanity. As well put in a letter by an insightful civic leader in Bismarck's time to a newly appointed minister of war "A piece of history has been entrusted to your hands" (Steinberg, 2011, 158). However the survival and species changing inhibition imperatives and, to a somewhat lesser but still large extent the thriving imperative, require radical changes in major historic processes. Otherwise bad futures are very likely, disastrous futures are quite possible, and great opportunities to thrive may be missed or at least unduly delayed with high costs.

The only this-worldly counterargument, other than trusting "history" which is a kind of magic belief, is that more or less spontaneous processes of a variety of social agencies, such as free markets, scientific communities, Agora-type improved mass democratic processes, and aggregates of individual choices, are very likely to produce desirable futures without the serious risks of deliberate future-shaping attempts by governments and political leaders. But, while such processes did in part work in the past, though at very high costs, they are clearly inadequate for coping with the emerging dangers and opportunities posed largely by likely misuses of science and technology.

A second stronger counterargument claims that letting politicians try to shape the future is likely to cause more damage than bring benefits. This is largely true if we assume the historic and contemporary qualities of politicians will continue to characterize future political leaders. But if this will be the case, humanity may well be doomed, or at least condemned to serious catastrophes. Therefore, returning to the leitmotif of this book, essential is a new genre of avant-garde politicians equipped to influence the trajectories of history for the better. This is not assured, failsafe or foolproof, but all other options are even more risky.

APPROPRIATE RATIOCINATION

The required train of thought for swerving history, and with adjustments also lesser attempts to influence the future trajectory of historic process, seems in the abstract straightforward. As indicated above but worthy repetition: They include mapping of alternative futures with the help of outlook approaches; evaluating them in terms of desirability or danger; identifying the main variable driving the future, with the help of appropriate studies and theories; selection of policy instruments which include future-shaping variables that are susceptible to some human control; and combining them into humanity-craft grand-policies. But all of this is very demanding and in part beyond present human knowledge and abilities.

Essential is at least construction of some kinds of models of historic processes including as many as possible of the components above, in discourse, prose, computer languages, and—most importantly—in the mind. But many factors can at best be known only as estimates and guesstimates, if at all; quite some known unknown have to be taken into account; preferences for desired futures are subject to disagreements and value changes; new drivers of the future are sure to emerge, such as supplied by science and technology; surprises are certain to occur, including inconceivable ones; and the relations between causes and effects are tenuous and contingent with random effects playing an important but unforeseeable role, making all models – explicit and tacit – doubtful, and grand-policies necessary based on them into fuzzy and often quite wild gambles for high stakes.

The need to take into account political factors, interest networks, cultural imaginaries, and resource scarcities further adds to complexities. Therefore, the process of pondering and making up the mind on swerving history is not "linear," but full of twists and turns. Nor is all of it explicit. But it can and should be largely systematic, while facilitating and seeking creative leaps.

In more technical language, the process should be open-ended, tentative, highly heuristic (which is the opposite of "algorithmic," including a lot of human discretion and hermeneutics that cannot be reduced to formulas or formal processes providing answers, or proving that no answer exists), partly intuitive and tacit, semi-structured, iterative, seeking creative options, and distinguished by steep learning curves. If carefully done, this is pondering on influencing future history at a high level of quality—as mandatory for avant-garde politicians. The maximum achievable quality is limited, but can be much higher than the usual future-impacting choices of the vast majority of the breeds of leaders who still dominate politics or various spontaneous social processes.

THESES ON HISTORY

To engage in swerving of history avant-garde politicians require a lot of high-quality "thinking-intuiting-in-history," including overall good comprehension, explicit and tacit, of the non-linear, underdetermined, and contingent rapidly changing dynamics of history and of its drivers and their extreme forms in an era of metamorphosis. To provide inkling of what is needed let me briefly present, following in the footsteps of Walter Benjamin though differently in contents, a set of selected main tentative theses on history relevant for the extraordinary mission of avant-garde politicians. But, as a tone-setter, I start with Walter Benjamin's thesis on the philosophy of history number XVIII :

> 'In relation to the history of organic life on Earth,' notes a recent biologist, 'the miserable fifty millennia of Homo sapiens represent something like the last two seconds of a twenty-four hour day. The entire history of civilized humanity would, on this scale, take up only one fifth of the last second of the last hour.' The here-and-now, which as the model of messianic time summarizes the entire history of humanity into a monstrous abbreviation, coincides to a hair with the figure, which the history of humanity makes in the universe (Benjamin 1974).

The set of theses that I suggest serve to illustrate what is involved in thinking-in-history as the basis for pondering on swerving historic processes. They also sum up some main ideas already presented and serve as a corridor into the following chapter. Here they are:

1. Knowing and understanding the past is difficult. "Facts" are infinite, so that only a selection from them, which is unavoidably biased by interests, cultures, theoretic assumptions, values, preconceptions, imaginaries, and availability, can be considered. And, even when all pertinent facts are known, as they never are, they are often ambiguous and the narratives which they form are always open to alternative compositions and interpretations, depending on personal ways of thinking and professional views and fashions. Still, knowing and understanding the past as far as possible is essential for comprehending humanity and present realities, however partially, and for thinking on alternative futures. But the principles of doubt and regarding all knowledge and understanding as-if and in part imaginary fully apply.

2. The question of whether historic processes known from the past are in part regular and thus permit generalization and formulation of theories of history is in debate. It seems that the answer is partly positive, on condition that theories on historic processes are contingent, limited to explicated domains, partly open, dependent on contexts, provisional, and viewed as doubtful.

3. Completely different is the discourse on the future, which cannot be "researched." As many historic processes are more contingent than deterministic, and as they change non-linearly, in part turbulently, and also somewhat chaotically, outlook is doubtful even if based on a very good understanding of the past, which usually is not available, and on good use of available outlook approaches, which is difficult. Still, the past is the basis of all outlooks, with the partial and debatable exception of imagination and foresight intuition. Therefore, knowledge and understanding of the past in terms permitting construction of at least somewhat plausible alternative futures and mapping of their drivers are essential for all serious endeavors to influence the future.

4. Philosophies of history differ very much from each other. A materialistic philosophy of history leads to very different conclusions than, for instance, Hegel's views on the "cunning of history," or the "end of history" views of Yoshihiro Francis Fukuyama, or religious views on the timing of the Day of Judgment and the "end of time." Political leaders who speak about "being on the right side of history," as if somehow they received insights into the deep secrets of historic processes, fool themselves that they know the unknowable or fool their publics, or both.

5. Broad theories of historic processes, such as on "rise and decline," are more enlightening than philosophies of history and provide bits for constructing models of historic processes, which however rudimentary and doubtful are essential for reason-based efforts to try and impact on the future for better in terms of values as changing with time. However all such models are fragmentary, culturally biases, and in between estimates, guesstimates, and speculations, to be regarded as provisional and in need of constant improvement and much doubt.

6. The anatomic and then cultural evolution of humanity passed through a number of transitions, all of which, after overcoming temporary setbacks, increased capacities to utilize nature and advance demographic, economic, social, and cultural development, while also impacting on the physical environment. The control of fire was, after the making of stone tools, probably the most important transition antecedent to the emergence of Homo sapiens. Ancient humans discovered fire more than a million years ago and sporadic uses of fire seem to have started by Homo Erectus more than 400 thousand years ago, with clear evidence of a much-used campfire used for cooking meat about 300 thousand years age being discovered recently in the Qesem Caves in Israel. Widespread controlled use of fire was probably achieved about 125,000 years ago.

7. Thanks to such achievement, Homo sapiens caused significant changes in its environments, which in turn changed human behavior, such as enabling, motivating, and also forcing migration into new territories and seeking of new food sources. Parts of the impacts, such as killing of animals needed for food, are aptly expressed in the term "future eaters" (Flannery 2002), a term that applies to parts of contemporary human practices.

8. Human development is largely shaped by cumulative cultural learning, stimulated by exchange of innovation between different societies, increasingly globally so. However, core innate features of humanity, as built into the genome, are mainly stable, though many of them are propensities and potentials realized in culturally shaped ways and also to an unknown but substantive extent by free will.

9. The brain is in many respects plastic and developing, subject to stable and in part rigid features. Consciousness and the mind are somehow embodied in the brain, but their nature and relationships with the brain are in debate and not really understood. Activities do influence brain and mind processes and result in measurable changes. But there surely are limits to the maximum capacities of the brain as presently constituted, though these are not known. It is an open question that cannot be answered whether maximum human brain capacities, with or without enhancement by human interventions, are sufficient for assuring a long-term future for the human species or not.

10. There are some differences between the brains of males and females. Throughout history they fulfilled different social roles and had different status in all societies, at least in part related to the child bearing tasks of women. Women were usually regarded as inferior in various respects. However, all this does not imply overall mental superiority or inferiority of either gender. Long-term results of increasing gender equality as a norm and at least partly of social and family practices are unknown.

11. Large-scale natural disasters, in part augmented or contained by human action, continue to be significant. Recent examples include the influenza pandemic of 1918–1919, and the 2009 Swine Flu scare. But, with the very low probability exception of a large body hitting earth and exterminating large parts of all advanced life forms, as happened in the past and as demonstrated by the 1994 comet hit on Jupiter which could have devastated earth if hitting it, or some geological mega-catastrophe such as a huge super-volcano eruption

or earthquake, extinction of humanity by natural disasters is very unlikely. Even a new mass-killing natural epidemic would spare sufficient humans to repopulate the earth. But the possibilities of extinction of humanity or large parts of it by human action, on purpose or accidentally, directly or indirectly, are becoming increasingly real and perhaps also more likely.

12. Mass education, public health services, increased social mobility and so on have changed much of human behavior. But core attributes seem stable. All deliberate efforts to bring about a "new human," by changes in social institutions, intense and novel forms of education, and also authoritarian means, failed. The USSR is a prime example. However science and technology is likely to supply tools that can change basic features of human beings. Results are inconceivable.

13. Historic processes are contingent, changing in part nonlinearly, and shaped by a fusion between linear determinism, probabilistic determinism, underdetermined possibilities, bounded random, "wild random" mutations, and phase leaps—together with human choice, which in turn is shaped by a similar variety of factors with the addition of an unclear measure of free will.

14. Present and foreseeable historic processes tend to be nonlinear and include mutations and radical transformations, largely due to human action and especially science and technology. These add up in an "era of metamorphosis."

15. Ongoing metamorphosis, peak creativity in science and technology, and unpredictable but possible major value innovations serve as main drivers of the future. They are likely to produce radically novel alternative futures, full with dangers as well as opportunities and leading towards inconceivability, including perhaps a Second Axial Age.

16. But there are many invariables which change very slowly, including core features of humanity imprinted by long evolutionary processes. Many social institutions, values, and deep cultural features also change slowly, though acceleration of transformations is likely. Such relative stabilities provide boundaries to metamorphosis, limit "chaos," and serve as bases for relative plausible outlooks which, in turn, enable deliberate human efforts to influence historic processes and impact on the future, though results will usually at least in part be different from intensions.

17. As historic processes have quite a momentum, human efforts to shift their directions require interventions achieving a critical mass sufficient for overcoming the momentum. But sometimes some aspects of historic processes of much importance to humanity become more elastic, such as following crises and catastrophes, reducing the intervention mass needed for changing their trajectory.

18. There is a debate on whether one can discern in history "progress," in terms of presently accepted values and morality. Clearly, there is some such process, such as in material qualities of life and human rights. But there is no reason to assume that "progress" in our terms is deterministically built into the processes of history. Rather, values should be expected to change radically, as they did throughout history, but there is no way to foresee their future contents.

19. Tool making has accompanied the human species from its very beginning. There has been constant advance in tool making, fully justifying calling the human species as in part Homo Faber, "toolmaker man". This process developed in spurs till the emergence of modern science and technology, reaching an unprecedented rate since the nineteenth century. It continues to accelerate. Cultural learning passed on such knowledge to future generations.

20. Consequently, human capacities to utilize, change and dominate nature have increased throughout human history, reaching peaks in the present epoch and sure to increase further in leaps and bounds thanks to science and technology. Overall, the increases in human capacities to impact on nature have been an advantage for the species, but this seems to change for the worse.

21. Modes of production have been closely related to tools. They exert much influence on societies and culture, but are in turn shaped by them. However important, they do not dominate cultures, societies, and historic processes for long.

22. Keeping records has been critical in the cultural evolution of humanity, enabling efficient interaction and diffusion of information, and passing on effectively cultural innovations from generation to generation. Writings, printing, computers, and electronic networks, such as the Internet and its changing modalities and proliferating uses, change some human realities dramatically. This process is continuing at an accelerating speed, with unknowable consequences.

23. Increasing populations accompany advances in tools, reaching unprecedented dimensions, accompanied by longer life expectancy, since the nineteenth century. The total number of humans that have ever lived has been estimated to be 110 billion. Approximately 7.2 billion, that is about 6% of all those people were alive in 2013.. The time spans needed since the middle of the twentieth century for global population to grow by one billion are becoming shorter, as a result of advancement in medicine and living standards. Concerning the future, United Nations projections in 2013 estimated the present global population to be about 7.2 billion, reaching 8.1 billion in 2025, and to increase to 9.6 billion in 2050 and 10.9 billion by 2100 (UN, Department of Economic and Social Affairs 2013, 1). The unreliability of demographic projections more than 10–15 years ahead throws doubt on such predictions. Still, such outlooks raise concerns on the carrying capacity of the earth, but it may well be radically enhanced by science and technology, up to geoengineering and molecular engineering.

24. Throughout history all knowledge and tools have been used for warfare and mass killing, some more and some less so in different periods. Given the increasing killing capacity of instruments supplied by science and technology, mass killings are to be expected, which may reach scales endangering large parts of humanity and perhaps the existence of the species. Only revolutionary changes in human institutions can change this mega-trend. Spontaneous cultural processes cannot be relied upon to do this on their own. Claims that there is a clear trend for the better may in part be well founded in some types of statistical data, but are far from fully reflecting realities and even less so can they indicate reliably what is likely to come.

25. There have been many rises and declines of civilizations and hegemonic powers. But some significant civilizations, with all their differences, have a relatively continuous history of more than 2000 years, with transformations, such as the Chinese, Iranian, and Jewish. Further rises and declines and changes in hegemony are sure to come, with Asian civilizations becoming increasingly important and probably dominant.

26. It is important to distinguish between the decline resulting in the disappearance of a major actor from history, as in the cases of Meso-American, American-Indian, and some African civilizations and states, and decline which brings about metamorphosis into a difference social structure with a viability of its own. The British and Dutch empires declined and disappeared, but the United Kingdom and The Netherlands are successful states.

27. The role of catastrophes in history raises interesting issues of much significance for the future. The most striking case within modern human history is the bubonic plague pandemic peaking in Europe and beyond in the years 1348 to 1350, known as "Black Death." According to relatively reliable estimates, about half of the European population was wiped out within four years. But recovery was relatively swift, with the availability of land and scarcity of labor benefiting parts of the survivors and their descendants, trust in superstitions and traditional medicine being undermined, and openness to new ideas increasing. Applied to the future of humanity, the species may survive major catastrophes and mass killings, though at very high costs in human suffering and with unpredictable consequences for the post-catastrophe future of humanity.

28. Transcendental and also magical beliefs and myths as well as changing worldviews and other imaginaries have accompanied humans from as early as evidence is available, and probably before. Related tribalism, fundamentalism, and fanaticism have been a main feature and driving force of history, for better and worth. They are sure to influence the future significantly, but may in part cause much damage up to endangering humanity. Therefore they require restrains.

29. Slavery in various forms was accepted as "obvious" till the eighteenth and nineteenth century, with its abolition in most of the world illustrating radical transformations in values. There is no reason to assume that values presently accepted as "obvious" and also "eternal" will not undergo transformation in an unknown future and in unknowable directions. On the contrary, the leap into a new epoch driven by science and technology, combined with globalization and other radically novel features, is likely to require and bring about radical changes in at least some major values.

30. In some cases there is a clear causal relationship between technological innovation and value changes, such as the impact of steam engines on the abolition of slavery. But often value changes, including radical belief system innovations, seem to be semi-autonomous phenomena, facilitated by social processes and individual creators, but not well understood. The amazingly rapid rise of Islam till temporarily contained and in part subjugated by the Christian West, and now rising again, is a striking example.

31. There have been periods of radical transformation in human consciousness, self-understanding, and belief systems. The most pronounced within known history is the so-called Axial Age, from about 600 to 200 CE, which is not fully explained. No signs of such a radical transformation can be identified in now-time. Future radical transformations may well produce a Second Axial Age with unknowable and also inconceivable features. But this is a speculation and at most a conjecture, not an outlook.

32. Greed, sexual aggression, envy, hostility, harsh competition, and violence accompany all of human history, with variations and ups and down. Solidarity, cooperation, empathy, and solidarity also accompany humanity all along its history. But they only seldom prevented for long large amounts of hostility and violence.

33. All human groups and societies have power structures and other forms of stratification, formal and informal, with superiors and inferiors. They can be more hierarchical or flat, but the higher up always receive more and those down below are usually exploited and neglected. Higher or lower positions are reached or allocated according to a variable mixture between ascription, merit, and "luck."

34. Leaders are a permanent feature of all human societies throughout history, with a few of their more elementary features shared with higher apes. Their selection and roles vary, but they always enjoy privileges and exert influence on their societies and its development. In some cases they serve as significant drivers of the future. But the quality of most leaders throughout history has been inadequate and toxic leaders abound. Given the increasing capability of humans to impact on the future, leaders, especially senior political ones, are sure to become more important drivers of the future, by action or non-action, for better or worse. Therefore improvement of their moral and cognitive quality is essential for the future of humanity including its survival.

35. Benevolence, compassion, and cooperation also characterize all of human history. But they were often confined to in-groups and tribes, in a broad sense of that term. Also, mass killings and subjugations were often done for the sake of "higher values" and ideologies sincerely accepted by the perpetuators of barbarism. This continues on smaller scales, but is likely to become more dangerous because of innovative and more effective mass-killing technologies which may be easily available.

36. For nearly all of human history wars and other bloody conflicts persisted, though moving between locations and taking different forms. There is no convincing reason to hope that they will disappear on their own or thanks to some spontaneous universal social and cultural processes.

37. Since the emergence of large and complex societies, lengthy periods of relative peace required hegemonic power structure and enforcement. Pax Romana is a prime example. Their lessons are relevant for the future.

38. Artistic creativity, with or without transcendental meanings, accompanies humanity for 40 thousand years and perhaps more, taking multiple forms. For at least the last three to four thousand years no qualitative progress can be discerned, though artistic creativity moves through stages. The same is true for literary creativity.

39. Human interaction and interdependence moved through periods of more and less intensity. But technologies make a big difference, with modern transportation and communication networks resulting in unprecedented degrees of multi-dimensional globalization the implications of which are just in the making. But geography, including for instance climate, access to the sea and distribution of important natural resources, continues to be an important factor, though less so than in the past and in other ways. Also, humanity is changing the very nature of "space," by creating cyberspace and moving beyond the earth.

40. No single factor drove history or dominated it in the past. Thus, in different periods and regions, means of production, values and ideologies, demography, climate, technology, warfare, elites, and leaders played a major role—always in a mix and with intense interactions.

41. The drivers of history are undergoing another transformation, with science and technology clearly being the dominant one. Science and technology are largely self-driven. Government policies and economic interests exert significant influence, but are themselves largely influenced by science and technology findings, elites, and establishments, which follow a dynamic of their own—the principle of which is "the more the better." This can in part be regarded metaphorically as the Sorcerer's Apprentice who lost control over his own powers, the Genie out of the bottle, and the Golem on his own.

42. The Annales School of history, as developed by Fernand Braudel and his followers, claimed that long-term history is beyond the influence of conscious actors, including revolutionaries. Instead relatively stable structures, both mental and environmental, determine the long-term course of events. This view was always partly exaggerated, with deliberate social action resulting sometimes in macro-historic consequences, however often unintended. It is increasingly and conspicuously false in our epoch, because of the rapidly growing impact potential of human actors on macro-history thanks to the instruments supplied by science and technology.

43. An illustration of major transformation very likely to come relatively soon, which can be predicted with high confidence, is a dramatic increase in leisure time of increasing parts of humanity, together with "unemployment" in the old sense, thanks to robotics, artificial intelligence, nano-technological 3M printing, and other human labor substituting devices. Assuring large-scale desirable uses of vastly increasing leisure time, while preventing dangerous misuses, is one of the major challenges facing humanity, though not the most dangerous one.

44. Most ominous of all is the emergence of human capabilities to terminate its existence as a species, or at least to bring about the extermination of large parts of humanity, by accident, neglect, or on purpose. Not less vexing, though differently so, are emerging capabilities to change the basic nature of human beings, as well as perhaps create life. These possibilities are completely unprecedented and constitute a total turning point in the evolution of humanity—for which nothing in history prepares us.

45. Therefore, it is very likely that a decisive global regime with a monopoly on mass-killing instruments is essential for preventing large-scale slaughters and assuring the survival of humanity. It is also required for controlling very disruptive technologies and in particular radical "human enhancement" which is sure to become more feasible thanks to science and technology.

46. Even more awesome is the likelihood of synthesizing life, first in the forms of cells that can replicate and evolve, but progressing to more complex self-evolving creatures. If successful, such endeavor will in some respects raise humanity to the level of a Creator, doing deliberately what happened somehow on the earth long ago. It is hard to image more total a transformation of humanity than acquiring the capacity to destroy itself, change its basic features, and create new forms of live. The only exception would be contact with extra-terrestrial sentinel beings, but this is extremely unlikely in the foreseeable future and perhaps for all of the lifespan of humanity, however long. But should this occur the implications are inconceivable.

47. All these and other theses concerning the future are conjectural, with presently inconceivable events and processes changing the trajectories of history being possible and also likely. Breakthroughs in space travel and a Second Axial Age changing human self-understanding are partly imaginable examples, the really inconceivable being by definition beyond available concept packages and mapping abilities, and probably beyond all but peak imagination.

DRIVER OF THE FUTURE: SCIENCE

Science is at present and in the foreseeable future one of the two main and most radical drivers of the future, the second being values. Science and technology are usually bundled together, all the more so because of some overlaps and partly open borders between them. But the deep and most critical driver is science, which serves as the basis of technologies and tools, however innovative the latter are also on their own. This is new in the history of humanity. Tool invention and uses were antecedents to the appearance of Homo sapiens, but science in the full sense of that term is very recent. It constitutes the modern tree of knowledge, bearing many fruits that are both nourishing and poisonous, depending on how they are used. It is also Prometheus unbound, giving humanity many forms of "fire," which can provide nourishing heat or burn to ashes Homo sapiens.

Physics and biology, as in part converging, are the basic sciences serving as the most important drivers of the future, together with sciences of materials and a combination between artificial intelligence studies and neurosciences. Synthetic biology and robots with artificial intelligence, together with nanotechnologies, will bring about radical transformations, in part foreseeable in outlines and in part inconceivable. However, they are of multiple and also contradictory usage, providing humanity with the capacity to terminate itself, change the features of being "human," reach peaks of pluralistic thriving, and also to transform worldviews if successful in synthesizing living organisms, enhancing substantively the intelligence of some animals, or producing "really intelligent" machines.

It is troubling that quite a number of books and articles preview in detail visions of all the blessings of future science and technology, while being quite sanguine in discussing the dangers, trusting human thought, values, and science to provide antidotes. Thus, the best seller by Michio Kaku, *Physics of the Future* (Kaku 2012), does not consider adequately the dangerous and perhaps fatal possible misuses of the new technologies that he predicts. And the few serious publications which do recognize fatal dangers, such as George Church and Ed Regis, *Regenesis: How Synthetic Biology Will Reinvent Nature and Ourselves* (Church and Regis 2012), put their trust in relatively mild countermeasures sure to fail. The really essential countermeasures, with all their partial harshness, such as globally rigorously enforced regulations, prohibitions, surveillance, and enforcement of limitations on science and technology and their products, are recognized only be very few authors, such as the already mentioned book by Robert L. Heilbroner (1991).

The central importance of science and technology in driving the future requires from avant-garde politicians, and indeed from all concerned about the future, to be literate in science and technology, their major trends, and impacts. At a minimum, they should be able to understand most articles in periodicals such as *Scientific American* and *Scientific American Mind* and be able to comment intelligently on their implications for humanity and its future. The fact that the vast majority of contemporary political leaders surely fail this not very stringent test is one of the manifestations of their inadequacy.

DRIVER OF THE FUTURE: VALUES

Values join science as main drivers of the future, but is an even more complex and in part enigmatic one. Value dynamics is not really understood. But some social conditions which breed ferocious fanaticism are known and their likely proliferation in an era of metamorphosis and its unavoidable transition crises can in principle be quite reliably predicted, though many of the specific instances and much of their contents cannot be foreseen and may in part be very surprising and also inconceivable.

The unanticipated results of the Krakatoa catastrophe on August 27, 1883, provide an interesting example. As a consequence of the catastrophe "not a few of these unhappy, dispossessed, and traumatized people eventually looked to…Mecca… This was a political and religious consequence of the disaster…that was to have the most profound and longest-lasting fallout, for the Indies, for Europa, and beyond" (Winchester 2005, 321).

Despite the opaqueness of value dynamics, the overall likelihood of belief systems serving as a main driver of the future should not be difficult to understand, having many historic precedents and contemporary examples. This also applies to the dangers posed by fanatic beliefs, all the more so when led by armed prophets and equipped with emerging mass-killing instruments. But many Western political leaders have great difficulties in overcoming optimistic assumptions on "progress" as understood by them and do not comprehend very different "others." Coping with ferocious fanaticism armed with products of science and technology will be a daunting challenge facing humanity, and avant-garde politicians in particular, closely associated and often merging with the need for strictly regulating science and technology and its products as well as dangerous true believers.

There are other important drivers of the future, such as cyclic climate changes independent from human action, natural calamities, demography, and more. Deliberate impacting on the future requires as full understanding of them as possible, which is all too often inadequate, all the more so as drivers of the future too change in an era of metamorphosis. But, as hopefully demonstrated in this book, enough can be known to influence deliberately some critical future trajectories, including swerving history at least somewhat on line with the existential imperatives. This is at the core of the extraordinary mission and the required qualities of the mind of avant-garde politicians.

CRITICAL INTERVENTION MASS

Essential for successfully swerving history is full understanding of the already posed need for critical intervention masses. The processes of history, however non-linear, ultra-dynamic, turbulent, and chaotic in part, have a momentum and often a very strong one. Therefore, influencing their trajectory requires not only selection of appropriate policy instrument, but also application of a critical mass of them. Small measures are in many situations useless.

The importance of this point justified giving three concrete examples from recent and current history, one a success, the second a failure, and the third still under debate.

The elimination of Polio in India, as part of the *Global Polio Eradication Initiative*, was achieved only thanks to a large scale comprehensive effort which reached the critical mass needed for eradication of this disease from a very large population. Debates in the White House on troop allocations for the war in Afghanistan clearly involved issues of the critical mass required for achieving desired results, though, as far as known (Gates 2014) not posed correctly in these terms. And the Israeli-Palestinian peace has to be considered in terms of the critical mass of regional peace agreements needed for calming the Arab-Islamic Israeli-Jewish conflict. Otherwise little that is sustainable for long can be achieved (Dror, 2011).

To move to your extraordinary mission, to prevent the production and diffusion of knowledge on how to produce mass-killing viruses in home laboratories, a few steps here and there are in vain. Needed is a large mass of education, ethical codes, incentives, prohibitions, surveillance, and enforcement on a global scale. And so on.

The trouble is that the requirement of critical mass interventions contradicts the habits and conveniences of "incrementalism," resource scarcities, and the ways of thinking of most political leaders. However, avant-garde politicians have to be fully clear in their mind about the need for critical intervention masses and act accordingly. Better are a few future-impacting endeavors with a critical mass than many efforts lacking the necessary mass and therefore useless. However, politically it may often be difficult to visibly neglect many pressing issues so as to concentrate limited resources on a few most important ones. Therefore, avant-garde politicians have to use fitting political stratagems, such as symbolic and minor efforts on many fronts serving as an umbrella for the concentration of efforts on a few selected ones.

SELECTIVE RADICALISM

Budgets, quality staffs, political support, institutional capacities, and other humanity-craft composing and implementation resources are limited. Therefore, the intervention strategy suggested to avant-garde politicians is "selective-radicalism" and in part "selective-revolutionary." It differs from incrementalism, which limits itself to small interventions with historic processes aiming at small improvements; and from comprehensive efforts to change main features of the future as a whole, as in visionary revolutions such as the French or the Communist ones. Instead, "selective-radical" interventions are limited to what is most important for avoiding catastrophes and improving some critical features of the future. However, these selective interventions are often "radical," aiming at a large swerve in the trajectories of history, up to being "revolutionary" in some domains and locations as may be required for bringing about necessary effects.

To provide three examples: (1) Preventing some forms of genetic research and technology development is not a total prohibition and does not prevent the advancement of knowledge, leaving free the vast majority of science and technology activities. But it is radical in overturning the norms and traditions of complete freedom of science and technology. (2) Imposing a few norms preventing the proliferation of instruments of mass killing on all countries is a narrow step, leaving state sovereignty intact in most domains. However, it is a revolutionary step in imposing norms on states also without their agreement and against their will. (3) Facilitating values of duties and responsibilities does not change the main notions of human rights and ideas of human thriving, and is in line with main religious and other value traditions. But it is a significant swerve away from unbalanced concentration on rights without concern for duties and responsibilities.

Following a selective-radical and, when necessary, selective-revolutionary strategy in efforts to swerve the trajectory of historic processes makes the task less impossible, both in terms of required understanding of historic processes and needed intervention masses. Therefore, this strategy not only is recommended as preferable, but is often the only perhaps feasible and still effective one.

PIVOTAL CHOICES

The Chinese scholar Xunzi, one of the main successors of Confucius, presented pivotal choices well in a saying attributed to Yang Zhu, a Chinese philosopher, during the Warring States Period (475—221 BCA) when classical Chinese statecraft was highly developed:

> As Yang Tzu once lamented at a crossroads: if a man makes an error of half a step in the wrong direction, when he awakens to the fact, he will have made a blunder of a thousand li (Knoblock 1990, 161).

A pivotal choice is one which has, or at least is plausibly expected to achieve significant impacts on future history. Pivotal choices, as integrated into series of earlier and follow-up choices and sub-choices, are an important feature of history. This is true in scientific research, but especially pronounced in choices by political leaders "where the buck stops." Coping well with opportunities, dangers, and crises enables and often requires critical choices, with a non-choice also being a choice. To assure as far as possible high quality of such choices preparatory pondering is required, together with time-compressed pondering when a situation ripens.

STEEP LEARNING CURVE

Often, swerving history involves nets of choices over time with plenty of opportunities to adjust decisions to changes in situations and learning from interim results. Therefore, needed are constant assessments of relevant situations and processes, and steep learning curves.

Changing the mind so as to adjust to changing situations and learning from results does not come spontaneously. In addition to facing dissonance reducing tendencies, as discussed, it requires constant efforts to monitor and evaluate actual development. And, most difficult of all, essential is mental capacity to changing the mind after having invested a lot in crystalizing a choice, and changing grand-policies and large projects after they have become in part "facts," without rushing into doing so. Therefore, as far as possible, flexible choices and grand-policies that are easier to correct should receive priority over more rigid ones, even when inferior in other respects. This is also a main way for coping with thick uncertainty and improving the unavoidable nature of choices as fuzzy gambles, as discussed in the next chapter.

LEARNING FROM HISTORY

One more matter requiring further consideration is learning from history. Therefore, let me add some further comments on ways to learn from history by avant-garde politicians.

Very important is "reenactment," as proposed by Robin George Collingwood (1946, 282-302). It involved trying to get into the mind of selected historic senior decision makers, understanding how they arrived at choices, evaluating their mental processes, and learning from such cases how to upgrade pondering in one's mind. This is useful and doable for mentoring avant-garde politicians and self-learning on their part, and is in my experience often found interesting and stimulating by them.

Beyond such specifics, an avant-garde politician needs an overall sense for the dynamics of history. This can be only achieved by lifelong diverse readings in history, with care to pick the best from a very large number of publications and to avoid the proliferating superficial stories written for a mass market.

Also essential are outstanding thinkers-in-history professionals and literati on the staffs of avant-garde politicians, who in addition to their contribution to humanity-craft composing should also serve informally as mentors helping their bosses understand historic processes, with special attention to prevent them from grossly misusing history.

MODELS IN THE MIND

Swerving history, in all its forms, is at the core of the extraordinary mission of avant-garde politicians. But it is very difficult and demanding. Not only has an avant-garde politician to think and intuit in terms of alternative futures, causal nets, rise and decline, and so on, but needed in the mind, as already mentioned, are inclusive and at least somewhat systemic models of the historic processes shaping the future of issues at stake, however tentative and pluralistic, with their multiple variables and complexities. Dividing issues into sub-issues can help, but does not reduce the need for a holistic image of relevant domains in the mind, as an essential basis for pondering, making up the mind, and acting.

The model in the mind will be qualitative, rudimentary, tentative, and always as-if and accompanied by doubt. It has to be dynamic, learning, and operational. Such models should include multiple dimensions and a variety of images. And necessarily they are based on proto-theories, such as on social change and on rise and decline.

This is far from simple. The model required understanding of historic processes which in large parts is not available, all the more so on a period of metamorphosis. Furthermore, the components of the model and their interactions include much ambiguity and are complex, with a lot of non-linearity, thick uncertainty, inconceivability, and so on.

However, this is not an excuse for not working hard on comprehending salient historical processes. Having in the mind at least a mental proto-model of the historic processes shaping a given domain, however rudimentary and provisional, is a must for avant-garde politicians as an essential basis for pondering on influencing historic trajectories. It should include different perspectives, probable drivers, alternative futures, multiple assumptions, and so on, together with many question marks. And the model should be learning, being constantly adjusted to actual developments and new understandings.

This is a requirement which an avant-garde politician should first of all recognize and accept, and then try to satisfy as far as possible, with the help of high-quality staffs. There is a clear and sharp dividing line between avant-garde politicians seeking to have in the mind plausible models of salient historic process and developing them as much as possible, and the vast majority of historic and contemporary political leaders who are not aware of this need or have in the mind very wrong models. You know on which side of this line you have to be.

An essential feature of the required models is an adequate reflection of the contingency of historic processes and the thick uncertainty built into them, as all the more pervasive in an epoch of metamorphosis. Therefore, even choices based on "perfect" models fully isomorphic with reality are necessarily fuzzy gambling. All the more so are choices based on models which necessarily reflect historic processes only in part and often not validly not only "fuzzy gambles," but often "wild fuzzy gambles." This is a bitter but unavoidable feature of choice built into the very nature of historic processes and the limits of human comprehension, as discussed in the next chapter.

CHAPTER 16
BOUNDED FUZZY GAMBLING

EXEGESIS ON MACHIAVELLI

Central for much of Machiavelli's thinking is the triangle "*Fortuna, Occasione, Virtù,*" and what to do to reduce the impacts of Fortuna for the worse. Given a modern interpretation, this triangle is crucial for upgrading the quality of an avant-garde politician as a "fuzzy gambler for high stakes," as taken up in this chapter.

Machiavelli claimed that those who fail because they lack virtù blame bad luck instead themselves. As put in his poem "Fortuna" "She [Fortuna] is blamed quickly for whatever fault You have; and if you find some good, you think it is your own, your virtue's bright result" (Tusiani 1963, 114).

Striking is the experience-based opinion of Machiavelli, resulting from living in an era of "enormous upheavals...being observed every day—events beyond human conjecture" (Machiavelli 2008, 84), that much of what seems to be bad luck is the result of human inability to adjust to new situations. "Machiavelli was aware of the transformations that were changing the world and warned of the need to adapt the institutions and rules of political life to them" (Vivanti 2013, VIII). But, according to Machiavelli "no man is so prudent that he knows how to adapt himself to this fact, both because he cannot deviate from that to which he is by nature inclined, and also because he cannot be persuaded to depart from a path after having always prospered by following it" (Machiavelli 2008, 85-86).

Political leaders with virtù can protect themselves against Fortuna which "turns her impetus towards where she knows no dikes and dams have been constructed to hold her in" (Machiavelli 2008, 84-85). The most infamous and also most interesting recommendation of Machiavelli how to do so is "that it is better to be impetuous, because Fortuna is a woman, and if you want to keep her under it is better to beat her and force her down" (Machiavelli 2008, 86-87).

Leaving aside Machiavelli's views on women, which were accepted at his time, the exegesis I propose is that in order to cope with uncertainty a critical mass of intervention with historic processes is necessary, which is forceful enough to overcome bad circumstances. As already mentioned, this recommendation is of paramount importance for impacting on the future-shaping processes of history. But, of course, as Machiavelli know very well from his own life narrative, nothing that humans can do eliminates the very large role of "Fortuna" in human affairs, which is further amplified in an era of metamorphosis.

SCALES OF LIKELIHOOD

Whatever the evolutionary causes may be, the human mind has difficulties pondering correctly in terms of uncertainty.

Gambling and games of chance are very early activities of humans. They could have stimulated the study of probabilities, but apparently did not. Modern probability theory began to develop in the eighteenth century, in part in conjunction with insurance of marine trade (Hacking 2006). Probability theory is a highly developed field with many applications to phenomena of large numbers, including some important for many of the ordinary missions of avant-garde politicians, such as select issues of demography, public health, welfare, and more. Modern developments, such as fuzzy, modal, and temporal logic, add to uncertainty conceptualization and scaling. However, most extraordinary and many ordinary tasks of avant-garde politicians face thick uncertainty however bounded by limits of the possible (hence the term which I often use "bounded thick uncertainty"), which is, in the main, beyond the reach of mathematical and logical concept packages and theories in their present forms. Thus, to repeat what is of critical importance for you to know and understand, often recommended "subjective probabilities," "expected value calculations," and Bayesian inference are of little help with most of fuzzy gambling on complex humanity-craft issues, and their unsophisticated use can be very misleading. Similarly, findings of experimental psychology on serious fallacies of the mind in considering rather simple probabilistic problems are inapplicable to most of pondering on domains shrouded in thick uncertainty.

THICK BUT BOUNDED UNCERTAINTY

In dreams, an avant-garde politician may imagine being a captain on the bridge of a large ship, giving commands in which direction to travel according to a well-laid-out plan based on reliable maps and weather forecasts, leading to a designated harbor. But this as-if is very far from reality. More lifelike a dream is gambling in a special kind of casino: card games change from poker to bridge without the players being informed; roulettes occasionally become curved; high-stake three-dimensional chess games with computers are the rage, but suddenly behave as if they were a go game; robbers come in and shoot all players, or a mad millionaire appears and distributes four carat round brilliant-cut diamonds to all; payoff tokens become in the hands of winners high-value plaques or copies of promissory notes signed by them to be paid immediately; and an earth quake may destroy the casino and kill half the players or all are invited for two weeks in Honolulu at a luxury resort.

Looking at *Doctor Who* on BBC television should not fool an avant-garde politician, even in riotous hallucinations: In this universe, as understood now, there cannot be a "master of time." The future is in part inherently contingent, uncertain and underdetermined, qualitatively and not only probabilistically, with the partial likely exception of macro-cosmic and some physical processes.

I leave to theologians to consider how a transcendental entity can know all the past and the future, despite the contingent nature of much of the universe, including free human will. But no human being can escape from thick uncertainty. This has an already presented vast and also devastating implication: nearly all choices are "gambles;" and the vast majority constitutes "fuzzy gambles" with various degrees of "wildness".

Going beyond what has already been said, let me start with the idea of "random." A world which is fully deterministic meets the requirements of Laplace's demon. As explained by Pierre-Simon Laplace, in such a world someone who knows the precise location and dynamics of every atom can calculate the state of the world in the past and future for any given point in time. There exist no "alternative futures," only one future being both possible and certain. In this case, uncertainty is the result of our limited knowledge (a weakness of epistemology), not of the nature of reality (ontology).

This image of reality was largely accepted in the natural sciences till undermined by two scientific revolutions: evolution and quantum mechanics. In evolution it became soon accepted that what should be regarded as random mutations are a main driver. The situation was more complex in the physical sciences. In a 1926 letter to *Max Born*, Einstein wrote: "I am at all events convinced that He [God] does not play dice" (Baggott 2011, 78), a view which he continued to repeat. But the dominant present view in physics is that Einstein was wrong. Chance plays an important role in particle physics and the contingency nature of significant portions of reality is at present widely recognized by science.

If this is the case in the natural sciences, a fortiori random is legitimized in the social sciences, though not adequately taken into account in most of them. What from a human perspective are random events can have much impact on future human realities, including long-term ones, in contrast to many philosophies of history. Thus, when decisions by political leaders, who have other options, can result in a nuclear war with significant effects on much of humanity, the importance of what are in many respects random events can be tremendous.

Recognizing the importance of random in human affairs as inherent in reality, and not only a result of our inadequate comprehension, does not explain the nature of "random" to human minds hardwired to think in terms of causality. Humans seem bound to think in terms of causal models with some concessions to probabilistic causality. Surprisingly, this is still recommended, or taken for granted, in modern books (e.g., Sloman 2005), some of which continue to brush aside real randomness.

The Butterfly Effect metaphor is offered by chaos theory as a kind of "explanation" for random effects, with very minute causes that cannot be discerned assumed to have large consequences. But this is morphine helping minds unwilling to accept random effects as real by showing that what appears to us as if random is really causal. Often this is the case, but my recommendation is to ponder as if random is real. I tend to the view that real random is an important part of reality, however hard to comprehend and accept. In any case, at least this is an essential working assumption for high-quality pondering facing bounded thick uncertainty.

In most contemporary thinking, random is expressed in terms of probabilities of various outcomes. But this is much too simplistic for an avant-garde politicians (and many others) who face thick uncertainty, which includes not only lack of knowledge concerning the likelihood of different possible outcomes, but lack of knowledge concerning the qualities of different possible outcomes, such as alternative futures. Furthermore, included in thick uncertainty is often absence of second-order knowledge on the levels of our uncertainty concerning the future.

If most of the future were in the mostre extreme forms of thick uncertainty it would approximate "chaos," which is also a type of order though radically different from what we ordinarily call "order." In such situations, our choices would be "wild fuzzy gambles" and perhaps "chaotic gambles." If and when this is the case, then human intelligence and intuition have little to do other than let matters take their course. Or, if we feel a need to be active, we can make what is in reality an arbitrary choice, or perhaps decide with the help of a randomizer—it makes no foreseeable difference. Alternatively, it would be best to allocate all mental and material resources to strengthening antifragility, however hard and perhaps impossible if the future is really completely opaque, as luckily is not the case. Reality is not chaotic, with the exception of some processes which for some time may approximate chaos. Rather, thick uncertainty too is usually "bounded" and most of the future is not beyond partial understanding.

Not everything can happen and quite some features of the future can be foreseen to some extent. Reality imposes strict, though not always known limits to what is possible within given time horizons. Most hypothetical possibilities are very unlikely to happen. And there are many invariances and slow and also regular changes. Therefore, random phenomena are confined within boundaries, partly knowable and also known.

To take an extreme example: while Hitler was a random mutation, he could not have occurred without many of the conditions prevailing in Weimar Germany. Without them, no random effect could have produced the Hitler regime. Nor, given those conditions, no random event could have produced in the short run a stable democracy in Germany.

To take up a more "normal" example, the future population of the earth within the next 50 years is very likely within a foreseeable range, though this range is quite large and there remains an unlikely but not impossible alternative future of sharp reduction in the number of humans, such as following a worldwide mass-killing epidemic. It follows that, given all that is underdetermined and depends on random, still thick uncertainty is not chaos but bounded, and the vast majority of choices are fuzzy gambles, not chaotic ones.

FACING FUZZY GAMBLING

Engaging in fuzzy gambling for the high stakes of human existence and welfare is very troubling. Many of the most important choices of avant-garde politicians are much fuzzier than a lottery, where ranges of outcomes and their probabilities are in part knowable, or horse betting, where the rules determining outcomes are clear and the likelihood of different outcomes can be estimated, or at least guesstimate within some range.

When genetic engineering, advanced artificial intelligence, global regulation of research and technology, forceful imposition of norms on states, rationing of pleasure machines, and similar humanity-craft grand-policies are at stake, the results of options are at least partly shrouded in rather loosely bound thick uncertainty. Therefore, while nothing can make fuzzy choices into failsafe or at least probabilistic decisions, maximal efforts to improve fuzzy humanity-craft gambles are imperative.

An avant-garde politician must understand the nature of thick uncertainty and of choices as fuzzy gambles. And understanding is not enough. You must also absorb emotionally the ideas and facts of thick uncertainty and fuzzy gambling. But this is dangerous unless much care is exercised. A political leader can easily slip into decisionism, thinking and feeling that if choices are fuzzy gambles then one can just as well follow gut feelings, instead of obfuscating the mind with complex approaches which do not undo the nature of choices as fuzzy gambles for high stakes. Or a decision maker may choose to dither and procrastinate, even if a little thought shows that this too is a fuzzy gamble, and often a very bad one.

The unavoidable pressures put on the mind by awareness of thick uncertainty, and of having to engage in fuzzy gambling, often for high stakes, easily cause additional serious errors. Some senior politicians seek escape into superstition, or misuses of religious beliefs, or extreme forms of wishful thinking, or trust in "luck," and so on.

A caveat is needed here. As already mentioned, self-deceptive clinging to optimistic assessments of the chances of success can strengthen will, effort, and readiness to make sacrifices, also by followers. These can under some uncommon conditions serve as "self-fulfilling prophecies," increasing the likelihood of success even if it remains small. This is especially important for revolutionary leaders. History provides some illustrations, such as the Communist takeover of Russia and the successes of Zionism. But history provides many more illustrations of dismal failures caused by avoidable illusions on success chances by senior leaders, not least the invasion of Russia by Napoleon Bonaparte and the attack on the United States by Japan in World War II.

Experienced decision makers know intuitively and also consciously that they are "gambling," though they usually refrain from telling so to their publics, often for good reasons. Even when they cannot explain their reasons for doing so, they are also right in being skeptical about using simplistic methods for coping with the thick uncertainties facing them. An avant-garde politician should know the findings of decision psychology on error propensities when facing uncertainty and the principles of probability calculus. But these will be of very limited help in improving pondering on fuzzy humanity-craft gambles and may also ruin them. What is really essential is, first of all, fuzzy gambling sophistication.

Many years ago I read a science fiction story (the author and publication details of which, to my regret, I failed to recover) on the inhabitants of a planet who were highly gambling sophisticated. Consequently, in all their complex choices and interactions with other civilizations, which did not share this unusual quality, they achieved superior results. This applies fully to an avant-garde politician.

Fuzzy-gambling-sophistication is not alchemy. It cannot make choices into non-fuzzy-gambles, but it will upgrade fuzzy gambling and significantly improve many outcomes. Taking into account the high stakes of some choices, up to the future of humanity, high-quality fuzzy gambling sophistication is a quality which is absolutely required in the minds of avant-garde politicians and must suffuse their pondering. Not less so, an avant-garde politician must know the main approaches to upgrading fuzzy humanity-craft gambling and use them fully, with the help of qualified advisors.

UPGRADING APPROACHES

Quite some ways for upgrading fuzzy gambles are available to those with the necessary knowledge and sophistication. But first, a maximum effort is required to make gambling less fuzzy by fully using the outlook approaches discussed in Chapter 11, without expecting more than they can provide. After doing so, a lot of bounded thick uncertainty is sure to remain, because of the inherent contingent dynamics of the processes of history, especially in an era of metamorphosis, and limits of our knowledge and understanding. Therefore, after all outlook efforts, choices remain fuzzy gambles of various degrees of "wildness". It is essential that you remain fully aware of this fact, despite claims to the contrary by the many uncertainty-unsophisticated experts and self-anointed "prediction experts."

To add what should be obvious, an avant-garde politician should not consider even for a moment seeking help from astrologers and other soothsayers, never mind whether these believe in their own chatter or are aware that they are hookers of the unaware.

After outlooks are exhausted, there are a number of main approaches that can upgrade fuzzy humanity-craft gambles. The first one involved rapid learning from parallel choices serving as quasi-experiments. Let us assume that we are planning to build a dam. Building the dam will take five years with an investment of 100 million dollars each year. If the dam is ready in five years, the total cost is 500 million dollars and all is well. But there is a problem: water flow studies show that there are two possible places for building the dam, one good, where the dam will be stable, and one bad, where flood waters will breach it. One more year of study is required for finding out which location is the good one. But every year of delay of finishing the dam involves a loss of 300 million dollars.

There are three ways to decide what to do. The first classical planning way is to wait one year so as to know for certain which location is good and then to build the dam there. In this case, the costs will be 500 million for building the dam plus 300 million losses as it will be ready only in six years, therefore, the total cost is 800 million.

The second way is more sophisticated and decides on the basis of an expected value calculation. By tossing a coin, a location to start building the dam now is selected. In this case (but not in others, as uncertainty on the success chances of two options does not mean that these are 50:50), it is correct to assume "as-if" we have a 0.5 probability of picking by lottery the good place. The expected value of the cost (for an investor having many such projects) is 500 multiplied by 0.5 (assuming we pick the correct place) + 600 multiplied by 0.5 (assuming we pick the wrong place, in which case building the dam at the correct place will cost 500 and we wasted 100 at the wrong place) + 300 multiplied by 0.5 (the penalty for the dam being ready one year late), total expected value of the cost is 700 million, that is 100 million less than if we waited a year for the results of the study.

The third way is very different and adopts the parallel trial approach. Based on models developed by Burton Klein at the RAND Corporation for deciding between solid fuel, liquid fuel, and mixed fuel missiles, we start to build the dam at once at both places. After one year we abandon the work on the wrong place and finish the dam at the good place. The cost is 100 million lost at the bad place + 500 million building the dam at the correct place, no delay in finishing the dam within five years, total cost for sure is 600 million. This is clearly the superior solution.

I ran this small exercise at workshops with senior politicians and planning professionals. In no case did participants propose the correct choice. The reason is clear: starting to build the dam at two places at once is on the face of it so absurd that it is not considered as a serious option. Only if one is familiar with advanced parallel trial strategies in situations with steep learning curves, such as in much of research and development, will the idea of starting implementing two "solutions" in parallel occur in the mind, calculations will be made and the correct option selected.

Let me add that at one of the workshops a participating prime minister took me aside at coffee and cakes time and said: "This is really striking. But when I have an occasion to apply this model I will invite you to explain to the mass media that I am not crazy to start building a dam at two places at the same time."

Even taking into account such political-media problems and other limitations, for instance vested interests hindering abandonment of inferior options already partly implemented, still this model illustrates a main approach to improving fuzzy gambling by reducing uncertainty thanks to accelerated learning based on parallel initial implementation of different options. This applies, for instance, in social experimentation with various welfare and employment policies tried in different localities. So-called "trial balloons" in politics belong to the same approach. When global policies are under consideration, trying different options in various countries and then changing all of them to the one proven best can significantly improve difficult choices facing thick uncertainty, assuming rapid learning is possible.

The example above demonstrates that fuzzy gambling choices can be improved. It also shows that this requires unconventional ways of pondering that are not "natural" to the human mind, but have to be learned, exercised, and become a habit of thinking and intuiting in the mind.

A second approach involves mapping of sensitivity to uncertainty. It has a simple and a more complex form. The simple but very useful form is always to consider options both optimistically and pessimistically. I would hesitate to recommend such an obvious idea were it not regularly ignored in practice. Let me testify on the basis of investigating top-level decision-making in a number of countries: in the vast majority of cases once minds begin to prefer an option pessimistic assessment of possible outcomes are discounted and also repressed; and if someone raises them very few really listen. Therefore, you should be especially careful not to discount outlooks which you do not like. Remember Cassandra and what happened to Troy!

The finding on propensities to repress pessimistic outlooks is important for two reasons. It reinforces the recommendation to insist on taking seriously into account optimistic and pessimistic assessments of option outcomes as an important way to improve fuzzy gambling which is not difficult to use once psychological barriers are dismantled. And it illustrates an important paradox which I have already mentioned on improving pondering on difficult choices: if the majority of choice processes were quite good then their improvement to very good would be difficult. But as pondering is often rather primitive, also when intelligent persons are involved, improvement from bad to quite good is often not very difficult. Thus, insisting on both optimistic and pessimistic assessments of options is not "sophisticated," but is very beneficial and doable.

But psychological resistance should not be underestimated. A personal experience will illustrate it in action. A prime minister with whom I worked a lot had an idea how to deal with a difficult issue, but I had doubts about it. When I had one of my personal meetings with him, I said, more or less: "Dear Arnold (not the real name), your idea is really interesting. Do you think that its success probability is somewhat near to 8 out of 10?" He responded: "Yehezkel, as always you put it very well, thank you." But I continued: "OK, but what will you do if the 2 out of 10 possibility of failure happens?" His face turned sour and he said "good question, but I must rush to a meeting—we will continue when meeting again." The experienced reader will not be surprised to learn that for nearly a month I was not invited to see the prime minister again.

The more complex though not very difficult form of sensitivity testing involves the preparation of outlooks for results of different alternatives given various future contingencies. Thus, in considering alternative industrial policies outlook is prepared for various assumptions on global economic developments, in the form of a sensitivity mapping table which shows the dependence of outcomes on different alternative futures.

		GLOBAL DEVELOPMENT	
	Stable	Prosperity	Crises
	OUTCOMES		
INDUSTRIAL POLICY			
A	good	excellent	very bad
B	very good	good	medium
C	good	good	good
D	medium	good	good
E	very good	very good	good

Clearly option E is superior under all the three assumptions concerning the future. This is a "dominant" alternative. If we have such an option, there is no need to try guesstimate the likelihood of the different states of the future—in any case E is the best option. But a dominant option is seldom available. Still, iterating option creativity with sensitivity mapping to stimulating efforts to develop less sensitive alternatives is a main way to upgrade fuzzy gambles.

Now, let us assume option E does not exist. Clearly option D is inferior, that is there exists an option better under all assumptions, in this case option C. Therefore, only an ignoramus picks option D (though this happens, such as an ill-considered compromise).

We are left with options A, B, C. Option C has the advantage of providing good results in all future situations, being "insensitive" to alternative futures. But option A provides excellent results in one alternative future and very bad ones in another. And option B in no case provides excellent or very bad results, performing very good, good, and medium in different futures.

Given this situation, the choice depends on lottery values: preferring a good result without any risks, which means in some sense not to gamble (in professional terminology, preferring "risk avoidance," without going into finer distinctions, such as maximin or minimax) leads to the choice of option C. Or if taking the risk of a bad result in order to have a chance of a good result is preferred, then either option A or B is selected, depending on further lottery value preferences.

A third approach deals with the very important problems posed by possibilities which have a very high impact but a very low or unknown likelihood. Here two common traps await the unwary, including many political leaders: The first one is to regard "strange" events as necessarily having a very low likelihood. However, there is a world of difference between not knowing the likelihood of a strange event and presuming to know that its likelihood is low—which is a positive statement that requires some support and cannot be based on the lack of knowledge of likelihood. Therefore, I use here the simplification of putting together "very low or unknown likelihood," which may be appropriate or inappropriate for different issues.

The second trap is the tendency to ignore or put at the end of the pondering and action agenda very low likelihood possibilities and also some with unknowable likelihood. This is understandable as a result of resource scarcities and current pressures, which also result in neglecting of problems till they become glaringly acute. But this is a serious error because of inattention to impact potentials.

Instead, necessary is an analysis which tries to guesstimate both likelihood and impacts, positive and negative, and then to determine priorities accordingly. Thus, contingencies with very low probability and low impact can be left aside. Contingencies with both high probability and high impact should receive high priority, as is usually done. Contingencies with high probability but low impact can receive low priority. The hard problem is posed by contingencies with low or unknowable likelihood but very high impact. The tendency in most domains, with the exception of security affairs, is to neglect such possibilities, but this may be a grave mistake. Much depends on lottery values and feelings about risks, but I tend to recommend high priority allocation to at least preparation of contingency plans and rapidly mobilizable action resources in case a high impact contingency realizes despite the low (or unknown, and therefore regarded as-if low) likelihood.

Another approach involves upgrading of "improvisation." Leaving aside its misuses, such as decisionism, do-ism, and simplistic pragmatism, improvisation implies rapid adjustment to changing situations. It is unavoidable when unforeseeable changes require rapid responses, as most pronounced in crises, but also in other situations. I return to improvisation and its derivatives below, when exploring entrepreneurial antifragility strategies which follow a similar line of reasoning in a somewhat different context.

There are a number of additional approaches to improving fuzzy gambling, such as structured "Devil's Advocacy," various simulation techniques, risk analysis, "mixed strategies," and more. These are for your staff to work out, while you evaluate their conclusions with an open mind and a lot of doubts. But, to improve insight into bound thick uncertainty and ways to improve fuzzy gambling, an avant-garde politician should personally participate in some staff work. As stated in a publication on improving intelligence analysis "involving policymakers in the alternative futures exercise is the most effective way to…sensitize them to key uncertainties. Most participants find the process … as useful as any finished product" (Center for the Study of Intelligence 2009, 34).

CONSTANT ADJUSTMENT

Choices only seldom take the form of a single critical and largely uncorrectable decision, though such pivotal choices, as discussed, do happen. Usually serious issues are handled by long-term policies, which include chains of choices over time. In such cases another major approach to improving fuzzy gambling is very useful, namely constant adjustments of decisions both to results and to changing situations, somewhat similar to learning from parallel trials and affiliated with improvisation.

To adjust choices to partly reduced uncertainty following the passage of time, a number of conditions must be met, including elasticity built into the policy; steep learning curves accompanying implementation of parts of the policy and the passage of time; continuous option innovation and creativity on how to adjust and improve policies in light of learning; decisiveness required for overcoming inertia; and primarily an ability of the mind to change earlier choices in light of learning from actual developments.

These requirements may look easy, but are often hard to meet: monitoring and evaluation of partial results are problematic and often resisted; good options for adjusting policies to intermediate results and changing conditions are scarce; and the psychological, organizational, and political costs of changing policies can be high and sometimes prohibitive. The dissonance-reducing tendencies, as discussed in Chapter 14, add further difficulties. Still, learning from intermediate results is a major way to improve fuzzy gambles.

COPING WITH LEAPING ENVIRONMENTS

A different perspective is supplied by strategies for coping with leaping environments. There is one wrong strategy, which is really a lack of a strategy, which I call "zero-strategy," and five strategies which fit in different mixes various situations as evolving with time.

The zero strategy misperceives changes as either more or less of the same that was before, or as not requiring any significant novel response other than "more of the same," till failure cannot be denied any more. Then come bad improvisations and panic responses.

A striking mega-example of central concern to avant-garde politicians is non-response to the phase shift in human capacities to shape its future including destroying itself. Pondering and action are clearly lagging being this unprecedented "to be, what to be, not to be?" existential issue facing humanity. There are some signs of awakening, such as the Doomsday Clock of the Bulletin of the Atomic Scientists, however partial; and some efforts concerning greenhouse effects, though inadequate and widely opposed. But, all-in-all, ignoring and grossly underestimating the paradigmatic transformation of the situation of humanity are the rule, posing the most fateful challenge of all for avant-garde politicians.

Given overcoming of the zero strategy, the first coping strategy recognizes significant changes more or less in real time and makes appropriate adjustments. But as these require time to be worked out, implemented, and take effect, a constant lag of measures behind dynamic realities is likely, with high costs.

Much better is the second strategy, which includes outlook that foresees important challenges in the making and engages in preemptive coping that prevents negative developments from maturing or reduces their costs, and utilizes new challenges as opportunities. But such outlook and preemptive action are difficult, because of limits of outlook possibilities and tyranny of the status quo (Friedman and Friedman 1984).

Very ambitious is the third strategy which tries to influence future developments instead of adjusting to them. Inhibiting some lines of science and technology development and their uses illustrates a major humanity-craft grand-policy that might do so. But this involves a lot of fuzzy gambling and meets much resistance.

The fourth strategy applies to single states and societies, but not to humanity as a whole. It tries to build membranes or a kind of *cordon sanitaire* protecting one's entity against bad impacts of changes elsewhere. Strict border controls and fences to prevent the entry of undesired refugees created by turmoil in other societies illustrate this strategy in action, including its many limits in an increasingly integrated global system with evolving humanistic values. Still, for some issues this strategy may work.

The fifth strategy is one of entrepreneurial antifragility, to change somewhat an already mentioned important idea of Nassim Nicholas Taleb (2012). This strategy in essence is an expanded and deepened version of crisis utilization. It involved constant search for opportunities provided by loosening of the rigidities of historic processes, and using them for implementing important policies which were not considered or had no chance of working under ordinary conditions. Distress, crises, and catastrophes are prime illustrations of such opportunities.

Thus, a major ecological catastrophe regarded widely as resulting from human activities may enable realization of essential environmental policies which cannot be agreed upon and actually implemented without the shock effects of a calamity. Or, to return to a harsher but crucial illustration, establishment of a decisive global regime preventing mass killing will probably become possible only following a local war using mass-killing weapons with large collateral damage to uninvolved countries, such as by nuclear fallout.

The entrepreneurial antifragility strategy requires constant monitoring of developments that may provide significant opportunities together with prepared outline plans on how to utilize them before the doors of opportunity close again. A striking example is provided by Chinese pondering by some elite groups in the Warrior State period preparing establishment of a unified Chinese empire (Pines 2009). However, the entrepreneurial antifragility strategy also applies to more mundane situations, as illustrated by some striking business successes which resulted from using failures as a jumping board to success.

Political leaders are usually more conservative in their mind, but there are exceptions as illustrated by some countries using the civil war in Syria to improve their geostrategic situation. It is up to avant-garde politicians to fully absorb the entrepreneurial antifragility strategy in their minds and using it fully. Opportunities to do so are sure to multiple due to crises built into metamorphosis, in addition to the problematic but important option of instigating carefully selected crises as already presented.

TIMING

The entrepreneurial antifragility strategy illustrates the importance of timing. Both delaying choice and action for too long and deciding and acting before adequate pondering or when situations are not ripe can be very damaging. Understanding of salient historic processes, as discussed in the preceding chapter, is essential for optimal timing of critical choices and humanity-craft grand-policies.

PUBLIC ATTITUDES

However desirable it is morally and as part of maturing to expose publics to the realities of fuzzy gambling, an avant-garde politician usually cannot declare on television "I have decided to choose the following fuzzy gamble to handle the serious problem…" Just imagine the devastating caricatures next day in the newspapers.

Human beings are not hardwired or taught to think and intuit in terms of thick uncertainty and fuzzy gambling. Presentation of weather forecasts in easy probabilistic language has been badly received in many societies. Inconsistency in attitudes to risk is the rule. Typical is a group of activists discussing a campaign against a food additive with very low probability of causing bladder cancer in rats if given in very large doses, while picnicking with bodies exposed on a very sunny beach, which surely increases the likelihood of developing melanoma.

Therefore, an avant-garde politician often has to cloak the true nature of choices as fuzzy gambles, hiding it in his mind and sharing it only with selected associates and advisors. All the more so you have to be doubly careful not to hide from yourself the true nature of important choices as fuzzy gambles for high stakes.

FUZZY GAMBLING ADVISORS

It is the duty of avant-garde politicians to try hard to become *Maestro Fuzzy Gamblers*. But even a maestro fuzzy gambler needs advisors who are fully qualified professionals in bounded thick uncertainty and fuzzy policy gambling. Listening to so-called "HiPPO—highest-paid person's opinion," as if celebrated and expensive pundits are sure to have reliable insights into the future, despite studies proving the opposite (Tetlock 2005), is a grave error. Instead strenuous search for advisors who can really help is essential, as discussed in Chapter 18. But first the problem of frequently having to hide from publics and also from unqualified or untrustworthy colleagues many truths, including about critical choices being fuzzy gambles, is taken up in the next chapter.

PART FIVE

PERSONAL RESOURCES

CHAPTER 17
PUBLIC INTEREST MACHIAVELLIANISM

MOOD-SETTER

The mind of an avant-garde politician requires as one of the most critical qualities a realistic comprehension of humans and humanity. To return to Machiavelli, who pioneered the need for such an understanding by senior political leaders in *The Prince*, his position is aptly condensed by Alan Ryan:

> The staying power of the *The Prince* comes from its sweeping statements about human nature, the role of chance, or *fortuna*, in political life, and, above all, its insistence on the need for a clear-sighted appreciation about how *men* really are, as distinct from the moralizing claptrap about how they *ought* to be... (Ryan 2013, 51-52, emphasis in original).

As discussed in earlier chapters, this includes recognizing not only the importance of values in the lives and actions of humans, but also the terrible propensity of humans to do horrendous harm to other humans while being convinced that they do so as a highly moral right and duty.

Staying with a realistic view of the world, avant-garde politicians need a lot of net power in order to fulfill their extraordinary mission and realize raison d'humanité, together with readiness to dirty their hands and do what in terms of personal morality is bad when essential for high-value public goods. As put famously by Michael Walzer when discussed the "clicking bomb" dilemma (the location and disarmament of which requires information which only the tortured person possesses):

> He orders the man tortured, convinced that he must do so for the sake of the people who might otherwise die in the explosions—even though he believes that torture is wrong, indeed abominable, not just sometimes, but always...When he ordered the prisoner tortured, he committed a moral crime and he accepted a moral burden. Now he is a guilty man. His willingness to acknowledge and bear (and perhaps to repent and do penance for) his guilt is evidence, and it is the only evidence he can offer us, both that he is not too good for politics and that he is good enough. Here is the moral politician: it is by his dirty hands that we know him. If he were a moral man and nothing else, his hands would not be dirty; if he were a politician and nothing else, he would pretend that they were clean (Walzer 1973, 167-168).

An avant-garde politician must accept such risks to his soul, while doing one's best to keep a moral balance in serving the missions. Helping to do so is the purpose of public interest Machiavellianism, as presented in this chapter.

NET POWER NEEDS

The famous Melian Dialogue in the *History of the Peloponnesian War by* Thucydides is very relevant for avant-garde politicians. Athens demanded a complete surrender from the city state in the small island Melos, while admitting that this demand was immoral. The Athenian argument was, according to the 1629 classical translation by Thomas Hobbes, that "they that have odds of power exact as much as they can and the weak yield to such conditions as they can get." Modern translations vary slightly, but the gist of all is that "the strong take what they can and the weak suffer what they must."

This statement is the basis of the "realistic" school of international relations, in contrast to the "idealistic" school which thinks that moral values impact strongly on events. For our purposes these approaches can be combined in the postulate that to impact on reality in accordance with raison d'humanité values, an avant-garde politician needs, in addition to the imperatives and value compass, a lot of net power. Therefore I start this part of the book, which deals with the personal resources of an avant-garde politician, with power. Its main thesis is that in order to mobilize the large amounts of power needed to fulfill the extraordinary mission an avant-garde politician needs to ponder and act according to what I call "public interest Machiavellianism". At the same time, an avant-garde politician must avoid becoming preoccupied with the need for power, as frequently happens to political leaders, such as in some opinions U.S. Presidents (Howell 2013).

To be more exact, required is a preponderance of "net power," that is a superiority of power compared to the strength of barriers and resistances. It is analogous to the concept of "net assessment" developed by Andrew Marshall at the Pentagon (Bracken 2006), a method which avant-garde politicians may well use, with adjustments, to evaluate their net power situation.

Avant-garde politicians labor to bring about radical changes in values, habits, institutions, and policies, as required by the existential imperatives. Comparable in this respect to revolutionary leaders, avant-garde politicians will be strenuously resisted in their endeavor by strong power holders, with the exception of situations of extreme crises when establishments and norms implode. They will be confronted with modern versions of the "perversity," "futility," and "jeopardy" accusations (Hirschman 1991). And, even worse, their measures will be meeting active and passive resistance by most actors having material or value interests in what must be subjected to some measures of constructive destruction, such as nearly unrestrained state sovereignty, unregulated science and technology, human rights without duties, overly very free markets, and so on.

Machiavelli was right also in recognizing the need for much freedom of action by political leaders having virtù in a period of turmoil (Bobbitt 2013). Avant-garde politicians need a net power advantage to make humanity-craft prevail, subject to strict safeguards, even if they move ahead with small steps.

To be added is the necessity to often lead from the front. Leading from the back is less power-consuming (Nye 2013), but often humanity-craft cannot be advanced only by "responding" when situations need radical reshaping in the face of strong opposition. All the more a lot of net power is needed.

"Power" includes a variety of ways to influence selected target populations to act according to the desires of the power holder. It is multidimensional and includes a large variety of *modi operandi* combined in various mixes, such as convincing others to wish to do what the avant-garde politician regards as necessary, personal charisma, incentives, and various forms and measures of force. But I will not engage in discourse on the nature of power, its roots, and the ways of using it. Nor will I take up various forms of power, such as actual versus potential power, owned versus borrowed power, "smart power," and so on, as discussed in the literature (e.g., Jouvenel 1949; Lukes 2005; Nye 2008). Rather, our concern is with meeting some of the special net power needs of an avant-garde politician beyond those of most mainstream political leader.

Usually the term "Machiavellianism" is used condemnatory, though with a lot of hypocrisies and without understanding the writings of Machiavelli, as if his main subject is giving advice on gaining power in unsavory ways to satisfy personal egocentric goals. I use the term quite differently, as clarified by the adjective "public interest." "Public interest Machiavellianism" refers to the quality in the mind of an avant-garde politician and the derived principles, strategies and stratagems which enables gaining of the power needed for the extraordinary mission, in contrast to personal purposes.

I start with the need to invigorate politics and then exploring catastrophes as providing "opportunities," as extensively discussed by Machiavelli, for augmenting and exercising power which is exceptional in scope and potentials. After doing so I proceed to strategies for acquiring and keeping power, which are more in line with the usual uses of the term "Machiavellianism," though I expand upon them.

DANGEROUS KNOWLEDGE

Writing this chapter was an exciting, challenging but not pleasant chore. Nor is studying it intended to call for applause. Whoever finds this chapter as a whole "enjoyable" is not fit to become an avant-garde politician. I deal with the unavoidable necessity of avant-garde politicians to behave to some extent immorally in order to mobilize and maintain the power essential for fulfilling their missions. This puts the being of an avant-garde politician to a hard moral trial: How to maintain personal morality and fulfill missions which are highly moral while dirtying and also bloodying mind and hands.

I hesitated about this chapter, not because it is likely to be badly received by those who do not understand the nature of power and its essential roles in human affairs. This does not disturb me. What really troubles me is the possibility that the recommended strategies will be misused by no-good and also toxic political leaders. But without frankly discussing at least some of the ways to meet net power needs this book loses touch with reality. In any case evil rulers have thriven throughout history and are likely to do so until a new global regime is erected. A Hitler does not need this chapter to learn how to gain and maintain a preponderance of net power, nor did his master propagandist Paul Joseph Goebbels.

REINVIGORATING POLITICS

As recognized by qualified observers (e.g. Naim 2013), politics is less and less a "Noble Science" (Collini, Winch, and Burrow 1984). Its overall standing is declining, also in well-structured states and in the world as a whole. Conspicuous corruption and tendencies towards plutocracy, in part because of the institutional corruptions of very expensive political campaigns, make politics ignoble. Large corporations, mass media conglomerates largely controlled by financiers, multibillionaires using their resources to influence unduly politics, civic society activists who in part are rather fanatic, celebrities who get most of the attention, non-governmental organizations (NGOs), social networks, street power—these are among the actors eroding the net power of political institutions and politicians, sometimes for the better but often for the worse. This is also the effect of judicial activism, client and publicity seeking lawyers and trust in "thick law," which in part impact for the better, as does appropriate global law, but in undue measures increasingly interfere with the legitimate autonomy of politics and paralyze some essential functions of political leaders and governments.

Free capitalist markets, however beneficial, also contribute to the decline of political power. The thesis of the transformation of nation states into market states (Bobbitt 2003, 665-807) is correct only in part, underrating as it does the continuous importance of politicians in making some critical choices according to their discretion, the importance of entrepreneurial roles of governments (Mazzucato 2013) and much more. But markets do dominate much of governance and erode the autonomy and authority of politics—often for the better but also often for the worse.

Some features of modern culture which degrade the image of politics are also significant, as illustrated by many movies in which politics and governments are depicted as evil, or at least incompetent. But the main cause of the decline of the public standing of politics is the visible failure of political leaders and institutions to deliver what public want and need, because of both unrealistic public expectations and low quality performance of politics. And inappropriate behavior of far too many political leaders adds to the growing disrepute of politics.

Failing performance and also corruption are increasingly exposed to the public, thanks to more "open government" combined with "the right to know." Distrust, often justified, in "they up there surely know what they are doing," is spreading. What Tacitus called in his *Annals* (Book 2, 36) "arcana imperii" (the secrets of government) have not disappeared, but are less accepted as valid explanations of what on the face of it look like—and often really are—fiascos, or at least gross incompetence.

Exaggeration must be avoided. Politics is very important and continues to be in charge of future-shaping choices, sometimes successfully so and often not. Some decline in the net power of politics may be for the better, especially in countries where it was bloated and misused. However, many of the agencies who took over power from politics are not benevolent. The overall decline in "capacities to govern" hinders coping with important issues. And the glaring inadequacies of truly global net political power prevent handling of issues of paramount importance for the future of humanity.

Gaining the net power avant-garde politicians need cannot be isolated from the standing of politics as a whole. Reinvigorating politics is therefore both a condition for their success and a main task facing them. This requires significant changes in political institutions (Dror 2002). But the emergence of high quality avant-garde politicians visibly acting in the interest of humanity is essential for reinvigorating politics and will help bringing it out, while enabling required reforms of political structures and processes.

INFLUENCING PUBLIC OPINIONS

An avant-garde politician needs a lot of support. Therefore understanding how views, imaginaries, and attitudes of various audiences form and change is essential. They vary between different cultures, periods, and publics, with religion, for instance, being important or marginal. All the contradictory features of human beings discussed in Chapter 10 come into play, such as the mix between hedonistic and idealistic motives and the new psychology of multitudes based on Internet.

Most political marketers cannot supply the comprehensions which you need. Some reading on political culture (e.g., Welch 2013), political fictions (Ezrahi 2012), and political psychology (e.g., Lakoff 2009 and a selection from Huddy, Sears, and Levy 2013) can help. But it seems that public opinion shaping processes are undergoing rapid changes, as a result of globalization, mass media, economic development, value transformations, and so on. The most single novel factor that seems to impact on public opinions and also behavior, is the rapidly evolving Internet, including the various social and other nets. Naïve views that these promote "democracy" have been refuted by interesting though limited studies (Marwick 2013), but it is too early to evaluate longer-term implications of Internet and related technologies on your potential to mobilize support in novel ways.

An avant-garde politician who succeeds to pioneer new Internet power-mobilizing modalities will gain a clear advantage. But to do so, or at least not to be lagging behind, an avant-garde politician must be knowledgeable on available and emerging Internet uses and their impacts on political psychology, and have outstanding advisors who are both fully familiar with these domains and creative.

RESHAPING "COMMON SENSE" IMAGINARIES

Much more fundamental and difficult, but essential, is reshaping widespread notions, understandings, imaginaries, and so on of public issues, which constitute accepted "common sense." New "common sense" views of public issues are essential for realizing the existential imperatives. Therefore changing accepted imaginaries relevant to the existential imperatives is necessary for the extraordinary mission of avant-garde politicians and part of their tasks.

Even more essential are efforts to facilitate and encourage intense feelings of human communality. This involved, in addition to already discussed measures, appropriate myths and imaginaries emphasizing the idea of one "Family of Humans," as pioneered by the famous exhibition of photography *The Family of Man* at the Museum of Modern Art, New York in January 1955 (Steichen, ed. 2002). It has been followed by many publications, TV programs, etc. But the potentials of modern multimedia are far from being fully utilized to advance a worldwide feeling of human communality galvanizing efforts to ensure a thriving future for all of humanity. These are essential bases for the needed Humanity Constitution and for humanity-craft as composed by avant-garde politicians.

I recommend to avant-garde politicians the views of Bruno Latour (2004) and others regarding single creators and elites as the main producers of "common sense" understandings. Public processes adopt and change one or another version of common sense and its practical implications and add to them. But very doubtful are views regarding the *Agora* and other public spaces as main producers of common sense, popular imagination, and other reality-comprehending imaginary, as proposed by Yaron Ezrahi (2012, 87-94), following Giambattista Vico (2000). Instead avant-garde politicians should, together with other mobilized opinion leaders, engage intensively in adjusting common sense understanding to the requirements of survival and thriving of humanity, such as accepting the long-term future of humanity as a main concern of politics.

To support the view presented above it is enough to follow the state of public opinions as revealed by various studies of the Pew Research Center, such as on human evolution (Pew Research Center 2013a) and on America's place in the world (Pew Research Center 2013b). As clearly shown by such and many additional studies, in the US and other countries, both the comprehension of issues by large parts of the public and the policies supported by a majority are doubtful, to put it mildly (but those of large parts of contemporary political elites are not necessarily of better quality).

Spiritual–cultural leaders are essential for this partly cultural-revolutionary task. But avant-garde politicians can do a lot by their pronouncements, demonstrative actions, and educational policies—thus also gaining the support and building up the net power essential for their extraordinary mission.

CATASTROPHES

Using crises as opportunities, and sometimes instigating them to create conditions for applying antifragility, have already been discussed. To be added are some comments on extreme crises which deserve to be called "major emergencies" and also "catastrophes," because of their scale and impacts.

These are unusual situations when an avant-garde politician needs special powers and also instruments of force, beyond the confines of usual legal and moral norms. As recognized already in the Roman Republic such situations require some form of "constitutional dictatorship," limited in time and accompanied by safeguards. Most modern democracies have provisions for constitutional or other special emergency regimes. Whatever the legal situation may be, when dire necessity arises, as discussed in Chapter 3, avant-garde politicians must do what is necessary for ensuring public safety and the integrity of societies, including emergency use of decrees and force, also outside and beyond the law.

As serious crises are sure to come in an era of metamorphosis, avant-garde politicians should prepare suitable legal bases for emergency action within their domains, which meet needs effectively while preventing abuses of power. But in the absence of such legal stipulations you still have to act as may be essential, taking personal responsibility for doing so, giving accounts afterwards, and also being judged if necessary after the emergency passes.

With or without special powers, the exigencies of crises and especially catastrophes (Aradau and Munster 2011; Kalyvas 2009; Kolbert 2014) provide prepared avant-garde politicians with opportunities which they can and should use not only to contain damage, but to advance major portions of their extraordinary mission as a whole, thanks to increasing elasticity of historic processes (Olson 1984). Similarly, they have unusual possibilities to build up their power, thanks to changes in public attitudes toward leaders who prove themselves (Alkeson and Lonna Rae Maestas 2012) and use appropriate language games (Rycker and Don 2013). Avant-garde politicians should use such opportunities to the full, within the limits of basic norms.

STRATEGIES

To help mobilize, maintain, and expand the needed net power and illustrate the praxis of public interest Machiavellianism as a main resource for doing so, I recommend the following strategies to be selectively used by avant-garde politicians:

1. As far as possible, present frankly the three existential imperatives and your policies and actions for advancing them, in understandable and attractive form, and mobilize support for them in terms of both long-term self-interest of relevant public and their descendants, and the needs of humanity as a whole.

Both ethics and utilitarian considerations, as well as your endeavor to mature humanity, require giving priority to bona fide efforts to explain the needs of humanity and mobilize support for the measures needed to advance them. The three existential imperatives are a good basis for doing so. But the efforts must be in languages and stories understandable by relevant public and attractive to them, and presented as serving their self-interest, as well as that of their children and grandchildren, and of their nation and civilization as well as humanity.

2. Be visibly different from other politicians, presenting conspicuously those features of an avant-garde politician which can gain support, while downplaying what may be disapproved by those on whom you depend.

An avant-garde politician is different from other politicians on one hand and from most of the actual or potential supporters on the other hand. Presenting this difference in a favorable light is often a good way to mobilize and maintain power. But people are apt to dislike someone who seems "strange." A lot depends on local cultures. Thus, in some seeming frugal can be admired, while in others it can be regarded as stupid. When societies are in trauma they seek superior "heroes." But in stable situations they prefer more "ordinary" political leaders. Therefore be selective in putting forth being "special" as a way to gain and keep power.

Still, taking into account the intense competition for power, an avant-garde politician will not succeed without presenting unique features. However which parts of uniqueness to show or hide requires constant adjustment to changing feelings of relevant public.

3. Deeds often speak louder than words.

Never mind the sales pitch of self-anointed "strategic advisors," who market politicians as if they were a cosmetic cream. The impacts of spins, spots, declarations, photo shows, and so on are limited and dissipate soon unless based on visible deeds.

An avant-garde politician faces a hard dilemma between deeds meeting public demands and those which are necessary for the extraordinary mission. Satisfying current demands will gain support, while investing in research that may lead to clean energy probably will not count for much when elections come. Therefore, if enlightening the public to the need for sacrifices now for the future will not work, public interest Machiavellian measures are often essential, such as camouflaging necessary but unpopular action, blaming international pressures for them, and promising rapid benefits also when this is unlikely.

4. Unique marketing.

Deeds are critical, but this does not make marketing yourself and your policies superfluous. You need unique promotion providing a competitive advantage over mainstream politicians, who often spend all their energy on world games and image manipulation.

What is "unique promotion" depends on what others are doing and what instruments are available to you, such as the creative use of Internet, as discussed. In addition novel uses of computer games and chat rooms, tailor-cut appeals to potentially supportive audiences, and discrete uses of your global roles may help to mobilize support.

5. *Look authentic and frank, also when not fully being so.*

Being trusted is an essential asset in the long run, but there are different ways to achieve it. Telling the truth is not only ethically required, but the only solid basis for building lasting trust. Do not promise what you cannot deliver. But this does not mean telling all of the truth all the time when this can be harmful to the missions. And lying is sometimes necessary, given humanity as it is, though you must keep it to a minimum. In all circumstances you must look authentic and frank, also when not being so, if necessary with the help of masks and theatrical performance.

6. *Reveal yourself as much as possible, but wearing well-fitted camouflage when necessary.*

An avant-garde politician should present as much information on one's way of life, beliefs, policies, finances, and so on, as an ethical norm but also in order to gain support; all the more so as most prevailing political leaders avoid doing so. This of course depends on having nothing personal to hide, as should be the rule for avant-garde politicians. Writing readable books which serve as a kind of "personal manifest" is often helpful. But often, as noted, you have no choice other than wearing masks, such as when advancing parts of the extraordinary mission which your constituency does not care about, or when some situations are dangerous but telling so will make them worse. If so, make sure the mask fits you well and is not transparent.

Regretfully, public interest Machiavellianism often requires "masks" and "costumes," taking largely the form of an appropriate demeanor which presents what mobilizes support and hides what causes opposition. However, the masks and costumes used by avant-garde politicians should be quite different from the self-marketing habits of the vast majority of political leaders, being more effective while distorting less of the truth. Therefore you need innovative "camouflage" advisors.

More is needed. Thus, private tutorials in theater role playing may be advisable if you lack relevant experience, so as to learn how to show seemingly authentically emotions which are not really felt. But these are techniques and behavioral skills outside the scope of this book.

7. *Do not hesitate to selectively scold relevant publics and make demands from them, together with explaining the reasons and trying to mature their understanding.*

In all too many societies the public gets much less from its leaders than is possible and needed. In other societies political leaders promise the impossible and distribute goodies for which the public and future generations will pay dearly. As an avant-garde politician you should avoid these two evils and serve the present and future public to the best of your abilities within the limits of stubborn facts of reality.

Make this clear to salient parts of the population, scolding and demanding as difficult situations and the needs of the future may require, while explaining yourself in understandable language and trying to upgrade the maturity of the audiences.

8. Be frank when crises strike and the public is frightened.

The recommendation of a study of the great influenza pandemic of 1918–1919, which according to the best estimates killed about 50 million people (other estimates range between 20 and 100 million) fully applies to nearly all crises:

> Those in authority must retain the public's trust. The way to do that is to distort nothing, to put the best face on nothing, to try to manipulate no one (Barry 2005, 462).

Care must be taken to convey a true picture, but in ways limiting panic. Classified information must not be divulged. But a credible posture during crises, in addition to being a part of good crisis coping, is an important investment in building and maintaining trust and thus reinforcing the power which you need.

9. When essential, downplay your commitment to humanity-craft.

A difficult problem is how to maintain the needed support while giving much weight to the extraordinary mission for which constituencies often do not care, including the future of the human species. Here a tragic choice is built into the being of an avant-garde politician. But, whatever mix between satisfying local, current and short-term demands and taking care of the long-term future of the human species you may adopt, your extraordinary mission demands doing a lot which you cannot reveal without being disabled.

Therefore quite some Machiavellian misrepresentations may be unavoidable, so as to build an image of yourself concentrating on the welfare of constituencies while in fact devoting much attention, efforts, and resources to ensuring a thriving future to all of humanity. This involves using a number of fitting stratagems, such as symbolic and minor efforts on many fronts covering up the concentration of efforts on a few selected ones.

However, you should not fully hide your commitment to raison d'humanité, even when necessary to downplay it. Rather, trying to gain public support for it by encouraging human communality is a duty.

10. Do not take public opinion polls seriously.

Democratic leaders are often influenced by public opinion polls, usually not for the better. In many non-democracies too studies of public opinion are regularly made, though not published, and these do influence decisions.

In principle public opinion should not cause an avant-garde politician to deviate from a correct course of action. But this may be impractical, because you need support and have to be elected or selected, otherwise you cannot serve the extraordinary mission. However, paying attention to most of the opinion polls is not the key to power, because of their low validity.

Contrasting two forms of opinion surveys will clarify this claim. On one extreme are telephone polls in which a relatively small number of respondents selected by some kind of random process are asked simple questions, such as "do you agree with such and such or support the policies of so and so, yes or no?" The advantage of this method is being cheap. The disadvantage is low validity, if any. Even when used to indicate trends, such polls do not deserve much attention because of their unreliability, never mind statistical claims concerning small "error margins."

Quite different is another type of survey: A carefully selected sample reflecting different social strata is interviewed, or at least asked to fill in a detailed questionnaire, which poses the same substantive question in different formulations, provides alternatives including open answers, and examines the intensity of the views expressed by the respondents and their stability. The disadvantage of such studies is their high costs. Their advantage is their relatively high level of validity, though they too cannot foresee changes in public opinion with time and events.

Without going into other public opinion study methods, such as focus groups and "milking" of social networks, I recommend being wary about their findings. Similarly do not give credence to claims that "big data" will provide reliable information on views of the public. Unless used in very sophisticated ways, as is usually not done, "milking" mainly reflects thin surface preferences. These are useful for selling easily read trade books and designing popular TV programs, but are not relevant for your main concerns.

However, do not ignore the bandwagon effect of published opinion polls and similar studies. If their findings are widely publicized they may influence public opinions temporarily.

11. Don't be unduly impressed by various demonstrations of "the will of the people," "street action," and aroused masses, unless justified on their merits or demonstrating sustained real power.

Relying on a new type of "militant" (Badiou 2012) and similar "signs from the future" (Zizek 2012, 127 ff.) is often a delusion, as illustrated by the fate of most such activists and signs, even if they mobilize a lot of temporary street power, as in parts of the "Arab Spring."

But an avant-garde politician should be wary about revealing his doubts about such campaigns and demonstrations. They can sometimes have positive results or provide opportunities to do what is needed but is not feasible without militants and street pressure. The situation is different in revolutionary circumstances. Detailed discussion of coping with them, using them, and also sometimes initiating them is beyond the scope of this book. But their existence should be recognized by avant-garde politicians, sometimes instigated, and utilized when appropriate.

12. Think through and script in your mind how to address the public, while looking spontaneous.

Consider carefully how to address the public and script it in your mind, or if necessary use a prompter, till appropriate ways of addressing various publics becomes a part of your tacit knowledge and intuition. Keep control of all who want to stage master your appearances, so that they meet your needs and not their ego requirements. Also remember, too many appearances may devaluate them.

Subject to adjustments to a particular public, demonstrate an eye-to-eye and "I–you" relationship, nearly never speaking from above; base your appeals on a mix between emotions and reasoned arguments, in a simplified version of classical rhetoric, often using "stories;" take into account needs for amusement and release of tension, but in emergencies the public needs reassurance and awaits appeals for effort and heroism; demonstrate confidence in the public, together with sharing apprehensions; and appeal to self-interest, as noted, and tribal feelings, with altruism and global concerns added as much as the public can bear.

Festivals or commemorative occasions require a different "high" and grave style for inspiring the public. Studying Lincoln's Gettysburg address (Wills 2006) and other famous historic speeches (MacArthur, ed. 2013) may be of help, though your addresses should express your own being. In all case, your appearances should look authentic and, with special exceptions, spontaneous, never mind how much they are planned.

13. Delicately play on the "hero" theme.

"Heroes" are a fundamental part of human mythologies (Campbell 2008) and the image of being a hero played a major role in political leadership in former times, leading to the "great man in history" theory, propagated by Thomas Carlyle in a series of lectures between 1837 and 1840 (Carlyle 2011).

Whatever the role of outstanding personalities in history may be, it is a mass-psychological fact that people need "heroes" to admire, and also to somewhat worship. An avant-garde politician has to use this trait of seeking heroes to build up power. But do so gingerly, as in most societies sports and movie stars are viewed as "heroes" and not political leaders. In nearly all totalitarian states too personality worship, as of Joseph Stalin in the Soviet Union, is out of fashion.

Leaving aside accidental events, you can promote some elements of being a modern type of "hero" based on having conspicuous personal merits and achievements. But do not overdo it. You must delicately "play" on this motive, as if it were an old and fragile violin, capable of producing a wonderful melody, but only in the hands of a maestro.

In any case, you need personal courage and should demonstrate it. An avant-garde politician is sure to make enemies, because of endangering widely accepted values, vested interests, powerful persons, and strong organizations. This may make you a target for bodily attacks. Furthermore, political and ideological violence is widespread globally and may become more so. Therefore, even an avant-garde politician who takes reasonable precautions is at some physical risk in relatively peaceful societies and much more so in turbulent and violence-prone ones.

Only in special cases can you be fully protected, and this is burdensome and never failsafe. You cannot be an avant-garde politician for long and hide all the time in a bunker or armored car. Therefore, you need a lot of courage based on the moral conviction that the missions are worth taking personal risks and also endangering your family.

Occasionally getting out of an armored car and shaking hands with admirers, even if your personal security details oppose it, illustrates what is needed. This does not imply being reckless. You owe to your mission, family, yourself, and supporters to take reasonable precautions. But demonstrating courage is important for maintaining power, while also being a virtue fitting an avant-garde politician.

Luck can be very helpful. A spontaneous act of bravery can help a lot to accumulate power. But such incidents must not be staged. If any "spin doctor" offers to "arrange" such an event which will look good on TV without any real risk, kick him out!

14. Pay special attention to global forums.

Global forums, such as meetings of select global NGOs, UN conferences, global business meetings, and so on, can help mobilize power. They are also crucial for taking care of the future of humanity. Therefore you should facilitate them and selectively participate, but take care not to identify with the rich and with egotistic interest groups, or marginal and "crackpot" ones. Also, be careful not to harm your power bases at home, by appearing too "cosmopolitan."

15. Take into account the age structure and economic situation of your potential supporters.

More than half of the world's population **is** under 30 years of age, but this differs between countries in some of which the population is aging, because of decreasing birth rates and longer life expectancy. You should adjust some of your appeals according. Also, there is much difference between situations of large-scale youth unemployment and suffering of the retirees and of widespread economic prosperity.

Younger age cohorts, and to some degrees their parents, constitute a public radically different from the growing number of the elderly, who necessarily are worried about their health and maintenance. If employment chances are good, the younger generations are likely to be more receptive to humanity-craft, such as reducing pollution. However, if most of the youth are unemployed and pessimistic about their future, and parents are desperate about the prospects of their children, then speaking about "the future of humanity" will backfire.

If the elderly are an important part of the populations the support of whom you need, you cannot expect them to get excited over the long-range future of the species. Therefore, adjusting your appeals to age structures and economic situations (as well as peace or war, and so on) as changing with time is mandatory.

16. Be on the side of the many in need, without unnecessarily alienating the powerful, but do not hesitate to criticize the latter when appropriate.

A power mobilizing and maintaining strategy which often combines a high level of morality with utilitarian effectiveness is to take the side of the needy. They suffer not only from material deprivations but also from "political poverty," are disorganized, do not have spare energy to engage in political activity, and often are controlled by power brokers. All the more so, potentially they are an important source of support. This requires credible acts demonstrating that you really care about the needy and empathize with them, as you should, without appearing sentimental. Going to expensive gourmet restaurants and then addressing a conference on poverty, as I saw some senior politicians doing in New York before a UN meeting, is morally despicable and power-wise stupid.

However, with the exception of revolutionary situations, it is neither necessary nor wise to pay special attention to those in need and mobilize their support by viciously attacking the powerful. When necessary then measures painful to the powerful have to be taken, but without superfluous and provocative demagogy.

17. You need money and other resources. A lot of "give and take" cannot be avoided. But remain strictly within the law, provide the public with maximum information on finances, and never trade away what makes you an avant-garde politician.

One of the serious problems of politics, which is very acute especially in democracies and aggravated by the importance of mass media, is the dependence of political power on money. Once you have power then mobilizing money is easier, though it is still difficult and requires much caution. But the initial steps in trying to mobilize power are every difficult and money is hard to get.

Unless one is very rich and willing to use private money for politics, or has a spouse or parents able and willing to do so, an avant-garde politician has no choice but to engage in a lot of "give and take" in order to mobilize the money without which it will often be impossible to build up the needed power. But you must remain strictly within the law, avoid getting money or other "goodies" from disreputable sources, maintain full accounts, and try to go public about the sources of resources. And adopt a strict "red line" never to bargain away the extraordinary mission, though hiding and camouflaging it is often necessary.

18. Be and appear to be a "fighter," but not a "hater."

For better or worse, most of the public admires a "fighter." Therefore demonstrate occasionally being one, including engaging selectively in confrontational politics, and also in revolutionary appeals and action when appropriate. One cannot wear successfully the mask of a modern-day Samurai while shying away from confrontations.

Being a fighter is different from being a "hater." With the exception of absolute evil, an avant-garde politician should hate no one deep down in the mind, though one may and sometimes should dislike and detest persons who deserve it morally. These are also the recommended public postures: demonstrating the ability to cope with adversaries, willingness to fight for what is right, and readiness to wage devastating wars against enemies as long as there is no war-preventing global regime, but hating only what is absolute evil.

While showing hatred and encouraging hating may gain support, avoid doing so unless absolute evil is confronted. As your mission involves advancing human communality and maturing the public, deeply felt hatred against others who are not totally evil is counterproductive in the long run.

19. Make revolutionary appeals when the situation so requires, moving on to revolutionary leadership and action when necessary and feasible. But otherwise hide the partly revolutionary nature of the extraordinary tasks.

As already argued, you need some attributes of a revolutionary in order to bring about radical changes in thinking, feelings, and action as required for the extraordinary mission. But appearing as a revolutionary depends on circumstances. In many cultures and situations you should hide all revolutionary portions and camouflage them as some kind of "new-conservatism" and "restoration," while in others you may have to put on the mask of a revolutionary in order to mobilize power even if no revolutionary action is justified or intended.

BEARING MORAL COSTS

The need to use quite some Machiavellianism, however for the public interest, can easily demotivate excellent candidates from choosing to become avant-garde politicians. I return to this danger in the epilogue, but one critical point must be made here: If good candidates refuse to pay the moral price and other Faustian bargains involved in being avant-garde politicians then the field is abandoned to the less scrupulous, with dismal results for humanity. Therefore, you should be an avant-garde politician with full awareness of moral and other costs, regretting them and feeling pain about them, but not hesitating to do what your missions require, as indicated in the quote of Michael Walzer at the beginning of this chapter.

CHAPTER 18
HELPMATES

HILLEL THE ELDER

A well-known saying of a famous Jewish Mishnaic sage, Hillel the Elder, states "If I am not for myself, who is for me? And if I am only for myself, what am 'I'? And if not now, when?" (*Pirkei Avot, Chapters of the Fathers*, also called *Ethics of the Fathers*, Chapter 1, section 13 or 14, depending on the version). The three segments of this saying are the subjects of this and the next two chapters.

The first segment is directed at the innermost philosophy of an avant-garde politician as the most precious personal resource, to be discussed in the next chapter. The second segment emphasizes that an avant-garde politician alone cannot accomplish anything, but needs "helpmates." It is considered in the present chapter. The third segment emphasizes the need for "Action Now!" as Churchill put it in his instructions during the Second World War. I take this commandment up when discussing in the Epilogue the personal critical choice of suitable readers and other candidates whether yes/no to try in earnest to become an avant-garde politician.

I first discuss "helpmates" in an expanded sense, applying it to an avant-garde humanity elite and to partners. Then this chapter discussed "helpmates" in a narrower sense, ranging from computer-www systems and office to family and a range of advisory staffs. But, first, some societal prerequisites have to be mentioned.

SOCIETAL PREREQUISITES

Essential for an avant-garde politician are first of all societal resources, such as populations, a minimum degree of public order, cultural and material capital, and state institutions. Also essential are an at least partly sociotechnical culture, a more or less shared sense of public interest and public goods; a somewhat functioning political culture and regime, and a machinery of governance which provides at least fair capacities to govern.

If these are missing and the situation is one of failed states, civil wars, and social disintegration, then the first task is state and society building, ensuring safety, establishing political order, mobilizing and augmenting resources, achieving some satisfaction of basic human needs, and setting up a working governance machinery. Only after succeeding in these tasks can an avant-garde politician take up in earnest the extraordinary tasks. But state and society building are separate endeavors, not considered in this book, which takes the existence of at least some measure of the societal prerequisites for granted.

GLOBAL AVANT-GARDE HUMANITY ELITE

Though the concept borders on the "politically incorrect" in many contemporary societies, a global avant-garde humanity elite is essential as a basis and "helpmate" of avant-garde politicians. It may also be a necessary basis for the emergence of an adequate number of avant-garde politicians to make a real difference to the future.

Such an elite is more than an avant-garde global agency (Ypi 2012), or a collection of NGOs interested in some parts of raison d'humanité. I do not subscribe to most of the view of Ludwig von Miser expressed in a letter to Ayn Rand on January 23, 1956 (shortly after publication of *Atlas Shrugged*), where he wrote: "You have the courage to tell the masses what no politician told them: you are inferior and all the improvements in your conditions which you simply take for granted you owe to the efforts of men who are better than you" (Mises 1956). But it is true, as already stated, that a tiny minority largely shapes the future of the many, within constrains imposed by overall social structures and with mass processes also impacting on the future, sometimes importantly so.

This view is not popular nowadays, especially in Western democracies, understandably so, but it is valid. It fully applies to an global avant-garde elite, consisting of separate individuals and groups cohering with time into an interacting and cooperation global network, probably based largely on Intranet.

Some parts of an global avant-garde elite are in the making, though they are disparate and lack essential elements, such as avant-garde politicians. Facilitating their development into an active collective agency participating in shaping the future for the better is one of the functions of avant-garde leaders. Such a constantly growing elite which in substance, never mind names, is a global avant-garde humanity elite, is essential for the extraordinary mission of avant-garde politicians and serves as a basis, power provider, reference group, "helpmate," and partner. But care must be exercised to keep the elite open while insisting on commitment to broad notions of raison d'humanité and high personal quality.

PARTNERS

A political leader is a single module in a number of networks having a variety of architectures. There have been some political leaders who worked without equals, from the top down, largely dominating the public and institutions critical for their activities. But this is unusual. Even powerful political leaders in authoritarian regimes depend a lot on partners, however subordinated. In democratic countries top leaders usually all the more so depend a lot on colleagues, with much give-and-take, compromises, power struggles, and so on. This fully applies to the vast majority of avant-garde politicians.

In most situations you can achieve desired impacts on the future only by being part of what Shakespeare called a "band of brothers" (*King Henry V*, Act 4, Scene 3), as illustrated in the book by Joseph J. Ellis "founding brothers" (Ellis 2002).

Your "brothers and sisters" (please note my addition) may be your political partners and also adversaries, members of shared global informal networks and elites, discourse groups, and so on. But without being a member of mutual support clusters sharing at least in part commitment to raison d'humanité, only single avant-garde politicians may be able to advance their extraordinary mission. As a rule avant-garde politicians need partners. Therefore building a variety of "brotherhoods" and "sisterhoods" and associating and also "bonding" with them is essential.

Six guidelines may help doing so: (1) keep your internal autonomy intact, (2) mutual trust, despite unavoidable disagreements, is essential, (3) frank discourse and mutual critique is the rule, (4) to "get" one has to "give", (5) friendly personal relations are part of the glue needed for cooperation, but (6) keep in a corner of your mind a measure of doubt and also suspicion.

Moving on to helpmates in a narrower sense, I start with the still strange-sounding "computer-WWW systems."

COMPUTER-WWW SYSTEMS

No avant-garde politician, including the most outstanding ones, can achieve much without a variety of personal helpmates. If I had written this book 10 or more years ago I would have started with your office, including a short passage on decision support systems (DDS). But now I start with a forward look and discuss first of all your Computer-WWW Systems (CWS in short).

The opinion is sometimes expressed that World Wide Web networking will develop into a kind of "global super-brain" based on advanced cybernetics, qualified to cope with the problems of humanity. If and when this happens then the idea of avant-garde politicians will require redesign. But aggregating in networks the minds of human beings as they are now, with many elements of "herd mentality," is more likely to result in a lot of nonsense, chatter and stupidity than new wisdom.

However, integrating in intense networks highly qualified persons may provide insight beyond most of presently available individual and group potentials, operating as a kind of "super think tank." Serious work on such lines is done, for instance, at the *MIT Center for Collective Intelligence*. Avant-garde politicians should facilitate such endeavor and be a pioneer in using them.

Also, you should build your own "pondering network" of suitable intellectuals and doers. Meeting personally with as many of them as possible is important, within and beyond the global elite as discussed above. But you will often achieve a lot by integrating your network into your CWS.

Other important components of your CWS include:

- Access to clearly flagged diverse information sources, as well as searches for additional ones, together with predictive search engines, which can partly foresee what information and analyses you need.

- Classified multilayer access to intelligence data and analyses, providing you with choice how far to go into raw material and detailed data or concentrating on summaries and comprehensive analyses, depending on your access permits, habits of mind, and concerns.

- Advanced interacting decision support systems, which help pondering by posing questions and commenting critically on your responses, run simulations on various issues and options, provide pondering schema, may suggest models of select historical processes, and more.

- Salient artificial intelligence tools are becoming available, which may apply heuristics to defined issues and provide tentative options and choice suggestions, and with further advancement may interact dynamically with your pondering.

User-friendly interactive computers in your private study and office and a mobile "super iPhone" can serve as convenient interfaces, together with additional ones that will become available, such as "computer glasses." But what really matters is your mind becoming habituated to using increasingly potent CWS as if they are nearly an extended part of it. This will come more naturally to the next generation which from young age interfaces freely with devices which their parents hardly dare to touch. But, whatever your age, you must preserve your mental agility and use CWS fully.

Obviously to be added are secure multimedia communication channels to all whom you may like to contact, either directly or through your office. All such and other equipment should be secured against unauthorized access. But this may be difficult in view of the potentials of sophisticated cyber-attacks and surveillance. You cannot be completely sure that all the secure lines, encrypted data transmissions, internal Intranets, and so on are completely protected against penetration. Again, some doubts should occupy a corner of your mind on this matter too, and extra precautions are required for very sensitive materials, communication and discourse. But at the same time full record keeping is advisable, with some exceptions for supersensitive matters.

YOUR OFFICE

Your office includes your personal working room together with meeting rooms, and a number of assistants and secretaries. In a broader sense it also includes your advisory staffs, but I focus here on your office in a narrower sense, discussing advisory staffs separately.

Having a well-run office is essential and does not require new work habits such as CWS. Still, optimizing your office will take quite some efforts. Its staff has much power, because it serves as gatekeepers to you. Intrigues run wild in it, together with personal competition for your attention. You should restrain them and not tolerate any "intimate relations" and cliques.

Your office is privy to very sensitive information, in part classified and in part personal and delicate. The best defense against leaks and soft types of blackmails is to do nothing which should not become known, but this is unrealistic even for the most virtuous of avant-garde politicians. Therefore only very trustworthy persons should work in your office and leaks should be harshly sanctioned.

No "friends" who think that you owe them something or who are ambitious climbers should be tolerated near an avant-garde politician. Your office and advisory staffs are not the place to exercise mercy. Whoever does not meet demanding requirements to the full must get out, the sooner the better. You are personally responsible for having a well-running office, even if you have a reliable Chief of Staff. Without strict oversight by you trouble is sure to come.

Your office is also in charge of monitoring implementation, together with a variety of line units. I will return to this important function later.

INTELLIGENCE UNITS

Much information, and also disinformation, is supplied by colleagues, advisory staff, and line units. A variety of organizations and civic society bodies too supply plenty of information, as lobbying groups also presume to do, however biased. For parts of humanity craft and many of the ordinary tasks, the needed information is available in open sources. However intelligence services are cardinal for security, some external relations, and select domestic issues. Therefore an avant-garde politician must know how to utilize them best.

The first rule is not to expect or demand from intelligence units what they cannot supply. They cannot enter the minds of decision makers, with the partial exception of largely speculative psychological profiles which make interesting readings but cannot be relied upon. Nor can they usually foresee trend shifts and many future events. But they can structure and somewhat reduce thick uncertainty and provide important insight and outlooks, if their staff is highly qualified, including in uncertainty sophistication, which often is not the case.

Intelligence units cannot be fully useful to you if they are not familiar with your concerns, interests, intentions, and agenda. This requires close liaison, probably with the help of an intelligence advisor in your staff whose commitment is first of all to the avant-garde politician, but who enjoys the trust of the intelligence community.

A dangerous pathology is adjustment of intelligence analysis and outlooks to what they think their boss wants to hear, with or without signals from him and his staff. This is all the more prevalent and easy because of the ambivalence of most of intelligence interpretations. Having a variety of intelligence units working independently on the same issue reduces this danger, but is very costly, causes a lot of friction, and may not be feasible.

Let me add a special cautioning on domestic intelligence units. They are essential however problematic. I leave aside legal and moral issues which differ between jurisdictions. But all domestic intelligence units necessarily possess a lot of extremely sensitive information on senior decision makers, including avant-garde politicians, a fact which you should keep in mind.

A problem with all types of intelligence units is that they like to control access to their sources and products. In part this is justified, but often this is a form of "turf war." It is up to you to make sure that all who need access to intelligence in order to help you should have it, subject to strict vetting and clearances, overriding all resistances as far as your authority reaches.

Intelligence units will become even more important when sensitive humanity-craft grand-policies begin to be implemented. Selective surveillance on local and global scale of science and technology, markets, profiled individuals, and more, however limited to what is really needed and protected against unauthorized access and misuse, is essential for implementing the imperatives. New global intelligence organizations and enlarged local ones will have to be set up and supplied with legal authority as well as limits and oversight, together with partly new instruments and work methods. This will be strenuously resisted by many parts of civic society, interest groups, and also politicians, with or without good reasons, as illustrated by discussions on U.S. National Security Agency global surveillance programs, which in some respects are minor compared to what raison d'humanité requires globally subject to strict safeguards.

FAMILY

Moving to the closest helpmates, the most multifunctional, sensitive, and delicate one is the family. Spouse, but also children, can make or break an avant-garde politician emotionally, morally, intellectually, and politically. Therefore you must be prudent in founding and building your family and establishing its relationship with your being an avant-garde politician. The family must realize that the mission comes often first and identify with this order of priority, however painful this may be to all concerned.

The main support that you need from your family, which it can and should provide, is emotional. Loving the avant-garde politician, providing solace in painful moments, and reassurance when under attack—these illustrate prime forms of passionate support. They should go together with frank criticism. But strictly to be avoided are family pressures trying to influence policies, appointments, and other acts related to the missions. Nor should the family ask to share sensitive and secret information.

This is not all. In western cultures, spouse and children can be very helpful with political competition and gaining public and mass media support, mainly, but not only, when elections approach. However an avant-garde politician should not press the family to become politically engaged more than essential if they are unwilling, otherwise the more important emotional relationship will be undermined. For sure, you should strictly behave in a manner which befits an intimate family. Infidelity is totally out of bounds, even if tolerated in a given society.

An avant-garde politician, and persons considering becoming one, should bear all this in mind when choosing a life companion or considering changing one. In any case, choosing a life companion is a fuzzy gamble. But a future or acting avant-garde politician should try not to get carried away by momentary feelings. Choosing a life companion who is very ambitious in a demanding profession is risky. And choosing a mate also eager to become a politician is asking for a lot of trouble. Beware: A former life partner who becomes an enemy can easily ruin you totally.

I said as much as I possibly can, not being a marriage and family counselor. But I have seen too much trouble caused to otherwise well-qualified political leaders by inappropriate family life to avoid the subject. Some of the advice rendered above contradicts notions of romantic love on first sight, as accepted in western mass culture. But family is much too critical an intimate helpmate to exclude its founding and maintenance from pondering and foresight, in addition to hot emotional attraction and one or another version of love.

To balance this somewhat cold discourse, let me mention that there are many instances of wives and husbands, or other life partners, advising political leaders well, often much better so than the staff, while also being an emotional pillar. This is an ideal which an avant-garde politician should strive for. But such a partnership requires deliberate efforts, which do not come easily, and quite some luck, which is not available on command.

No avant-garde politician should be misled by political leaders and their spouses demonstrating affection in public, dressing glamorously, campaigning in common, the spouse engaging in good and uncontroversial causes, and the couple seeming to be a paradigm of harmonious partnership. The truth is often very different, though more or less hidden from public gaze, with the willing or prescribed cooperation of the mass media. Building a happy family life, or at least avoiding an unhappy one, should as far as humanly possible not be left by an avant-garde politician to chance or hormones.

HERMITAGE

Whenever I get to know a high level political leader I try to get invited to what serves as a "hermitage," such as a private study or retreat facility, because it reveals much about the person. How is the working space? What are the dominant colors? Which books are within easy reach? Does a compute show signs of much use? What painting and sculptures are in it How is seating arranged? Is there a small bar or an espresso machine? What about a world globe? Is there a white board? How is the washroom? —these are some of the questions in my mind when trying to look around so as to learn to know the politician better.

Paying attention to the design and interior of your hermitage is worth quite some efforts on your part.. Bear in mind that your pondering environment influences its quality. Therefore your commitment to the future of humanity should, I think, be reflected symbolically in your hermitage. Examples are the Blue Marble photograph of the Earth, a multi-layer globe of the Earth, a "tree of life" representing the evolution of life leading to Homo sapienss, or whatever you like.

Obviously you need your personal pondering aids, such as the CWS, and perfect but screened safe communication devices. Access to your hermitage should be strictly controlled, but according to your guidelines and not the favors of the unavoidable gate keepers.

"GREY EMINENCES"

A difficult issue is posed by informal private advisors who are very close to an avant-garde politician, being a kind of "grey eminences" acting behind the scenes. A relatively well-studied example is "Colonel" Edward Mandell House, who served as President Woodrow Wilson's confidant during the First World War—not always, it seems, for the better (George and George 1964). A different and very interesting example is Father

Joseph who advised Cardinal de Richelieu, as insightfully described by Aldous Huxley (Huxley 1941). The term "grey eminence" apparently first referred to Father Joseph.

You are entitled to get advice from whomever you trust. Multiple credible sources enrich pondering and improve choice. But the quality of a private advisor is critical, all the more so when he or she really influences you. This is not a situation for taking risks. Better to forgo a perhaps very useful private advisor who may mislead you or cause otherwise trouble. Very strict vetting is essential, also when you are sure that you know someone inside-out. Having a lot of personal contacts with you may easily activate skeletons hidden in closets. And do not let any personal advisor interfere in any way with the working of your professional advisory systems.

PROFESSIONAL ADVISORY SYSTEMS

As an introduction to professional advisory systems, let me mention that in a study of mine of the advisory staffs of 43 heads of governments all around the world, I found that none was adequately equipped for pondering on complex policy issues, and even less so global ones. But most of the top-level political leaders at least had the valid instinct not to fill their staffs with dysfunctional experts in obsolete knowledge and narrow techniques, who would have done more bad than good. I only regret that most of that study was sponsored by one international and one multinational organization which prevented publication of the findings as "being too sensitive."

Of the formal helpmates, most important of all is the professional advisory system, on which an avant-garde politician largely depends. It is composed of a number of circles or layers, of which the crucial one is the personal professional advisory staff. Its functions, which are in part shared by all of the advisory system, include providing both general and focused knowledge and understanding, so as to improve the veracity of the world in your mind; helping with ways of pondering and intuiting, such as coping with bounded thick uncertainty; providing comprehensions, novel options, outlooks, analysis, and recommendations; compensating for biases and fallacies of the avant-garde politician, by vigorous remonstration; and, much more problematic, in hours of need provide some emotional support.

To these the special functions of political and marketing advisors, never mind how called, must be added, namely to help you gain and keep power, increase acceptance of your policies and decisions, get mass media delicately to support you and your policies, and improve relations with the powerful and the public at large—in line with the preceding chapter.

The selection and motivation of the inner circle of professional advisors and your interface with them are of paramount importance for your successes or failures. The following principles may help to get the best out of your personal professional staff:

1. The inner circle should be compact, say a maximum of 10 to 15 persons, with some movement in and out and participation of additional advisors on specific issues.

2. Their professional and personal composition should include a mix between generalist-professionals, an ethics advisor (with some other title), a political and marketing advisor, and a number of broad-spectrum professionals in science and technology, human species, socio-economic issues, security affairs, and whatever else is central to your domain.

3. Very important is inclusion of at least one advisor each excelling in thinking-in-history, policy composing, processes of the mind, and human species issues. Amazingly, this is often not the case.

4. All of the advisors need comprehensive perspectives, broad knowledge, deep understanding of complex processes, comprehension of what an era of metamorphosis is all about, , some literacy in policy composing and science and technology, much innovativeness, and at least a modicum of creativity.

5. Advisors should be selected on their merits, with strict exclusion of friends who think that the avant-garde politician owes them something.

6. Political and marketing advice should be kept separate with some overlaps, with care not to let it override the professional policy advice.

7. Discretion is a duty of all advisors. Leaks should be investigated and guilty advisors should be immediately fired, and if appropriate punished.

8. Competition between advisors for your attention and trust is unavoidable. But intrigues should be condemned and sanctioned.

9. Those who never spend time in the proximity of political leaders do not realize how important personal relations are in the working of their aids, staff, and assistants. It is up to the avant-garde politician to ensure good collegial relations despite unavoidable, and also useful, disagreements and competition.

10. Some specialization between advisors is necessary. But they should work on main issues as a pluralistic team.

11. An epigram formulated by Ludwig Wittgenstein applies: "[a]s if someone were to buy several copies of the morning paper to assure himself that what it said was true" (*Philosophical Investigations* §265). This should not be the case with your advisors. They need different perspectives and views, within shared commitment to the imperatives.

12. You should maintain close contact with the advisors, but not dominate their thinking. Instead, encourage and demand that they remonstrate with you, up to the adage of the Ottoman sixteenth century poet and scholar Kinalizade Ali Celebi "true friendship means to look on a friend's work with the eye of an enemy" (Fleischer 1986, 43), and as advocated by the Confucian ethics on advising rulers.

13. The advisors should also help to self-bind the avant-garde politician, in line with the already discussed Odysseus and the Sirens metaphor. "Yes Sir" advisors should be dismissed. But impudence should not be tolerated and too much intimacy should be avoided.

14. Emotional support should not be expected or demanded from the professional advisors, with the exception of specially stressing situations as mentioned above.

15. An avant-garde politician should understand the hopes and ambitions of the advisors and reward good work. But a close eye should be kept on advisors with political ambitions.

16. A "senior advisor," accepted as such by all of the staff, should coordinate work and solve personal problems, but without strong hierarchical authority other than your backing. The structure of the inner circle of advisors should be flat and relations collegial, with minimum barriers between them and the avant-garde politician.

SPECIAL ADVISORS

Some observations on special advisors will supplement what has been said. Let me start with a spiritual advisor, as distinct from an ethics advisor who is a member of the personal professional staff and who considers the ethical aspects of main policy issues, and not your personal ethics. However unconventional my advice may be, as already recommended an avant-garde politician needs a personal spiritual advisor, but some other title should be used. He should be freely available to you and also have access at his initiative, but does not necessarily serve on a full time basis.

Spiritual advisors, taking different forms, such as court priests in the West and Confucian advisors in China, have a long history. But they are out of fashion in modern Western culture. After extensive looking around I found only one case of a formal ideology advisor who in effect served as a spiritual advisor on select issues to a Prime Minister, though there seem to have been a few informal ones. But the harsh moral dilemmas facing you, such as in relation to public interest Machiavellianism, require a spiritual advisor helping you to clarify them to yourself. However the spiritual advisor should in no way serve as your psychologist.

The spiritual advisor should be a mature person of impeccable reputation with a strong background in a relevant field, such as moral philosophy, theology, or humanities. But what counts most is his personality and ability to build a confidential, empathic but not sentimental or too personal relation with you.

Please pay attention to the term "social-economic" which I use for a needed professional advisor. Standard economic advisors are easily available, but they ignore crucial social aspects. Therefore needed is a social-economic advisor. But these are hard to find, all the more so as social policy thinking and economic policy thinking tend to take place in different mental worlds and are bound to dissimilar and often conflicting disciplines.

Security advisors are very different from military advisors, needing a broad "national security" perspective integrating all types of security and external relations, including sometimes also domestic security. This leads to complex issues, up to the possible need in some situations for a "national security staff" as a major part of the advisory system of a high level avant-garde politician, together with a "domestic policy staff," with some overlaps. Related are various types of situation rooms and crisis coping facilities. These need careful design fitting specific conditions, which need separate discussion (for an important example, though specific to the United States, see Rothkopf 2006).

The political and marketing advisors, under whatever name, are in many respects the opposite of the ethics advisor, having to look out after image and power. They are an essential part of the personal staff, in addition to often heading a "communication" unit. But their influence must be restrained, all the more so because of the pathological tendency to give increasing weight to politicking and marketing at the cost of substantive decision quality.

To give an illustration, in a Western country which is relatively very good in policy planning, I found at a repeat lengthy consultative visit after five years a big difference introduced into the policy units: a number of public relations experts were added and in the work guidelines marketing considerations were given much weight, pushing substantive considerations down in the hierarchy of attention. When I confronted them, the policy planners complained bitterly that their political heads were much more interested in "marketing," while the politicians whom I asked just shrugged their shoulders.

Nearly none of the advisory staffs of heads of governments with which I worked had a science and technology advisor. When issues obviously involving science and technology were on the table, relevant experts were called in. Also, special science advisory units were often located somewhere in the machinery of government. But this does not meet the needs of taking a close look on the science and technology aspects of nearly all important policy issues and of recognizing the emerging critical problems posed by science and technology. Therefore a top quality broad gauged science and technology advisor should be in the professional advisory staff, with a supporting small unit as may be necessary.

Essential as a member of the inner circle of professional advisors is what I call, lacking a better term, a human species advisor. I mean an outstanding professional advisor on the evolution and nature of humanity as a species, with broad perspectives on the alternative futures of humanity. This advisor is crucial for the extraordinary mission of an avant-garde politician. Probably some conventional title is needed for this advisor, depending on circumstances.

Critical is an outstanding policy pondering and composing advisor, who can also advise on decision processes and crisis coping. This advisor should provide professional guidance to the advisory system as a whole and help evaluation of the assessments, analyses, and recommendations provided by them and by other units.

Also needed are legal advisors. And additional ones may be required on domains of concern to a specific avant-garde politician. Some can be attached from relevant ministries for a fixed or open-ended period. This is fine if their main function is liaison. But having advisors whose loyalty is first of all to their regular positions instead of the avant-garde politician is risky.

A note on legal advisors (for full disclosure, let me mention that, inter alia, I have a full Israeli and American legal education and was admitted to the Israeli Bar): they should, first of all, help avoid clearly illegal acts. Then their job is to help implement policies by putting them into suitable legal forms and defending them in courts. But they are advisors, not decision makers. If an avant-garde politician chooses to ignore their advice and takes the risk of doing so, this is acceptable. Furthermore, as many legal matters are in dispute, getting second and third legal opinions is often advisable.

EXTERNAL COUNSEL

The third circle of helpmates includes additional sources of advice, but at arm's length from the avant-garde politician and working largely with and through the personal professional staff, with some direct contacts with the avant-garde politician as needed. Essential are compact policy planning units throughout the machinery of government working as enclaves of professional excellence on major policy domains and issues, think tanks, and pools of intellectuals and professionals available on call.

Furthermore, an avant-garde politician should periodically converse with a diversity of knowledgeable persons, look around with wide open eyes and mind, and engage in a lot of readings other than official papers. Thus, if selectively done, he can benefit from a plenitude of pluralistic counsel.

OPERATIONAL PRINCIPLES

All these, with obvious additions such as discourse with partners, add up to the overall formal and informal advisory system of an avant-garde politician. Some principles apply to that system as a whole, in addition to those already discussed. Thus:

- Creativity is essential, but is not necessarily provided even by the best of professional staff. Therefore you and your staffs should strenuously search for new perspectives, unconventional ideas and novel options. As already noted, neither being famous nor being a pleasant personality matters when creativity is at stake.

- As in part indicated, but in need of repetition for emphasis, periodic personal meetings between you and select thinkers, researchers, artistic creators, and so on, in private or in small groups, are essential for enriching your mind. So are study and pondering workshops shared by your advisors and outside professionals and thinkers, if possible with your personal participation.

- Majority opinions are not necessarily correct. Differences of opinions between knowledgeable professionals signify real uncertainty, the question "who is right?" being inappropriate and misleading.

- Positive redundancy is needed when very important issues are at stake, with separate units working on them without contacting one another.

- While structures and work processes as well as some standard procedures are important, the quality of the professionals and their commitment to their tasks are the crucial factors determining the worth of their products.

- Some rotation between diverse advisory positions, academic and research institutions, and, in some cases, line positions is essential for constant improvement of professional competence and should be a part of your personnel policy for the advisory system.

- In most cases, a kind of Chief of Staff managing all of the advisory system is needed, who combines recognized professional authority with a wide open mind and a soft hand.

To conclude, please note that you have to guide, motivate, monitor, and supervise your advisory systems, while encouraging creative thinking, counter-conventional view, frank expression of opinions, and also remonstrations. Also, you can and should initiate staff work fitting your experience and needs. Thus, President Dwight D. Eisenhower prompted "Project Solarium" for exploring three main grand-strategies for dealing with the Soviet Union (Pickett, ed. 2004). Probably Eisenhower would not have done so without his rich military experience with staff work, but all avant-garde politicians should try and gain some staff work experience, or at least learn by closely observing it. This helps a lot to benefit from professional advisors without being their captive.

CHECKING IMPLEMENTATION

Still in need of exploration is checking implementation of decisions. The theory and practice of assuring implementation require a book of its own. However, your office and parts of the staff should fulfill a major role in ensuring good implementation. Advice and decisions should include clear allocation of responsibility for implementation, with time tables and road signs that can serve as progress indicators to be checked regularly. When appropriate, special implementation regimes, such as project structures, should be set up. The political and marketing advisors should be alert to political, public and mass-media critique of wrong or inadequate implementation, which often provides useful information not otherwise available. And your office has to keep a record of all decisions and follow-up their implementation, though this will involve quite some frictions with line units in charge of execution.

BUDGETING

Implementation leads to the last and very important point that must be raised here, namely budgeting. An option without cost calculation or at least plausible estimations is an idea, but not a real alternative for action-oriented pondering and choice. A decision intended for implementation without resource allocation is a delusion, or worse—a fraud. All implementation requires adequate resources, in budgets and also human and political wherewithal. Therefore, costing and budgeting are an integral part of action-oriented advice, pondering, and making up of the mind. Accordingly, all advisors must be cost and budget conscious and budgeting experts are an important part of the decision and implementation machinery. Furthermore, budgeting methods have to enable systems costing and provide clear bridges between decisions and specific allocations, in some kind of "performance budgeting" format.

Always be aware that costing estimates of intended projects, acquisitions, studies and so on tend to be too optimistic, with actual costs often being very much in excess of predicted ones. Take this into account when making your decisions otherwise your priorities may easily be subverted by unexpected resources scarcities stemming from relying on doubtful cost estimates.

Macro-economic and macro-social implications of budgets and other financial instruments must also be taken into account, with the help of social-economic advisors and appropriate budgeting units.

YOU DEPEND ON YOUR STAFF

However good and even outstanding an avant-garde politician you may be, the quality of your pondering, choices and actions depend a lot on the merits of your staff, its efforts and the effectiveness of your interface with its members. Therefore, you should pay much attention to recruiting and maintaining an excellent staff, motivating it to do its very best, and being open to its inputs. Fulfilling your missions well largely depends on it.

CHAPTER 19
INNERMOST PHILOSOPHY

CALLING-RELATED

All human beings have some kind of life philosophy, primitive or high-brown, implicit or explicit, considered or absorbed without much thought, partial or comprehensive, spiritual or materialistic, narrow or comprehensive, shared with others or relatively unique, stable or changing. An avant-garde politician shares with other thinking and self-aware persons the need for a more or less considered life philosophy. But our concern is with innermost philosophy closely related to the calling of an avant-garde politician, leaving other parts of life philosophy, however important, aside.

The calling-related inner philosophy cannot spring readymade from your mind, neither can it be easily acquired in some supermarket of ideas. Instead, it has to be consciously brooded over and deliberately designed and developed, with much contemplation, musing, soul-searching, self-examination and pondering, consciously as well as intuitively and tacitly. The life partner, spiritual advisors, religious mentors, and similar counselors can be of help, as can selective readings. But the job of developing the innermost calling-related philosophy is up to each avant-garde politician so as to fit personality and situations, though there are core parts which are recommended for all of them, which are presented in this chapter.

I divide the innermost calling-related philosophy, which I call in this chapter simply "innermost philosophy," into a number of facets. Some are more conscious or subconscious and different ones come to the fore with changes in moods and situations. But all of them should reverberate throughout the mind of an avant-garde politician, adding up to a holistic "melody."

MAIN FACETS

Some of the facets have been discussed in other contexts. But they need reiteration here for providing a coherent view, which also serves to sum up some main ideas of the book, while adding a deeper level.

Good dose of existentialism

A philosophy which has much to contribute to an avant-garde politician is existentialism, whether in its more secular version, as for instance developed by Jean-Paul Sartre and Albert Camus, or in its more religious version, as first presented by Søren Kierkegaard. Existential philosophy has various versions, but one core element shared by nearly all of them, which is of paramount importance for the innermost philosophy of an avant-garde politician, is taking full responsibility for one's life—for what one is, does and becomes. This involves seeking maximum "authenticity" in the sense of personal autonomy, in addition to remaining a fully social actor. To formulate it differently, your personal philosophy involves increasing the role of conscious decisions in the amalgam of choice and chance which forms the trajectory of your life.

Borrowing from different schools of existentialism, three additional elements are of special importance: (1) giving meaning to the world and oneself, with or without accepting a transcendental foundation; (2) choosing deliberately the values to which one is committed and with which to relate to one's "facticity," which in the case of an avant-garde politician include the existential imperatives, raison d'humanité and a selection from the proposed value compass, with freely chosen additions; and (3) "existence precedes essence," in the sense that the way one shapes one's existence defines one's "being," but leaving open the issues of having a "soul" and related beliefs and feelings.

To be added is personal orientation towards the future. What one should and will become and do in the future is what really matters, without spending much energy on bewailing or applauding the past, though repentance for committed sins, in one sense or another, and learning from the past for the future, are required.

Being an avant-garde politician dominates nearly all of life

The innermost philosophy of an avant-garde politician requires a being dominated by the mission and calling, as freely chosen. Everything else comes second and third. If for some reasons a person does not wish this dominance, then being an avant-garde politician in the full sense of that term is an inappropriate choice.

This does not exclude other life contents, if they do not contradict the missions or consume personal resources needed for them. Thus, warm family life, religious worship for those who want it, painting or writing a novel and so on are fine and also useful for personal integrity and mental health. But they must not displace the missions in any way.

Tenacity

The innermost philosophy of an avant-garde politician requires and should provide a large measure of personal tenacity and also "hardiness," to stand against pressures, distractions, and also paralyzing feelings of inadequacy in the face of fateful wild fuzzy gambles.

Very appropriate is the statement of Max Weber in his *Politics as a Vocation* lecturer already quoted in part, applying words attributed to Martin Luther to politicians. They need "an ethics of responsibility…where he says 'Here I stand, I can do no other'" (Weber 2004, 92). This mental posture fully expresses the tenacity required from an avant-garde politician as a mandatory part of innermost philosophy.

Meaning of life and gearing for death

Whatever may be your transcendental beliefs, a significant part of the meaning of life is provided by being an avant-garde politician and a feeling that, however long or short, your life has a deep meaning beyond and above your embodied self. This should ease bearing the trials of life, however in part painful, while persistently adhering to the missions.

Facing the certainty of death is a dominant feature of life, implacably influencing one's moods, feeling, and actions. Preparing for exit from being an avant-garde politician is a must, as discussed in the next chapter. Much of the attitudes to death necessarily depend on transcendental beliefs beyond the scope of my discourse. But being an avant-garde politician should provide significant help in facing death with serenity, thanks to having lived meaningfully and used life for the better.

Being aware of being a partner, however minuscule, in genesis

Consciousness of being a partner, however minute, in creation, up to the level of participating in genesis, provides the being of an avant-garde politician with a distinct and distinguished place — however hidden — in the history of humanity, the world, and, in some sense, the universe.

Being a speck of protoplasm infinitely small in comparison with the world and all the more so the universe, and occupying an infinitesimal part of space-time, but nevertheless still regard oneself as a partner in creation, this is quite something. Hence the outstanding importance of this feature for all of the innermost philosophy, with in part dangerous implications. It can easily make an avant-garde politician feel much too important, while it should make him grateful and humble. The dangers of hubris and overbearing are serious and can become devastating. Toxic rulers throughout history who viewed themselves as Masters of History are a red light. Therefore, this feature of the innermost philosophy needs a strong antitoxin in the mind, as discussed next.

Humbleness and gratitude

It is easy for an avant-garde politician to develop the vice of hubris. Not only does the sense of taking part in creation drive the mind towards megalomania if not counteracted, but an avant-garde politician can easily come to believe that it is due to outstanding talents, distinguished virtues, and iron determination that one becomes what one is and takes part in very ambitious endeavors. This is factually partly wrong, morally contemptible, and self-destructive in results.

Factually, without underrating the importance of deliberative efforts in making oneself into an avant-garde politician, for becoming one essential are suitable genetic endowments, a nurturing environment, and a lot of luck. Therefore it befits the innermost philosophy to be grateful for circumstances beyond one's making playing a major role in becoming an avant-garde politician, instead of being self-conceited.

A hefty dose of self-irony belongs to this tune, helping not taking oneself too seriously. Otherwise an avant-garde politician can easily slide down on the slippery slope of ponderous self-importance and feelings of infallibility, which are among the most vicious vices.

Self-identity as belonging to a new aristocracy of duty and service

No avant-garde politician is alone in being one; otherwise there would be no hope for the extraordinary mission. There are future-impacting political leaders as predecessors, other avant-garde politicians as partners and colleagues, and future avant-garde politicians as successors. Thus, one is a single link in a net expanding over space and time. Also you are part of an emerging global humanity elite. This is important for self-identity. It is even more important for preventing a sense of isolation from pervading the innermost philosophy, all the more so as large parts of the life of an avant-garde politician may cause quite some feeling of being alone with a mission impossible.

Instead, the innermost philosophy should include a strong sense of belonging to an aristocracy of merit which has a long history and becomes of growing fateful importance, even if partly contrarian and not widely recognized. It entails duties and services rather than privileges, encourages some measures of abstemiousness instead of "having a good time", emphasizes a sense of personal responsibility, and seeks satisfaction in a mission well performed without expecting external rewards. Therefore, a "philosophy of aristocracy" characterizes more than a little of the innermost philosophy of an avant-garde politician.

Working for a better human future is the intrinsic and only worthwhile reward

Not only is fame ephemeral and seeking of it and hedonistic rewards of office poisonous to the being of an avant-garde politician, but in terms of the innermost philosophy only intrinsic rewards should matter. These include the feeling and knowledge, in good conscience, that one is doing one's very best to increase the likelihood of a good future for humanity.

While consequentialism applies to the values which an avant-garde politician strives to realize, what matters in the innermost philosophy is the effort, not the actual results. The underlying reason, which by now will be clear to you, is the absence of a necessary causal relation between efforts and results. This is due to contingency and the nature of choices as fuzzy gambles, which often defy the best efforts.

This melody in the mind leads directly to the next two ones, related to some versions of stoicism, but contradicting them in important tones.

Stoic enthusiasm

Implied in the tune discussed above are some pessimism and a measure of "acceptance" on the scope of impact on the future for better which an avant-garde politician can actually achieve, as distinct from the quality of his efforts which depend on her. Therefore needed in the innermost philosophy is a large measure of stoic enthusiasm.

This may seem to be an oxymoron, but is not, having instead a clear and consistent meaning, though deviating in part from stoicism: an avant-garde politician should be enthusiastic about the missions and working very hard to realize as much of them as possible. But the avant-garde politician must also be "stoic," expecting many failures and be able to accept them without reducing the strength of commitment to the missions and of efforts to realize them.

The essence of the idea is very well put in the Serenity Prayer, probably written by Reinhold Niebuhr. The best known formulation includes the following passages:

> God grant me the serenity
> to accept the things I cannot change;
> courage to change the things I can;
> and wisdom to know the difference.

I should not presume to improve on it, but nevertheless I add a verse addressed primarily to avant-garde politicians:

> Together with the ability to make some things which
> appear unchangeable but need change,
> into amendable to change by my exertions.

Stout inner citadel

The facet above, together with the need for much inner autonomy, lead to the metaphor of a stout inner citadel at the center of your innermost philosophy. Taking this image from a book by Pierre Hadot on Marcus Aurelius (Hadot 2001), I use it to refer to the virtue of inner strength, fortitude, a lot of autonomy of the mind, a good measure of equanimity, and also tranquility under pressure.

This is an absolutely required tune in the innermost philosophy. The mission of an avant-garde politician includes a lot of moving against accepted opinions, up to radicalism, contrarianism, and revolutionary portions. All the more so, an inner citadel is essential. But it must not be an impregnable fortress which is isolated from reality and ultimately condemned to ineffectiveness.

The citadel has open doors and large windows. Its inner architecture, furniture, library, and other contents include the qualities of the mind with various additions. Family resided in it and many guests visit. There is much communication with the outside, and the mind spends most of the time in the external world. Still the citadel, though not being a fortress, has hard and high walls. Having such an inner citadel is a key feature of the mind of an avant-garde politician central to innermost philosophy.

Renovated enlightenment

A somewhat renovated version of enlightenment is required in the innermost philosophy of an avant-garde politician. It includes, inter alia, much but not full trust in reason, combined with appreciation of intuition and aesthetics; rejection of all kinds of quasi-magical thinking; seeking of empirical evidence or other justifications for images of the world in the mind, with awareness of their limitations; and constant searching for more knowledge and understanding.

However, some important departures from "enlightenment" up to a measure of iconoclasm are also needed in the innermost philosophy. These include doubts about the maximal scopes of "reason" and especially "rationality," skepticism about the "wisdom of masses," rejection of trust in the inevitability of "progress" and the universal applicability of Western type democracy, subjection of "natural human rights" to essential duties and responsibilities, doubts about both actual and proposed "political fictions," and emphasis on a human species perspective instead of nearly exclusive focus on individuals.

Cosmopolitism

I have in the main eschewed the term "cosmopolitism" because of various associations and connotations which do not fit what I have in mind, preferring instead "human communality" and similar concepts. However, it fits a major need in the innermost philosophy of an avant-garde politician, with cosmopolitism serving as a basic world view pervading the mind, with or without additional meanings as one may prefer (Brock and Brighouse, eds. 2005; Held 2010; Brown, Wallace and Held, eds. 2010).

Tolerance

A good dose of tolerance for what one does not like or understand is essential, as long as it does not contravene raison d'humanité. This applies, for instance, to regime differences. An avant-garde politician is not in charge of making all countries into democracies, as long as the values of public acceptance of a regime, absence of aggressive fanaticism, and protection of basic human rights are realized. This also applies to some gender differentiation, if a large majority of a society, including its women, agrees on different rules of behavior for males and females, for instance on religious matters.

Selective social critique

To balance and supplement the tunes above, the innermost philosophy of an avant-garde politician should be critical of much of social and cultural realities, even when tolerating them and not acting to change them beyond the requirements of raison d'humanité.

This recommendation stems from the necessity for orders of priority and values of pluralism. The future of humanity is not ensured, destitute is widespread, mass killings take place, and other realities contradicting the existential imperatives, raison d'humanité and central parts of the value compass are rife. Also, future values may well be more or less different from widely accepted contemporary ones. Therefore, social critic should be rooted in the innermost philosophy of an avant-garde politician, but selectively and focusing on what is most important for the extraordinary mission.

Principle Hope

A hopeful tune is essential for all of the melody of the innermost philosophy. Unless an avant-garde politician is in some respects optimistic, in line with the train of thought of the three volumes *Principle of Hope* by Ernst Bloch, published originally between 1954 and 1959 (Bloch 1995), devoting oneself to the missions is impossible. Only saints can perhaps give their life for a cause having no this-worldly chance whatsoever, also not in the distant future, and most of them do so with the hope for heavenly endorsement.

Avant-garde politicians are not and cannot be saints. But they must be somewhat hopeful about the future of humanity in order to cling to the missions. I think this is not an illusion: There is hope for the future of humanity, though we cannot be sure about what will be.

Therefore, the Principle Hope is recommended not as a useful self-deception, but as quite likely having a realistic basis, making its inclusion in the innermost philosophy justified in terms of truth value and not only psychological utility.

Containing Anxiety and Fear

I have met quite a number of political leaders who suffered from undue anxiety and fear, often resulting in psychosomatic symptoms. This is understandable in view of the pressures to which they are subjected. Thus, facing much thick uncertainty and knowing that one engages in fuzzy gambling for high stakes can easily result in extreme and also paralyzing anxiety. Therefore containing anxiety and fear is a must for avant-garde politicians, but not eliminating it. Thus, to return to the example above, not caring about the risks of fuzzy statecraft gambles easily results in irresponsibility up to recklessness. Therefore, a good measure of apprehensions and worries is needed, but not intense anxiety and fear.

Anxiety as a general feeling and fear on particular issues are universal human emotions which easily become disabling (Freeman and Freeman 2012). You have much to worry about, concerning the future of humanity and your domains of activity, the outcomes of critical fuzzy humanity-craft gambles and other matters related to your demanding missions. You also share with all humans worries about your family, health and other personal matters. But you must keep anxiety and fear contained so as not to contaminate your missions.

The reassurances you can and should get from your philosophy of life as a whole are beyond the scope of this book and depend on your personal faiths. But your innermost philosophy should serve as a bastion against disabling anxieties and fears.

Your spiritual advisor should be concerned about your anxieties and worries and assist in handling them. Maintaining good mental hygiene, as discussed, can be very helpful. And, if necessary, you can get discrete professional assistance.

Whatever it takes, you must keep anxiety and fear within boundaries, so as not to endanger your being an avant-garde politician. Recognition of their dangers and willingness to act against undue anxiety and fear are, therefore, an important part of knowing and handling yourself and of your Delta test discussed below, crucial to your innermost philosophy.

A measure of distance from worldliness

I hesitate somewhat about this quality, but still regard it as an essential part of the innermost philosophy. The term "worldliness" is here used in a secular meaning. An avant-garde politician should know about but not get lost in the more mundane, hedonistic, egotistic, and animalist aspects of much of "worldliness," which often seem to dominate cultures and also political leaders. Instead required is a kind of mental frugality, even when enjoying a gourmet meal.

Pervasive doubts

Nearly last, I return once more to doubts as a required tune of the innermost philosophy, accompanying all the melody of the mind. It includes doubts about oneself, including paradoxically some doubts about the innermost philosophy itself.

Doubt as an encompassing mood and attitude on all that is in the mind is essential, being justified by the limits of validity of imaginaries, thoughts, feelings, pondering, and so on. Doubts on all inputs provided to the mind are justified because their veracity and the trustiness of their providers are not ensured. And, only if an avant-garde politician has a lot of painful doubts about himself, though not a paralyzing overload of them, will efforts to climb higher on the arduous path towards becoming more of a peak avant-garde politician, as required, never stop.

Virtual privileged historian as a judge of oneself applying a Delta-test

The above-mentioned need for doubts about oneself, combined with doubts about the ability of humans to know themselves, leads directly to the necessity for a kind of hall of mirrors, or alter ego, built into the innermost philosophy which can serve as a resident of the mind evaluating the avant-garde politician, including primarily the mind itself. Much of what has been said in this book on required qualities, including in this chapter, can serve as criteria for self-evaluation, and should be so used. But needed in your innermost self is an overriding "judge." My candidate for that important role is a virtual privileged historian.

A "privileged historian" is one who knows all the truth about an avant-garde politician, his mind, feelings, pondering, choices, actions, and impacts. The question which an avant-garde politician must ask himself is what such a historian is likely to write about him in, say, 50 years. In other words, an avant-garde politician should try to simulate in the mind the privileged historian and thus learn where to remake oneself—as a basic attribute of the innermost philosophy.

The main test which an avant-garde politician should apply in the mind to oneself is a Delta-test: has she done the maximum she possibly can to influence the future for the better in terms of the imperatives and other main values she believes in after careful consideration, including working hard to upgrade her qualities as needed for making a real difference to future history within her domains of activity, small or large as they may be?

Spending periodically a day or two in solitude, searching your soul in terms of the Delta-test, perhaps assisted in part by your spiritual advisor and, when appropriate, by evaluations of your main policies and their impacts prepared by independent professionals, as well as other pertinent inputs, is not only strongly recommended but essential for continuing and upgrading your being an avant-garde politician. Doing so and learning from it are, therefore central to your innermost philosophy.

MULTIFARIOUS BUT INTEGRATED

Please do not be anxious about the apparent complexity of the proposed innermost philosophy. Being a thinking and self-conscious human and in particular an avant-garde politician faces demanding existential as well as transcendental issues, which cannot be reduced to a monolithic song of life. But the tunes of your innermost philosophy, as in part presented in this chapter, are not a dissonant collection of contradictory noises. They add up to a multifarious but integrated composition that can be summed up in a symphony of the mind helping in advancing towards becoming more of a compleat avant-garde politician, though reaching perfection is beyond human capacities.

CHAPTER 20
Afterglow

EXIT IS CERTAIN

However well an avant-garde politician is doing, exit is unavoidable. You should prepare for the inevitable, so that, first of all, successors are qualified to continue your mission subject to their views. Secondly, to enable you to continue contributing to raison d'humanité in other ways, and thus prolong your extraordinary mission by being an active "emeritus" avant-garde politician. And thirdly to continue having a full life. But first comes exiting.

Leaving aside the possibility of sudden death or incapacitating, there are a number of possible modes of exiting. You may resign, be pushed honorably out from office, or be dismissed brutally.

Very few political leaders resign, also when clearly becoming unable to fulfill their mission because of personal reasons, such as declining health, or political and other constraints making it impossible for them to do what they regard as essential. Not resigning on time is a manifest symptom of prevalent "non-ethics" of political leaders. An avant-garde politician should follow other norms. As already proposed, when reaching the conclusion that you cannot fulfill the main parts of the missions any longer and this is likely to be irreversible, you should resign, while trying to help a worthy successor take over.

Reaching the conclusion that one cannot fulfill any longer the missions is hard for an avant-garde politician fully devoted to them. Many mental processes are at work to deny such realities and to plant illusions in the mind that soon the situation will improve. And all who have a vested interest in the avant-garde politician continuing in the position will argue that she is well able to do so. Therefore you need both cold self-evaluation and family and other truth-speaking advisors, such as spiritual advisors and medical caretakers, who will speak out clearly when reaching the conclusion that the time has come for you to resign.

Clinging to the altars of power when one cannot any more fulfill the missions is an unforgivable abomination. Even worse is continuing in office after having engaged in behavior clearly disqualifying an avant-garde politician, such as grossly abusing power.

I may be out of tune with modern culture, but sexually misusing the office, as done among many other political leaders by some U.S. Presidents, should have caused them to seek treatment or resign. And those who knew about it were duty-bound to inform the public. But let me take a less debatable case: In an hour of weakness you accepted a handful of blood diamonds "as a personal sign of respect." If you have not informed within a day the judicial authorities about this failure of yours, given the diamonds for safekeeping to your lawyers, acted to have the person who gave them to you arrested and accused of attempted bribery, and told the public about the incident with the explanation that you were in such a shock that it took you a day to act properly, then you should offer to resign forthwith.

Let me take an in-between case in which I was personally involved: An Israeli Committee of Investigation having judicial powers, of which I was a member, found three top level leaders personally responsible for seriously mismanaging a war. Only one of them accepted some responsibility and resigned. This is how an avant-garde politician should behave. If found responsible for serious failures by an independent inquiry, your resignation should follow without delay.

CONFLICT OF INTEREST

In one of my workshops for top level political leaders in a Latin American country, I included a crisis exercise with a scenario of the daughter of the President being kidnapped and the kidnappers demanding the release of many terrorist prisoners who for sure would return to kill many civilians and perhaps also destabilize the country. The credible kidnappers threatened to torture the girl to death if their demands were not accepted, but to release her safe and sound if the prisoners were granted freedom.

The workshop participants considered and suggested various options, all of them doubtful or clearly bad. But the President of the country, who was present at the exercise but did not participate in it, interrupted the discussion saying that of course he would immediately resign his position and swear not to return to political life. He gave three reasons: (1) if he continues to serve as President necessarily he would be deeply involved emotionally in the dilemma and unable to make a choice on the merits of the issue, and even if he did so, this would not seem credible and he would be blamed for whatever he decides. (2) If he delegated the decision to his deputy, or would resign, but many would believe that he would return to office, this would unduly influence whoever would be in charge of the decision, and even if not, the decision would still be widely regarded as thus influenced. (3) If he ceased for ever being president, the kidnappers might realize that they no longer possess a strong bargaining asset and that their demands would be refused. This might well cause them to release the daughter unharmed so as at least to gain a good public image.

This case in various forms is far from unrealistic. A relevant episode, about which I read later, was described by John S. D. Eisenhower, the military historian son of Dwight D. Eisenhower. As a young major in the US Army during the Korean War he sought a combat position. He discussed this with his father, at that time a candidate in Presidential elections, who agreed. "However, he had a firm condition: under no circumstances must I ever be captured. He would accept the risk of my being killed or wounded, but if the Chinese Communists or North Koreans ever took me prisoner, and threatened blackmail, he could be forced to resign the presidency. I agreed to that condition wholeheartedly. I would take my life before being captured." (Eisenhower 2008).

An avant-garde politician can be entangled by circumstances beyond his control in a strong conflict of interest. In such situations, resigning from the position may be the best option, leaving open the possibility of returning to serve or not, depending on circumstances.

The overall conclusion is that if there is a minor conflict of interest, you must detach yourself from related decisions; but if there is a major conflict of interest which cannot be eliminated quickly, then you may have to resign even if not pressed to do so.

There are additional ways to leave your position, such as losing elections without a chance to return to office, or being subjected to a constitutional limitation on length in office. But, however you exit, there are many options what to do that fit an ex-avant-garde politician, all of which are enhanced if you prepare for them in advance. But before exploring them, the duty to prepare successors and ease transitions need consideration.

PREPARING SUCCESSORS

The easiest way to exit may well be to die at a mature age while still being a successful avant-garde politician. But you cannot count on it. However unpleasant it is for most persons to think about death, you are duty bound to prepare for it and for other contingencies that may incapacitate you.

Quite a number of political leaders had sudden massive strokes or cerebral hemorrhages and were succeeded by persons whom they did not trust, with good reasons, and whose rise to power they could have prevented while still being in good health. Stalin succeeding Lenin despite the latter's wishes is a case in point. Therefore, as far as possible you should take care of readying worthy successors and prepare their way to power when you exit in one way or another. True, you may be nurturing competitors who will try to displace you. But this is a small risk, if you take some precautions, and one that you have to take.

Preparing future avant-garde politicians is a very significant part of your job also without thinking on sudden exit. Many avant-garde politicians are needed. Getting experience and mentorship are essential for development of the needed qualities. But this is difficult unless acting avant-garde politicians and their advisors on their behalf engage in training interns and tutor avant-garde politicians in-the-making. Therefore, actively seeking suitable candidates and cultivating future avant-garde politicians is an important part of your mission, while also preparing for your demise.

This was done to a limited extent throughout history, as illustrated by the adoption and preparation of successors by some Roman emperors and special schools and tutoring for princes in Middle Ages Europe and elsewhere. Later, with dynastic succession becoming unimportant and elections or party selection becoming the main gate to political leadership, targeted preparation for senior political leadership became limited to a number of party schools, mainly in single party countries, and socialization in "political families."

To be mentioned in this context is the unique French École Nationale d'Administration (ÉNA), established in 1945 by Charles de Gaulle and imitated, not very successfully, in a number of countries; university programs directed in part at students wishing to enter politics or other senior public offices, such as the PPE (Philosophy, Politics, and Economics) program at Oxford University; and some public policy programs, such as at the Kennedy School at Harvard University and the Blavatnik School of Government at Oxford University.

These are important long-term attempts to improve the qualities of politicians, but very inadequate ones. Many political leaders do not undergo such learning experiences. And, however better than nothing, the curricula and learning methods of such and similar programs are at present far from adjusted to the qualities needed by avant-garde politicians. Therefore, initiating and facilitating learning programs fitting the requirements of avant-garde politicians in-the making and encouraging suitable candidates to participate in them are a main long-term ways to fulfill your duty to develop cohorts of avant-garde politicians.

Addition steps include:

- Identification of suitable candidates, with or without political experience, and taking them for a kind of internship in your office, while also encouraging them to choose politics as their vocation and prepare themselves by salient studies.

- Helping suitably qualified persons to advance their political career so as to ripen them for senior office.

- If feasible, designating one or two qualified avant-garde politicians, formally or informally, as your successors, and preparing them by sharing information and involving them in relevant missions, discourses, and staff work.

- Giving priority in all such endeavor to young promising candidates, women, and persons from social strata under-reflected in the political elites.

- Taking care not to prefer persons similar to you and sharing your views, but rather to advance "fresh thinkers" who will be innovators.

TRANSITION

Whether you are happy with the persons taking over your position or not, you should ease the change-over and help them enter office, also if you oppose their views. The exceptions include clearly incompetent or evil politicians, whom you should publicly expose and resist.

Assisting transitions includes, as far as possible, a shared overlap period in which you introduce the successors to what they need to know; preparation of "transition books" summing up relevant information and detailing running projects and policies; encouraging your assistants and staff to continue working for your successor if asked to do so, and help new assistants and staff to move into their positions; strictly avoiding hiding of official information, destruction of documents, deletion of electronic data and so on, even if sharing it with your successor carries some risks; and putting yourself at the disposal of your successors for frank discourse, personal confidential advice, or any other assistance they want.

A unique case is Singapore, where Lee Kuan Yew, after serving as Prime Minister, but in reality as the founder and ruler, for three decades and then leaving the position, continued serving as "Minister Mentor", a position created by his son Lee Hsien Loong, when the latter became the nation's third prime minister. This served well the long-term thriving of Singapore. There is something to learn from this experience, which should be viewed as one particular "best practice." But it is very doubtful whether a similar transition arrangement is feasible in Western type democracies and hardly so in other contemporary regimes.

It is worth mentioning in this context that in China party schools for preparing leaders are highly developed, and careful vetting and grooming of candidates for taking over senior positions seems, after Mao Zedond, to be practiced to an impressive extent, though reliable information is scarce.

If you have any experience at the higher levels of politics you will know that actual transitions are in the vast majority of cases very different from what I recommend. Frank hostility, mass resignation of staff even if requested by the successor to remain, and destruction or removal of official material—these are the rules, with few exceptions. And cooperation between incoming and former top level political leaders seems to be very scarce. This, for example, seems to be so with most U.S. Presidents, with only few instances of real cooperation between new and former ones (Gibbs and Duffy 2013).

Yehezkel Dror

CONTINUING MISSIONS

You are out of office and feel a big empty and painful space inside yourself, missing the surges of adrenalin and opportunities to steer history. T. S. Elliot catches it well in *The Elder Statesman*:

> Former statesman 'contemplating nothingness' when looking at the empty pages in his engagement book, 'Now I've no more to say, and no one to say it to….fear of the emptiness before me' (Elliot 1973, 16-17).

Even if you left honorably, receive a good pension, and perhaps are appointed to some honorific position, nothing compares with being an avant-garde politician. A revealing study, though limited, tends to show that former senior political leaders move into sunset instead of moving on into afterglow (Theakston and Vries 2012). The question facing you is really a hard one: What to do with yourself?

Depending on your environment and personal situation you can fully retire, as discussed below. You can seek a position in business, giving your name and connections in return for a lot of money. But, assuming you are in good mental shape, I have another suggestion: continue to contribute to the future of humanity. While many opportunities available to an acting avant-garde politician are now closed, being out of office opens before you other ways that did not exist before.

First of all, you can and should openly and loudly advocate radical measures necessary for the long-term existence and thriving of humanity, however unacceptable by the public and contradiction widely accepted "common sense." Limiting state sovereignty, adding human duties and responsibilities to human rights, imposing limits on some types of scientific research and technology development, and moving forward with the establishment of a Global Authority—these illustrate measures which you can now advocate and advance loudly and clearly without apprehensions about losing power.

You do not have to act alone. You can cooperate with suitable non-governmental organizations, though you should keep distance from the crackpot ones. Organizing a new one, in cooperation with like-minded former avant-garde politicians and other leaders, is an important possibility, in an improved and more radical humanity-craft directed form than the *Club of Madrid* composed of former Presidents and Prime Ministers of different countries.

A second important contribution of yours after leaving active politics is to write up and otherwise pass on your accumulated knowledge and understanding, which must not be lost. Writing a kind of "avant-garde politician testament," as was often done in the past, is a good possibility. Frank diaries and memoires, such as to some degree the three volumes by Richard Crossman in the UK (1975; 1976; 1977) and the three volumes by Henry Kissinger in the United States (1999; 2011a; 2011b), and other presentations of personal experience, such as by Helmut Schmidt (Schmidt, Janich, and Gethmann 2008) and Michael Ignatieff (2013), to give a few examples out of many, do pass on to future avant-garde politicians and other future-impacting leaders, advisors, and tutors important lessons of experience. Not less important, though quite scarce, are admissions of serious errors, such as by Robert McNamarra (1996).

Providing advisory services for free or a reasonable honorarium, running workshops, and teaching humanity-craft courses and seminars at universities are additional recommended options. Even if you lose your position dishonorably, you can regain respect by repenting and contributing to public policy, as illustrated partly by Richard Nixon, but this is difficult and may be impossible.

On the "not to do" side, you should refrain from giving self-laudatory lectures and write self-complimenting books to glorify your name and make a lot of money. And misusing your knowledge and connections to provide lobbying services for groups and enterprises not committed to raison d'humanité is corrupt.

FULL RETIREMENT

Full retirement means leaving the public arena. You can engage in private business as long as you avoid conflicts of interest. Spending time with your family, which has seen very little of you while you were an active avant-garde politician, may be a wonderful option. And, if you wish to grow roses or plant vegetables, tour the world, make up on what you missed in literature and museums, etc., these too are very worthwhile.

Starting to play on some instrument, or at least acquiring the ability to enjoy music, is an attractive option. Without trying in earnest you cannot know what you may be able to accomplish. As demonstrated in a striking book (Marcus 2012), learning a new and creative skill, such as music, is possible also at an advanced age and can provide worthy contents to the rest of life.

If you feel bitter about being thrown out of office unjustly, still you can express your feeling artistically or literarily. An example, with all the differences in culture and situations, is provided by the impressive seventeenth century Chinese "artful recluse," who disengaged from active life to paint and write poetry after hostile rulers took over. This is well put in the preface to a beautiful book, based on an exhibition at the Santa Barbara Museum of Art: "The scholar-painters...knew the models of the past...they understood the philosophical, moral, and social implications of worldly disengagement...they recognized that they lived in a period of crisis...Awareness prompted self-reflection…and a desire to voice a response that asserted a sense of self. Poetry and painting were essential media for this purpose" (Sturman and Tai 2012, 8).

Your work does not have to break the market at Sotheby or hang in the Louvre, not are you expected to give piano concerts and write bestsellers. If some local gallery likes to show what you accomplish and some reading clubs invite you to discuss your book, this is quite an accomplishment. And if you, your family, and friends are the only ones to enjoy what you paint, sculpt, write, or play, this too is a lot and may provide you with a bright sense of accomplishment, after having done your share as an avant-garde politician. This is superior in many respects to remaining for too long in the dark and red arenas of power and politics till death makes you depart.

AFTER DEATH

Your legacy to the future is your Delta, the impact for the better on historic processes. This is all that really matters, together with your spiritual and educational effects on your successors and descendants. Fame, as already discussed, is ephemeral, as are institutions called after your name. Certainly you should oppose having your name used in this way while you are still alive, as if this will make you "immortal."

You cannot control what happens after you die and trying to do so is often futile. Seeing a hospital or research institute called by your name may impress your grandchildren while they are still childish, but much better if they are proud of your achievements as an avant-garde politician and further contributions of yours to humanity after your retired.

Humans like rituals and need them, even if fully mature. Otherwise I would recommend to you a simple burial and a humble inscription on your grave stone. But leave this to your mourning family and ambitious politicians eager to use and misuse posthumously your name and reputation. Taking care of the material needs of your surviving parents, spouse, and descendants is important, but too much may be worse than providing them with what they really need. Saying more would trespass on what is for you to decide.

Knowing that afterglow is possible after ending service as an avant-garde politician is one of the legitimate consideration in deciding whether to try and become one. This life-shaping critical choice is taken up next, in the Epilogue.

EPILOGUE
EITHER/OR

CRITICAL LIFE CHOICE

If you are a student deciding what subject to take, a business executive seeking a more meaningful life, a politician striving to upgrade oneself, or in a similar situation of facing critical choices what to make of yourself, this book opens before you the existential choice of yes/no making an effort to join the "shapers" of the future through political action. Given some prerequisites, you can try to become an avant-garde politician, though success is far from assured.

A human being is born, created, or thrown into life, as one person from about seven to eight billion living in the 21st century, and of more than 100 billion of humans who ever lived up to the beginning of the twenty-first century. By human reckoning, a particular person being born is the result of a chain of events of extremely low probability, going back to generations of mating, child bearing, and survival. And being what one becomes is in large part determined by a further combination of circumstances of very low probability.

If one thinks about all these, as one periodically should, the question what life path to choose, or to change with maturing, becomes all the more pregnant with complex meanings and difficult dilemmas. Little wonder that the vast majority of human beings tend to drift into one of the few "obvious" living options, ignoring the much larger range open in the modern world to those not satisfied with a standard menu.

The version of existential philosophy which I recommended emphasizes the multiplicity of open options, within constraints, and recommends deliberate choice based on careful pondering. This fully applies, to use the *Either/Or* terminology of Søren Kierkegaard, to either choosing to try and become an avant-garde politician or preferring other possibilities. The nature of the climb to become an avant-garde politician and acting as one has been, I hope, sufficiently clarified in this book to permit you to consider this option seriously.

MANY OPTIONS

There are many ways of life to choose from, including drifting along if this is what you really want. There are also many morally and emotionally good options, such as finding fulfillment in family and with friends, research, arts and humanities, business, the professions, teaching, handicrafts, and many other occupations. Blue collar work too is praiseworthy and can be very satisfying in appropriate social and physical environment.

If you strive for significantly impacting for the better on the human future, again there are various possibilities, however demanding, such as science and technology, spiritual and cultural renewal, pastoral mentoring, social or economic entrepreneurship, and literary and artistic creativity. Just consider the large impact on history of the 1852 novel *Uncle Tom's Cabin* by Harriet Beecher Stowe to realize the many ways in which a single person, without any institutional affiliations and social power, can make a large contribution to the future, if one has the talents and opportunity, makes a concerted effort and Fortuna smiles. And smaller contributions also count.

I am not here to convince, urge, exhort, preach, and certainly not hector you. The options are many. But avant-garde politicians are critical and becoming increasingly so. Therefore, if you are constituted of suitable stuff and feel the calling, I suggest that you make a determined effort to become an avant-garde politician as your passionately chosen destiny. But be aware of the many risks and costs.

Take into account that deciding to try and become an avant-garde politician determines most of what life will be and mean for you. It requires an arduous ascend on a steep trail and a dangerous one for your soul, and sometimes for your body too. But it is worth the effort and risk if you feel a fire in your bones urging you to do so. This book can serve as one of your Sherpa, but the choice with all the involved sweat and blood are yours.

With all the joys of taking part in creating a better future and many other satisfactions of being an avant-garde politician, the personal price is high. You will have little time and patience for your mate and children, be quite alone in your inner self, face many bitter disappointments, and necessarily make many Faustian bargains that easily corrupt your soul. Also, you may find out that you lack the essential potentials. And, even if you have them in surplus, you may easily fail.

Therefore, choosing to try and become an avant-garde politician is a gamble, a worthwhile one, but still a rather wild throw of not clearly marked neither well balanced dices with your future partly at stake.

REQUIREMENTS

No-one can be sure about having the potentials to become an avant-garde politician. Available knowledge in the psychology of special abilities does not provide reliable findings on what is needed. Many different and largely unknown genes are probably involved in providing the unusual innate features conductive to becoming an avant-garde politician. Future-impacting political leaders throughout history have come from very diverse backgrounds, succeeded or failed in a variety of unique circumstances, with luck always playing a large role. However, a number of requirements can be mapped, on the basis of historic experiences, relevant theories, and examination of the challenges faced by avant-garde politicians. This has been done throughout this text. But, to help you consider the option of trying to become an avant-garde politician, let me sum up a number of salient observations:

- It is trifle to discuss obvious initial requirements, such as some kind of high level intelligence, much curiosity and learning ability, a minimum of human relation skills, a largely "open mind," a lot of energy, strong will power, and innovativeness. But it makes no difference what mixtures of inheritance and environment provide you with these qualities. It is enough if you or those who know you best do believe that you have what it takes, or will be able to acquire it with efforts and help.

- A few future-impacting political leaders overcame harsh initial conditions and broke out from poverty and discrimination. But their number is small. Therefore, do not let a bad starting line stop you from trying the climb. But be aware that you will have to work even harder than other strivers and your chances of being successful are often lower, unless you can make your disadvantage into a winning asset, which is sometimes possible.

- Take care not to be misled by the proliferating populist publications claiming that with enough effort and willpower there are no limits to what nearly everyone can become. This is incorrect. Only a very small part of humanity carries in the back bag the scepter of power. Scarce innate talents and propensities, as well as unusual determination and will power, are essential. And a lot depends on luck.

- The inner potentials to become an avant-garde politician do not depend on race or gender. But educational and social environments do make a difference. And historical conditions, as changing with time, shape significantly the actual chances of persons with different qualities and life narratives becoming avant-garde politicians.

- A number of social prejudices may make it harder for you to become an avant-garde politician. Thus, despite much talk and some action to the contrary, if you are female you face in many societies handicaps. And if you have what is regarded as a physical deformity this will make it hard for you to become an avant-garde politician, human beings suffering from stupid prejudices despite all talk to the contrary. Race, caste, and other ascribed characteristics, as well as age, money, and other factors other than your inner qualifications are also likely to influence significantly your success chances.

- During the climb you have to pass many reality tests, moral, cognitive, emotive, and behavioral, which may easily disqualify you. Repeated failures indicate that you probably cannot become an avant-garde politician. But, before giving up, try and try again.

- Do not trust formal tests presuming to evaluate your fitness for political leadership, including apparently sophisticated ones such as group projects and survival tracks. None of them predicts your performance under real life conditions. I know personally glaring cases of officers selected on the basis of very sophisticated screening methods which they passed brilliantly, who failed miserably under enemy fire, while some NCOs who were not accepted for officer's training received field commissions for leadership on the battle field, making up for the missed training later.

If, after considering all that has been said, you take to heart the adage by Theodor W. Adorno "he who dies in despair has lived his whole life in vain" (Claussen 2008, 12), and do not despair of the possibility of becoming an avant-garde politician, you have to prepare yourself for this option. Let me try to be of help, starting with some suggestions for students who consider seriously going into politics and strive to become outstanding leaders of the avant-garde politician type.

FOR STUDENTS

First, a personal confession: I had very good graduate students at universities, courses, and workshops in many countries. Some of them asked in private for my advice whether they should try and enter politics. Up to about 15 years ago I recommended, with some hesitation, not to do so, explaining that most members of parliaments, local councils, and similar office holders do not really have much influence on critical choices and the chances of reaching senior positions of real impact are very slim, given the competition. Furthermore, so I said, the merits which make outstanding students will in most countries be a disadvantage in politics, where rougher qualities provide an advantage. And, so I continued, to succeed in politics one has to excel in Machiavellianism and self-marketing, which are very likely to corrupt morally. Having power will do so even more. Better to become a professional, or scholar, or intellectual, or artist, or human services provider, and so on, and thus find fulfillment while maintaining personal integrity and doing something good.

But I changed my mind. After having had many additional opportunities to observe first-hand the hot corridors of power and thinking a lot both on politics and on humanity and its future, I reached the conclusion that developing an improved type of politician, what I now call "avant-garde politician," is essential for the future of humanity. Furthermore, an avant-garde politician can exert meaningful influences in many positions of various types, achieving impact on the future for the better on a small scale being also important. Therefore, I recommend to my best students to take the risk and move into politics and related activities, while developing the qualities needed for becoming the kind of politician which humanity urgently needs.

If this is what you chose to try, I suggest that you go to as good a university as you can and study till you have a second degree, perhaps changing universities and the countries in which they are located so as to expose yourself to different cultures and teachers.

If you choose or are obliged to take a few years off for military service or some kind of "peace corps," this will be a very enriching experience contributing much to your qualities as an avant-garde politician. And if you feel like spending a couple of years learning a manual occupation, or one of the arts, this in no way closes the way to becoming an avant-garde politician and can enrich your ways of becoming one, though you will have to acquire later necessary academic–professional knowledge and understanding. Life expectancies are long enough to enable taking roundabout ways which have much to offer with time, rather than sticking from early on to what seems to be the shortest route.

When going to a university, as you should, you have to decide what to study. Your interests are a paramount consideration. Thus, if you are interested in astrophysics do take it. Making a living is also an important consideration. If you have reasons to assume that you will make good money as a lawyer and you do not loath this profession, choosing law is a reasonable choice. And so on.

Any subject which you study seriously and with good teachers up to an advanced degree can provide you, if you make enough of an effort, with ways of knowledge and understanding very important for an avant-garde politician. But the subjects you study will also implant in your mind concepts and ways of reasoning which you may have to adjust and also forget in part in order to be an avant-garde politician. Thus, mechanical engineering may habituate you to think in terms of certainty and calculated risks, law may make you assume that the legal world reflects reality and that legal procedures are adequate for getting at the "truth," analytical philosophy may make you believe too much in positivism, and so on.

Therefore there are many advantages in picking a study package providing you with knowledge and understanding directly relevant to becoming and being an avant-garde politician, such as politics, economics, philosophy, public policy, history, and social sciences. In any case, whatever your main study subjects may be, you have to acquire basic knowledge in these domains, as well as good science and technology literacy and familiarity with theories of evolution and the history of the human species. You also need numeracy and acquaintance with the fundamentals of statistics.

Needless to say, wide reading of history and biographies of outstanding politicians and also peak thinkers and creators will do you a lot of good. Readings on leadership are essential, but you should be very selective because many of the bestsellers are misleading. Much insight can be gained from outstanding dramas on leaders, such as by Friedrich Schiller (as well discussed by Immer 2008, regretfully available only in German). The recommended readings following this Epilogue provide further guidance.

Knowing well a number of languages is an important advantage and often a necessity one. In Europe, you should not dream of becoming an avant-garde politician without knowing your mother language, English, and at least one more European language and preferably more. In the United States you should know also Spanish and one more language. And so on.

Knowledge of languages is not only useful for communication and a valuable Machiavellian asset, but also improves the quality of your mind. Every language has unique concepts and "games" of its own. This is the reason why even the best of translations cannot fully convey all of the meanings of the original.

You need to know more about the world than you can learn from living in one country, looking at geographic TV channels and doing some traveling. Living for at least two years while you are still young in a country with a different major culture is strongly recommended. Thus, if you grew up in a western country you should try to spend two years in an Asian one, and the reverse. And if you grew up in a country with a culture that is neither European nor Asian, say in Africa or the Middle East, spending three years divided between European and Asian countries is strongly recommended. You can try doing so while studying, choosing universities accordingly.

Another quality which you should start exercising while still young is leadership. This involved gaining practical experience, which will also test your aptitude for becoming an avant-garde politician. You can start gaining leadership experience in high school, or in a youth movement, going on for political or civic volunteering, periods of internship, and junior leadership positions in public and political organizations. Participating in election campaigns is a good learning opportunity. And engaging in student leadership, while learning to do so (Burchard 2009; Komives et al. 2011; Komives, Lucas, and McMahon 2013), is strongly recommended. But be careful with whom to associate. Observing various "strange" groups in action is enriching, but joining should be reserved for groups with whom you feel affinity and which will not cause trouble later on.

Exceptions include situations which really call for revolutions. In those cases, which do exist though their number is limited, joining a revolutionary group while you are still young is very important for learning to be a revolutionary avant-garde politician and building up a record helping to climb the ladder of leadership. But extreme selectivity is essential. Most "revolutionary" youth groups in affluent societies are a sham, even when participants take them seriously till moving from a student culture to a job. Keep distance from them.

Student years are the time for broad interests, such as in arts, wide readings, adventurous trips, diverse social experiences, and much more. However, if you seriously consider being an avant-garde politician as your life mission do not get sidetracked too much. Some sports, yes, but not a lot. Some "green" or "animal rights" activities are OK, but within measure and without fanaticism. A little New Age experimentation, at home or in India, may be fine. But joining a sect or spending months in a Tibetan monastery—do not even dream of it!

Very important is participating in young leadership programs and other leadership training activities. Only a few of them are of high quality, but all interaction with other youngsters interested in leadership will teach you a lot, about yourself no less than about others and about leadership in general.

AGES 35 TO 45

Moving on to ages around 35 to 45, you are ripe to consider changing your life and can try to become an avant-garde politician. Your life experience may make you a very good candidate for doing so. But you have to make up for what you missed doing at an earlier age, as discussed above. And, much more difficult, you must unlearn many skills and habits which are trained incapacities for an avant-garde politician.

ACTING POLITICIANS

If you are an acting politician, you may either reject most of what is said in the book, or you are mentally and emotionally ready to upgrade yourself by becoming more of an avant-garde politician. Being already active in politics you have many opportunities to do so which are denied to others. It all depends on your will and is mainly up to you.

APPEAL TO THE BEST

This book is in part a call for "action now!" as Churchill used to write on his urgent instructions, as already mentioned. Let me accordingly conclude with an appeal to the best of the best, in a pluralistic meaning, among the younger and older, women and men: Do consider seriously serving humanity as a high-quality politician, whether more or less in line with the model proposed in this book. Humanity needs you, is calling for you, and relies on you!

RECOMMENDED READINGS

This list of annotated recommended books represents my personal preferences, without necessarily agreeing with the various authors. Many items will be overtaken by new publications, though I suggest up-to-date ones. Readers are urged to check whether newer editions or more recent reputable books covering the same ground are available.

The recommended books provide broad treatments which can serve as gourmet meals for your mind, not "takeout" portions of fast food. They add up to quite a lot, but without much reading one cannot be an avant-garde politician. This is all the more true for students considering becoming avant-garde politicians or their advisors as a main part of their life meaning, or who want to understand what should be the nature of political leadership in the emerging epoch of metamorphosing humanity.

The list is for choosing and picking. Explore what interests you and read what appeals to you. But without a lot of diverse readings you cannot become and constantly improve yourself as an avant-garde politician.

Surnames of authors and publication date are provided, full information being included in the bibliography. The readings are presented as sets more or less in the order of chapters, with deviations, by order of dates of publication or recommended order of reading. Additional publications, included some recommended for reading, are cited in the text.

As a first aperitif, start with Wood (2006). Then proceed to Heilbroner (1991) and Weber (2004). Read "Science as a Vocation," and then study closely "Politics as a Vocation." Also relevant is the overall spirit of Ypi (2012), though I disagree with much of its content.

A second aperitif which introduces you to the serious dangers facing humanity includes Bostrom and Ćirković, eds. (2012), Newitz (2013) and Marchetti and Moyle (2010), together with the by now classic Rees (2003).

A third and last aperitif, especially for readers lacking personal experience in the corridors of power, starts with Blight and Lang (2012), which illustrates a political leader's readiness to start a nuclear war because of strongly held beliefs. Imagine such leaders equipped with biological weapons that can kill most of humanity and you gain insight into the main rationale of my book. Bovens and Hart (1998), Scott (1998), and Clark (2013) further demonstrate the inability of most prevailing types of political leader is to cope with an era of metamorphosis. For a different stimulating perspective on leadership and politics, read Schmitt (2007), and then Balakrishnan (2002). Some further insight into the realities of politics is provided by Ignatieff (2013).

Essential is understanding of politics in depth. I take for granted familiarity with some mainstream books in political science, political psychology, political sociology, constitutional law, and so on, together with personal knowledge based on experience which you have to acquire. But essential is familiarity with cutting-edge approaches deviating from introductory texts. Two recommended books which provide necessary unconventional perspectives, though I disagree with parts of them, are Ezrahi (2012) and Welch (2013).

Moving on to the main reading dishes, despite major differences between political and other leaders a convenient introduction is Grint (2010). Much can be learned from Heifetz (1995), Saar, with Hargrove (2013), and Rotberg (2012) who discusses some proto-avant-garde politicians. A comprehensive introduction to leadership theories is provided by Northhouse (2013). Still worth careful reading is Burns (1978). For Chinese views on leadership, read Guo (2002).

Interesting on "calling" and related shaping of the self is Goldman (1988), to be followed with Goldman (1992).

Classical moral sermons to rulers are illustrated by Muntzer (2010). Modern Mirrors for Rulers include Morris (1999) and Lord (2003). On the crucial context of capacities to govern and proposals for institutional reforms needed for bringing to the fore high-quality political leaders, recommended are Dror (2002) and Grover (2013).

Christian (2011) and Diamond (1999) provide macro-historical perspectives. On human evolution in relation to science and technology, recommended are Johnson and Wetmore, eds. (2009), Lightman, Sarewitz, and Desser, eds. (2009), and Allenby and Sarewitz (2011). An interesting different view is presented by Finlayson (2009).

On value issues read MacIntyre (2002). On value application to concrete choices recommended is Sandel (2009a). On moral issues posed by science and technology start with Sandel (2009b) and Janicaud (2005). To get deeper into issues of human enhancement continue with Buchanan (2011), to be compared with Agar (2010).

If you have not done so, read Emmanuel Kant, *On Eternal Peace*, in one of its English translations. Relevant for setting up a Global Authority is Pines (2009). On the United Nations, read Kennedy (2007). Important is Urquhart (1995), which illustrates challenges faced by global governance in the past, but, however difficult, these are relatively easy compared to novel ones emerging quickly.

On debates concerning the nature of consciousness I recommend Revonsuo (2010) and Blackmore (2010). On the mind itself, start with Pinker (2009), and continue with

Brockman (2011b). Intuition is well discussed in Klein (2013). A different perspective is supplied by Groopman (2007). On cultural differences read Nisbett (2003). Concerning the autonomy of the mind recommended is Guignon (2004). To get a sense for benefits and dangers of mental aberrations, read Shenk (2005) and Ghaemi (2011).

You can easily find biographies of political leaders in which you are interested. As a starter, I recommend Arana (2013), Debray (1994), Bergére (2000), Dusen (1969), Anderson (2010), Read (2005), White (2010), and Vogel (2011). Though somewhat outdated, also recommended is Downton, Jr. (1973). Illustrating the difficulties of arriving at realistic images of early rulers who became mythical persons is Allen (2012).

Obligatory readings include at least one biography of a toxic leader, such as Adolf Hitler. Start with Stolfi (2011), to be followed by a fascination discussion of the impact of Richard Wagner's *Nibelungen Ring* on the dream world of Hitler (Kohler 2001), which could easily have resulted in using a doomsday weapon, if he had one, in preference to letting the Third Reich lose the war.

Reading at least one penetrating book on Nazi Germany, such as Evans (2006), will provide essential insight into the nature of absolute evil and the ease, in some circumstances, of making an educated and culturally creative society adopt predatory fanaticism. Important are Goldhagen (2009) and Browning (1992).

On worlds in the mind I suggest Horowitz (2009), and then Ramo (2009). Important is Vertzberger (1993).

On humans from a psychological perspective read Gross (2012). Artistic creativity as a major factor in human nature and history is beautifully presented in MacGregor (2011).

The pioneering book on alternative futures which repays reading is Jouvenel (1967). Essential readings include National Intelligence Council (2012). Also relevant are Singh (2012), Smil (2012), and Gore (2013), though they miss a lot. Reliable reviews and recommendations on relevant books are presented in Michael Marien's global foresight books website http://www.globalforesightbooks.org/bio.htm.

On rationality and reason read Elster (2008). Concerning pondering, reading some chapters selected by you from Holyoak and Morrison, eds. (2013), and from Moran, Rein, and Goodin, eds. (2008) is recommended.

A good text in policy analysis, though more is needed for pondering on humanity-craft, is Dunn (2011). Strategic planning is discussed in Lampel et al. (2013), but some important issues are not taken up. A mind-stretched book illustrating the use of theory of games applied metaphorically to complex issues is Williams (1987)). On policymaking as a whole you may like to read Dror (2003). Sayers (1979) and Schon (1991) deal with creativity and professionalism respectively.

On swerving history, essential readings include Braudel (1982), Hawthorn (1991), and Ferguson (2011). On rise and decline, I recommend Toynbee with Somervell (1946, 1957). Fascinating case studies include Israel (1995) and Wald (2014), which is also distinguished by interestingly surveying main theories of rise and decline. A modern text worth reading is Diamond (2011), though over-influenced by contemporary concerns with environmental issues. Importantly dealing with the rise and decline of an ideological-political history-changing still influential global movement is Priestland (2010), indicating what may happen again unpredictably. Priestland (2013) explains history in a different way, illustrating the importance of frames of thinking and concept packages for presenting and understanding the past.

On science and technology, books which can help you acquire essential literacy are Boysen et al. (2011), Brockman (2011), Church and Regis (2012), Dexler (2013) and Kaku (2012). Contemplative-philosophic is Fuller (2011). A recommended mind stretcher is Scientific American (2013b), though parts are already becoming outdated, illustrating rapid advances, or changes of mind, in some exciting domains of physics.

On uncertainty read Taleb (2011). Important is Dewar (2002). Interesting but not applicable to thick uncertainty is Kahneman (2011). You have to study and try to apply the very important book by Taleb on antifragility (2012).

On power, recommended is Lukes (2005). Rereading *The Prince* by Machiavelli and reading Bobbitt (2009; 2013), and then doing a mental exercise applying them to modern conditions are salutary. Reflections by modern practitioners of power are represented by Powell (2010). An unusually realistic perspective is provided by Scharfstein (1995).

Essential knowledge in political psychology and marketing is provided by Sears, Huddy, and Jervis eds. (2003), and Lees-Marshment, ed. (2011), together with Lakoff (2009) and Brockman (2011a). But I think all of them are rapidly becoming at least in part outdated because of changing mass media, Internet impacts, now types of "crowds," and shifting public agendas. I have not found any book to recommend on the emerging new political psychology.

On advisors, a pleasure to read is Huxley (1941). On advisors in action I recommend Sorensen (1963), though it presents too rosy a picture. Important is George (1980). On science advisors recommended is Jasanoff (1998), though it is somewhat narrow and outdated. Interesting on outside and mixed outside-inside advisors are Neustadt (2000) and Sorensen (2008). But both books relate in part to specific features of President John F. Kennedy and his entourage.

There is plenty of literature on advising the U.S. President, the U.S. National Security Council, and so on—experiences which influence quite a number of countries, even if not fitting well. I recommend Rothkopf (2006) and Patterson (2010). A relevant and interesting UK report is Parker et al. (2010).

On existentialism recommended are Flynn, T. (2006) and Solomon, ed. (2005). Obligatory reading is Hadot (2001). Also recommended is Hadot (1995). Interesting insights are provided by Heidegger, as conveniently presented in Inwood (1997). Important is Storr (2005). Also recommended are the *Meditations* of Markus Aurelius, available in many editions, and the private diary and notes of Hammarskjöld, available in Hammarskjöld (2003).

On self-monitoring and improvement, read Sloterdijk (2013), and then Kekes (1992) and Hutter (2005). On self-knowledge Hatzimoysis, ed. (2011) covers the ground. If you are interested in your "self", read relevant chapters from Gallagher 2011. As a warning not to overstay in office, Post (1995) is recommended.

From all the many diaries and memoirs by political leaders I recommend two. The first are the three volumes of *Diaries of a Cabinet Minister* by Richard Crossman (1975, 1976, 1977), which describe in fascinating details his experience inside the British government, including much information never revealed before. He used to dictate frankly every week on a tape recorder his experiences. After his death his diaries were published in three volumes, with the courts overruled government objections. They served as raw material for the British TV series *Yes Minister* and *Yes Prime Minister*.

The second quite different but highly important diaries are the three volumes of *White House Years* by Henry Kissinger (2011a, 1999, 2011b, in this order), which present much statecraft wisdom in action. Different but revealing is Ignatieff (2013).

It may be worth your while to do some readings on rhetoric. Recommended as starters are Toye (2013); and, if you feel you are a radical, Gandio (2008).

The following books relating to the Finale conclude this list of readings: Eagly and Carli (2007), Damon (2009), and Komives et al. (2011).

Going beyond readings, throughout the book I mention a number of movies which illustrate well some main issues. Seeing them is well worth your time, while also being enjoyable. Let me add one more film you must in my view see, perhaps more than once (as I did), and ponder about, if you have not already done so: *A Man for All Seasons*, based on Robert Bolt's play of the same name about Sir Thomas More, directed by Fred Zinnemann and released in 1966.

BIBLIOGRAPHY

This bibliography provides details of all publications cited in the text and included in the recommended readings. Nearly all of the included books are in English, with the exception of a few pertinent ones in German. When appropriate I add information on the original versions and other details.

6, Perri, Diana Leat, Kimberly Seltzer, and Gerry Stoker. 2002. *Towards Holistic Governance: The New Reform Agenda*. New York: Palgrave.

Abbott, Edwin A. 2009. *Flatland: An Edition with Notes and Commentary*. Cambridge, UK: Cambridge University Press.

Agamben, Giorgio. 2005. *State of Exception*. Chicago: University of Chicago Press.

Agar, Nicholas. 2010. *Humanity's End: Why We Should Reject Radical Enhancement*. Cambridge, MA: MIT Press.

Ahrens, Joachim, Rolf Caspers, and Janina Weingarth, eds. 2011. *Good Governance in the 21st Century: Conflict, Institutional Change and Development in the Era of Globalization*. Cheltenham, UK: Edward Elgar.

Akerlof, George A., and Robert J. Shiller. 2010. *Animal Spirits: How Human Psychology Drives the Economy, and Why It Matters for Global Capitalism*. Princeton: Princeton University Press.

Algrant, Christine Pevitt. 2002. *Madame de Pompadour: Mistress of France*. New York: Grove Press.

Alkeson, Lonna Rae, and Cherie D. Maestas (2012). *Catastrophic Politics: How Extraordinary Events Redefine Perceptions of Government*. Cambridge, UK: Cambridge University Press.

Allen, Charles. 2012. *Ashoka: The Search for India's Lost Emperor*. New York: Overlook Press.

Allenby, Braden R., and Daniel Sarewitz. 2011.*The Techno-Human Condition*. Cambridge, MA: MIT Press.

Anderson, Benedict. 2006. *Imagined Communities: Reflections on the Origin and Spread of Nationalism*, Revised Edition. London: Verso.

Anderson, Jon Lee. 2010. *Che Guevara: A Revolutionary Life*. London: Bantam.

Aradau, Claudia, and Rens Van Munster. 2011. *Politics of Catastrophe: Genealogies of the Unknown*. New York: Routledge.

Arana, Marie. 2013. *Bolivar: The Epic Life of the Man Who Liberated South America*. New York: Simon and Schuster.

Arendt, Hannah. 2006a. *Denken ohne Geländer*. Munich: Piper Verlag.

Arendt, Hannah. 2006b. *Eichmann in Jerusalem: A Report on the Banality of Evil*. New York: Penguin.

Athanassoulis, Nafsika. 2013. *Virtue Ethics*. New York: Bloomsbury Academic.

Babich, Babette E. 2007. *Words in Blood, Like Flowers: Philosophy and Poetry, Music and Eros In Holderlin, Nietzsche, And Heidegger*. Albany, NY: State University of New York Press.

Badiou, Alain. 2005. *Metapolitics*. London: Verso.

Badiou, Alain. 2012. *Philosophy for Militants*. London: Verso.

Baggott, Jim. 2011. *The Quantum Story: A History in 40 Moments*. Oxford: Oxford University Press.

Balakrishnan, Gopal. 2002. *The Enemy: An Intellectual Portrait of Carl Schmitt*. London: Verso.

Barber, Benjamin R. 2013. *If Mayors Ruled the World: Dysfunctional Nations, Rising Cities*. New Haven: Yale University Press.

Barber, James David. 2009. *The Presidential Character: Predicting Performance in the White House*. New York: Pearson Longman.

Barry, John M. 2005. *The Great Influenza: The Epic Story of the Deadliest Plague in History*. New York: Penguin.

Bar-Tal, Daniel. 2013. *Intractable Conflicts: Socio-Psychological Foundations and Dynamics*. New York: Cambridge University Press.

Basl, John and Ronald L. Sandler eds. 2013. *Designer Biology: The Ethics of Intensively Engineering Biological and Ecological Systems*. Lanham, MD: Lexington.

Bass, Bernard M., and Ronald E. Riggio. 2006. *Transformational Leadership*, Second Edition. London: Lawrence Erlbaum.

Bellah, Robert N., and Hans Joas, eds. 2012. *The Axial Age and Its Consequences*. Cambridge, MA: Harvard University Press.

Benjamin, Walter. 1974. *Über den Begriff der Geschichte*. Gesammelte Schriften I:2. Frankfurt am Main: Suhrkamp Verlag. Written in 1940.

Bergére, Marie-Claire. 2000. *Sun Yat-sen*. Stanford: Stanford University Press.

Berggruen, Nicolas, and Nathan Gardels. 1913. *Intelligent Governance for the 21st Century: A Middle Way between West and East*. Cambridge, UK: Polity.

Berlin, Isaiah. 2013. *The Hedgehog and the Fox: An Essay on Tolstoy's View of History*, Second Edition. Princeton, NJ: Princeton University Press.

Birger, Fredriksen, Sing Kong Lee, and Chor Boon Goh. 2008.*Toward a Better Future: Education and Training for Economic Development in Singapore Since 1965*. Washington, DC: Word Bank Publications.

Blackmore, Susan. 2010. *Consciousness: An Introduction*. London: Hodder Education.

Blight, James G., and Janet M. Lang. 2012.*The Armageddon Letters: Kennedy/Khrushchev/Castro in the Cuban Missile Crisis*. Lanham, MD: Rowman & Littlefield.

Bloch, Arthur. 2003. Murphy's Law: The 26th Anniversary Edition. New York: Berkeley Publishing Group.

Bloch, Ernst. 1995. *The Principle of Hope*, 3 volumes. Cambridge, MA: MIT Press. Published originally in 1954–1959.

Bobbitt, Philip. 2003. *The Shield of Achilles: War, Peace, and the Course of History*. New York: Anchor Books.

Bobbitt, Philip. 2009. *Terror and Consent: The Wars for the Twenty-first Century*. New York: Penguin.

Bobbitt, Philip. 2013. *The Garments of Court and Palace: Machiavelli and the World That He Made*. New York: Grove.

Boroujerdi, Mehrzad, ed. 2013. *Mirror for the Muslim Prince: Islam and the Theory of Statecraft*. New York, Syracuse: Syracuse University Press.

Boserup, Ester. 1981. *Population and Technological Change: A Study of Long-Term Trends*. Chicago: University of Chicago Press.

Bostrom, Nick, and Milan M. Ćirković, eds. 2012. Global Catastrophic Risks. Oxford: Oxford University Press.

Bourdieu, Pierre. 1998. *Practical Reason*. Cambridge, UK: Polity.

Bovens, Mark, and Paul T. Hart. 1998. *Understanding Policy Fiascoes*. New Brunswick: Transaction.

Boysen, Earl, Nancy C. Muir, Desiree Dudley, and Christine Peterson. 2011. *Nanotechnology For Dummies*. Hoboken, NJ: Wiley.

Bracken, Paul. 2006. "Net Assessment: A Practical Guide." *Parameters*, Vol. 36, Issue 1, (Spring): 90-100.

Braudel, Fernand. 1982. *On History*. Chicago: University of Chicago Press.

Brock, Gillian, and Harry Brighouse, eds. 2005. *The Political Philosophy of Cosmopolitanism*. Cambridge, UK: Cambridge University Press.

Brockman, John, ed. 2011a. Is *the Internet Changing the Way You Think: The Net's Impact on Our Minds and Future*. New York: Harper Perennial.

Brockman, John, ed. 2011b. *The Mind: Leading Scientists Explore the Brain, Memory, Personality, and Happiness*. New York: Harper Perennial.

Brockman, Max, ed. 2011. *Future Science: Essays From the Cutting Edge*. Oxford: Oxford University Press.

Brousseau, Eric, Tom Dedeurwaerdere, and Bernd Siebenhüner, ed. 2012. *Reflexive Governance for Global Public Goods*. Cambridge, MA: MIT Press.

Brown, Garrett Wallace, and David Held, eds. 2010. *The Cosmopolitanism Reader*. Cambridge, UK: Polity.

Brown, Lester R., and Hal Kane. 1994. *Full House: Reassessing the Earth's Population Carrying Capacity*. New York: Norton.

Browning, Christopher R. 1992. *Ordinary Men: Reserve Police Battalion 11 and the Final Solution in Poland*. New York: Harper.

Buchanan, Allen. 2011. *Better than Human: The Promise and Perils of Enhancing Outselves*. Oxford: Oxford University Press.

Budgen, Sebastian, Stathis Kouvelakis, Slavoj Zizek, and David Fernbach. 2007. *Lenin Reloaded: Toward a Politics of Truth*. Durham, NC: Duke University Press.

Burchard, Brendon. 2009. *The Student Leadership Guide*, Fourth Edition. Garden City, NY: Experts Academy Press.

Burckhardt, Jacob. 1990. *The Civilization of the Renaissance in Italy*. London: Penguin. First published in German in 1860.

Burger, Dionys. 1983. *Sphereland: A Fantasy About Curved Spaces and an Expanding Universe*. New York: Harper and Row.

Burgess, Anthony. 1962. *A Clockwork Orange*. New York: Norton.

Burns, James Macgregor. 1978. *Leadership*. New York: Harper and Row.

Busemeyer, Jerome R., and Peter D. Bruza. 2012. *Quantum Models of Cognition and Decision*. Cambridge, UK: Cambridge University Press.

Butler, Judith P. (2005). *Giving an Account of Oneself*. New York: Fordham University Press.

Calabresi, Guido, and Philip Bobbitt. 1978. *Tragic Choices: The Conflicts Society Confront in the Allocation of Tragically Scarce Resources*. New York: Norton.

Caldwell, David, Mark A. Hall, and Caroline M. Wilkinson. 2010. *The Lewis Chessmen: Unmasked*. Birmingham: NMSE Publishing.

Calinescu, Matei. 1987. *Five Faces of Modernity: Modernism, Avant-garde, Decadence, Kitsch, Postmodernism*, Second Edition. Durham, NC: Duke University Press.

Campbell, Joseph. 2008. *The Hero With a Thousand Faces*. Novato, CA: New World Library.

Cannadine, David. 2013. *The Undivided Past: History Beyond our Differences. New York, NY: Knopf.*

Carlyle, Thomas. 2011. *On Heroes, Hero-Worship, and The Heroic in History.* Charleston, SC: Create Space, first published 1840.

Carrel, Laurent F. 2010. *Leadership in Krisen: Ein Leitfaden für die Praxis. 2nd ed., Wiesbaden: Gabler.*

Center for the Study of Intelligence. 2009. *A Tradecraft Primer: Structured Analytical Techniques for Improving Intelligence Analysis.* Washington, DC: US Government.

Chouliaraki, Lilie. 2013. *The Ironic Spectator: Solidarity in the Age of Post-Humanitarianism.* Cambridge, UK: Polity.

Christian, David 2011. *Maps of Time: An Introduction to Big History.* Berkeley: University of California Press.

Christian, David, Cynthia Brown, and Craig Benjamin 2013. *Big History: Between Nothing and Everything.* New York: McGraw-Hill.

Church, George, and Ed Regis. 2012. *Regenesis: How Synthetic Biology Will Reinvent Nature and Ourselves.* New York: Basic Books.

Cirincione, Joseph 2013. *Nuclear Nightmares: Securing the World Before It Is Too Late.* New York: Columbia University Press.

Clark, Christopher. 2013. *The Sleepwalkers: How Europe Went to War in 1914.* New York: Harper.

Claussen, Detlev. 2008. *Theodor W. Adorno: One Last Genius.* Cambridge, MA: Harvard University Press.

Cochran, Gregory and Henry Harpending 2010. *The 10,000 Year Explosion: How Civilization Accelerated Human Evolution.* New York: Basic Books.

Codevilla, Angelo M. 2009. *Advice to War Presidents: A Remedial Course in Statecraft.* New York: Basic Books.

Cohen, Michael D., James G. March, and Johan P. Olsen. 1972 "A Garbage Can Model of Organizational Choice." *Administrative Science Quarterly* 17(1):1-25.

Collingwood, Robin George. 1946. *The Idea of History.* Oxford: Oxford University Press.

Collini, Stefan, Donald Winch and John Burrow. 1984. *That Noble Science of Politics: A Study in Nineteenth-Century Intellectual History.* Cambridge, UK: Cambridge University Press.

Cooper Jr., John Milton. 2011. *Woodrow Wilson: A Biography.* New York: Vintage.

Cottington, David. 2013. *The Avant-Garde: A Very Short Introduction. Oxford: Oxford University Press.*

CQ Researcher. 2013. *Global Issues. Thousand Oaks, CA: CQ Press.*

Crossman, Richard. 1975. *The Diaries of a Cabinet Minister, Volume 1: Minister of Housing, 1964–1966.* London: Hamish Hamilton.

Crossman, Richard. 1976.*The Diaries of a Cabinet Minister, Volume 2: Lord President of the Council, 1966–1968.*London: Hamish Hamilton.

Crossman, Richard. 1977 *The Diaries of a Cabinet Minister, Volume 3: Secretary Of State For Social Services 1968–1970.* London: Hamish Hamilton and Jonathan Cape.

Csikszentmihalyi, Mihaly. 2008. *Flow: The Psychology of Optimal Experience.* New York: Harper.

Csikszentmihalyi, Mihaly. 2013. *Creativity: The Psychology of Discovery and Invention.* New York: HarperPerrenial. First published 1996.

Damon, William. 2009. *The Path to Purpose: How Young People Find Their Calling in Life.* New York: Free Press.

Dawkins, Richard. 1997. *Climbing Mount Improbable.* New York: Norton.

Dawkins, Richard 2006. *The Selfish Gene: 30th Anniversary Edition--with a new Introduction by the Author.* Oxford: Oxford University Press

Debray, Regis. 1994. *Charles De Gaulle: Futurist of the Nation.* London: Verso.

Dennett, Daniel C., and Linda LaScola (2013). *Caught in The Pulpit: Leaving Belief Behind.* Congruity Publishing (no location supplied).

Dessler, Andrew, and Edward A. Parson. (2010). *The Science and Politics of Global Climate Change: A Guide to the Debate.* Cambridge, UK: Cambridge University Press.

Deutsch, David 2011. *The Beginning of Infinity: Explanations That Transform the World.* New York: Viking.

Deutsch, David, and Artur Ekert 2013. "Beyond the Quantum Horizon." *Scientific American, Special Collector's Edition—Extreme* Physics—*Probing the Mysteries of the Cosmos,* Vol. 22(2):102-107.

Dewar, James A. 2002. *Assumption-Based Planning: A Tool for Reducing Avoidable Surprises.* New York: Cambridge University Press.

Diamond, Jared. 1999. *Guns, Germs, and Steel: The Fates of Human Societies.* New York: Norton.

Diamond, Jared. 2011. *Collapse: How Societies Choose to Fail and Survive.* London: Penguin.

Diamond, Jared M. 2013. *The World Until Yesterday: What Can We Learn from Traditional Societies?* London: Penguin.

Divers, John. 2002. *Possible Worlds.* London: Routldge.

Dorling, Danny. 2013. *Population 10 Billion.* London: Constable and Robinson.

Downton, Jr., James V. 1973. *Rebel Leadership: Commitment and Charisma in the Revolutionary Process.* New York: Free Press.

Drexler, K. Eric 2013. *Radical Abundance: How a Revolution in Nanotechnology Will Change Civilization.* New York: PublicAffairs.

Dror, Yehezkel. 1980. *Crazy States: A Counterconventional Strategic Problem*. Milwood, NY: Kraus.

Dror, Yehezkel Dror. 2002. *The Capacity to Govern: A Report to the Club of Rome*. London: Routledge.

Dror, Yehezkel. 2003. *Public Policymaking Reexamined*. New Brunswick: Transaction. First published 1968.

Dror, Yehezkel. 2011. *Israeli Statecraft: National Security Challenges and Responses*. New York: Routledge.

Duggan, William. 2013. *Strategic Intuition: The Creative Spark in Human Achievement*. New York: Columbia University Press.

Dunn, William N. 2011. *Public Policy Analysis*, 5th Edition. Cambridge, UK: Pearson.

Dusen, Henry P. Van 1969. *Dag Hammerskjöld: The Man and His Faith*. New York: Harper.

Duve, Christian De, with Neil Patterson. 2010. *Genetics of Original Sin: The Impact of Natural Selection on the Future of Humanity*. New Haven: Yale University Press.

Eagly, Alice H., and Linda L. Carli. 2007. *Through the Labyrinth: The Truth About How Women Become Leaders*. Cambridge MA: Harvard Business School Press.

Ehlers, Eckart, and Thomas Krafft, eds. 2010. *Earth System Science in the Anthropocene: Emerging Issues and Problems*. Berlin: Springer.

Eisenhower, John S. D. 2008. "Presidential Children Don't Belong in Battle," *New York Time*, September 27, 2008.

Eisenstadt, Shmuel N. ed. 1986. *The Origins and Diversity of Axial Age Civilizations*. Albany, NY: State University of New York Press.

Elias, Norbert 1992. *Time: An Essay*. Oxford: Blackwell.

Elliot, Thomas Stearns 1973. *The Elder Statesman*. London: Faber and Faber.

Ellis, Joseph J. 2002. *Founding Brothers: The Revolutionary Generation*. New York: Vintage.

Elster, Jon. 2008. *Reason and Rationality*. Princeton: Princeton University Press.

Emirates Center for Strategic Studies and Research. 2005. *With United Strength: Shaikh Zayid Bin Sultan Al Nahyan: The Leader and the Nation*. Abu Dhabi: Emirates Center for Strategic Studies and Research.

Etzioni, Amitai. 1994. *Spirit of Community*. New York: Touchstone.

Etzioni, Amitai. 1997. *The New Golden Rule: Community And Morality In A Democratic Society*. New York: Basic Books.

Evans, Richard J. 2006. *The Third Reich in Power*. New York: Penguin.

Ezrahi, Yaron. 2012. *Imagined Democracies: Necessary Political Fictions*. Cambridge, UK: Cambridge University Press.

Fagan, Brian. 2009. *The Great Warming: Climate Change and the Rise and Fall of Civilizations.* London: Bloomsbury Press.

Fayol, Henry. 1949. *General and Industrial Management.* London: Pitman. First published in French in 1916.

Featherstone, David. 2012. *Solidarity: Hidden Histories and Geographies of Internationalism.* London: Zed Books.

Ferguson, Niall. 2011. *Virtual History: Alternatives and Counterfactuals.* London: Penguin.

Ferguson, Niall. 2012. *Civilization: The West and the Rest.* London: Penguin Books.

Festinger, Leon et al. 1956. *When Prophecy Fails.* Minneapolis, MN: University of Minnesota Press.

Finer, Samuel Edward. 1999. *The History of Government from the Earliest Times: Ancient Monarchies and Empires; The Intermediate Ages; Empires, Monarchies and the Modern State* (3 Volumes). New York: Oxford University Press.

Finlayson, Clive 2009. *The Humans Who Went Extinct: Why Neanderthals Dies Out and We Survived.* Oxford: Oxford University Press.

Flannery, Tim F. 2002. *The Future Eaters: An Ecological History of the Australasian Lands and People.* New York: Grove Press.

Fleischer, Cornell H. 1986. *Bureaucrat and Intellectual in the Ottoman Empire: The Historian Mustafa Ali (1541–1600).* Princeton: Princeton University Press.

Flynn, James R. 2012. *Are We Getting Smarter?: Rising IQ in the Twenty-First Century.* Cambridge, UK: Cambridge University Press.

Flynn, Thomas R. 2006. *Existentialism: A Very Short Introduction.* Oxford, UK: Oxford University Press.

Ford, David F. 2011. *The Future of Christian Theology.* Hoboken, NJ: Wiley-Blackwell.

Ford, David F. 2013. *Theology: A Very Short Introduction.* Oxford: Oxford University Press, 2013.

Forrester, Jay Wright. 1969. *Urban Dynamics.* Cambridge, MA: MIT Press.

Fox, Douglas. 2011. "The Limits of Intelligence." *Scientific American*, 305(1): 20-27.

Freeman, Daniel and Jason Freeman (2012). *Anxiety: A Very Short Introduction.* Oxford: Oxford University Press.

Friedman, Milton, and Rosa Friedman. 1984. *The Tyranny of the Status Quo.* New York: Houghton Mifflin.

Friedman, Thomas L. 2007. *The World Is Flat: A Brief History of the Twenty-first Century.* Third Edition. New York: Picador.

Fromm, Erich. 1973. *The Anatomy of Human Destructiveness.* New York: Holt.

Fromm, Erich. 1994. *Escape from Freedom.* New York: Bolt.

Fromm, Erich. 2005. *To Have or To Be?* Revised Edition. London: Bloomsbury Academic.

Fukuyama, Francis. 2006. *The End of History and the Last Man, with a new afterword.* New York: Free Press. First published 1992.

Fukuyama, Francis, ed. 2008. *Blindside: How to Anticipate Forcing Events and Wild Cards in Global Politics.* Washington, DC: Brookings Institution.

Fukuyama, Francis. 2012. *The Origins of Political Order: From Prehuman Times to the French Revolution.* New York: Farrar, Straus and Giroux.

Fuller, Steve. 2011. *Humanity 2.0: What it Means to be Human Past, Present and Future.* New York: Palgrave Macmillan.

Gallagher, Shaun, ed. 2011. *The Oxford Handbook of The Self.* Oxford: Oxford University Press.

Gandio, Jason Del. 2008. *Rhetoric for Radicals: A Handbook for 21st Century Activists.* Gabriola Island, Canada: New Society Publishers.

Gardam, Judith 2011. *Necessity, Proportionality and the Use of Force by States.* Cambridge, UK: Cambridge University Press.

Gardner, Howard, with Emma Laskin 2011. *Leading Minds: An Anatomy of Leadership.* New York: Basic Books.

Garrett, Laurie. 2013. "Biology's Brave New World: The Promise and Perils of the Synbio Revolution." *Foreign Affairs* (November/December). http://www.foreignaffairs.com/ articles/140156/laurie-garrett/biologys-brave-new-world (accessed October 25, 2013).

Gates, Robert M (2014). *Duty: Memoirs of a Secretary at War.* New York: Knopf.

George, Alexander L. 1980. *Presidential Decisionmaking in Foreign Policy: The Effective Use of Information and Advice.* Boulding, CO: Westview Press.

George, Alexander L., and Juliette George. 1964. *Woodrow Wilson and Colonel House: A Personality Study.* New York: Dover.

Ghaemi, Nassir. 2011. *A First-Rate Madness: Uncovering the Links Between Leadership and Mental Illness.* London: Penguin.

Gibbs, Nancy, and Michael Duffy. 2013. *The Presidents Club: Inside the World's Most Exclusive Fraternity.* New York: Simon and Schuster.

Gigerenzer, Gerd. 2007. *Gut Feelings: The Intelligence of the Unconscious.* New York: Penguin.

Ginsburg, Tom. 2012. *Comparative Constitutional Design.* Cambridge, UK: Cambridge University Press.

Gladwell, Malcolm. 2005. *Blink: The Power of Thinking Without Thinking.* Boston, MA: Little, Brown.

Gobet, Fernandt, Jean Retschitzki, Alex de Voogt (2012). *Moves in Mind: The Psychology of Board Games.* New York: Psychology Press.

Goethe, Johann Wolfgang. 1998. "Zum Shakespears Tag". In *Werke*, hersg.von Friedmar Apel u.a. Frankfurt am Main und Leipzig: Wissenschaftliche Buchgesellschaft.

Goldberg, Elkhonon. 2001. *The Executive Brain: Frontal Lobes and the Civilized Mind*. Oxford: Oxford University Press.

Goldhagen, Daniel Jonah. 1997. *Hitler's Willing Executioners: Ordinary Germans and the Holocaust*. New York: Vintage.

Goldhagen, Daniel Jonah. 2009. *Worse Than War: Genocide, Eliminationism, and the Ongoing Assault on Humanity*. New York: PublicAffairs.

Goldin, Ian. 2013. *Divided Nations: Why Global Governance is Ffailing, and What We Can do About It*. Oxford: Oxford University Press.

Goldman, Harvey. 1988. *Max Weber and Thomas Mann: Calling and the Shaping of the Self*. Berkeley, CA: University of Californian Press.

Goldman, Harvey. 1992. *Politics, Death, and the Devil: Self and Power in Max Weber and Thomas Mann*. Berkeley, CA: University of Californian Press.

Gore, Al. 2013. *The Future*. New York: Random.

Gould, Stephen Jay. 2007. *Punctuated Equilibrium*. Cambridge, MA: Harvard University Press.

Grint, Keith. 2010. *Leadership: A Very Short Introduction*. Oxford: Oxford University Press.

Groopman, Jerome. 2007. *How Doctors Think*. Boston: Houghton Mifflin.

Gross, Richard. 2012. *Being Human: Psychological and Philosophical Perspectives*. London: Hodder Education.

Grover, William F. 2013. " Deep Presidency: Toward a Structural Theory of an Unsustainable Office in a Catastrophic World—Obama and Beyond," *New Political Science* 35 (3):432-448.

Grube, Ernst J. 1992. *A Mirror for Princes from India: Illustrated Versions of the Kalilah Wa*. Mumbai: Marg Pubns.

Guignon, Charles. 2004. *On Being Authentic*. London: Routledge.

Guleng, Mai Britt. 2013. "The Narratives of The Frieze of Life. Edward Much's Picture Series." In*Edward Munch 1863–1944*, ed.: Skira Rizzoli. Milano: Skira editore, 128-139.

Guo, Xuezhi. 2002. *The Ideal Chinese Political Leader: A Historic and Cultural Perspective*. Westport CT: Praeger.

Guterl, Fred. 2013. *The Fate of the Species: Why the Human Race May Cause Its Own Extinction and How We Can Stop It*. New York: Bloomsbury.

Hacking, Ian. 2006.*The Emergence of Probability: A Philosophical Study of Early Ideas about Probability, Induction and Statistical Inference*, Second Edition. Cambridge, UK: Cambridge University Press.

Hadot, Pierre. 1995. *Philosophy as a Way or Life: Spiritual Exercises from Socrates to Foucault*. Oxford: Blackwell.

Hadot, Pierre. 2001. *The Inner Citadel: The Meditations of Marcus Aurelius*. Cambridge, MA: Harvard University Press.

Hamilton, Cllive. 2013. *Earthmasters: The Dawn of the Age of Climate Engineering*. New Haven: Yale University Press.

Hammarskjöld, Dag. 2003. *Markings*. New York: Knopf.

Hardt, Michael and Antonio Negri 2005. *Multitude: War and Democracy in the Age of Empire*. New York: Penguin.

Harris, Sam (2012). *Free Will*. New York: Free Press.

Hatzimoysis, Anthony, ed. 2011. *Self-Knowledge*. Oxford: Oxford University Press.

Hauser, Mark. 2009. "The Origins of Mind." *Scientific American*, September, 24-29.

Hawking, Stephen W. and Leonard Mlodinow. 2011. *The Grand Design*. New York: Bentam.

Hawthorn, Geoffrey. 1991. *Plausible Worlds: Possibility and Understanding in History and the Social Sciences*. Cambridge, UK: Cambridge University Press.

Hazleton, Lesley. 2013. *The First Muslim: The Story of Muhammad*. New York: Riverhead.

Heifetz, Ronald A. 1995. *Leadership Without Easy Answers*. Cambridge, MA: Harvard University Press.

Heilbroner, Robert L. 1991. *An Inquiry Into The Human Prospect: Looked at Again for the 1990s*. New York: Norton.

Held, David. 2010. *Cosmopolitanism: Ideals and Realities*. Cambridge, UK: Polilty.

Highfield, Roger. 2013. "3D Printing: Manufacturing Enters a New Dimension—The 3D Printer is Threatening to Change the World in Ways We Can Barely Imagine." *The World Today* (October and November):14-16.

Hilger, Matthew, and Ian Taylor. 2007. *The Poker Mindset: Essential Attitudes for Poker Success*. Suwanee, GA: Dimat Enterprises.

Hirschman, Albert O. 1991. The *Rhetoric of Reaction: Perversity, Futility, Jeopardy*. Cambridge, MA: Harvard University Press.

Hoffer Eric 1951. *The True Believer: Thoughts on the Nature of Mass Movements: Thoughts on the Nature of Mass Movements*. New York: Harper.

Hofstadter, Douglas and Emmanuel Sander. 2013. *Surfaces and Essences: Analogy As the Fuel and Fire of Thinking*. New York: Basic Books.

Hölldobler, Beret and Edward O. Wilson. 2008. *The Superorganism: The Beauty, Elegance, and Strangeness of Insect Societies*. New York: Norton.

Holyoak, Keith J., and Robert G. Morrison, ed. 2012. *The Cambridge Handbook of Thinking and Reasoning*. New York: Oxford University Press.

Horowitz, Alexandra. 2009. *Inside of a Dog: What Dogs See, Smell and Know*. New York: Scribner.

Howell, William G. 2013. *Thinking about the Presidency: The Primacy of Power*. Princeton: Princeton University Press.

Huddy, Leonie, David O. Sears, and Jack S. Levy, eds. 2013. *The Oxford Handbook of Political Psychology, Second Edition. Oxford: Oxford University Press*.

Huizinga, Johan. 1971. *Homo Ludens: A Study of the Play-Element in Culture*. Boston, MA: Beacon Press. First published in Dutch in 1938.

Hulme, Mike. 2009. *Why We Disagree About Climate Change: Understanding Controversy, Inaction and Opportunity*. Cambridge, UK: Cambridge University Press.

Hunt, Earl. 2010. *Human Intelligence*. Cambridge, UK: Cambridge University Press.

Huntington, Samuel P. 2011. *The Clash of Civilizations and the Remaking of World Order*. New York: Simon and Schuster. First published 1996, based on a 1992 lecture and a 1993 article.

Hutter, Horst. 2005. *Shaping the Future: Nietzsche's New Regime of the Soul and Its Ascetic Practices*. Lanham, MD: Lexington Books.

Huxley, Aldous. 1941. *Grey Eminence: A Study in Religion and Politics. New York: Harper*.

Ignatieff, Michael. 2013. *Fire and Ashes: Success and Failure in Politics*. Cambridge, MA: Harvard University Press.

Ikenberry, G. John. 2011. *Liberal Leviathan: The Origins, Crisis, and Transformation of the American World Order*. Princeton: Princeton University Press.

Immer, Nikolas. 2008. *Der inszenierte Held: Schillers dramenpoetische Anthropologie*. Heidelberg: Universitätsverlag Winter.

Innerarity, Daniel. 2012. *The Future and Its Enemies: In Defense of Political Hope. Stanford: Stanford University Press. First published in Spanish in 2009*.

International Commission on Intervention and State Sovereignty. 2001. *The Responsibility to Protect: Report of the International Commission on Intervention and State Sovereignty*. Ottawa: International Development Research Centre.

Inwood, Michael. 1997. *Heidegger: A Very Short Introduction*. New York: Oxford University Press.

IPCC. 2013. *Intergovernmental Panel on Climate Change. Climate Change 2013: The Physical Science Basis—Final Draft Underlying Scientific-Technical Assessment*. Geneva: IPPC. http://www.climatechange2013.org/images/uploads/WGIAR5_WGI-12Doc2b_FinalDraft_All.pdf (accessed October 2, 2013).

Israel, Jonathan I. 1995.*The Dutch Republic: Its Rise, Greatness, and Fall 1477-1806*. Oxford: Oxford University Press.

Janicaud, Dominique. 2005. *On the Human Condition*. London: Routledge.

Jasanoff, Sheila. 1998. *The Fifth Branch: Science Advisers as Policymakers.* Cambridge, MA: Harvard University Press.

Jasanoff, Sheila. 2005. *Design in Nature: Science and Democracy in Europe and the United States.* Princeton: Princeton University Press.

Jasanoff, Sheila. 2013. *Science and Public Reason.* New York: Routledge.

Jaspers, Karl. 1963. *The Atom Bomb and the Future of Man.* Chicago: University of Chicago Press. First published in German in 1958.

Jaspers, Karl. 2010. *The Origin and Goal of History.* New York: Routledge. First published in German in 1949.

Joas, Hans. 2000. *The Genesis of Values.* Chicago: University of Chicago Press.

Joas, Hans. 1996. *The Creativity of Action.* Chicago: University of Chicago Press.

Joas, Hans. 2013. *The Sacredness of the Person: A New Genealogy of Human Rights.* Washington, DC: Georgetown University Press.

Johnson, Deborah G. and Jameson M. Wetmore, eds. 2009. *Technology and Society: Building Our Sociotechnical Future.* Cambridge, MA: MIT Press.

Jouvenel, Bertrand de. 1949.*On Power: The Natural History of Its Growth.* New York: Viking.

Jouvenel, Bertrand de. 1967.*The Art of Conjecture.* London: Weidenfeld and Nicolson.

Joy, Bill. 2000. "Why the Future Does not Need Us." *Wired* (April). http://www.wired.com/wired/archive/8.04/joy_pr.html (accessed 25 November 2013).

Kaebnick, Gregory E. and Thomas H. Murray, eds. 2013. *Synthetic Biology and Morality: Artificial Life and the Bounds of Nature.* Cambridge, MA: MIT Press.

Kagan, Robert. 2004. *Of Paradise and Power: America and Europe in the New World Order.* New York: Vintage.

Kahneman, Daniel. 2011. *Thinking Fast and Slow.* New York: Allen Lane.

Kaku, Michio. 2012. *Physics of the Future: How Science Will Shape Human Destiny and Our Daily Lives by the Year 2100.* New York: Anchor Books.

Kalyvas, Andreas. 2009. *Democracy and the Politics of the Extraordinary: Max Weber, Carl Schmidt, and Hanna Arendt.* New York: Cambridge University Press.

Kaplan, Robert D. 2003. *Warrior Politics: Why Leadership Demands a Pagan Ethos.* New York: Random House.

Kaplan, Robert D. 2012. *The Revenge of Geography: What the Map Tells Us About Coming Conflicts and the Battle Against Fate.* New York: Random.

Kateb, George. 1994. *The Inner Ocean: Individualism and Democratic Culture.* Cornell: Cornell University Press.

Kaufman, Scott Barry, ed. 2013. *The Complexity of Greatness: Beyond Talent and Practice*. New York: Oxford University Press.

Kekes, John. 1992. *The Examined Life*. University Park, PA: Pennsylvania State University Press.

Kelsen, Hans. 1949. *General Theory of Law and State*. Cambridge, MA: Harvard University Press.

Kennedy, Paul. 2007. *The Parliament of Man: The Past, Present and Future of the United Nations*. New York: Penguin.

Kennedy, Paul. 2013. "The Great Powers, Then and Now." *International Herald Tribune*, August 8, 6.

Kepnes, Steven *(2013).The Future of Jewish Theology*. Hoboken, NJ: Wiley-Blackwell.

Keynes, John Maynard. 1965. *General Theory of Employment, Interest and Money*. New York: Harcourt, Brace. First published in 1965.

Khanna, Parag. 2011. *How to Run the World: Charting a Course to the Next Renaissance*. New York: Random.

Kissinger, Henry. 1999. *Years of Upheaval*. New York: Simon and Schuster.

Kissinger, Henry. 2011a. *Years of Renewal*. Reprinted Edition. New York: Simon and Schuster.

Kissinger, Henry 2011b. *White House Years*. Reprinted Edition. New York: Simon and Schuster.

Klein, Gary. 1999. *Sources of Power: How People Make Decisions*. Cambridge, MA: MIT Press.

Klein, Gary. 2013. *Seeing What Others Don't: The Remarkable Ways We Gain Insights*. New York: PublicAffairs.

Knoblock, John. 1990. *Xunzi: A Translation and Study of the Complete Works*, Volume II. Stanford, CA: Stanford University Press.

Kolbert, Elizabeth (2014). *The Sixth Extinction: An Unnatural History*. London: Bloomsbury.

Kohler, Joachim. 2001. *Wagner's Hitler: The Prophet and His Disciple*. Cambridge, UK: Polity.

Komives, Susan R., John P. Dugan, Julie E. Owen, et al. 2011. *The Handbook for Student Leadership Development*. San Francisco: Jossey-Bass.

Komives, Susan R., Nance Lucas, and Timothy R. McMahon. 2013. *Exploring Leadership: For College Students Who Want to Make a Difference*. San Francisco: Jossy-Bass.

Koonz, Claudia. 2005. *The Nazi Conscience*. Cambridge, MA: Harvard University Press.

Kuhlmann, Meinard. 2013. "What Is Real?" *Scientific American* (August), 309 (2):40-47.

Kuhse, Helga and Peter Singer, eds. 2012. *A Companion to Bioethics*, Revised Edition. Hoboken, NJ: Wiley-Blackwell

Kupchan, Charles A. 2012. *No One's World: The West, the Rising Rest, and the Coming Global Turn*. New York: Oxford University Press.

Kurzweil, Ray 2006. *The Singularity is Near: When Humans Transcend Biology*. New York: Penguin.

Kurzweil, Ray. 2013. *How to Create a Mind: The Secret of Human Thought Revealed*. London: Duckworth Overlook.

Lakoff, George. 2009. *The Political Mind: A Cognitive Scientist's Guide to Your Brain and Its Politics*. New York: Penguin.

Lampel, Joseph B, Henry Mintzberg, James Quinn, Sumantra Ghoshal. 2013. *The Strategy Process: Concepts, Contexts, Cases*, Fifth Edition. Cambridge, UK: Pearson.

Lanier, Jaron. 2013. *Who Owns the Future?* New York: Allen Lane.

Laski, Harold J. 1931. *The Limitations of the Expert*. London: The Fabian Society.

Latour, Bruno. 2004. *Politics of Nature: How to Bring the Sciences into Democracy*. Cambridge, MA: Harvard University Press.

Latour, Bruno. 2013. *An Inquiry into Modes of Existence: An Anthropology of the Moderns*. Cambridge, MA: Harvard University Press.

Lawrence, Joanne T., and Paul W. Beamish, eds. 2013. *Globally Responsible Leadership: Managing According to the UN Global Compact*. Los Angeles: Sage.

Lees-Marshment, Jennifer, ed. 2011. *Routledge Handbook of Political Marketing*. New York: Routledge.

Leitner, Michael, Sara Leitner, and associates. 2004. *Leisure Enhancement: Instructor's Manual*, Third Edition. New York: Routledge.

Lenin, Vladimir. I. 2005. What Is To Be Done? Burning Questions of Our Movement. New York: International Publishers, 2005. First published in Russian in 1902.

Levinas, Emmanuel. 2006. *Humanism of the Other*. Champaign, IL: University of Illinois Press. First published in French in 1972.

Lewin, Leonard C. 1967. *Report from Iron Mountain on the Possibility and Desirability of Peace*. New York: Dial Press.

Lightman, Allen, Daniel Sarewitz, and Christina Desser, eds. 2009. *Living With the Genie: Essays on Technology and the Quest for Human Mastery*. Washington, DC: Island Press.

Linnér, Sture and Sverker Åström. 2008. *UN Secretary-General Hammerskjöld: Reflections and Personal Experiences*. Uppsala, Sweden: Dag Hammerskjöld Foundation.

Linstone, Harold A. 1984. *Multiple Perspectives for Decision Making: Bridging the Gap between Analysis and Action*. Amsterdam: Elsevier Science.

Lockley, Steven W. and Russell G. Foster, Sleep: *A Very Short Introduction*. Oxford: Oxford University Press, 2012.

Lomi, Alessandro, and J. Richard Harrison, ed. 2012. "The Garbage Can Model of Organizational Choice: Looking Forward at Forty." *Research in the Sociology of Organizations, Volume 36*. Wagon Lane, UK: Emerald Group Publishing.

Lord, Carnes. 2003. *The Modern Prince: What Leaders Need to Know Now.* New Haven: Yale University Press.

Lukács, Georg. 1962. *Die Zerstörung der Vernunft.* Luchterhand: Neuwied-Berlin, 1962.

Lukaćs, Georg. 2009. *Lenin: A Study on the Unity of His Thought.* London: Verso. First published in German in 1924.

Lukas, John. 2001. *Five Days in London: May 1940.* New Haven: Yale University Press.

Lukes, Steven. 2005. *Power: A Radical View.* New York: Palgrave Macmillan.

MacArthur, Brian, ed. 2013. Book *of Historic Speeches.* London: Penguin.

Maccoby, Michael. 2007. *Narcissistic Leaders: Who Succeeds and Who Fails.* Cambridge, MA: Harvard Business Review Press.

MacGregor, Neil. 2011. *A History of the World in 100 Objects.* London: Allen Lane.

Machiavelli, Niccolò. 2003. *Discourses on Livy.* Oxford: Oxford University Press,

Machiavelli, Niccolò. 2008. *The Prince.* Oxford: Oxford University Press.

MacIntyre, Alasdair. 2002. *A Short History of Ethics: A History of Moral Philosophy from the Homeric Age to the Twentieth Century.* New York: Routledge.

MacMillan, Margaret (2010). Dangerous Games: The Uses and Abuses of History. New York: Modern Library.

MacMillan, Margaret (2013). *The War That Ended Peace: The Road to 1914.* New York: Random.

Mann, Thomas. 1999. *Doctor Faustus: The Life of the German Composer Adrian Leverkuhn As Told by a Friend.* New York: Vintage. First published in German in 1947.

Manyka, James, Michael Chui, Jacques Bughin, Richard Dobbs, Peter Bisson, and Alex Marrs. 2013. *Disruptive Technologies: Advances That Will Transform Life, Business, and the Global Economy.* San Francisco, CA: McKinsey Global Institute.

Marchetti, Michael P., and Peter B. Moyle. 2010. *Protecting Life on Earth: An Introduction to the Science of Conservation.* Berkely, CA: University of Californian Press.

Marcus, Gary. 2012. *Guitar Zero: The New Musician and the Science of Learning.* New York: Penguin.

Marean, Curtis W. 2013. "When the Sea Saved Humanity." *Scientific American -Special Collector's Edition: What Makes Us* Human. Vol. 22, No. 1. Winter, 52-59.

Martinez, Michael E. 2013. *Future Bright: A Transforming Vision of Human Intelligence.* New York: Oxford University Press.

Marty, Martin E., and R. Scott Appleby. 2004. *Fundamentalisms Comprehended.* Chicago: University of Chicago Press.

Marwick, Alice E. 2013. *Status Update: Celebrity, Publicity, and Branding in the Social Media Age.* New Haven: Yale University Press.

Masters, Roger D. 1999. *Fortune Is a River: Leonardo da Vinci and Niccolò Machiavelli's Magnificent Dream to Change the Course of Florentine History*. New York: Penguin.

Mayer-Schönberger, Victor, and Kenneth Cukier. 2013. *Big Data: A Revolution That Will Transform How We Live, Work and, Think*. New York: *Houghton Mifflin Harcourt*.

Mazzucato, Mariana. 2013. *The Entrepreneurial State: Debunking Public vs. Private Sector Myths*. New York: Anthem Press.

McGilchrist, Iain. 2012. *The Master and His Emissary: The Divided Brain and the Making of the Western World*. New Haven: Yale University Press.

McMeekin, Sean 2013. *July 1914: Countdown to War*. New York: Basic Books.

McNamara, Robert S. 1996. *In Retrospect: The Tragedy and Lessons of Vietnam*. New York: Vintage Books.

MCRIT et al., ed. 2013. *Flagship: Forward Looking Driving Change—Report Trends, Policies and Future Challenges in Economics, Demographic, Legal, Social and Environmental Field and Their Territorial Dimensions*. Rome: ISIS.

Meadows, Donella H., Dennis L. Meadows, Jorgen Randers, and William W. Behrens III 1974. *The Limits to Growth: A Report for the Club of Rome's Project on the Predicament of Mankind*. New York: Universe Books.

Meadows, Donella H., Jorgen Randers, and Dennis L. Meadows 2004. *Limits to Growth: The 30-Year Update*. White River Jct., Vt: Chelsea Green Publishing.

Meier, Christian 1980. *Die Ohnmacht des allmächtigen Dictators Caesar: Drei biographische Skizzen*. Berlin: Suhrkamp.

Mele, Alfred R. ed. 1997. *The Philosophy of Action*. New York: Oxford University Press.

Michael, Donald N. 1968. *Unprepared Society: Planning for a Precarious Future*. New York: Basic Books.

Milgram, Stanley. 2009. *Obedience to Authority: An Experimental View*, Reprinted Edition. New York: Harper Perennial Modern Classics.

Mintzberg, Henry. 1994. *Rise and Fall of Strategic Planning*. New York: Free Press.

Miscamble, Wilson D. 2011. *The Most Controversial Decision: Truman, the Atomic Bombs, and the Defeat of Japan*. Cambridge: Cambridge University Press.

Mises, Ludwig Von. 1956. Letter to Ayn Rand of 23 January. http://en.wikipedia.org/wiki/Atlas_Shrugged (accessed July 30, 2013).

Mitford, Nancy. 2001. *Madame de Pompadour*. New York: New York Review Books Classics.

Moran, Lord (Dr. Charles McMoran Wilson). 1966. *Churchill: Taken from the Diaries of Lord Moran*. Boston, MA: Houghton Mifflin.

Moran, Michael, Martin Rein, and Robert E. Goodin, eds. 2008. *The Oxford Handbook of Public Policy*. New York: Oxford University Press.

Yehezkel Dror

More, Max and Natasha Vita-More, eds. 2013. *The Transhumanist Reader: Classical and Contemporary Essays on the Science, Technology, and Philosophy of the Human Future.* Malden, MA: Wiley.

Morgan, Michael L. 2008. *On Shame.* New York: Routledge.

Morris, Dick, 1999. *The New Prince.* Los Angeles: Renaissance Books.

Muller, Richard A. 2009. *Physics for Future Presidents: The Science Behind the Headlines.* New York: Norton, April 12.

Muller, Richard A. 2013. *Energy for Future Presidents: The Science Behind the Headlines.* New York: Norton, April 12.

Muntzer, Thomas. 2010. *Sermon to the Princes.* London: Verso.

Murray, Charles. 2006. *In Our Hands: A Plan To Replace The Welfare State.* Washington, DC: American Enterprise Press.

Naam, Ramez. 2013. *The Infinite Resource: The Power of Ideas on a Finite Planet.* Lebanon, NH: University Press of New England.

Nagel, Thomas. 1989. *The View from Nowhere.* New York: Oxford University Press.

Nagel, Thomas. 2012. *Mind and Cosmos: Why the Materialist Neo-Darwinian Conception of Nature is Almost Certainly False.* Oxford: Oxford University Press.

Naim, Moisés. 2013. *The End of Power: From Boardrooms to Battlefields and Churches to States, Why Being In Charge Isn't What It Used to Be.* New York: Basic Books.

National Intelligence Council. 2008. *Global Trends 2025: A Transformed World.* Washington, DC: Superintendent of Documents, US Government Printing Office.

National Intelligence Council. 2012. *Global Trends 2030: Alternative Worlds.* Charleston, SC: CreateSpace.

Neustadt, Richard E. 2000. *Preparing to be President: The Memos of Richard E. Neustadt.* Washington, DC: AEI Press.

Newitz, Annalee. 2013. *Scatter, Adapt, and Remember: How Humans Will Survive a Mass Extinction.* New York: Doubleday.

Nisbett, Richard E. 2003. *The Geography of Thought: How Asians and Westerners Think Differently…and Why.* New York: Free Press.

North, Helen. 1966. *Sophrosyne: Self-Knowledge and Self-Restraint in Greek Literature.* Ithaca, NY: Cornell University Press.

Northhouse, Peter G. 2013. *Leadership: Theory and Practive.* Sixth Edition. Los Angeles: Sage.

Nowak, Martin A., with Roger Highfield. 2012. *SuperCooperation: Altruism, Evolution, and Why We Need Each Other to Succeed.* New York: Free Press.

Nye, Joseph S. Jr. 2008. *The Powers to Lead: Soft, Hard, and Smart.* New York: Oxford University Press.

Nye, Joseph S. 2013. *Presidential Leadership and the Creation of the American Era.* Princeton: Princeton University Press.

O'Connor, Timothy, and Constantine Sandis, eds. 2013. *A Companion to the Philosophy of Action.* Malden, MA: Wiley-Blackwell.

OECD. 2011. *Future Global Shocks: Improving Risk Governance.* Paris: OECD, Reviews of Risk Management Policies.

Olson, Mancur. 1984. *The Rise and Decline of Nations: Economic Growth, Stagflation and Social Rigidities.* New Haven: Yale University Press.

Orford, Anne. 2011. *International Authority and the Responsibility to Protect.*

Cambridge, UK: Cambridge University Press.

Parker, Geoffrey. 2000. *The Grand Strategy of Philip II.* New Haven: Yale University Press.

Parker, Simon, Akash Paun, Jonathan McClory, and Kate Blatchford. 2010. *Shaping Up: A Whitehall for the Future.* London: Institute for Government.

Patterson, Bradley H. 2010. *To Serve the President: Continuity and Innovation in the White House Staff.* Washington, DC: Brookings Institution Press.

Payne, Richard J. 2012. *Global Issues, Fourth Edition. Cambridge, UK: Pearson.*

Peikoff. 2012. *Understanding Objectivism: A Guide to Learning Ayn Rand's Philosophy.* New York: New American Library.

Peter, Laurence J., and Raymond Hull. 2011. *The Peter Principle: Why Thinks Always Go Wrong.* New York: Harper.

Pew Research Center. 2013a. *Public's Views on Human Evolution.* Washington, DC: Pew Research Center.

Pew Research Center. 2013b. *America's Place in the World 2013.* Washington, DC: Pew Research Center.

Pew Research Center. 2013c. *Living to 120 and Beyond: Americans' Views on Aging, Medical Advances and Radical Life Extension.* Washington, DC: Pew Research Center.

Pereboom, Derk, ed. 2009. Free Will. Indianapolis, IN: Hackett.

Pickett, Willliam P. ed. 2004. *George F. Kennan and the Origins of Eisenhower's New Look: An Oral History of Project Solarium.* Princeton: Princeton University, Princeton Institute for International and Regional Studies, Monograph No. 1.

Pines, Yuri. 2009. *Envisioning Eternal Empire: Chinese Political Thought of the Warring States Era.* Honolulu: University of Hawai'i Press.

Pinker, Steven. 2009. *How the Mind Works,* reissues Edition. New York: Norton.

Pinker, Steven. 2011. *The Better Angels of Our Nature: The Decline of Violence in History and Its Causes.* New York: Penguin.

Planck, Max. 1949. *Scientific Autobiography and Other Papers*. New York: Philosophical Library.

Plato. 1995. *The Statesman*. Cambridge: Cambridge University Press.

Pohl, Rüdiger F. ed. 2012. *Cognitive Illusions: A Handbook on Fallacies and Biases in Thinking, Judgement and Memory*. New York: Psychology Press.

Post, Jerrold M. 1995. *When Illness Strikes the Leader: The Dilemma of the Captive King*. New Haven: Yale University Press.

Postrel, Virginia. 1999. *The Future and Its Enemies: The Growing Conflict Over Creativity, Enterprise, and Progress*. New York, NY: Touchstone.

Powell, Jonathan. 2010. *The New Machiavelli: How to Wield Power in the Modern World*. London: The Bodley Head.

Power, Samantha. 2002. *A Problem from Hell: America and the Age of Genocide*. New York: Basic Books.

Priestland, David. 2010. *The Red Flag: Communism and the Making of the Modern World*. London: Penguin.

Priestland, David. 2013. *Merchant, Soldier, Sage: A History of the World in Three Castes*. London: Penguin.

Prigogine, Ilya. 1997. *The End of Certainty: Time, Chaos and the New Laws of Nature*. New York: Free Press.

Prothero, Donald R. 2011. *Catastrophes!: Earthquakes, Tsunamis, Tornadoes, and Other Earth-Shattering Disasters*. Baltimore, MD: Johns Hopkins University Press.

Ramo, Joshua Cooper. 2009. *The Age of the Unthinkable: Why the New World Disorder Constantly Surprises Us and What to Do About It*. New York: Little, Brown.

Rand, Ayn. 1999. *Atlas Shrugged*. New York: Plume, first published 1957.

Raven, Peter H., David, M. Hassenzahl, and Linda R. Berg. 2012. *Environment*, Eighth Edition. Hoboken, NJ: Wiley.

Read, Christopher (2005). *Lenin: A Revolutionary Life*. London: Routledge.

Rees, Martin. 2003. *Our Final Hour: A Scientist's Warning*. New York: Basic Books.

Retschitzki, Jean and Alex de Voogt. 2012. *Moves in Mind: The Psychology of Board Games*. New York: Psychology Press.

Revonsuo, Antti. 2010. *Consciousness: The Science of Subjectivity*. New York: Psychology Press.

Richardson, Robert C. (2007). *Evolutionary Psychology as Maladapted Psychology*. Cambridge, MA: MIT Press.

Robinson, Andrew. 2011. *Genius: A Very Short Introduction*. Oxford: Oxford University Press.

Root, Hilton L. 2013. *Dynamics among Nations: The Evolution of Legitimacy and Development in Modern States*. Cambridge, MA: MIT Press.

Rostow, Walt Whitman. 1960. *The Stages of Economic Growth: A Non-Communist Manifesto*. Cambridge: Cambridge University Press.

Rotberg, Robert I. 2012. *Transformative Political Leadership: Making a Difference in the Developing World.* Chicago: University of Chicago Press.

Rothkopf, David. 2006. *Running the World: The Inside Story of the National Security Council and the Architects of American Power.* New York: PublicAffairs.

Ryan, Alan. 2013. *On Machiavelli: The Search for Glory.* New York: Liveright.

Rycker, Antoon De and Zuraidah Mohd Don, eds. 2013. *Discourse and Crisis: Critical perspectives.* Amsterdam: John Benjamins Publishing.

Saar, Shalom Saada, with Michael J. Hargrove 2013. *Leading with Conviction: Mastering the Nine Critical Pillars of Integrated Leadership.* San Francisco: Jossey-Bass.

Sahlberg, Pasi. 2011. *Finnish Lessons: What Can the World Learn from Educational Change in Finland?* New York: Teachers College Press.

Sandel, Michael J. 2009a. *Justice: What's the Right Thing to Do?* New York: Farrar, Straus and Giroux.

Sandel, Michael J. 2009b. *The Case against Perfection: Ethics in the Age of Genetic Engineering.* Cambridge, MA: Harvard University Press.

Sarkar, Shrii Prabhat Rainjan. 2012. *Neo-Humanism: Principles and Cardinal Values, Sentimentality to Spirituality, Human Society.* Corona, NY: Ananda Marga Publications.

Sayers, Dorothy L. 1979. *The Mind of the Maker.* San Francisco: HarperSanFrancisco.

Scharfstein, Ben-Ami. 1995. *Amoral Politics: The Persistent Truth of Machiavellism.* Albany, New York: State University of New York Press.

Schiff, Stacy. 2011. *Cleopatra.* London: Virgin Books.

Schlosser, Eric. 2013. *Command and Control: Nuclear Weapons, The Damaskus Accident, And The Illusion of Safety.* New York: Penguin.

Schmidt, Helmut, Peter Janich, and Carl Friedrich Gethmann. 2008. *Die Verantwortung des Politikers.* München: Wilhelm Fink Verlag.

Schmidt, Markus, Alexander Kelle, Agomoni Ganguli-Mitra, Huib de Vriend eds. 2009. *Synthetic Biology: the technoscience and its societal consequences.* New York: Springer.

Schmitt, Carl. 2006. *Political Theology: Four Chapters on the Concept of Sovereignty.* Chicago: University of Chicago Press, first published in German in 1922.

Schmitt, Carl. 2007. *The Concept of the Political: Expanded Edition.* Chicago: University of Chicago Press. Originally published in German 1927.

Schon, Donald A. 1991. *The Reflective Practitioner: How Professionals Think in Action.* Farnham, UK: Ashgate.

Schulman, Paul R. 1981. *Large Scale Policy Making.* Westport, CT: Praeger.

Schwinge, Erich. 1983. *Der Staatsmann: Anspruch und Wirklichkeit in der Politik.* München: Universitas.

Scientific American. 2013a. "pecial Collector's Edition: What Makes Us Human." 22(1).

Scientific American. 2013b. "Special Collector's Edition: Extreme Physics—Probing the Mysteries of the Cosmos." 22(2).

Scientific American Mind. 2012. "Special Collector's Edition: His Brain, Here Brain—How we're different." 21(2).

Scientific American Mind. 2013. "Special Collector's Edition: 187 Illusions." 22(3).

Scott, James C. 1998. *Seeing Like a State: How Certain Schemes to Improve the Human Condition Have Failed.* New Haven: Yale University Press.

Searle, John. 2010. *Making the Social World: The Structure of Human Civilization.* New York: Oxford University Press.

Sears, David O., Leonie Huddy, and Robert Jervis, eds. 2003. *Oxford Handbook of Political Psychology.* New York: Oxford University Press.

Seielstad, George A. 2012. *Dawn of the Anthropocene —Humanity's Defining Moment*, Kindle Edition. Alexandria, VA: American Geosciences Institute.

Selznick, Philip. 2002. *The Communitarian Persuasion.* Washington, DC: Woodrow Wilson Center Press.

Shafir,Eldar, ed. 2013. *The Behavioral Foundations of Public Policy.* Princeton: Princeton University Press.

Shenk, Joshua Wolf. 2005. *Lincoln's Melancholy: How Depression Challenged a President and Fueled His Greatness.* Boston: Houghton Mifflin.

Siege, Eric. 2013. *Predictive Analytics: The Power to Predict Who Will Click, Buy, Lie or Die.* Hoboken, NJ: Wiley.

Simonton, Dean Keith. 1994. *Greatness: Who Make's History and Why.* New York: Guilford Press.

Singh, Sarwant. 2012. *New Mega Trends: Implications for our Future Lives.* New York: Palgrave Macmillan.

Skira Rizzoli. 2013. *Edward Munch 1863–1944.* Milano: Skira editore.

Slauter, Eric. 2011. *The State as a Work of Art: The Cultural Origins of the Constitution.* Chicago: University of Chicago Press.

Sloman, Steven. 2005. *Causal Models: How People Think About the World and its Alternatives.* New York: Oxford University Press.

Sloterdijk, Peter. 2013. You Must Change Your Life. Cambridge: Polity.

Smil, Vaclav. 2012. *Global Catastrophes and Trends: The Next Fifty Years.* Cambridge, MA: MIT Press.

Smith, Jean Edward 2012. *Eisenhower in War and Peace.* New York: Random House.

Solomon, Robert C., ed. 2005. *Existentialism*, Second Edition. New York: Oxford University Press.

Sorensen, Theodore C. 1963. *Decision-Making in the White House: The Olive Branch or the Arrows.* New York: Columbia University Press.

Sorensen, Theodore. 2008. *Counselor: A Life at the Edge of History.* New York: Collins.

Stavrakakis, Yannis.1999. *Lacan and the Political.* New York: Routledge.

Steinberg, Jonathan. 2011. *Bismarck: A Life.* Oxford: Oxford University Press.

Steinbock, Bonnie, ed. 2009. *The Oxford Handbook of Bioethics.* New York: Oxford University Press.

Steichen, Edward, ed. 2002. *The Family Of Man.* New York: The Museum of Modern Art.

Stolfi, R.H.S. 2011. *Hitler: Beyond Evil and Tyranny.* New York: Prometheus.

Stong, Tracy B. 2012. *Politics without Vision: Thinking without a Banister in the Twentieth Century.* Chicago: University of Chicago Press.

Storr, Anthony. 2005. *Solitude: A Return to the Self.* New York: Free Press.

Sturman, Peter C., and Susan S. Tai. 2012. *The Artful Recluse: Painting, Poetry, and Politics in Seventeenth Century China.* New York: Prestel.

Subirós, Pep, ed. 2011. *Jane Alexander Surveys (from the Cape of Good Hope).* New York: Museum for African Art.

Suganami, Hidemi 1989. *The Domestic Analogy and World Order Proposals.* Cambridge, UK: Cambridge University Press.

Taleb, Nassim Nicholas. 2007 *The Black Swan: The Impact of the Highly Improbable.* New York: Random.

Taleb, Nassim Nicholas. 2010. *The Bed of Procrustes: Philosophical and Practical Aphorisms.* New York: Random.

Taleb, Nassim Nicholas. 2012. *Antifragile: Things That Gain from Disorder.* New York: Random House.

Tan, Jason, and Ng Pak Tee, ed. 2005. *Shaping Singapore's Future: Thinking Schools, Learning Nations.* Singapore: Prentice Hall.

Taylor, Charles. 1992. *Sources of the Self: The Making of the Modern Identity.* Cambridge, MA: Harvard University Press.

Tegmark, Max. 2014. *Our Mathematical Universe: My Quest for the Ultimate Nature of Reality.* New York: Knopf.

Tetlock, Philip E. 2005. *Expert Political Judgment: How Good Is It? How Can We Know?* Princeton, NJ: Princeton University Press.

Theakston, Kevin, and Jouke de Vries, eds. 2012. *Former Leaders in Modern Democracies: Political Sunsets.* New York: Palgrave Macmillan.

Toscano, Alberto. 2010. *Fanaticism: On the Uses of an Idea.* London: Verso.

Toye, Richard (2013). *Rhetoric: A Very Short* Introduction. Oxford: Oxford University Press.

Toynbee, Arnold. 1963a. *A Study of History: Volume 7A: Universal States.* New York: Oxford University Press.

Toynbee, Arnold. 1963b. *A Study of History: Volume 7B: Universal Churches.* New York: Oxford University Press.

Toynbee, Arnold J., with David Churchill Somervell. 1946. *A Study of History, Vol. 1: Abridgement of Volumes I–VI.* Oxford: Oxford University Press.

Toynbee, Arnold J., with David Churchill Somervell. 1957. *A Study of History, Vol. 2: Abridgement of Volumes VII–X.* Oxford: Oxford University Press.

Tuchman, Barbara W. 2004. *The Guns of August.* New York: Presidio Press. First published in 1962.

Tusiani, Joseph. 1963. *Lust and Liberty: The Poems of Machiavelli.* New York: Ivan Obolensky.

Twain, Mark. 2012. *King Leopold's Soliloquy a Defense of His Congo Rule, Charleston, SC: Forgotten Books.* First published 1905.

Tyldesley, Joyce. 2009. *Cleopatra: Last Queen of Egypt.* London: Profile Books.

Unamuno, de Miguel. 1978. *The Tragic Sense of Life in Men and Nations.* Princeton: Princeton University Press. First published in Spanish in 1913.

United Nations Global Compact Office. 2011.*Global Compact: Corporate Sustainability in The World Economy.* New York: United Nations.

United Nations, Department of Economic and Social Affairs, Population Division. 2013. *World Population Prospects—The 2012 Revision: Key Findings and Advance Tables.* New York: United Nations.

Urquhart, Brian. 1995. *Hammarskjold.* New York: Norton.

Vaziere, Simine and Timothy D. Wilson, eds. 2012. Handbook of Self-Knowledge. New York: Guilford Press.

Vertzberger, Yaacov Y.I. 1993. *The World in Their Minds: Information Processing, Cognition and Perception in Foreign Decisionmaking.* Stanford: Stanford University Press.

Vickers, Sir Geoffrey. 1995. *The Art of Judgment: A Study of Policy Making.* Thousand Oaks, CA: Sage. First published 1965.

Vico, Giambattista. 2000. New Science. London: Penguin. First published in 1725 in Italian.

Vivanti, Corrado. 2013. *Niccoló Machiavelli: An Intellectual Biography.* Princeton, NJ: Princeton University Press.

Vogel, Ezra F. 2011. *Deng Xiaoping and the Transformation of China.* Cambridge, MA: Harvard University Press.

Vrabie, Ioan I. 2011. *Differential Equations: An Introduction to Basic Concepts, Results and Applications*, 2nd Edition .Singapore: World Scientific Publishing Company.

Wacquant, Loïc. 2005. "Habitus". *International Encyclopedia of Economic Sociology.* London, Routledge, 315-319.

Wald, Shalom Salomon. 2013. *Rise and Decline of Civilizations: Lessons for the Jewish People.* Boston: Academic Studies Press.

Walzer, Michael. 1973. "Political Action: The Problem of Dirty Hands." *Philosophy and Public Affairs* 2 (2):160-180.

Weber, Max. 2001. *The Protestant Ethic and the Spirit of Capitalism. London: Routledge.* First published in German as two essays in 1904 and 1905, and consolidated into a revised book published in 1920.

Weber Max. 2004. *The Vocation Lectures: Science as a Vocation, Politics as a Vocation.* Indianapolis, IN: Hackett, published originally in German in 1919.

Welch, Stephen. 2013. *The Theory of Political Culture.* Oxford: Oxford University Press.

White, Ronald C. Jr. 2010. *Lincoln: A Biography.* New York: Random House.

Widdows, Heathen. 2011 *Global Ethics: An Introduction.* Durham, UK: Acumen.

Wildavsky, Aaron. 2005. *The Nursing Father: Moses as a Political Leader.* New York: Shalem Press. First published in 1984.

Wilde, Lawrence. 2013. *Global Solidarity.* Edinburgh: Edinburgh University Press.

Will, George F. 1983. *Statecraft As Soulcraft: What Government Does.* New York: Simon & Schuster.

William H. McNeill. 2011. *Maps of Time: An Introduction to Big History.* Berkeley: University of California Press.

Williams, John Davis. 1987. *The Compleat Strategyst: Being a Primer on the Theory of Games of Strategy*, Revised Edition. Mineola, NY: Dover.

Wills, Garry. 2006. *Lincoln at Gettysburg: The Words that Remade America.* New York: Simon & Schuster.

Winchester, Simon. 2005. *Krakatoa: The Day the World Exploded: August 27, 1883.* New York: Harper.

Wolff, Martin. 2014. "Failing elites threaten our future." *Financial Times*, January 14.

Wood, Bernard. 2006. *Human Evolution: A Very Short Introduction.* Oxford: Oxford University Press.

Woodcock, George. 1976. "Editorial: Historians And Biographers," *Canadian Literature, No. 70, Autumn.*

World Economic Forum. 2014. *Global Risks 2014.* Geneva: World Economic Forum.

Wouters, Jan, Stephanie Bijlmakers, Nicolas Hachez, Matthias Lievens, and Axel Marx, eds. 2013. "Special Issue: Global Governance and Democratic Legitimacy: A Bottom-up Approach." *Innovation: The European Journal of Social Science Research* 26(3).

Wright, Diana, and Donella H. Meadows 2009. *Thinking in Systems: A Primer.* New York: Routledge.

Ypi, Lea. 2012. *Global Justice and Avant-Garde Political Agency*. Oxford: Oxford University Press.

Zimbardo, Philip. 2007. *The Lucifer Effect: How Good People Turn Evil*. New York: Random.

Zizek, Slavoj. 2012. *The Year of Dreaming Dangerously*. London: Verso.

www.ingramcontent.com/pod-product-compliance
Lightning Source LLC
Chambersburg PA
CBHW081356270326
41930CB00015B/3323